Digital Rights Management

Business and Technology

William Rosenblatt, William Trippe,
and Stephen Mooney

M&T Books
An imprint of Hungry Minds, Inc.

Best-Selling Books • Digital Downloads • e-Books • Answer Networks •
e-Newsletters • Branded Web Sites • e-Learning

New York, NY • Cleveland, OH • Indianapolis, IN

Digital Rights Management: Business and Technology

Published by
M&T Books
909 Third Avenue
New York, NY 10022
www.hungryminds.com

Library of Congress Control Number: 2001096080

ISBN: 0-7645-4889-1

1B/TR/RQ/QR/IN

Distributed in the United States by Hungry Minds, Inc.

Distributed by CDG Books Canada Inc. for Canada; by
Transworld Publishers Limited in the United Kingdom; by
IDG Norge Books for Norway; by IDG Sweden Books for
Sweden; by IDG Books Australia Publishing Corporation
Pty. Ltd. for Australia and New Zealand; by TransQuest
Publishers Pte Ltd. for Singapore, Malaysia, Thailand,
Indonesia, and Hong Kong; by Gotop Information Inc. for
Taiwan; by ICG Muse, Inc. for Japan; by Intersoft for
South Africa; by Eyrolles for France; by International
Thomson Publishing for Germany, Austria, and
Switzerland; by Distribuidora Cuspide for Argentina; by
LR International for Brazil; by Galileo Libros for Chile;
by Ediciones ZETA S.C.R. Ltda. for Peru; by WS
Computer Publishing Corporation, Inc., for the
Philippines; by Contemporanea de Ediciones for
Venezuela; by Express Computer Distributors for the
Caribbean and West Indies; by Micronesia Media
Distributor, Inc. for Micronesia; by Chips Computadoras
S.A. de C.V. for Mexico; by Editorial Norma de Panama
S.A. for Panama; by American Bookshops for Finland.

For general information on Hungry Minds' products and
services please contact our Customer Care department
within the U.S. at 800-762-2974, outside the U.S. at 317-
572-3993 or fax 317-572-4002.

For sales inquiries and reseller information, including
discounts, premium and bulk quantity sales, and foreign-
language translations, please contact our Customer Care
department at 800-434-3422, fax 317-572-4002 or write to
Hungry Minds, Inc., Attn: Customer Care Department,
10475 Crosspoint Boulevard, Indianapolis, IN 46256.

For information on licensing foreign or domestic rights,
please contact our Sub-Rights Customer Care department
at 212-884-5000.

For information on using Hungry Minds' products and
services in the classroom or for ordering examination
copies, please contact our Educational Sales department at
800-434-2086 or fax 317-572-4005.

For press review copies, author interviews, or other
publicity information, please contact our Public Relations
department at 317-572-3168 or fax 317-572-4168.

For authorization to photocopy items for corporate,
personal, or educational use, please contact Copyright
Clearance Center, 222 Rosewood Drive, Danvers, MA
01923, or fax 978-750-4470.

 is a trademark of Hungry Minds, Inc.

 is a trademark of Hungry Minds, Inc.

About the Authors

Bill Rosenblatt is president of GiantSteps/Media Technology Strategies, a consulting firm (`www.giantstepsmts.com`) whose clients include content providers, digital media technology companies, and investment firms. Bill bridges the gaps between business and technology in the digital media world. He brings content providers expertise in areas such as content management, rights management, streaming media, and cross-media publishing, and he provides technology vendors with market strategy, business development, and product management services.

Before founding GiantSteps, Bill was chief technology officer of Fathom, an online content and education company backed by Columbia University and other scholarly institutions. He has been a technology and new media executive at McGraw-Hill and Times Mirror Company, and he served as manager of strategic marketing for media and publishing at Sun Microsystems. He was also one of the architects of the Digital Object Identifier (DOI), a digital rights management related standard.

Bill is a frequent speaker and writer on media technology topics. He is the author of several technical books and has written articles for *EContent* magazine, *Salon, CNN Interactive, Journal of Electronic Publishing,* and other periodicals. He is president of Princeton Broadcasting Service, Inc., a member of the Software & Information Industry Association (SIIA) Digital Rights Management Working Group, and a member of the advisory boards of Seybold Seminars and several startup companies.

Bill holds degrees from Princeton University and the University of Massachusetts. He lives in New York City.

Bill Trippe is president of New Millennium Publishing (`www.nmpub.com`), a Boston-based consulting practice formed in 1997. Bill has more than twenty years of technical and management experience in electronic publishing, content management, and SGML/XML and related technologies. He brings a unique blend of strategic and hands-on knowledge of the products and trends that are shaping the publishing and content technology marketplace. In addition to his role at New Millennium, Bill is associate editor of *The Gilbane Report,* the XML columnist for *Transform*, and a regular contributor to the magazine *EContent*.

Stephen Mooney is founder of Stephen Mooney & Associates, a consulting company advising technology providers, rightsholders, aggregators, and others on new approaches to intellectual property licensing. Steve has more than fifteen years of consulting, negotiating, sales and licensing experience in the publishing and information industries. He concluded numerous license agreements with Fortune 500 corporations while with Copyright Clearance Center, and was vice president of business development at Yankee Rights Management. He chairs several standards committees, including DOI-EB (Digital Object Identifier for E-Books), the Identifier Working Group of the Open E-Book Forum (OEBF), and the SIIA DRM Working Group. He is a regular speaker at conferences on rights management issues. Steve is admitted to the bar in New York and Massachusetts.

Credits

Acquisitions Manager
Chris Webb

Senior Project Editor
Jodi Jensen

Technical Editor
Mark Walter

Copy Editor
Dana Lesh

Project Coordinator
Nancy Reeves

Cover Design
© Noma/Images.com

Supervisor of Graphics and Design
Shelley Lea

Graphics Specialist
Kelly Hardesty

Proofreader
Mary Lagu

Indexers
Tom Dinse and Johnna VanHoose Dinse

To Margot Lorraine Rosenblatt, whose birth during the writing of this book served as the most welcome distraction imaginable.   —Bill Rosenblatt

To Michele, for her patience and encouragement.   —Bill Trippe

To my wife Amanda, son Billy, and daughter Betsy.   —Stephen Mooney

Acknowledgments

We would like to thank several people who took time out of their busy schedules to offer their thoughts on DRM and the media marketplace, most notably Bob Meltzer of ASTM, and Gordon Hardy, David Jost, and Avi Lev at Houghton Mifflin Company. Thanks to John Stubbs for his important insight into SDMI and the online music market, Brad Husick for valuable information about ICE, Sean Murphy for expertise on intellectual property law, Natalie Lustig for her research into software piracy, and Jessica Lustig for all manner of help and support. Thanks also to Mark Stefik of Xerox PARC for the inspiration of his research and writings.

Several executives at DRM vendors were also generous with their time and resources, including Kirstie Chadwick of DigitalOwl, Meg Fisher (formerly of Reciprocal), Jim Hickey of Authentica, Martha Nalebuff of Microsoft, Trish Naudon and Vanessa Erhard of Digital World Services, Carol Risher and Prasad Ram of Savantech, Mark Sarbiewski of InterTrust, and David Sidman of Content Directions. They were extremely generous with their time and offered thoughtful and interesting perspectives on the technology and business of digital rights management.

We would also like to acknowledge cooperation and assistance from vendors' marketing, PR, and legal staff, including: John Bjerke, Joyce Fowler, and Linda White (Adobe); Lyndon Holmes and James King (Aries Systems); Yalan King (ContentGuard); Marty Moe (ebrary); Esteban Yepez (Elisar); Diana Holm (FileOpen Systems); Remi DuBois, Justin McCarthy, and Brian Queen (IBM); Ruth Lindley (InterTrust); Ann Naumann (iCopyright); Meredith Friedman (Infraworks); Erin Curtis (Kinecta); Kimberly Strop (Liquid Audio); Greg Benson and Dave Roth (MediaDNA); Peter Hanschke (NetActive); Joanne Simpson (Phocis); Ben Rotholtz and Tahir Sharif (RealNetworks); Tony Telloni (Reciprocal); Daniel Raskin (RightsCenter); Kendra Nemeth (RightsMarket); Laura Higgins and Vera Zlidenny (SealedMedia); and Chris Doherty (ViaTech).

Finally, we would like to express appreciation to our technical editor, Mark Walter, for his valuable feedback on the manuscript.

Preface

This book is about a subject that has been lurking in the underbrush of the digital information world for many years and is finally coming to the forefront. Rights management is, in some ways, the ugly beast that content providers — publishers, broadcasters, market researchers, consultancies, major corporations, and others — have wanted to keep in the closet. The Internet has forced the closet door open; really, it has eliminated the door itself. What used to be relatively simple is now uncomfortably complex. What used to be a source of moderate business overhead is now a significant undertaking. What used to be the province of lawyers, agents, and administrators is now also the domain of technologists. Content providers need to understand and embrace rights management in order to play in the Internet age.

What Is Digital Rights Management?

The term *digital rights management* (DRM) was coined by some combination of vendors, their marketers, and industry analysts in the late 1990s. Thus it's less relevant to ask, "What does DRM mean?" than to ask, "What is it that has come to be called DRM?"

We take a broad view of the meaning and scope of DRM. When you create content (information), you inherently control a set of rights to that content — to see it, change it, print it, play it, copy it, excerpt it, translate it into another language, and so on. Traditionally, those rights have accrued from three sources:

- ◆ **Legal:** Rights that you get either automatically under law (such as inherent copyright) or by some legal procedure (such as applying for a patent)
- ◆ **Transactional:** Rights that you get or give up by buying or selling them, such as buying a book or selling a manuscript to a publisher
- ◆ **Implicit:** Rights defined by the medium that the information is in

The most important thing to remember about DRM is that the first two sources of rights haven't changed much with the advent of technologies such as the Internet, cell phones, and MP3 files. Various parties have called for a complete gutting and replacement of the standing intellectual property (IP) law, but this hasn't happened and isn't going to. As discussed in Chapter 3 of this book, legislators have responded to new technologies by adding a couple of new laws instead, such as the Electronic Signatures Act and the Digital Millennium Copyright Act.

Transactions haven't changed much, either — regardless of the fact that they can be performed over the Internet. The same laws apply, the same money is used, and the same goods can be bought and sold. What's really changed is the implicit nature of rights when applied to traditional media. The Internet has made these implicit rights explicit. This engenders problems as well as opportunities for content providers as well as for consumers.

To understand what we mean by the *implicit rights* of traditional media types, consider this: If you buy a book at a bookstore, you're given some rights to the content in the book. Some are legal: It's a breach of copyright law to make copies of the book and sell them. Some are transactional: You paid some money for the right to read the book, to lend it, or to give it away.

But most of the rights derive from what's easy and what's hard to do with the technology of a printed book.

It's easy to read a book; that's what books were designed for. It's also easy to give a book to someone else (in most cases). However, it's not that easy to make a copy of the book; it's even harder to change the contents of the book — regardless of whether those activities are legal. For that reason, publishers haven't been too worried about people doing these things.

The Changing Attitude Toward DRM

Although publishing has been around for centuries, publishers' attitudes towards rights have changed dramatically in the last decade. Technology has imposed two inflection points on the industry: The first was putting content in digital format, as opposed to physical forms such as print, vinyl, and videotape. Digital content can be copied with perfect fidelity: Unlike in legacy media, a copy of a copy of a copy of a copy is just as good as the original. The second inflection point is the Internet, which eliminates the need for physical media to distribute digital content. Instead of distributing it on floppy disks, CDs, DATs, MiniDiscs, or Zip drives, digital content can be sent from place to place instantaneously and extremely cheaply.

In other words, digital network technologies have dramatically decreased the cost of manipulating, copying, and distributing content. There are all kinds of things that you can do to content in digital form now that were too time-consuming or expensive to do before. This makes content production and distribution easier for publishers and other content providers, but it also makes piracy easier for pirates.

Digital rights management refers to *controlling* and *managing* rights to digital intellectual property. The need for control and management has increased now that digital network technologies have taken away the implicit control that publishers get with legacy media.

At first, unsurprisingly, content providers were concerned with digital network technologies' effects on piracy. They became interested in technologies — mostly borrowed from the world of commercial software distribution — that would take digital content and reintroduce the types of limitations on manipulation, copying, and distribution that physical media contain.

These early DRM technologies didn't catch on, mainly because they were too cumbersome to use. At one level, they merely replaced one data distribution problem — the content — with another — the software required to use the content. In other words, vendors produced software that effectively gave digital content on the Internet some of the same properties as physical content with regard to the ease of exercising rights such as view, copy, and change. But the software brought new problems: distributing, maintaining, and getting consumers to install and use it. So the software introduced a level of complexity that users didn't welcome.

This type of DRM technology still exists today; in fact, recent developments in the music industry are making it potentially more important than ever. As this book goes to press, the five major recording labels are preparing to roll out the MusicNet and pressplay services, which offer digital music to consumers through subscription services that involve DRM technology. With the weight of legal victories against the likes of Napster and MP3.com behind them, the record companies are hoping that consumers will accept by fiat two flavors of proprietary DRM technology, from Microsoft and RealNetworks, as opposed to the single SDMI standard that the music industry attempted to float but has largely abandoned. It will take some time for the market to decide.

Opportunities through DRM

As content providers have begun to be more familiar with the Internet and with rights issues, they are coming to realize three things: First, rights management concerns much more than the distribution of content to consumers. A publisher or content provider is only one link in a chain that also includes content creators (authors, photographers, musicians, and so on), manufacturers, distributors, and so on. Managing rights really means managing them throughout the entire chain.

Secondly, and more importantly, content providers have begun to understand that rights management is as much about the opportunity inherent in new business models as it is about preserving the business of old ones. They are realizing that physical media formats have defined limits on opportunity, not just piracy. For example, people may not want to purchase an annual subscription to an expensive scientific journal, but they may be interested in one or two articles. It's hard to do that with print journal publishing, but network digital technology makes it much easier. Publishers can increase revenue by adding this type of capability, of which rights management is a necessary component.

Similarly, there are many music fans (like one of us) who are fed up with the homogeneity of broadcast radio and would pay a monthly fee to listen to good, commercial-free music in their favorite genres, but have little interest in owning lots of albums and even less in going to the trouble of picking them and putting them on a music-playing device. It takes rights management technology to provide this type of service.

Publishers can also provide their content to third parties that add value to the content by repackaging it, adding it to larger collections of content, and so on. In the world of legacy publishing, these so-called secondary publishers have had to set up very expensive operations to serve this market opportunity. Networked digital technology dramatically lowers barriers to entry — as long as rights are managed properly. In today's environment, publishers are learning that content brands transcend location and delivery media: It pays to get content in front of your intended audience, wherever they may be. If part of that audience is best served by another venue — another publication, another Web site, another service — then the best thing to do is to license content to that other venue. This, once again, is a rights management issue.

The third thing that content providers have come to realize is the opportunity inherent in learning more about the audiences for their content. There's only so much that you can learn about readers of physical media. If they buy books at bookstores, they can do so using anonymous cash, so you have no idea who they are. In the world of magazines, you know something about your subscribers, but there's no way of knowing which articles they read, which ads they look at, and with whom they share the magazines. And, of course, television networks sometimes go to extraordinary lengths to find out who's watching.

Networked digital technology makes it possible to find out with unprecedented precision who is consuming what content and when. In fact, sometimes the information on content use is worth more than the content itself. If you manage and control rights to content, it's only a small step beyond that to tracking its usage.

Rights management also applies to businesses that don't sell content as their primary source of revenue. More and more types of businesses depend on information as an accompaniment to the products and services that they sell — from management consulting and banking to manufacturing. The construction industry, for example, depends on plans and specifications for buildings, roads, and bridges that someone wants built. Construction firms bid on projects, and documents are created and shared among different participants in the process. It's important to distribute these artifacts digitally while ensuring that only authorized parties get access. The same is true in the aviation industry for building today's complex aircraft, in financial services for research documents that are sent only to top customers, in pharmaceutics for managing drug regulatory documentation processes, and in many other fields.

We feel strongly that DRM solutions will eventually spill over from pure content industries to all these other fields. In fact, some noncontent industries already use document management systems that have certain aspects of DRM built in.

Digital rights management differs from traditional rights management because it needs to be proactive instead of reactive, and it needs to be explicit and comprehensive instead of letting the medium determine the rights.

An entire industry is emerging of technologies that perform digital rights management. These comprise several different types of functionality, such as the following:

- Systems that content providers can use internally for defining, organizing, and managing rights
- Systems for distributing content to consumers in a controlled way (the original types of DRM solutions and the ones that get the most press because they are meant to address piracy)
- Systems for managing access to content within an enterprise, such as a corporation or educational institution.
- Systems for licensing and distributing content to other publishers in a controlled way
- Systems for measuring content usage

The market for these technologies came into focus in the mid-1990s and has been growing slowly ever since. Many vendors have come and gone; leaders have yet to emerge. But most people agree that even though the Internet was built with an "information wants to be free" environment in mind, DRM is becoming a more and more fundamental idea in the evolution of digital content; because of this, the market should grow rapidly. Recent (June 2001) research by IDC predicts that the market for DRM technology and services, which it measures as $96 million in 2000, will be $200 million in 2001 and ultimately $3.5 billion in 2005 — an annual growth rate of over 100 percent.

The Origins of DRM Technology

As mentioned earlier, the identification of a type of technology for controlling the copying of content in digital form came about with the rise of the Internet. Before that, making unauthorized copies of digital files was a problem that originated in the software industry.

Software piracy continues to be a problem for vendors to this day. Yet it wasn't much of an issue in the days before the PC (pre-1980s), when computers were mostly large machines for multiple users — minicomputers and mainframes. Yet ironically, key components of what we now call DRM technology arose out of the mini/mainframe environment. On every large computer system, individual users maintain their own sets of files. Each of those files has permissions on them, allowing different users the rights to do certain things with those files, such as read them, write (change) them, run them (for files that are themselves programs), and delete them. On the most sophisticated systems, each of those permissions could be assigned (or not assigned) to different classes of users, including the creator of the file, members of a defined group of users, and "everyone."

In Chapter 4 (and throughout this book), we call this specification of who can do what to or with a file a *rights model*. Developers of rights models for DRM certainly took their inspiration from file permission schemes for multiuser operating systems. Incidentally, this technology didn't go away with the advent of PCs: On the contrary, every Web and database server that you use today has it. The computers themselves just got smaller and more powerful.

When personal computers came out in the late 1970s through the early 1980s, software was distributed on floppy disks. Nowadays, with most software packages too large to fit on 1.44MB floppies, CD-ROM is the most popular physical medium for software distribution. Floppies were easily duplicated, and today's cheap CD-RW (writeable CD) drives have made CD-ROM software relatively easy to pirate as well. Software vendors have devised various schemes, including warning messages ("guiltware" or "scareware"), product ID keys stickered onto the CD-ROM boxes ("naziware"), and the infamous dongles (hardware device that attach to PCs' printer ports) to stem the tide of piracy, with mixed success.

Local area networks (LANs), which became widespread in the late 1980s, engendered new possibilities for piracy. Now, instead of making copies of floppy disks, it was possible to make copies of files on other people's machines or on central file servers. Certainly it was easy to copy software that way. Software vendors tried hard to create tools that would administer software licenses among the dozens, hundreds, or even thousands of users in a corporation or other institution. This proved to be extremely difficult in the Microsoft Windows environment, although it was easier in the UNIX environment.

Controlling access to digital files via encryption came up around this time. On mini and mainframe computer systems, it was often possible to encrypt files in an ad hoc manner (for example, through the UNIX `crypt` command). Encryption provided an extra measure of protection: You needed to know a password in order to unencrypt the file. File compression programs such as PKZIP also provided encryption, which supposedly helped software vendors copy-protect their distributions (although PKZIP's particular type of encryption has been judged to be weak).

The first well-known application of encryption for what you could call "content" was for type fonts. Fonts used to be expensive: They would cost up to a few hundred dollars apiece. (This was before Microsoft began to throw a few dozen of them in with every version of Microsoft Office.) When a font file was on a server on a LAN, everyone could use it — either by copying it or by referring to it on the server. In the early 1990s, fonts were typically distributed on CD-ROMs. Two vendors, InfoSafe and CDMax, responded to this by inventing technology that encrypted files on CD-ROMs, required users to have decryption keys to use them, and charged users according to what they used.

It was a relatively small step from encrypted files on CD-ROMs to encrypted files on the Internet. Although the Internet had been around for much longer, most people identify 1994 as the year when it started on its meteoric rise to commercial prominence. The threat of piracy became all too clear to publishers.

Three developments took place within the two years after 1994 to create the paradigm that we now know as *digital rights management*. Two of these were the first well-known DRM systems from commercial vendors: infoMarket from IBM and a system from the startup company Electronic Publishing Resources (EPR). IBM's infoMarket was a combination of two things: One was a technology for strictly controlling content rights and distribution called Cryptolope. As its name implies, Cryptolope was an "envelope" that used encryption to keep content inaccessible to those who didn't provide the proper consideration, such as paying for it. The other was a set of software that enabled IBM's customers to create marketplaces on the Web for content distributed in that way.

EPR took a slightly different approach. Whereas IBM's infoMarket was all software, EPR designed an entire end-to-end system for distributing digital content that included hardware devices on the client side. They spent an alleged $25 million in research and development to invent this technology and, just as importantly, apply for many patents on it. Neither IBM's infoMarket nor EPR's hardware devices were very successful, but the technologies live on: Bits of infoMarket have survived in IBM's Electronic Media Management System (EMMS; see Chapter 11), and EPR moved its technology from hardware to software and renamed itself InterTrust — now one of the biggest names in DRM.

The third major development that catalyzed the DRM paradigm was the publication of the paper "Letting Loose the Light: Igniting Commerce in Electronic Publication," by Dr. Mark Stefik, a researcher at Xerox PARC research labs. This landmark paper defined what you could call the "techie's view" of DRM for all time. It said, in essence, that it should always be possible to strictly define and control who can do what to a piece of content, when, on what devices, and for how much money or other form of consideration.

"Letting Loose the Light" defined something called a *trusted system.* A trusted system is a device that holds some data and implements a precisely defined set of behaviors on that data. There is no way to access or modify the data other than to go through the trusted system. Trusted systems, Stefik said, would be the only feasible way to implement digital rights management because general-purpose computers have too many security holes. Stefik left some room for interpretation about the form of the trusted system, but he implied that it should take the form of a convenient, dedicated device, such as a smart card that plugs into a PC, music player, or other device.

In addition to defining the trusted system, Stefik defined a programming language for expressing rights to content, who gets them, what they cost, and so on — what we call a *rights model* in this book. This language was called Digital Property Rights Language (DPRL).

We call Stefik's paper the "techie's view" of DRM because it envisions a world where all content rights are defined and controlled by automated processes. It doesn't allow for any ad-hoc content rights transactions among humans that publishers may want to allow, or may even depend on, such as passthrough (making a few copies of a magazine article for colleagues around the office) and fair use (see Chapter 3). On the contrary, Stefik says, in his 1999 book *The Internet Edge: Social, Technical, and Legal Challenges for a Networked World,* that even these types of content "transactions" can and should be covered under rights management technology. Some intellectual property law experts disagree, suggesting that the idea of tight control of content access rights runs counter to copyright law – in particular, to the First Sale Doctrine (see Chapter 3).

After publishing "Letting Loose the Light" (which appeared, among other places, in Stefik's 1996 book *Internet Dreams: Archetypes, Myths, and Metaphors*), Stefik and colleagues from Xerox traveled around and talked to publishers, record companies, and consumer electronics manufacturers about implementing DPRL and the trusted systems concept.

Certain people within Xerox entertained the idea of implementing DPRL language interpreters in the company's printers, copiers, and scanners so that their tasks could be performed in a way that respects copyright. Although no vendor of a media-producing or media-consuming technology wants to build devices that restrict their own actions, Xerox may have been "inspired" by legal actions such as the 1991 lawsuit that the Association of American Publishers coordinated of seven publishers against Kinko's for unauthorized copying of academic materials.

Xerox never did follow through on DPRL-enabling their devices, but they did create a division called Xerox Rights Management to build software around the DPRL technology. Xerox eventually spun Xerox Rights Management out, and after a change in management, it became ContentGuard, Inc. As discussed in Chapter 6, ContentGuard modified and commercialized the DPRL technology, naming its variation XrML (Extensible Rights Markup Language).

Since 1996, many DRM vendors have come and gone. Most have targeted the publishing industry and have implemented technology designed to run on standard PCs and over the Internet. One early exception was Wave Systems, of Lee, MA, which implemented DRM technology in hardware. Wave Systems invented the EMBASSY processor, sort of a "DRM on a chip," and tried without much success to sell it to PC manufacturers, who would then build the chip into their PCs.

Nowadays, as shown in this book, the DRM market is dominated by software players because of the total dominance of PCs and their ilk (for example, Macintoshes) as devices that access the Internet. Grafting DRM technology onto these technologically mature platforms has its problems. But as more and more post-PC Internet access devices are invented, such as PDAs, cell phones, and Internet music devices, DRM technology will have more opportunities to be integrated at the ground floor. Meanwhile, the software vendors aren't standing still, either. DRM has come a long way from its origins in operating system file protection.

Is This Book for You?

This book was designed to help you chart a confident course through the technologies, business issues, and solutions in an industry in a constant state of flux. We show you the principles behind digital rights management: the existing content provider environments in which the industry was born, the new business models that are possible through DRM solutions, the fundamentals of the relevant technologies, and how to combine it all into solutions that make sense for your business.

If you are looking for a *Consumer Reports*-style guide to various DRM vendors' solutions, this may not be the best place to look. We do examine specific vendors' technologies, to be sure, but because vendors and their offerings change so frequently, we feel that you should consider supplementing this book with some of the more frequently updated periodicals and research journals that touch on the subject. These are listed under "Further Reading," later in this Preface.

If you read this book first, you can place vendor hype, as well as industry news and analysis, into a unique framework of understanding and cut through biases and temporalities. You'll be able to compare apples to apples.

The primary target audience for *Digital Rights Management: Business and Technology* is business and technology decision makers at content-providing businesses, including publishers, broadcasters, consultancies, investment firms, market researchers, and many other types of businesses that generate or handle a lot of information. We wrote this book because there is no other place to get comprehensive information about the principles underlying DRM, as opposed to the latest vendor hype or technology fads.

This book will also be of interest to people who work on the technology side of the industry. If you are a technologist, you will find this book useful for learning about the business issues that concern content providers. Publishing people are a tightly knit community with a reputation for not trusting technology vendors unless they "talk the talk" and demonstrate that they have "been there and done that." They tend not to buy technology solutions unless and until they are proven in the field. After reading this book, you will be able to fine-tune your technology offerings for your target market and be better able to explain their value to potential customers. You may even also find out more about what your existing and potential competition is doing.

Finally, this book will appeal to those third parties with a vested interest in the world of digital content technology: investors, analysts, venture capitalists, consultants, and so on. Read this book to get more insight about DRM in one place than has heretofore been available, at any price.

Above all, you will find that this book offers analysis and opinions borne of the decades of content business and technology experience of its authors. Collectively, we have worked both sides of the fence — as publishers and as technology vendors — and as third-party consultants, analysts, and investment advisors. You will find no vendor hype, no publishers' paranoia, or pipe dreams here — just information analysis that you can trust, with implicit emphasis on the wheat rather than the chaff.

From a technical standpoint, this book doesn't presuppose deep technical expertise in areas such as encryption, security, XML, Internet technologies, and content formats. It will help you, but isn't strictly required, to have a high-level understanding of processes for content publishing in any format, intellectual property rights, Internet fundamentals, and the essentials of system architecture and integration. The legal- and technology-oriented chapters contain pointers to more detailed information, as does the bibliography.

How This Book Is Organized

Digital Rights Management: Business and Technology is organized into three parts. Here are descriptions of each part and of the chapters in each.

Part I: The Business of DRM

Chapter 1: Where We Came From: Content Rights in the Predigital World

This chapter is an overview of how intellectual property rights have been handled in the world of physical media, with examples from the publishing, music, and film industries. Chapter 1 describes legacy rights clearance organizations such as the CCC, ASCAP, and BMI.

Chapter 2: Bits and Nets: New Businesses, New Possibilities

This chapter discusses new business models that the networked digital technology makes possible. These include paid downloads, subscriptions, pay-per-view and pay-per-listen, usage metering, peer-to-peer, superdistribution, and selling rights instead of the actual content.

Chapter 3: Help from the Government: Law and Technology

Chapter 3 is a summary of the various types of intellectual property law, with an emphasis on copyright and licensing and an explanation of how the law relates to rights management. This chapter also contains descriptions of recent relevant legislation, including the UCITA, DMCA, European Copyright Directive, and Electronic Signatures Act, as well as some of the important recent court decisions related to content rights

Part II: The Technology of DRM

Chapter 4: Rights Models: Representing Rights as Bits

In this chapter, we present the fundamentals of rights models, which are frameworks for describing intellectual property rights in computer systems that support rights transactions. Chapter 4 explores how rights models support new Internet-based business models as well as how they fall short of being able to support some content business models from the physical world.

Chapter 5: DRM Building Blocks: Protecting and Tracking Content

Chapter 5 contains explanations of our DRM reference architecture and primary technology components of digital rights management systems, with an emphasis on consumer-oriented DRM. Chapter 5 includes discussions of encryption and watermarking technologies.

Chapter 6: Technology Standards: Leveling the Playing Field

This chapter discusses the role of open standards in DRM, with detailed information on the most important emerging standards, including the Digital Object Identifier (DOI), Extensible Rights Markup Language (XrML), Information and Content Exchange (ICE), and the Secure Digital Music Initiative (SDMI).

Chapter 7: Proprietary Core Technologies: The Heavyweights

Chapter 7 is a look at the most prevalent core technologies in the DRM world today, including offerings from InterTrust, Verance, Digimarc, Preview Systems, Reciprocal, Adobe, and the heaviest of them all, Microsoft.

Part III: DRM Solutions: Putting It All Together

Chapter 8: Get What You Need: Determining Requirements

This chapter shows you how to gather requirements for your digital rights management application: It includes some general thoughts about requirements definition, along with laundry lists of the types of decisions that you will need to make when choosing a DRM approach.

Chapter 9: Implementation Options: Build, Buy, Integrate, and Outsource

In this chapter, we explore the differences between raw DRM technology and DRM solutions, including options for buying off-the-shelf packages; integrating components; building your own DRM solution from scratch, and outsourcing all or part of your DRM technology. Chapter 9 also includes advice on how to choose the best approach for your needs.

Chapter 10: Plug and Play: Integrating DRM

Chapter 10 discusses how to integrate digital rights management technology with various types of content production processes and systems that you may already have in place, such as editorial systems, content management, sales, marketing, and finance.

Chapter 11: Additional DRM Solutions

Chapter 11 contains descriptions of many of the vendors of digital rights management solutions, beyond those discussed in Chapter 7, whose technologies are based on the DRM reference architecture discussed in Chapter 5. We examine DRM solutions for text and PDF, corporate documents and e-mail, music, and multiple media.

Chapter 12: DRM-Related Solutions

Chapter 12 is a survey of solutions that are related to DRM but do not conform to the DRM reference architecture. We discuss internal rights management systems for publishers and entertainment companies, online rights exchanges, DRM-enabled search technologies, syndication software packages, syndication hubs, and content distribution services.

Chapter 13: Epilogue: The Future of DRM

In Chapter 13, we offer some final thoughts on the future of digital rights management, discussing business models that will and won't work, technologies that still need to be built, and perspectives on the development of the DRM market.

Further Reading

The best places to go for further and more up-to-date information about digital rights management are the various magazines and journals that cover digital media technology. The most appropriate ones for you depend on which specific segment of the content industries you occupy; here are some suggestions:

- **For publishing:** *EContent* magazine (www.econtentmag.com), and if you can afford a subscription, the *Seybold Report* (www.seyboldreports.com).
- **For music and video:** StreamingMedia.com (www.streamingmedia.com), and if you can afford it, Webnoize (www.webnoize.com).
- **For corporate information:** The *Gilbane Report* (www.gilbane.com).

The Bibliography lists several interesting research reports, white papers, and so on, in addition to those works specifically cited in this book.

If you have thoughts or questions, we invite your correspondence. You can contact us at the following addresses:

Bill Rosenblatt
GiantSteps Media Technology Strategies
200 West 57th St., Suite 305
New York, NY 10019
(212) 956-1045
billr@giantstepsmts.com
www.giantstepsmts.com

Bill Trippe
New Millennium Publishing
1 West Foster St.
Melrose, MA 02176
(781) 662-6672
btrippe@nmpub.com
www.nmpub.com

Stephen Mooney
Stephen P. Mooney & Associates LLC
Cottage Place, Suite 207
218 Boston Street
Topsfield, MA 01983
(978) 561-1036
stephenpmooney@yahoo.com

And now, we invite you to read on and explore the field of digital rights management with us. We hope that you find it to be as fascinating a subject as we do, and we hope that this book is helpful to you and to your business.

Contents

Part III: DRM Solutions: Putting It All Together 169

Part I

The Business of DRM

Chapter 1

Where We Came From: Content Rights in the Predigital World

In this chapter, we take a look at the ways that rights to content have been managed — or not managed — before the advent of technologies such as digital media formats and the Internet. Many people, especially those who work for digital rights management technology vendors, like to think that DRM technology is revolutionary; so everyone who handles digital content should just throw out his old ways of doing business and adopt DRM-enabled business models. Unfortunately, that's not how it works. The creation and movement of content depend on systems and processes that are based on long-standing business custom or legal constraints.

What came before digital rights management? Careers have been built on the premise that such a question is tantamount to heresy because what, many may ask, could past rights management efforts — done on paper after all — possibly have to tell us about *digital rights management*? Actually, quite a bit.

Traditional Rights Management

Answering the question of whether DRM is something fundamentally new requires a brief examination of how content rights were addressed in the predigital world. Surely content rights were successfully exploited long before anybody had heard of the Internet. But do all copyrights fall within the scope of a rights management system, whether digital or not?

Numerous forms and fashions of copyright infringement flourished well prior to the advent of the Internet and to our being collectively wired. In fact, a variety of mechanisms arose in the predigital publishing, music, and film industries to address such infringement. We examine some of those efforts in this chapter and posit what these old rights management (ORM) systems have to teach us in considering where and when to apply DRM.

What sorts of rights and accompanying transactions have and have not been addressed by rights management systems traditionally? Is it simply a matter of applying DRM systems to all rights transactions? What should we retain from the proven nondigital approaches? Actually, our experience with content rights in the predigital world provides not just a guide but clear tests to determine whether it's appropriate to apply digital rights management systems to particular rights and transactions.

Rights management terminology

Many of the following terms, now associated with digital rights management, were established long before anybody ever heard of *digital* rights management:

- **Rightsholder:** A legal entity (person or company) owning rights in intellectual property (copyright, trademark, patent, and so on). Rightsholders bargain for the use of their rights. If a rightsholder is licensing rights, he is said to be a *licensor*. If he is selling his rights outright, he is said to be *seller* or *grantor*.

- **User:** A legal entity that intends to make use of intellectual property rights. If a user is licensing rights from a rightsholder, she is said to be a *licensee*. Is she is buying rights outright, she is said to be a *buyer* or *grantee*.

- **Content owner:** A term often used interchangeably with *rightsholder*. This term is somewhat imprecise, because a content owner may not own all rights to the content. For example, a content owner may be able to exercise every conceivable right in North America and have no rights at all to the very same content in the European Union. He is, nevertheless, still sometimes referred to as the *content owner*.

- **Rights transaction:** Another imprecise term for commercial purposes because it can refer to many things. For example, if you buy a copy of the *Los Angeles Times* at a newsstand, you have entered into a rights transaction. The *Los Angeles Times* (as the grantor/rightsholder) sells intellectual property rights (that is, a particular copy of the paper) to you (as the user/buyer/grantee). That's a rights transaction.

  Now, let's say that you're interested in sending a copy of an article in that particular edition of the *Los Angeles Times* to five hundred people at work. You call the paper, and you negotiate a reasonable fee. You pay the paper the fee and get the right to distribute the article. In this case, the *Los Angeles Times* (as the licensee/rightsholder) licenses intellectual property (that is, an article) to you (*as* the user/licensee).

  It turns out that your boss is so impressed that he decides to buy the *Los Angeles Times* outright. In addition to the plant, equipment, and customary commercial aspects of the transactions, yet another rights transaction ensues: to buy the intellectual property of the *Los Angeles Times*. Rights transactions, then, run the gamut from the simple (buying a newspaper) to the complex (buying a business); and they may involve licenses, both express and implied.

- **Agent:** A legal entity (person or company) authorized by a rightsholder to enter into a rights transaction on behalf of the rightsholder. For rights transactions that are less central to a rightsholder's everyday business or that, perhaps, somebody else can perform more efficiently, rightsholders often employ agents. For example, if the people at the *Los Angeles Times* are too busy to sell an edition of the paper to you directly or to negotiate a license for five hundred copies of an article, they can use agents to carry out these tasks. A real-world example, which we discuss in the section "Old Rights Management Systems" later in this chapter, is the Copyright Clearance Center (CCC), the authorized agent of thousands of publishers for entering into certain rights transactions on publishers' behalf.

- **Royalties:** Monetary compensation to a rightsholder or his agent for the use of intellectual property rights.

- **Rights management:** Business processes that for legal and commercial purposes track rights, rightsholders, licenses, sales, agents, royalties, and associated terms and conditions.

- **Digital rights management:** Rights management that uses digital technology and applies to intellectual property in digital form.

Rights management for every type of transfer?

Do all rights transfers need to be "managed" by some system? No. Take a look at a few examples from the predigital world that should continue to be handled by people rather than systems for the foreseeable future.

Songwriters and record companies

Let's imagine that Jerry, a well-known songwriter, writes a new song and makes a multimillion-dollar commercial arrangement with a recording and distribution company. Under the terms of the deal, Jerry transfers certain rights to the song to the company.

Aspects of this sale are a type of transfer, but does Jerry need a rights management system (whether ORM or DRM) to manage this rights transfer? Absolutely not. Because it is a multimillion-dollar deal, Jerry's lawyer is more than willing to devote whatever time is necessary to ensure that the deal is negotiated properly; and Jerry's agent or business managers will ensure that the agreement is carried out according to its terms.

Jerry doesn't need a rights management system to facilitate the broad distribution and secure use of his work, and this is true whether Jerry's song is pressed on vinyl records or CDs or distributed electronically via the Internet. The recording company very well may need such a system for digital distribution, but Jerry probably doesn't need it — at least not within the four corners of this particular transfer.

Jerry has completed a rights transfer without the need for a fancy rights management system, and this is true whether Jerry's deal is made in 1950 or in 2000. Because a lot of money is involved, automated rights management is simply not required and, indeed, could inhibit the successful completion of Jerry's agreement, which — because of its sheer complexity — must result from the interactions of human beings, not machines. The amount of money involved in a given transaction, then, may well be a factor in determining whether an automated rights management system (ORM or DRM) is required.

ORM and DRM systems are not particularly focused on the type of infringement that is most likely to befall Jerry at the prepublication stage. Just as the transfer of Jerry's rights to a publisher involves human interaction primarily, so too would infringement at the prepublication stage. Somebody could steal Jerry's work and attempt to pass it off as his own.

Preventing such an act of infringement is really just a matter of keeping one's work away from prying eyes or "sticky fingers." If Jerry composes his work on a computer, he probably employs some sort of security to protect his files, but such protection is not a DRM system per se. Thus, protection of Jerry's song at the prepublication stage won't be solved by a rights management system but simply by Jerry's discretion. Once again, this doesn't necessarily apply to the recording company's distribution of Jerry's song, which is an altogether different transaction.

Jerry is but one example to illustrate our first premise: Rights management systems don't apply to every type of transaction. We have also discovered two factors that are relevant in determining whether a rights management system should be applied to a particular rights transaction. The first factor is the value of the transaction: If the value is very high, it's likely to be monitored by people rather than automated systems. (And if it's very low, it's likely not to be monitored by anything at all.) In Jerry's case, the transaction was well worth his personal involvement and that of his agents. The second factor is whether the completion of the transaction will result in the increased opportunity for potential infringement.

Broadcast monitoring

As another example of rights management, consider broadcast monitoring systems. These systems monitor broadcast television and radio signals for the presence of certain pieces of content — such as advertisements and songs — that have been watermarked (tagged in a way that humans can't perceive) for such detection. One reason for implementing a broadcast monitoring system is so that an advertiser can ensure that the ads it pays for actually receive airtime. If the ads don't run, the system notifies the advertiser, who can then get the broadcaster to issue a "make-good" ad later. This is fine for run-of-the-mill advertisements. But if the ad is an $800,000 Super Bowl commercial, you can bet that many pairs of eyes will be on TV sets to make sure that the ads actually run. Despite that, broadcast monitoring is a fruitful application of watermarking technology, as the discussion in Chapter 7 indicates.

> **CROSS REFERENCE:** Broadcast monitoring systems are discussed in more detail in Chapter 7.

Publishing rights and permissions

In publishing, many rights transactions have traditionally been handled through publishing companies' Rights and Permissions departments. Surely the Great American Novel would not be sold nor bought through these traditional rights management processes, because its value calls for individual attention at higher echelons within a publishing company. Rights and Permissions departments routinely process requests from other publishers to use pieces of content, such as illustrations, tables, or quotations in educational and professional works.

Rights and Permissions departments have long been the mainstay of rights efforts in publishing. They have been engaged in rights management for decades: They determine whether publishers own particular rights; they license those rights for a fee; and, sometimes, they seek permissions for the publisher who employs them.

Rights and Permissions departments in large publishing companies are often the butts of jokes in the industry because the tasks that they perform are often cumbersome and inefficient. Yet the last laugh may be on the DRM technology companies that have worked themselves to death attempting to automate rights and permissions functions. The opportunity is there: Large publishers employ battalions of people to manage the sea of paperwork involved in requesting rights, granting rights, and processing contracts — often armed with nothing more than PCs with word processors and spreadsheets. Automating these functions would surely reduce costs and increase efficiency significantly.

Yet implementing systems to automate rights and permissions has proven to be prohibitively disruptive and expensive. An informal mid-1990s survey of CEOs from book and journal publishing companies showed that they were either unwilling to bear the cost and disruption of automating the processes, or they were in deep denial that they had a problem in this area. We attempted to build such a system at a textbook publishing company around the time of that survey, only to be told that the projected cost of implementation was more than double the expected financial return from the system.

The biggest problem is that no two publishers handle rights and permissions the same way, making it difficult for a vendor to create a single system that it can sell to more than one or two publishers. This means that rights and permissions systems must be built as custom software, which is the most expensive (and risky) type of software possible.

Vendors continue to attempt to serve this market opportunity. Some, such as the CCC and iCopyright, serve it by automating certain permissions tasks that are common, such as obtaining reprints of newspaper and magazine articles. Others, such as Savantech, REAL Software Systems, Rightsline, and Vista Computer Services, have built systems that cover a broader range of rights and permissions tasks. All these vendors are discussed in Chapter 12; the CCC is discussed in more detail in its own section, later in this chapter.

Time will tell whether any one (or more than one) of them becomes a de facto standard in the market, the way vendors such as SAP and Oracle have become standards for financial systems. At this point in time, spending a lot of money on technology in an effort to bring rights and permissions into the 21st century seems unlikely to be worthwhile. Depending on the financial return, your current system may be just fine. Looking at the costs and benefits of any DRM system is essential.

Old Rights Management Systems

We have determined that there are transactions to which rights management systems don't apply. Now we take a look at rights management systems that existed before *digital* rights management, which are called *old rights management systems* (ORMs).

The technological menace of the 1950s

Whereas we worry about the Internet today, a half century ago, fears of copyright owners were fanned by the advent of a technological menace that appeared in offices across the United States during the 1950s and 1960s: the photocopier. Photocopying of copyrighted materials became a great concern to the publishing industry, and it seemed especially difficult to address. Unlike the example about Jerry's song transaction that I used in the preceding section, the amount of money involved with any one photocopy is relatively small. As a simple business matter, it's simply not worth pursuing a royalty when the royalty itself is far less than the cost of collection. Furthermore, the materials that could be photocopied were everywhere. People subscribed to copyrighted materials; and they were readily available at home, in the office, or at a library.

Fears about the photocopying of copyrighted materials, in fact, were a major impetus to the movement in the 1960s and 1970s to overhaul the Copyright Act of 1909. The revised copyright law was passed in 1976 and went into effect in 1978. Although the act didn't address the development of private sector rights management systems per se, the legislative history did refer to the possibility of such a system developing. Congress suggested that workable clearance and licensing procedures be created to facilitate photocopying of copyrighted works. This led to the creation of the Copyright Clearance Center, Inc. in 1978.

The Copyright Clearance Center

The Copyright Clearance Center (CCC, www.copyright.com) developed licensing systems to grant permissions to users of copyrighted materials and collect royalties for publishers. CCC created an effective rights management system — albeit simply for photocopying, but still successful — long before the advent of the Internet. Although CCC initially addressed only the photocopying of text materials, CCC successfully built a rights management system by gathering the same set of rights from thousands of publishers and aggregating them into one license agreement that a copyright user could sign. Significantly, CCC doesn't enforce copyright but has built a rights management system that relies on companies and individuals respecting the law and abiding by what, in large measure, is the honor system.

No single publisher could afford to approach any users of very low-value rights because the cost of conducting the transaction would, in the overwhelming majority of cases, be far more than any royalty received. However, by aggregating the rights and royalties, CCC successfully built a viable rights management business model, fully twenty years before the term became popular. Pricing and royalty distribution were initially determined by actual surveys of the photocopying of copyrighted material, and the survey procedures themselves became a science. The notion behind the surveys is to base price on something that approaches actual use, a principle that is well understood in DRM circles today.

In its corporate licensing program, CCC traditionally aggregated survey data to get the average cost of copying in a given industry. CCC asked prospective licensees for certain employee information to come up with a price. At one time, this involved a determination of, for example, the number of employees involved in research and development activities; but in recent years, the focus has shifted to the numbers of exempt and nonexempt employees.

CCC's licensing program has been most successful in the corporate market. In addition, users may report copies to CCC on a copy-by-copy basis over the Internet and pay "by the copy."

Significantly, CCC is not the only photocopy-compliance alternative available. Users are always free to arrange separate agreements with publishers, purchase reprints, secure permissions through document suppliers, or not copy at all.

Today, CCC is the largest licensor of text reproduction rights in the world. It provides licensing systems for the reproduction and distribution of copyrighted materials in print and electronic form. CCC manages rights relating to over 1.75 million works and represents more than 9,600 publishers and hundreds of thousands of authors and other creators, directly or through their representatives. CCC-licensed customers in the United States number over 10,000 corporations and subsidiaries (including 92 of the Fortune 100 companies), as well as thousands of government agencies, law firms, document suppliers, libraries, academic institutions, copy shops, and bookstores.

CCC is a member of the International Federation of Reproduction Rights Organizations (IFRRO) and has bilateral agreements with Reproduction Rights Organizations (RROs) in 13 countries worldwide. Other major RROs include the Copyright Licensing Agency, Ltd. (CLA), United Kingdom; CanCopy, Canada; Copyright Agency Limited (CAL), Australia; and Verwertungsgesellschaft WORT (known as VG WORT), Germany.

We need to consider the factors in CCC's success, but before doing so, let's take a brief look at music as well as at possible government-run alternatives to rights management in the predigital world.

The music industry

Two organizations have dealt with collective music licensing in the United States: the American Society of Composers, Authors, and Publishers (ASCAP, www.ascap.com), founded in 1914, and Broadcast Music International (BMI, www.bmi.com), founded in 1940. Both provided road maps to CCC during the course of its formation. A third organization, SESAC (www.sesac.com [the acronym denotes an outdated French phrase]), started out as a licensing agency for classical music in Europe and has only recently started representing pop music composers and publishers in the United States. Composers and publishers choose which of these organizations they want to represent them.

ASCAP

ASCAP, a membership association of songwriters, lyricists, composers, and music publishers, grants businesses permission to perform music publicly. ASCAP provides licenses to users and royalties to members through a collective licensing system not unlike CCC's in concept. ASCAP is based on the premise that individual composers cannot possibly monitor the hundreds of thousands of businesses that use music, nor can business owners locate and negotiate with all the owners of the music that may be used.

Businesses may obtain the right to perform songs through ASCAP; their licensees include television and radio networks and affiliates, cable and satellite networks and systems, public broadcasters, Web sites, colleges and universities, night clubs, taverns and restaurants, fitness and health clubs, private clubs, hotels, trade shows, shopping malls, amusement parks, airlines, stores, and music users in a wide variety of other industries. Fees vary among industries but are consistent within a given industry. Essentially, every playback of recorded music in a public setting generates fees. Some of these public settings are obvious, whereas others are less obvious:

- Radio broadcasts.
- Soundtracks for television programs.
- Background music for shopping at supermarkets and other stores.
- Music played at nightclubs.
- Hold music for telephones.
- Background mood music at restaurants.
- Music played at company events, such as management conferences and sales meetings.

ASCAP's view is that music is a tool for making businesses more successful. It shouldn't, therefore, be free. Furthermore, the creators of the music should have the right to give or not give permission for its use in any public performance.

BMI

Like ASCAP, BMI represents songwriters as well as film, television, musical theater and classical music composers, and, of course, music publishers. BMI was founded in 1940 as an American performing rights organization. It collects money from the businesses that use music in the course of their day and then pays out that money as royalties to the composers and publishers of the songs and compositions that they play. BMI collects license fees on behalf of those American creators that it represents, as well as for the thousands of creators from around the world who have chosen BMI for U.S. representation. Like ASCAP, BMI has reciprocal agreements with similar performing rights organizations around the world.

The three music-licensing agencies have recently made forays into collecting fees from Web sites that stream music on the Internet. Initially, many music sites — especially startups not affiliated with record companies or traditional broadcasters — didn't take them seriously and viewed their attempts to collect money as nothing more than extortion. The matter isn't entirely resolved, but now it seems that the licensing agencies are gaining legitimacy in collecting fees for Internet use. For example, they've had more success in collecting increased fees from traditional broadcasters who stream their signals onto the Internet and already pay them anyway.

Another important licensing and collecting organization in the music industry is the National Music Publishers Association (NMPA) and its subsidary, the Harry Fox Agency (HFA). NMPA represents "mechanical" rights, which are the rights to reproduce and distribute recorded music. It also collects fees licenses for "synchronization rights" to use recorded music in movie soundtracks, commercials, and so on.

The rights management experiences of CCC, ASCAP, SESAC, and BMI offer lessons to those considering building and implementing DRM systems; and those lessons are examined in more detail in the section, "Lessons from ORMs," later in this chapter. But the old rights management systems don't offer the only possible solutions to collecting royalties for rightsholders — rights can be managed through strictly legal mechanisms. The following section offers two examples of these legal mechanisms.

Legal alternatives to ORMs

The systems used by ASCAP, SESAC, BMI, and CCC are not the only alternatives to addressing rights issues. Two proposals involving significant government intervention in rights transactions are considered from time to time: a compulsory license and the so-called *umbrella statute*.

Compulsory licensing

Under a compulsory licensing scheme, the rightsholder is unable to withhold permission from the user, provided the user pays an established royalty rate. Compulsory license agreements are often established when the exclusive right of the copyright owner isn't firmly established or when a greater societal good is identified.

Where can a good case for compulsory licensing be made? Of the millions of people in sub-Saharan Africa infected with HIV/AIDS, almost none have access to promising AIDS drugs because of the cost. Anti-AIDS drugs are developed by pharmaceutical companies and are the subject of patent rights. Patents are discussed in Chapter 3, but suffice it to say that pharmaceutical patents grant a 17-year monopoly to the patent holder, who is free to charge what the market will bear. There is a conflict between the human benefits that distribution of anti-AIDS drugs would have in sub-Saharan Africa and the rightsholder's monopoly. Let's say that a cure for AIDS were developed. It could be argued that a compulsory licensing scheme should be instituted. Under a compulsory licensing scheme, the pharmaceutical company would be stripped not only of the option not to license but probably also of its power to set the price. Situations such as these can lead to great tension, not to mention legal battles.

Although determining the price for property conveyed has traditionally been left to the parties, compulsory licensing requires the establishment of fees by entities such as a copyright tribunal (that is, the government), which promulgates rules and sets fees. Whether the parties will deal is not an issue with respect to copyright works covered by compulsory licenses; indeed, the works covered by such an arrangement must be made available to the user. The Copyright Act provides for the following four compulsory licensing arrangements:

- Cable television
- Phonograph records
- Broadcasting
- Satellite dishes

As with the ORMs, compulsory licensing arrangements are implemented when the transaction costs of dealing are high in relation to the likely licensing fee that the parties would negotiate on their own.

At first blush, compulsory licensing appears to be a reasonable and fair arrangement. The user gets rights, the copyright owner gets paid, and the risk of litigation, at least in theory, is diminished because the compulsory license forces agreement. The establishment of compulsory licensing in the pre-DRM world begs the question as to whether another compulsory licensing amendment should be added to the Copyright Act so that DRM may be specifically addressed. Such an amendment would clearly be inappropriate. The practical difficulties of such a system would outweigh the benefits. It would bring the government into the transaction. Because the fees would likely be established by the government, or at least with government oversight, the heart of the agreement would be left to a nonparticipant in the transaction. Moreover, such a system would not account for changes in circumstances that will inevitably arise.

Finally, compulsory licensing is not the most effective way to promote the purpose of copyright, which is the progress of science and the useful arts. Reward to the copyright owner is a secondary consideration, but compulsory licensing would ascribe far too little importance to such rewards by leaving no room for the natural give and take between copyright owners and users. Could the greater societal good of progress of the arts and sciences be advanced by adding yet another bureaucratic agency? We think not.

The umbrella statute

An approach somewhat more benign is the *umbrella statute,* which is proposed from time to time. Under the umbrella statute, the only remedy that a rightsholder could receive for copyright infringement is a reasonable copying fee, provided that he belongs to a collective licensing society such as CCC or ASCAP. Clearly, the umbrella statute would encourage copyright owners to place their works in collective licensing arrangements. Failure to do so would result in the copyright owner being able to recover only a reasonable copying fee (as opposed, for example, to much larger statutory damages available under current law). In this way, the umbrella statute mimics incentives that the law provides to copyright owners to register their works with the Copyright Office. By encouraging parties to participate in a collective licensing arrangement, the umbrella statute appears to be a workable mechanism.

Suppose, however, that an umbrella statute were in force with respect to certain electronic rights. If a particular copyright owner refused to make his works available, the umbrella statute would prevent that copyright owner from being awarded more than a reasonable copying fee. This is contrary to the spirit of American law, which has traditionally provided much wider remedies to copyright owners whose rights are infringed.

Lessons from ORMs

After considering the various approaches taken by CCC, ASCAP, and BMI to the management of certain rights in the predigital world, as well as schemes such as an umbrella statute or compulsory license, we draw the following conclusions about rights management systems generally, whether in the digital world or not.

Government provides the forum, not the solution

We offer this lesson first because we feel so strongly about it. Direct government intervention in the rights management solution or agreement, as with compulsory licensing, may be necessary in certain areas where the use provides secondary revenues to the rightsholder. But otherwise, government intervention is not appropriate for digital rights management generally, as agreements should best be left to the parties involved. CCC, ASCAP, and BMI have demonstrated that even some secondary uses of copyrighted works (photocopying, background music, and so on) may be effectively handled in the private sector. Solutions such as compulsory licensing or the umbrella statute are, for the most part, not appropriate in DRM settings.

Focus on particular rights

CCC focuses on photocopying; ASCAP focuses on music licensing to businesses. Within the realm of all possible copyrights, these are actually quite narrow. By sticking to their respective areas, these organizations developed niche rights businesses that have not only proven enormously successful but have also resulted in their being the market-makers and "go-to" organizations within their niches. Both DRM vendors and rightsholders using DRM systems should appreciate the importance of focus and not reaching too broadly in applying new DRM technologies.

Aggregation is key to economic viability

ASCAP, CCC, SESAC, and BMI succeed because it's not economically worthwhile for rightsholders to pursue their respective niches. The transactions costs in any one instance exceed any reasonable anticipated royalty. Rightsholders have figured out that farming out these licensing opportunities makes the most economic sense for them.

This is every bit as true for DRM systems and services. Just because somebody offers a DRM service that could address all possible rights transactions doesn't mean that you should use it for that purpose. Such systems may tempt a rightsholder to manage photocopying rights or certain rights to music internally, but the system itself should not be the only rationale for doing so. You need to be placed correctly in the market to exploit particular rights. It may be that you can efficiently exploit all your rights some of the time, but adopting a DRM system doesn't necessarily give you the ability to exploit *all* your rights *all* the time.

Advantages in collective action

It's possible that DRM service providers can offer advantages to rightsholders through collective action. Certainly economies of scale have been created in this manner. The predigital world is replete with examples of this. A bookstore or music store is really nothing more than a collection of rights from hundreds of publishers and recording companies. An online store is not really all that different in this respect. By bringing materials together, rightsholders can take advantage of an aggregated audience. Rights aggregated into a book or an electronic publication ultimately come to be traded separately in certain cases, and the development of such a "rights market" is the sort of collective action that rightsholders may take.

Your core business

What are you in business to do? What is your mission in life? In the case of text publishers, their mission is to publish books or journals and to get people to buy or subscribe to them. Sure, they own the photocopy rights, but collecting royalties for photocopying is not their core business, so farming it out makes sense. Similarly, recording companies are interested in getting people to buy their recordings — on CD, DVD, or whatever. Collecting royalties for music playing in elevators is not their main mission, so they farm this task out to ASCAP. Be aware that this dynamic continues in the digital world; DRM doesn't change anything in this regard. Always ask, "What's my core business?"

Predigital Industry Organizations

As you consider how to apply some of these lessons to DRM, you also need to be aware of certain important organizations that began in the predigital world and whose experience is projected into the digital world. Some of the more notable industry groups are discussed in this section.

Authors: CISAC

Founded in Paris in 1926, the CISAC (the International Confederation of Societies of Authors and Composers — the abbreviation actually stands for the French name, Confédération Internationale des Societes d'Auteurs et Compositeurs) is a nonprofit organization that represents a total of more than two million creators of music, literature, visual arts, and other types of content.

Authors don't belong to CISAC on an individual basis; instead, the societies that represent them on a national basis become members of CISAC. Authors' societies include ALCS (Authors Licensing and Collecting Society) in the United Kingdom and the Authors' Guild in the United States. CISAC coordinates work among its member societies that have, for several decades, effectively established a system of reciprocal representation founded on a basic contract defined by CISAC.

The standardization of technical exchanges of information between societies and the harmonization of industry practices are important CISAC functions. CISAC is currently deploying the Common Information System (CIS), a world network of databases and standards for the identification of works and participants in the creative process. CIS is aimed at improving member society management by setting up more secure and efficient procedures while also enabling the tracking of the use of works in the digital sphere and, in particular, on the Internet.

Music: RIAA

The Recording Industry Association of America (RIAA) functions as an advocacy group for the recording industry generally and "fosters a business and legal climate that supports and promotes members' creative and financial vitality" (www.riaa.com). The membership of RIAA includes companies that create, manufacture, and distribute approximately 90 percent of all sound recordings produced and sold in the United States (not counting illegal copies, of course).

RIAA has engaged in many legislative efforts to prevent what it views as the censorship of music, surely a rights issue at one level. The RIAA is interested in preventing censorship as a free speech issue, but also because banning sales would limit sales opportunities for its member organizations. In the wake of numerous school shootings across the country, many efforts have been launched to prevent certain music from influencing minors in negative ways. Banning certain kinds of music is not the answer, according to RIAA. The organization has been lobbying Congress against restrictive measures and working with the artists themselves to educate both lawmakers and the public about the negative effects of such measures. The RIAA believes that voluntary warning labels on albums with explicit lyrics — which were put in place around 15 years ago over the RIAA's objections — are enough. The RIAA has been working actively to prevent such measures as ratings for concerts that are similar to ratings for movies, national standards (instead of local community standards) for decent versus indecent material, and state initiatives to prevent sales of albums with warning labels on them to minors.:

Although the music censorship debate is often viewed as a free speech issue, it is also a rights issue. In theory, DRM systems could make it possible to keep certain music from certain users (for example, children) in certain circumstances. A similar debate is under way within the library community with regard to the installation of filtering software on library computers to prevent patrons who are minors from viewing pornography. The technology in each case has implications for intellectual property rights.

RIAA's solution is parental involvement and control. This was, of course, the only option available in the predigital world, and it was easier in some respects to implement. As DRM technologies come to bear on such problems (the so-called V-Chip, which can block the reception of certain television programs, is but one example), what were purely free speech issues become in some respects rights issues: If I am prevented from exploiting my intellectual property by a given technology, does that not proscribe my exclusive rights under copyright law?

In recent years, RIAA has also gotten heavily involved in more explicit DRM issues, related to music piracy. The advent of the MP3 file format — which enables good-quality music to be compressed into relatively small digital files — and software such as Napster and Gnutella have scared the record companies half to death with the prospect of revenues sharply diminishing from piracy. To combat this, RIAA and the major record labels started the Secure Digital Music Initiative (SDMI) in 1999. See Chapter 6 for details on SDMI, but the punch line is that this effort to create standards for copy-protected digital music distribution through cooperation among the record companies, consumer electronics manufacturers, and DRM technology vendors looks like it won't pan out.

Regardless of the specifics of SDMI, RIAA is a predigital industry body that is having an increasing impact on how intellectual property rights are exercised in the market.

Movies: MPAA and MPA

Two groups formed in the predigital world impact the exploitation of intellectual property rights expressed in film: the Motion Picture Association of America (MPAA) and the Motion Picture Association (MPA).

According to its Web site, MPAA was formed in 1922 as a trade association of the American film industry. Its initial focus was on cultivating a positive image for the film industry. MPA was formed in 1945 to represent the audiovisual industry worldwide and function as "a little State Department" to address a wide range of activities affecting the film industry overseas. The focus of these groups is increasingly turning to rights for television, cable, home video, and future means of delivering audiovisual works not yet invented. MPAA is the entity of greater interest to those interested in DRM because it has directed a comprehensive antipiracy program since 1976. The focus of this, according to MPAA, is to perform the following:

♦ Strengthen industry security measures.

♦ Strengthen existing copyright protection through legislative activity.

♦ Assist local governments in the investigation and prosecution of piracy cases.

♦ Provide technical support in the criminal and civil litigation generated by such investigations.

The MPAA's Web site points out that videocassette copying remains a common form of piracy of audiovisual works in the United States. Policing such piracy obviously becomes increasingly difficult in the digital world, particularly as broadband access becomes more widely available across the country. Broadband, usually made available to homes through cable modems or DSL access, enables the transmission of digital video files that, due to their large size, cannot be feasibly transmitted on traditional dial-up connections to the Internet. Thus, it's likely that the preponderance of the piracy of video works will shift from VCRs to digital duplications over time, as more and more people get Internet access through broadband connections.

Still, it's worth noting that most long-form video programming, such as cybercasts of concerts, is currently sent through streaming technology (see Chapter 5) rather than through file downloads, which would measure in the gigabytes. Streaming technology is considerably harder to exploit for piracy, although that too will change over time. MPAA will eventually become engaged in efforts that employ DRM services and systems that identify, track, and monitor these valuable works.

Intellectual Property Tracking

The predigital world offers several models for tracking intellectual property, perhaps the best known of which are the International Standard Book Number (ISBN) and the International Standard Serial Number (ISSN). This section discusses how these systems came to be.

Readers of books and periodicals often note the ISSN or ISBN without knowing its intended purpose. It's not important for you to understand the intricacies of these systems; but we offer some background here to provide an historical overview for the future importance of unique identifiers to intellectual property in digital environments. Even in those environments, identifiers ideally will be transparent to users. But this background information may be of interest to information professionals.

ISBN

W.H. Smith, a large book retailer in the United Kingdom, decided in the mid-1960s that it needed to computerize its warehouse facilities. To do so, it decided to adopt a standard numbering system for tracking its books. Consultants and other experts in the U.K. book industry developed the Standard Book Number (SBN), which was instituted in the United Kingdom in 1967. The International Organization for Standardization (ISO) established a committee to study the possible adoption of the SBN for international use. Representatives from Europe and the United States met in London in 1968, wrote and circulated a report, and met again in Berlin in 1969. The result was the International Standard Book Number (ISBN), which was approved as an ISO standard in 1970 as *ISO 2108*. The ISBN has not changed all that much since, although it has been applied to more than simply books (even to a particular line of teddy bears). The International ISBN Agency is based in the Staatsbibliothek zu Berlin (Berlin State Library); its principal functions are the following:

- Promote and supervise the worldwide use of the ISBN system.
- Approve the definition and structure of group agencies.
- Advise on the establishment and functioning of group agencies.
- Allocate range identifiers to group agencies.
- Advise group agencies on the allocation of international publisher identifiers.

The ISBN is employed in 150 countries, and major ISBN agencies are run in the United States by R.R. Bowker and in the United Kingdom by Whitakers. The functions of each local ISBN agency, according to the International ISBN Agency, are the following:

♦ Promote participation of the ISBN system within its area.

♦ Manage and administer the affairs of the group.

♦ Decide, in cooperation with publishers and their representative agencies, the range of publisher prefixes required.

♦ Allocate publisher prefixes to eligible publishers and maintain a register of publishers and their prefixes.

♦ Decide, in consultation with publishers and their representative agencies, which publishers will assign numbers to their own titles and which will have numbers assigned to their titles by the group agency.

♦ Advise publishers on the correct and proper implementation of the system.

♦ Provide materials and resources that ensure the proper implementation of the ISBN standard.

♦ Make computer printouts of ISBNs available to publishers that number their books and have check digits already calculated.

♦ Inform publishers of any invalid or duplicate ISBNs assigned by them.

♦ Provide technical advice and assistance to publishers and ensure that standards and approved procedures are observed in the group.

♦ Assist the book industry in the use of the ISBN in computer systems.

♦ Handle relations with the International ISBN Agency on behalf of all the publishers in the group.

ISBNs consist of "ISBN" followed by ten digits. (By 2006, ISBNs will have up to thirteen digits.) The ten-digit number has four distinct parts:

1. **The group identifier:** Identifies the geographical area, country, or language area.

2. **The publisher prefix:** Identifies the publisher who published the book.

3. **The title identifier:** Identifies a specific edition of a specific publication of the publisher.

4. **The check digit:** Provides a statistical means to verify the authenticity of the overall ISBN.

ISSN

International Standard Serial Numbers (ISSNs) apply to serials. Serials are publications that usually bear a date or volume/issue number, such as newspapers, magazines, journals, and annual reports and directories – that is, materials published in installments. Unlike ISBNs, however, information can't be gleaned from an ISSN except for the identity of the particular serial. ISSNs contain eight digits and, as with ISBNs, the last digit is a check digit. According to the Library of Congress, ISSNs provide the following advantages:

♦ ISSNs provide a useful and economical method of communication between publishers and suppliers, making trade distribution systems faster and more efficient.

♦ ISSNs help the accurate citing of serials by scholars, researchers, abstracters, and librarians.

- As a standard for numeric identification code, the ISSN is eminently suitable for computer use in fulfilling the need for file update and linkage, retrieval, and transmittal of data.

- ISSNs are used in libraries for identifying titles, ordering and checking in, and claiming serials.

- ISSNs simplify interlibrary loan systems and union catalog reporting and listing.

- The U.S. Postal Service uses ISSNs to regulate certain publications mailed at second-class and controlled circulation rates.

- The ISSN is an integral component of the journal article citation used to monitor payments to the Copyright Clearance Center.

- All ISSN registrations are maintained in an international database.

Although the ISSN is an identifier without evident meaning, the Library of Congress rightly observes its many practical uses in daily life. Imagining such advantages in the digital environment led publishers and others to construct the next identifier we examine in this chapter: DOIs.

DOI

ISBNs and ISSNs are now deeply ingrained in the publishing industry. Yet they have various inadequacies as identifiers, particularly with respect to identifying digital content. In Chapter 6, which covers DRM-related standards, we mention that various identifiers have been invented to cover different types of intellectual property, ranging from books and periodicals to journal articles and musical works.

The Digital Object Identifier (DOI), which was invented in 1997 under the auspices of the Association of American Publishers (AAP, the trade association for book and journal publishers in the United States), is the first identifier that is applicable to *all* types of content, whether online or offline. The system that underlies DOI has certain special properties that make it ideal for identifying content on the Internet.

Chapter 6 provides details about the DOI, which is off to a promising start, especially in the book and journal publishing industries. The journal publishing community embraced DOIs through CrossRef, a nonprofit organization set up to provide reference linking among journal articles using DOIs. In the book industry, the AAP commissioned a study by Andersen Consulting (now Accenture) on numbering and metadata in the emerging eBook market; the study recommended the adoption of the DOI as the preferred numbering scheme. An article in the November 29, 2000 issue of *The Seybold Bulletin* proclaimed that the book community's endorsement of DOIs would give the numbering scheme significant momentum and called for the DOI's adoption in the magazine, newspaper, and Web publishing markets as well.

Predigital Rights: Indications of Quality

In addition to particular rights management solutions and industry organizations, the predigital world offered everyone in the intellectual property chain certain implicit assurances about quality. That is, it was relatively easy to judge the quality of a particular product — text, video, or music — just by looking at it or knowing where it came from. Before the Internet, it was relatively easy for users to judge the quality of information. They could examine a particular publication, know its reputation, and make judgments accordingly. The same was true of music. Because distribution was so closely controlled, it was relatively easy for users to assess what they were getting before making a commitment. This, in turn, enhanced the reputation of the rightsholder, for users accorded good providers market respect and loyalty.

However, Internet users either will not or cannot readily identify *quality* information. Because what rightsholders sell is more likely to be *quality* information than that provided by unauthoritative sources, a user's inability or unwillingness to determine quality threatens rightsholders' ability to manage rights effectively. At the February 2001 meeting of the Professional and Scholarly Publishing (PSP) Division of the AAP, Dr. William Arms of Cornell suggested that American children use the Yahoo and About Web sites for research. According to Arms, undergraduates avoid the use of libraries in part because the Web is so readily available to them. So tThe risk that students will use inaccurate or simply mediocre information is high.

Consider this example of how indications of quality are not always clear: The *New York Times* is a traditional newspaper of high quality. The arduous process of research in a paper world would give even the unacquainted some assurance that the *New York Times* is an esteemed newspaper. However, on the Web, information contained in the *New York Times* may not appear to be all that different than that which appears in the *Drudge Report.* The ease with which the unacquainted may reach either the *New York Times* or the *Drudge Report* in an electronic environment yields no clue as to which is the more valuable. How is a user to know that the *New York Times* is the more valuable? And if a user doesn't know that, how can she make an informed decision as to the value of the information? She is in no position at all to avail herself of the quality information that you may be selling.

Only you can define your marketing presence. Who are you? What is your clear mission, market, and focus? Do you know it? Do your employees know it? Do your customers know it? Is it written down somewhere? If your answer to the latter four questions is *yes*, you are well positioned to market yourself and your intellectual property to the world. If you answer *no* to even one of the four questions, you should consider remedying the situation immediately. And only you can provide editorial direction targeted toward your market.

"Everything depends on a chain of reputation," according to Arms. In publishing, as in other businesses, an aspect of reputation is a quality brand and longevity. Being around a long time really helps, and Arms cites a publisher who has said, "The only way that we build reputation is over time," and "Our greatest achievement is coming out on time, for over five years."

Rights management systems will help rightsholders who maintain trusted sources of content or develop new ones and communicate to customers that their content is of value. The mere act of going to the effort and expense of adopting rights management systems — even though such systems in the digital world may be cheaper and easier to implement than their analogs in the predigital world — says something to customers about your commitment to product quality. Saying that you care about controlling rights goes a long way toward differentiating your products from a product from a company who doesn't care about rights.

Chapter 2

Bits and Nets:
New Businesses, New Possibilities

Ways of distributing content, whether online or offline, are based on business models. The objective of this chapter is not to discuss the merits of all possible business models for online content distribution because that would require an entire book itself. For one thing, the question of what sizes of content to sell — because the Internet lets you sell any size at all, for example, individual textbook chapters, journal articles, and music tracks instead of entire books, journals, and CDs — is the subject of endless debate, and we don't venture far into that territory. Instead, we examine several online content business models that have been or could possibly be enabled or improved by digital rights management technology.

If you examine the early DRM systems, you will notice a paradox: DRM was originally intended to make the online world more like the offline world by inhibiting copyright infringement for digital content in ways that approximate the natural inhibitions that physical media place on copyright infringement. But in concentrating so much on copyright protection, early DRM solutions largely sidestepped successful *business models* from the offline world, instead placing the importance of copy protection ahead of the importance of business models. This is one of the reasons — though not the only one — why early DRM systems failed. They assumed the validity of business models that were unproven, hiding behind claims about the Internet being a new medium.

Years have gone by, and we understand a more about what business models will succeed or fail online. It shouldn't be surprising that some online business models are direct analogs of those from the offline world. Others have arisen because of the unique properties of the Internet; still others have come into being as a result of the expectations set by early Internet technologies.

As we examine these business models, you'll find that DRM works where it supports the business model, not the other way around. This may sound obvious, but it's worth stating anyway. Another obvious statement that's worth making is that business models derive from the customer. The customer may be empowered to do new things with new technologies, but otherwise, and for the most part, she's the same customer as she ever was.

In this chapter, we look at the following types of business models and examine how DRM applies to them:

- Paid downloads
- Subscriptions
- Pay-per-view and pay-per-listen
- Usage metering

- Peer-to-peer and superdistribution
- Selling rights

This chapter concludes with a few thoughts on choosing the right business models for your own business.

Paid Downloads

The original business model associated with DRM was the paid download. You went to a Web site, filled out some information, gave your credit card number, and got a file that contained some content in encrypted form. You downloaded a client application that decrypted the content and played or showed it or passed it to another application to do so. This is one of the few business models that early DRM systems such as IBM's Cryptolope supported.

Paid downloads are not a bad idea, and the business model makes sense because it's a direct analog to commerce in physical goods. You go to a bookstore and buy a book. Go to a music store and buy a CD or cassette. Go to a Web site and buy a piece of content. Paid downloads approximate this business model, and DRM technology makes it possible to approximate the *rights* model inherent in physical content purchases of this nature (as discussed in Chapter 4).

Yet DRM-enabled paid downloads on the Internet have not done very well. This is mainly because the technology has been too clunky. There are three problems:

- It's complex to purchase the content.
- It's even more complex to use the DRM technology.
- People are not comfortable reading books or listening to music on their PCs or Macs.

It's important not to overlook the first point: Often the barrier to purchasing content is the process, not the price. If you're a road warrior, this scenario is probably familiar to you: You show up at the airport only minutes before your flight takes off. You want to grab a newspaper to read on the plane, but there's a long line at the newsstand's cash register. Your conundrum: Do you try waiting in line to pay for the paper, skip the paper and board the aircraft, or just take the paper without paying? Come on, admit it — you've done the latter at least once in your life.

Similarly, given the choice between paid and free content downloads, many people opt for the free one out of convenience — not because they can't afford it. Several years ago, the two leading sources of information about consumer computer products on the Web were C|Net and ZDNet, the latter being the Web site of the publisher Ziff-Davis. C|Net offered its product reviews for free, whereas ZDNet required users to register and download product reviews from its esteemed *PC Magazine* labs. Someone we know was researching home printer/fax machines and looked at these two sites. He would be an enormous hypocrite to begrudge a publisher a couple of bucks for its content, but he just didn't want to be bothered with the registration form — so he chose C|Net.

Paid downloads will be more successful on the Internet when the three problems that we listed above are fixed. One approach is to offer paid downloads on PCs without DRM. Several newspapers and magazines are now offering paid downloads of archive articles through service providers such as QPass and ProQuest (see Chapter 12), but these are plain files, not using DRM technology, and they are short articles that people don't mind reading on their PCs. Another advantage of these services is that users need to register with them only once and can then download articles from any of the publications that use them. Another avenue to DRM-enabled paid downloads is to eschew the PC. Certain new handheld devices, such as eBook readers and portable music players, provide a better reading or listening experience than PCs. Plus, it is possible to build DRM technology directly into these devices, instead of retrofitting it, as has been necessary in the PC world. DRM technology is now firmly embedded into eBook readers. DRM's chances for success in music players are mixed because portable music players with good playback quality have been around since the Sony Walkman made its debut in the early 1980s; therefore, some retrofitting (of consumer attitudes as well as of technology) is necessary. Several DRM vendors are working with consumer electronics makers on this.

Nevertheless, there are isolated examples of paid downloads that involve both DRM technology and PCs. Some segments of the publishing market are early adopters of DRM technology because their content is timely, of high value, and unique. Market research fits this description — market research in the technology area, where the users are more likely to be comfortable with DRM clients, especially so. Computer industry market researchers such as G2 Computer Intelligence and the Aberdeen Group have used DRM technology to support paid downloads, often of documents in PDF format, for a while. A number of "boutique" newsletters in vertical industries — the kind that cost several hundred dollars a year for a subscription — are also experimenting with DRM-enabled paid downloads.

The music industry has also attempted paid downloads for a few years. The most successful technology vendor in that area has been Liquid Audio, which has a complete encoding and playback solution that incorporates both encryption and watermarking. Liquid Audio offers this as a turnkey solution to Web sites that want to sell music downloads. It includes the Liquid Player client, Liquid Store server, and Liquid Catalog of over 150,000 digital tracks of secure downloadable music in a wide variety of styles, encoded in Liquid Audio's format.

One of the earliest users of Liquid Audio technology was a company called N2K (which stands for "Need to Know"), which operated the Web site Music Boulevard. N2K offered a service called EMOD (Encoded Music on Demand), which used the Liquid Audio system. N2K merged with CDNow, which is a popular music purchase site at this writing. CDNow continues to offer paid downloads of music in Liquid Audio, although Liquid Audio has modified its technology so that its files can be exported for playback on other music players. CDNow tries to ameliorate the ease-of-use problem by giving users a step-by-step guide on "How to Download Music."

The paid download business model is now being considered by the film industry as well. Five major movie studios (MGM, Paramount Pictures, Sony Pictures, Warner Brothers, and Universal Pictures) recently announced plans for a joint venture that would allow users to download copies of feature films over the Internet for a fee. According to a story in the *New York Times* on August 17, 2001, the studios are doing this more as a defensive move than as a near-term revenue opportunity:

> The service . . . will be available only to those with high-speed Internet connections [and] is an attempt to get ahead of piracy problems that have plagued the music industry through services like Napster and which were beginning to be felt in the film industry with newer file-swapping services. . . . The venture is also seen by many studio executives as a first step toward true video-on-demand, when consumers will be able to watch any movie they want, whenever they want. Initially, the films will be available for download only onto personal computers, or television monitors linked to an Internet connection, but eventually video-on-demand service is expected to include cable television and other delivery systems. . . . The selection of films, and how much it will cost to download them, will be left to the individual studios. Studios that are not part of the venture will also be allowed to post films on the site. The average feature film is about 500 megabytes in digitized form and will take 20 minutes to 40 minutes to download.

Thus, the paid download model, the digital equivalent of buying a book, CD, or video in a retail establishment, will eventually become a mainstay of DRM business models on the Internet. It is most likely to work with high-value, time-critical content that is not available from other sources or as an alternative to subscription services for users who want only small tastes of the content being offered. It is *not* likely to work with small, low-value content that has free equivalents, such as most newspaper and consumer magazine articles. If nothing else, the cost of processing those small transactions is prohibitive and likely to remain so for a while.

Subscriptions

Subscription models are not currently related to DRM, but they will be in the future. The way a subscription model has traditionally worked online is that you sign up for a subscription and get a username and password that gives you access to a "subscribers only" part of a Web site. Nothing prevents you from copying the material that you find there and sending it to a million of your closest friends. But as with paid downloads, the lack of copy protection technology is mainly due to the technology not being easy enough to use vis-à-vis the value of the content. After DRM technology becomes more mainstream, we will see subscription services in which content is protected in such a way as to allow only paid subscribers to access it, no matter where it is.

Content providers love subscription models, and we are all familiar with how they work. For a set fee, often an annual fee, users receive copyrighted information on a regular basis — daily, weekly, monthly, quarterly. The foremost attractive feature of subscription models is the ability to predict revenue with a fair degree of certainty several quarters, and even years, in advance. This predictability makes subscriptions the DRM model of choice for many rightsholders, just as is the case in the paper world. And just as in the paper world, content providers are willing to trade off some absolute revenue in favor of the certainty of the revenue stream over time.

Yet on the Internet, consumers haven't fully embraced paid subscription models. We are aware of many individuals who gladly pay regular fees (and tips!) for the delivery of the *New York Times* to their doorstep each morning, but who take great umbrage at the thought of the *New York Times* charging a similar subscription fee for its online version. Many online periodicals, including *Slate* and *Inside.com,* flirted with paid subscriptions, only to retrench to the safe world of "free" — although in a sense, the online version isn't really free because you have to register and provide personal information, which is worth something.

Why will users pay for physical but not electronic delivery? As noted earlier, the technology is too hard to use. Habit and expectations also play a role. The Internet grew up with a frontier mentality of "Information wants to be free," to quote early Internet ideologue Stewart Brand. Expectations have been set. Although there are plenty of print newspapers that are free to readers, these have tended not to be "serious" newspapers — the sort of thing that you can grab from a flimsy wire stand while hurrying out the door of the local 7-Eleven (with the exception, of course, of the *Village Voice,* which is free for ideological as well as financial reasons). However, on the Web, free quality news information has existed in abundance since the Web became a significant presence in our lives. Thus, from the perspective of user expectations, it has been extremely difficult for any news organization to charge a subscription fee online. This phenomenon has repeated itself across the Web.

The other factor is the value, timeliness, and uniqueness of the information. As mentioned earlier, market research reports and industry newsletters rate highly in all three categories. Simpler forms of information, such as real-time stock quotes, fit this description too. These are all specialized information that particular groups of users *need*. In contrast, you don't *need* the *New York Times,* with all due respect to it. In a pinch, if you're interested in national or international headlines, a variety of other papers would be *good enough,* however much you may love the *New York Times.* And if you're just interested in what is going on in New York, the *Daily News'* new product the *Daily Express,* given out for free to Manhattan subway commuters during evening rush hour, may also be *good enough.* Even the *New York Times* is not sufficiently specialized to overcome the expectations of users that it ought to be free online.

WSJ.com, the *Wall Street Journal's* Web site, is one of the few exceptions to the preceding rule. Tens of thousands of people are willing to pay for subscriptions to it. This is mainly because the audience is more affluent than usual, and in many cases, they can charge the subscription fee to their companies as a business expense. Another well-known exception is *Consumer Reports Online.* People pay for subscriptions to that because it is closely related to making purchases, some of them of large consumer durables such as automobiles and dishwashers. A subscription to *Consumer Reports Online* is like an investment in product quality, just as a subscription to a report by a respected stock analyst is an investment in, well, one's investments.

Although *Consumer Reports* doesn't link its print and online subscriptions, the *Wall Street Journal* does. There was a time when the *Wall Street Journal* had a business model similar to the *New York Times:* You had only to register at `www.wsj.com`, and you had free access to the *Wall Street Journal* online. When the *Wall Street Journal* switched models and began charging a subscription fee, the number of subscribers fell markedly. This was all according to plan: Management at the *Journal* had always intended to charge for subscriptions to the site; they used the free site as a teaser, sort of as a try-before-you-buy offer.

Moreover, the paper used its online version to enhance the value of its print subscriptions.

The *Wall Street Journal* offers the following:

♦ An online-only subscription of $59 per year.

♦ An online subscription of $29 per year for users who subscribe to the print version of either the *Wall Street Journal* or *Barron's,* another esteemed publication of Dow Jones & Co. The annual print subscription to the *Wall Street Journal* costs $175.

These numbers lead to an interesting analysis of the subscription model. First of all, remember that a great number of users gladly "subscribed" to the *Wall Street Journal* when the price was free, just as is the case with the *New York Times* currently. When the *Wall Street Journal* began charging the foregoing subscription fees, these users dropped off. Should Dow Jones care that these people stopped being interested? Surely, had its business model relied on advertising revenue and had its advertisers been watching the numbers of eyeballs looking at the Dow Jones site, the precipitous drop in users would have spelled disaster for the *Wall Street Journal.* Although some were certainly sorry to see those readers depart when subscription fees were charged, the *Wall Street Journal* really shouldn't be concerned; its own subscription fees tell the tale.

Clearly, if a user wants just the information, the least expensive option is the $59 per year online subscription. The user pays less money, and at the same time, the *Wall Street Journal* saves the cost of production and delivery of the print newspaper. Everybody evidently wins.

Note, however, that there is another class of users who willingly pay subscription fees of $204 for *the very same information* in two forms — paper and online. Now, the $204 people can take their paper on the train and do all those wonderful things that you can do with paper that you can't do (at least not yet) with an electronic subscription. The fact, however, that they are willing to pay more than three times the cost as the online-only subscribers shouldn't be lost on those considering rights subscription models. There are groups of users for whom the subscription is worth the price, given who they are, the value that particular information has to them, and (to be fair) the depth of their company's largesse for business expenses.

The economist's term for these people is *price-elastic.* The *Wall Street Journal* has identified a group of price-elastic users, who not only pay more money for their subscriptions but are also highly attractive to advertisers. It has willingly forgone other users —people whose lives don't turn on the content in the *Journal,* but who may take a glance at the paper from time to time if it's free. These people offer Dow Jones nothing in terms of revenue or potential revenue.

Although the *Wall Street Journal* was a prominent example of a paid online subscription product for a fairly broad consumer audience, there have been many examples of paid online subscription products for specialized audiences, such as academic and professional fields. As a prominent example of the former, John Wiley & Sons' InterScience (`www.interscience.wiley.com`) is a collection of journals that Wiley has put up on the Web. Anyone can register for the site, do keyword searches for articles, and view citations, but only subscribers to the journals in question can view the full text of the articles.

Paid online subscriptions are also common among market research firms – once again, especially those in the technology sector, such as Forrester Research, Jupiter Media Metrix, and the Gartner Group. Large companies often buy these firms' research products, choosing which subject matter areas they want to receive and paying accordingly. The tricky issue with online subscriptions to academic and professional content is how to control institutional access. In some cases, companies purchase access for a set number of people, in an arrangement known as a *site license.* The company appoints an administrator (usually someone in the corporate library) to keep track of site licenses. The content provider may give the administrator a set number of user IDs, which she must dole out to people who need access to the content (Forrester's service works this way).

In other cases (such as Jupiter), only a single point of contact has a username and password for getting access to the content on the Web site, and the publisher trusts that person to distribute the information to those who need it in the company. This is analogous to a librarian controlling a single hard copy of the research. Just as people may infringe copyright by making photocopies of the hard copy, they may infringe the terms of the online content license by giving their username and password away to others in the company. That is a risk that research publishers such as Jupiter are willing to take – they have chosen to prioritize easy access (and simple pricing) for their customers. It's interesting to compare Forrester with Jupiter in this way: Jupiter, the newer and more Internet-focused research firm, emphasizes ease of use in its distribution model, while Forrester, the older firm, tends toward copyright control. The situation is quite analogous to the C|Net/ZDNet example cited in the section "Paid Downloads," earlier in this chapter.

Subscriptions in the music industry are currently rare, although not completely nonexistent. Some high-end music magazines have included music CDs with their monthly issues. Music clubs are sort of like monthly subscription services: You get a "Featured Selection" every month in the mail unless you explicitly say that you don't want it. But overall, the model in the music industry has been one of paying for products one at a time.

The primary obstacle to music subscription services is being able to offer enough of a catalog to make the service worthwhile. The major music clubs, Columbia House and BMG Music Service, are owned by a single major recording label (BMG), but they spend lots of time and effort negotiating the rights to sell other labels' music so that their catalogs of music for sale can contain rich selections. There is an expectation that any online music subscription service must offer a complete catalog of music — one that, at any rate, rivals the ad hoc catalog that was available on Napster before the court put a stop to it (see Chapter 3). This is a far more difficult thing to achieve than most people realize. In many cases, the major recording labels don't even have rights to their own recorded material, such as when a track on an album is an arrangement of a song that is not owned by the recording label.

One independent startup company that appears to be on the verge of licensing a mass of music material that is sufficient to power a subscription service is FullAudio (`www.fullaudio.com`). At this writing, FullAudio has negotiated deals with two of the five major recording labels — BMG and EMI — and is building a subscription service that uses Windows Media Player along with its built-in DRM technology.

Online music subscription services will definitely expand. A combination of technological limitations and court decisions affecting companies such as Napster has effectively forced the music industry into a paid-subscription model online. Because downloading individual music items from the Internet is prohibitively complex to music listeners other than the technically adept Napster/Aimster/Gnutella crowd, because metering plays and charging on that basis is too hard for the recording companies and potentially violates privacy, because subscriptions are easy to pay for, and because legal decisions by nontechnical judges and juries favor simplistic solutions, the industry is in the process of defaulting to a subscription model.

As a result, the five major recording labels are launching two online subscription services, PressPlay and MusicNet. We expect these to dominate the world of online music eventually — if two factors can be overcome. One is the constant state of flux of music rights ownership, as catalogs are continuously bought and sold. The other is antitrust considerations: The U.S. Justice Department already launched an investigation into the two services in August 2001, even though they had yet to launch at that time.

PressPlay, originally known as Duet, is a 50-50 joint venture of Sony Music and Universal Music (a division of Vivendi Universal). It will offer a subscription-based service that will be licensed to music outlets online. Yahoo became PressPlay's first licensee in April 2001, months before the service actually launched. PressPlay will use DRM technology, possibly licensing it from InterTrust.

CROSS REFERENCE: See Chapter 7 to find out more about the proprietary core DRM technologies, such as InterTrust, RealNetworks, and Reciprocal.

The other three major labels (Warner Brothers, BMG, and EMI) own MusicNet, along with technology vendor RealNetworks, whose audio format will be used for the music and whose RealMedia Commerce Suite will serve as the DRM technology for the service. MusicNet will feature music in both download and streaming formats. MusicNet will also be licensed to Web sites that want to offer music. Not surprisingly, one of its first licensees is AOL — the service of Warner Brothers' parent company, AOL Time Warner. MusicNet will enjoy the advantage of RealNetworks' installed based of *190 million* players worldwide. Both MusicNet and PressPlay are expected to launch by the time this book is published, although many in the industry are skeptical that they will launch before the end of 2001.

The other potentially important music subscription service is Napster. Napster offered, from the perspective of some users, the ideal music subscription service. Users accessed Napster's software to look for digital music files on the computers of other users. User A could download a music file from User B through Napster, and one "subscribed" in the sense that one had to register with Napster. User A and User B are said to be "peers" and "peer-to-peer" ("P2P") has been (in)famous ever since. The problem, of course, with that particular subscription model was that no money changed hands, and the recording industry claimed that Napster was facilitating the infringement of copyright law.

> **CROSS REFERENCE:** Chapter 3 provides an in-depth look at copyright law and technology.

Prior to the court decision, Napster had formed an alliance with Bertelsmann, the owner of BMG, and four days following the court decision, Napster and Bertelsmann issued a joint press release announcing the formation of Digital World Service (DWS). DWS is actually a DRM service provider (similar to others, such as Reciprocal) that focuses on back-end technologies such as financial transaction clearing; however, its inherent advantage is that it has corporate access to Bertelsmann's enormous war chest of content in all formats — including Random House and Bantam Doubleday Dell books, the large magazine chain Gruner+Jahr, and many others in addition to the BMG music labels.

DWS's primary initial task is to provide the technology that will turn Napster into a paid-subscription service that offers some level of content security. DWS will provide subscription payment processing services, and it is grafting a security component onto the MP3 files that Napster manages. DWS is modifying the Napster client so that it imposes this security for files that don't yet have it (thus eliminating the need to go through everyone's Napster-accessible files and re-encode them). We discuss DWS further in Chapter 11.

After the initial rollout, DWS will develop technology that enables more advanced business models on the new Napster, such as usage tracking, usage-based payments, and subscription renewals. It remains to be seen whether these models will work. It will be interesting enough to see whether the fee-based Napster will be as successful as the *Wall Street Journal*'s switch from free to fee. Certainly the demographics are vastly different.

The biggest concern with Napster will be the same as for PressPlay and MusicNet: its ability to include material licensed from other recording companies. As it stands now, Napster is allowed to manage only music files that aren't copyrighted, meaning recordings from unsigned bands and the like. Charging money for access to unknown music is a known loser. The legendary IUMA (Internet Underground Music Archive) has been doing this for free for years, and other sites such as garageband.com actually offer fans incentives (prize giveaways) to listen to unknown artists so that they can determine which bands to sign to their recording label.

One thing is for sure: Music subscription services of the future will definitely include DRM technology, unlike publishers' services such as the *Wall Street Journal*. Whereas newspaper and magazine content is short and depends more on context for its full value, music tracks are too valuable in their discrete forms and must be protected.

Pay-Per-View and Pay-Per-Listen

Pay-per-view is probably the oldest business model for "content" in the physical world: It applies to live events such as concerts and plays and to movies (provided that you don't stay in the theater to see the movie a second time). Furthermore, for nearly two decades, pay-per-view cable television has been a content delivery option in homes across the United States. Users willingly pay beyond their standard cable subscription rates for particular movies or sporting events that aren't interrupted by commercials.

Pay-per-listen has existed in music as well. Regrettably, we are old enough to remember jukeboxes as a common feature in bars and restaurants — whereas now they are found only in self-consciously "retro" joints such as Johnny Rockets and a few old watering holes here and there. There was a time when a user — we'll call him Frank — finding himself in a restaurant or bar would simply put a nickel in the jukebox and punch the code for Ella Fitzgerald singing "How High the Moon," and the song would play one time. Frank wouldn't expect to have any further right or access to the song for his nickel. Frank knew what he was getting — a one-time pay-per-listen. The expectations were clear and established.

Are today's online users likely to want the digital equivalent of a jukebox? Will Frank's son — let's call him Junior — gladly enter into a micropayment transaction in 2001 to hear "Behind the Paint" by Insane Clown Posse? It depends on the situation. We can imagine bars and restaurants of the near future having digital jukeboxes that retrieve music from a library hosted by one of the music services discussed earlier. Users will pay a quarter per listen or five for a dollar, just as they would with the analog jukeboxes with their gouged-up 45s. But will Junior pay a quarter (or anything) to listen to "Behind the Paint" on his PC, personal music player, or home broadband stereo component? We think not. Besides the issues of expectations and user inconvenience, the cost of processing such small financial transactions is, like paid downloads of short articles, too high.

Pay-per-view (or pay-per-listen) has been a business model that was supported by early DRM technology, but it has had no success. In the physical world, pay-per-view has hardly ever applied to published materials such as articles, books, or documents. Yet these are exactly the kinds of content that digital technology can convey and render easily. Pay-per-listen has also hardly ever applied to online audio content, although digital technology can now convey and render that relatively well. Digital technology is at best mediocre at conveying video content, which is the only type of media for which *home* pay-per-view has ever really worked.

DRM-enabled pay-per-view for video will have some success in the future, when the Internet gets better as a video delivery medium, but it will be limited. First of all, the Internet will have to get *a whole lot* better at distributing and rendering video content, or else people won't pay for it, no matter what it is. Beyond that, however, the success of DRM-enabled pay-per-view depends on the time sensitivity of the programming. If a program is time-sensitive, pirated versions will have little value. It may be possible to capture and redistribute a live streaming cybercast of a championship boxing match, but few will care enough to watch it later when they can see highlight clips on network television.

Bootlegs of a pay-per-view concert, such as a Madonna cybercast from Madison Square Garden, may be more interesting for later viewing, thereby requiring DRM technology to protect them. The most applicable content of all to DRM-enabled pay-per-view is movies, although even these are only applicable in certain instances. Outside of movie theaters, pay-per-view movies are appropriate for people in hotel rooms on business trips with nothing to do after dinner at the hotel restaurant or via room service. These services are known as video on demand (VOD), and they are typically powered by banks of videocassette players. In many cases, a movie will start every hour; this is known as NVOD or near-video-on-demand.

You can easily imagine a scenario in which a traveler in a hotel room (or another similar captive environment, such as an airplane or bus) is able to choose from a large library of movies on demand from a broadband network service licensed by the hotel chain. Such services should appear in the near future. They will be online pay-per-view services for which content will need to be protected — not from the road warrior in the hotel room, but from professional pirates who will seek out such services to do their dirty work. Similar services will be available in the home, but (as mentioned earlier) they are likely to be subscription-based, not pay-per-view.

Usage Metering

Usage metering works pretty well with gas, electricity, and other utilities. Usage patterns are long since established, and utility users have expectations about what is reasonable within a range. Metered-usage arrangements, however, tend to be more convenient to the owners of the goods or services whose uses are being metered. In most cases, people tend to favor fixed-price arrangements, because they are predictable.

Look at the changes in consumer telecommunications and Internet services: Pricing structures have gradually been shifting from usage metering to fixed rates. In the very old days, local phone service had per-minute or per-call pricing; now, most people (especially those in urban centers) pay monthly flat rates for local service. More recently, long distance phone service has changed from rates that depend on the city being called (although not necessarily on how far that city is away from you) to uniform per-minute rates for all service across the United States. Similarly, Internet access has changed from per-minute connect charges to flat monthly fees. America Online broke the mold for millions of users when they switched to flat monthly rates as a means of boosting subscribership – and they saw usage skyrocket beyond their capacity to handle it.

Flat-rate pricing lowers risk to consumers as it raises risk to producers. Just as there is a well-known risk-reward tradeoff in the investment world, most consumers are willing to accept slightly higher prices in exchange for predictability.

Sometimes metered-usage pricing is offered as an alternative to flat rates for those who don't anticipate heavy usage levels. Low-income people, for example, will sign up for a checking account at a bank that charges fees for each check written, instead of a monthly fee that is equivalent to more checks than they expect to write. Similarly, the same people may choose a phone service that bills them per local call instead of a flat fee for unlimited local calls, because they expect to carefully control their phone usage and therefore pay lower fees.

In the middle, between flat-fee and metered-usage pricing, is the type of tiered pricing scheme used by wireless phone companies. With these schemes, you usually get a certain number of minutes of talk time per month at a flat rate, with additional minutes available at a per-minute fee that varies according to the plan you buy. (For example, the incremental per-minute rate on a 1,000-minute-per-month plan will be lower than that for a 500-minute-per-month plan.) Wireless service providers arrived (probably reluctantly) at these pricing schemes after years of stagnant growth in subscribership due largely to the off-putting complexity of their metered-usage pricing plans.

Wireless Internet service providers currently offer tiered pricing, albeit based on kilobytes (KB) transferred instead of on minutes of use. For example, Palm has three tiers of pricing for its PalmNet service for the Palm VII, which depend on the volume of data you transfer. The two lower tiers have limits in data volume, along with per-KB rates for data transferred over the limits; the highest tier gives unlimited usage for $45 per month (at this writing). The obvious problem with this type of scheme is that consumers generally have no idea how many KB it takes to check a stock quote, a flight departure time, a weather forecast, or a business's street address – to name four typical uses of wireless Internet devices. Wireless Internet services will assuredly shift to more predictable pricing models in the future.

In the world of online content, there are a few services that enable users to pay metered-usage prices if they think they will use the services only sporadically. For example, SciFinder is a service of Chemical Abstracts Service, a division of the nonprofit American Chemical Society. SciFinder gives people in chemistry and related fields access to a large database of research from thousands of different sources. Users of SciFinder have two payment options: One is an annual institutional subscription fee, which provides unrestricted access to a certain number of individuals; the other is a metered-usage plan that charges by "task." Tasks are various types of search and browse operations. You can buy blocks of tasks, and the cost varies by volume. (Although, somewhat counterintuitively, it *increases* slightly with volume.)

DRM technology works well with metered-usage pricing because it is capable of doing the metering and reporting to a server exactly what the user is doing with the content. However, using DRM technology for usage metering is better applied to things other than pricing. Learning what your customers are doing with your content helps you determine which particular content items users find most interesting, which lets you perform tasks such as improve your editorial selection process or steer advertisers towards more highly trafficked content. Usage tracking is especially valuable for video content, to see how long people are viewing video clips and which segments are the most popular. For metering access to text and other forms of static content, tools such as WebTrends have been around for several years and are quite effective.

Yet usage metering raises privacy concerns, and for that reason, its appeal will be limited. Content providers should recognize the fact that their users' agreement (tacit or explicit) to have their usage metered is a form of consideration, just like money — and just like personal information that users supply on a registration form. It's easy to imagine content services that offer users the option of paying less (or paying nothing, or even *being* paid) in return for having their usage metered. Marketing people have done this for a long time in the form of focus groups and test-marketing initiatives.

Peer-to-Peer and Superdistribution

Superdistribution is multiple-step distribution, that is, passing an object along more than once. In reality, most content in the world goes through multiple steps of distribution or rights ownership. An author (for example, Steve Mooney) conveys rights to a book to a publisher (such as M&T Books), which prints the book and sends copies to distributors (such as Baker & Taylor), which in turn sends copies to bookstores (for example, Borders). The term *superdistribution* refers to multiple distributions of the same digital file, and most typically it refers to *peer-to-peer* rather than multitiered distribution.

Here is an example of superdistribution: Tom purchases a digital music recording online from Tunesco, Ltd. Tom has the rights to replay the recording to his heart's content. Tom decides to pass along the file to Dick. Dick can see what the file is but can't access it; he does, however, have enough information about the content to make a purchase decision. The file provides Dick with sufficient information so that Dick can connect to an online service, conduct a rights transaction with the rightsholder or his agent, and get access to the content either on terms similar to Tom's or on other terms that may be available to users generally. Thoroughly pleased with his experience, Dick passes the file on to Harry who goes through a process similar to Dick's.

A more advanced model of superdistribution (covered in more detail in Chapter 4) gives Tom the ability to act as a *reseller* of the music file and to reset the price to whatever he wants, perhaps subject to some constraints. Tom may try to mark up the price in order to make a profit, he may choose a different pricing model (for example, time-based access or a fee for single play instead of a fee for download), or he may lower or eliminate the price in order to get other consideration from his users. This is still considered superdistribution, but there's a fine line between what Tom is doing in this case and what Tunesco does. This type of superdistribution implementation is rare because the technologies and rights models get too complicated too quickly.

Two significant aspects of superdistribution make it differ from normal multitiered content distribution of the type exemplified by the preceding book example, as follows:

♦ It doesn't require participation in a particular community or within a proprietary network.

♦ It doesn't depend on the rightsholder or his agent defining a particular market before purchase. Indeed, it relies to a great degree, not so much on serendipity but on the fact that personal and business relationships foster the sharing of content in ways marketers cannot begin to fathom as a systematic distribution matter.

The latter point hasn't been lost on marketers in recent days. So-called "viral" marketing is all the rage: Businesses are adopting various techniques to get hype about a product to spread by word of mouth. Not only can this be very effective, but it can also be far, far cheaper than traditional mass marketing techniques. Trendy books such as Malcolm Gladwell's *The Tipping Point* and Seth Godin's *Unleashing the Ideavirus* have amplified this idea.

Peer-to-peer distribution has other aspects that go beyond superdistribution. Recall that superdistribution relies on Tom's initial "push" of the digital music file to Dick. With peer-to-peer distribution, Dick determines what he is interested in, looks for it, sees that Tom has it, and goes and gets it. Thus, peer-to-peer distribution need not rely on any understanding of interest between Tom and Dick. Indeed, they don't even need to know each other. The classic example, of course, is Napster, whereby MP3 music files were effectively made freely available to anybody with an Internet connection and sufficient bandwidth, as long as they registered with Napster.

DRM technology is vitally important in peer-to-peer and superdistribution models — for the simple reason that if a distribution model allows for content to change hands multiple times, there are that many more opportunities for a loss of control over rights to the content. DRM solutions that control rights through superdistribution (which several available ones do) must have airtight control mechanisms, including strong encryption, to work properly. We discuss this in more detail in Chapter 5.

However, superdistribution also poses that many more opportunities for users to be put off by inconvenience if the technology is not easy to use. Early DRM solutions (again, such as IBM's Cryptolope) included superdistribution features from the beginning. They were not successful. The chain is only as strong as its most technophobic link.

Selling Rights

In addition to the business models that involve online content distribution, there are several possible business models that involve the distribution of the *rights* to content rather than the content itself. In most cases, these involve rights transactions among businesses, such as publishers, who want to distribute each other's content or use portions of it in their works.

Most such transactions happen without much technology: They take place over the phone, via letters of permission, and face-to-face at big conferences such as the Frankfurt Book Fair for publishing and Western Cable for cable television. But in recent years, various schemes have been hatched to move the buying and selling of rights onto the Internet. In Chapter 12, we discuss a few businesses that use these schemes and are still running. Here is the story of one such scheme that is not. To paraphrase Joe Friday on *Dragnet,* the story that you are about to read is true, but the names have been changed to protect the insolvent.

In the late 1990s, a well-established, medium-sized company that distributed books and analog copies of music and videos decided that the time had come to cash in on the emerging market for the digital uses of copyrighted materials. Having served publishers successfully for decades, the company knew that it was especially well placed not only to build its own successful business models but also to show rightsholders how they could profit from these new and exciting technologies leveraged by the new business models that went along with them. Following a review of where this company went afoul, we'll take a closer look at business models that it considered and the market circumstances under which each can succeed and, in some circumstances, fail. We'll refer to this company by the fictitious name of *The Yesteryear Distribution Company.*

In the decades leading up to 1997, Yesteryear developed excellent relations with rightsholders who produced the text materials and analog recordings and videos that Yesteryear purchased. Its relations with the corporate and institutional customers to whom Yesteryear sold were equally sound. The classic middleman, Yesteryear performed its business so well that it came actually to anticipate precisely what materials its customers would want, even before a given customer himself knew of a particular need. Yesteryear thereby drove its profits.

Yesteryear's services were beyond the competence of most rightsholders, who tend to be dedicated primarily to the creation, editing, and marketing of their own materials. Yesteryear clearly added value to the stream of commerce of text and analog recordings. Success prompted Yesteryear to computerize its operations circa 1980, and the company came to rely on computerized operations totally by 1990. In fact, by the early 1990s, Yesteryear couldn't imagine conducting its business without sophisticated computer hardware and specialized software, much of which came to be developed from scratch by Yesteryear's growing cadre of software engineers and other computer experts, who drove much of the business thinking at Yesteryear.

The cadre eventually formed a full-fledged Information Technology (IT) department, which became the largest group of employees in the company save the warehouse staff. The IT guys always won all the softball games at Yesteryear summer outings, and they weren't at all shy about sharing their opinions as to how the business should be run. Because the IT folks had contributed so magnificently to the success of the company, senior management always listened.

In the mid-1990s, the director of IT convinced the president of Yesteryear that they needed a more significant online presence. IT argued that Yesteryear needed to give its customers direct access to Yesteryear's data about the copyrighted materials being offered for sale, about rightsholders, about the customer's own account, and even about the competition. Millions were spent to develop this capability, and the resulting online system was another overwhelming success. Productivity went up. Revenue per employee increased. Customers were happy.

Suppliers were happy. Shareholders were happy. The IT guys were happy, especially because they continued to win company softball games, and, most importantly, senior management was happy.

All was well at Yesteryear. The existing business became more efficient and, as a result, more profitable, directly as result of information technologies that were poised, it seemed, to move beyond merely making an existing business more efficient to actually transforming an industry. The unfettered but secure distribution of copyrighted works across the Internet seemed to be at hand.

However, this apparent opportunity also was thought to threaten Yesteryear's very existence. A series of internal meetings focused on what could, in fact, be a looming demon, one that threatened all that Yesteryear had built: The creation, secure distribution, and use of materials in digital form were topics about which Yesteryear knew almost nothing. Customers spoke with increasing frequency about digital distribution changing "everything within five years time" or "three years" or "two" or, as one of their most established customers pronounced in the late 1990s, "within eighteen months."

Although Yesteryear very effectively used computer systems to manage the distribution of text materials in paper form, as well as analog video and audio recordings, it had never seriously contemplated distributing such materials in digital form. Nor had it considered that rights associated with a given work could be separated from the work itself and, perhaps, traded separately.

Yesteryear's leaders reasonably foresaw threats as well as possibilities. Yesteryear management had rebuilt its business model in the mid-1990s at the behest of the IT department by moving customer service functions online. Now, those same software engineers and computer gurus urged the creation of a digital rights management business model that would "propel Yesteryear into the 21st century," solve its Y2K problems in the bargain, and — although spoken in somewhat more hushed tones — provide a real fun project for those IT guys. Management remembered that revising the business model around online computer systems had worked once and that IT had been their salvation when they went online and had made customer service more efficient, so they now believed that they could remake all aspects of their business — especially purchasing, distribution, and accounting.

"Why, by the year 2000," the president of Yesteryear announced in late 1997, "we could be getting 40% of revenues from digital distribution across the Internet," pausing to confirm with the director of IT, "It's called *superdistribution,* right? If we don't act now, somebody else will, and we will lose market share." Believing they had no choice, Yesteryear management concluded that they would be remiss not to act, that their shareholders would surely take them to task were they to refrain from acting, and that they would lose the chance of a lifetime if they did not take the next logical step. So in the late 1990s, they formed iyesteryear.com, a wholly owned subsidiary of Yesteryear, Inc., and, like the country cousin, merrily set out to Digital Rights City to make their fortune. But a funny thing happened on the way to the fortune. Their ultimate failure wasn't so much related to technology but to the fact that they chose the wrong business model at the wrong time.

Management was well aware that iyesteryear.com was no Microsoft. Although they had significant resources, they couldn't simply squander money, but they did have one thing that, at the time, appeared to be a significant competitive advantage. Evidently, the IT department had long been working on a secret software development project called *Yesterlicense,* an online system that could automatically conclude customized license agreements over the Internet after a rightsholder established terms and conditions, set fees, and added information ("metadata") that described a particular work with certainty.

Amazingly, Yesterlicense actually worked and impressed technical and business people alike. However, Yesterlicense didn't purport to deliver content but merely to complete transactions with regard to particular content. Although the distinction sounds subtle in the description, it is massive in the implementation. It took Yesteryear away from its traditional business model of being a *content sales* middleman to being a *rights licensing* middleman, something that it had never attempted before.

Yesteryear's management knew that Yesterlicense worked and could be applied to rights transactions. They knew that rights transactions were necessarily part of any conceivable form of secure digital distribution across the Internet, so they decided that the business question before them was simply to choose the appropriate class of rights transactions. Four broad areas were envisioned:

- ◆ Simple permissions transactions — for example, to make a photocopy of an article.
- ◆ Subsidiary rights transactions (or *subrights* for short), which are transactions on rights other than the primary one. Copyrights are severable into component parts. Let's say that we write *The Great American Novel.* The French translation rights, the North American distribution rights, and the audiobook rights are examples of subrights. A rightsholder may sell a subright, such as the French translation rights, while retaining every other conceivable right to the work. Following that transaction, the original rightsholder can still do everything *except* publish the work in French.
- ◆ The outright sale of a copyright.
- ◆ An online rights brokerage system encompassing all of the preceding that would mimic rights transaction activities that go on each year at industry events such as the Frankfurt Book Fair.

Yesteryear rejected the last three options as the place to start because simply announcing the availability of an online rights brokerage system or an online subrights trading system, or even a place online where copyrights could be bought and sold, wouldn't guarantee use. Those three areas involved significant amounts of money, and people might be reluctant to try a new online system with so much at stake. (Nevertheless, at least two companies nowadays, RightsCenter and RightsWorld.com, are trying this; see Chapter 12.) So Yesteryear based its business model on demonstrating a proof of concept through online permissions transactions, the first in the preceding list.

Applying Yesterlicense to permissions rather than actual delivery of digital content made a great deal of sense because

- ◆ Secure digital content wasn't yet sufficiently widely available across the Internet to begin distribution beyond proprietary networks.
- ◆ Yesterlicense included no encryption or other technical protection of content because it was merely a means to conduct license transactions.
- ◆ The market for permissions appeared to be unsatisfactory to rightsholders, who generally provide permissions services through Rights and Permissions departments or through agents; such processes are famously inefficient, costly, and time-consuming.
- ◆ Users are also generally not satisfied with the process whereby they secure simple permissions to, for example, photocopy an article from a journal.

Yesterlicense was perfectly suited to automate permissions processes and to bring the process directly under the control of the rightsholder, just as soon as the rightsholder fed pricing, terms and conditions, and data into the system. Users could use Yesterlicense to initiate a permissions transaction from a Web site, from the content itself, from a PDF file, or elsewhere on the Internet.

Yet the project failed completely after three years. Why? The Yesterlicense technology wasn't the problem — it really worked; although technology has since passed it by, at the time it was fine. The real problem was the false business premises on which iyesteryear.com was built. Yesteryear got the business model wrong, even though all the assumptions that it made at the beginning were, for the most part, correct. Why was the whole *less* than the sum of its parts?

First, Yesteryear got the money wrong. Iyesteryear.com planned to take 10 percent of royalties collected on behalf of rightsholders. It couldn't charge more than that because if it did, it would then be less expensive for rightsholders to go with traditional manual approaches. Under this model, then, iyesteryear.com paid out to rightsholders 90 cents out of every dollar collected before it covered a penny of its expenses. Furthermore, it incurred a substantial cost in educating the marketplace about why such a system was necessary, adding to the financial concerns. This didn't add up to profitability.

Second, and probably more importantly, before you are able to trade permissions online, you must be able to track and manage them internally. Rare indeed is the publisher that does this. Permissions management is a big, hairy problem of publishers (especially book publishers) in general. Solutions — a few of which are mentioned in the section "Internal Rights Management," in Chapter 12 — are complex and not yet widely adopted. Publishers would have had to do far too much work internally to be able to use a system such as Yesterlicense at all.

Finally, Yesteryear didn't focus on what it knows best, nor did it commit sufficient resources to turn itself into something new. Yesteryear was a content seller, not a rights licensor.

Yesteryear was the classic middleman, not a software developer or service bureau operator. This is not to say that it could never have been these things, but it embarked on a new business model either half-heartedly or unknowingly, and thereby failed.

Yesterlicense ended in failure, and iyesteryear.com went the way of all flesh and most Internet startups. Yesteryear had been a great success in its traditional business. It understood that developments out in the world threatened its well-being. It realized that investments were necessary to meet the challenges. It even developed a new software product that actually worked. Yesteryear had a position in the industry such that it could bring its new software product to market and not be a stranger coming in anew. But Yesteryear positioned itself and its product in exactly the wrong way and fell flat on its face, well prior to the "dot-bomb" fiascoes that hit the market in 2001.

Choosing the Right Business Model

The great advantage of the Internet is the flexibility and fluidity that it allows you in selecting a business model for distributing content. Try something. If it doesn't work, try something else; you can move on more quickly than in most offline media. Adopt multiple simultaneous business models if you have disparate audiences with different needs and ways of accessing your content. If your business models necessitate the use of DRM technology, pick DRM solutions that support *all* the business models that you can possibly think of, and then some. The Internet will evolve, as will your customers. You should, too.

Consider the many business models for music that we discuss in this chapter. A song recording is a single, indivisible unit (despite the fact that there may be a dance club version and an edited single for radio). It can be streamed over the Internet to a PC, downloaded into a portable music player, played over a home digital audio system, played in an Internet jukebox in a bar, selected automatically by genre as part of a subscription "digital radio" service, used as background music for some video content, and so on, and so on.

Each of these paradigms has a potentially distinct audience for it, one that you need to understand in terms of when, where, and how they want to access the music. The point is that if you want, you can embrace any or all of these business models for the same content simultaneously. In Chapter 10, we discuss some of the systems and processes that you would need to put in place internally in order to make this happen. If you're lucky, you can find a DRM system that handles all these situations and scales to meet your future requirements. If you're more typical of content providers nowadays, you will have to find and adopt monolithic systems for each distribution channel.

Also bear in mind that *money* is not your only consideration in deciding to distribute content online or to use DRM technology. Learning more about your users so that you can market more and better products and services to them can be just as important. When you build plans for new distribution channels (whether on- or offline), try to convince your management to add the value of consideration other than money into the return on investment (ROI) equation.

Finally, consider the lessons of Yesteryear. Take Clint Eastwood's advice and know your limitations. Be mindful of where you truly add value. Why should users, rightsholders, or anybody give money or personal information to you? Some of the business models reviewed in this chapter may suit you perfectly as a technical matter, but a particular technology, however elegant, won't save a bad business model from commercial demise, nor will it save a business that employs a good model at the wrong time or under the wrong circumstances. Digital rights management depends on the delivery of rights and/or content to a user from a rightsholder for consideration, and that depends on a carefully planned and well-considered model for conducting your rights and content business online.

Chapter 3

Help from the Government: Law and Technology

Within DRM circles, law and lawyers have the reputation of inhibiting business. We leave it to the lawyers to defend themselves. However, think about this: Laws are what provide us all with DRM business opportunities. Without certain laws, there would be no business opportunities and certainly no need at all to invest in, or even contemplate, building DRM technologies.

The rights that content providers seek to manage in digital rights management are creations of the law, and no such right is inherent or self-evident. You can clearly distinguish the rights that DRM addresses from the natural or human rights that grow out of human nature. Within Western tradition, these human rights are viewed as inherent, individual, and inviolable. This isn't the case with intellectual property rights, however, which are subject to legislative and judicial processes. Thus, the term *rights,* according to *Black's Law Dictionary*, is "an interest or title in an object of property; a just and legal claim to hold, use, and enjoy it or to convey it or donate it." The rights you have to manage — digitally and otherwise — exist only because the law created them. These rights are inherently creations of law.

Rights: Creations of Law

Much of DRM technology is about complying with contracts. It's important to understand the basics of certain intellectual property laws, particularly copyright law, but you also need to remember that DRM deals with contracts. A license is a contract, and you need to look to contract law and practice to get your business issues sorted out properly. Businesspeople generally are familiar with basic contract principles, although they may not think in legal terms. The sale of goods, for example, is built on a body of commercial law, and businesspeople develop an understanding of what "feels right" because the sale of goods is an everyday occurrence.

In the context of DRM, the basics of licensing are not all that different from licensing in other areas of business. Before we go into more detail, however, you should understand the basic types of intellectual property and which types are central to digital rights management. The four most common types are patents, trademarks, trade secrets, and copyrights. These types of intellectual property are explained in the following sections. Keep in mind that this is not a law book, so we're not trying to explain these property types in legal terms.

Patents

Patents protect novel and unique inventions or processes. After you patent your invention, nobody can use it without your permission, and you have essentially an unlimited monopoly for a period of years. You have to disclose the details of your invention to the world, but you can take legal action to prevent others from using it without conforming to your terms of use while your patent is active. After the patent time period expires, anyone can freely use your invention. The limited time frame in which to exploit a patent provides you with an incentive to create new inventions, and the time limit also ensures that everybody can benefit from your inventions in the long run.

Pharmaceutical companies offer a great example for how patents work in the real world. They patent new drugs, charge high prices while the patent is in force, generate great profits, and continually seek to invent new drugs because they know that today's cash cow will go "off patent" someday. When a drug goes off patent, anybody can make it, so the price falls, and the cash cow is gone.

In the DRM world, technology companies can patent DRM technologies and processes. Patents, however, are not generally the object of DRM systems and applications. Patent rights do play an increasingly important role in the *creation* of DRM technologies and systems, though. The interplay of various patent rights will affect, for good and for ill, the DRM systems and applications that develop over time.

Technology providers regularly claim that DRM is simply not possible without a license to this or that patent. Talk about the impact of contracts on the use of copyrighted works! These contentions indicate that access to certain copyrighted material can be conditioned upon a vendor having certain patent rights for a system, the function of which is simply to render the copyrighted work.

Such forces have led standards bodies, such as the Moving Picture Experts Group (MPEG), to form *patent pools*, whereby technology companies pool their various patents and agree to reasonable licensing terms. How these patent issues will play themselves out as DRM systems evolve remains to be seen. The process by which this happens will drive how patents affect DRM systems, and an important place to look for legal and business effects is MPEG-21.

The vision for MPEG-21 is to define a multimedia framework to enable the transparent and augmented use of multimedia resources across a wide range of networks and devices used by different communities. Although many elements currently exist to build an infrastructure for the delivery and consumption of multimedia content, there is no "big picture" to describe how these elements, either in existence or under development, relate to each other. The aim for MPEG-21 is to describe how these various elements fit together. The result is intended to be an open framework for multimedia delivery and consumption, with both the content creator and content consumer as focal points.

MPEG generally permits a number of encoding applications, ranging from video and multimedia CDs on a desktop computer to interactive TV and digital satellite networks. MPEG standards made interactive video on CD-ROM and digital television possible. MPEG facilitates the creation of intellectual property markets and has always been part of a formal standards process accredited by the International Organization for Standardization (ISO; the acronym derives from the French). As such, MPEG is open to all comers, provided that they are accredited to their national standards organizations. This implies that MPEG is completely open to the entry of a new group of players representing a new content type.

At the very least, those interested in practical examples of how legal and commercial forces play themselves out in the DRM space can learn from MPEG's success. Were DRM technology vendors to fail to account for the MPEG big picture, how the various elements of multimedia content relate to electronic publications, and particularly the effect of patent rights in this mix, they could fall short of the goal to create and maintain commercial and legal frameworks to promote the successful adoption of DRM systems and applications.

Trademarks

Trademarks protect logos, trade names, and symbols used to identify a company's products or services, which could be sounds and smells in addition to graphical symbols. Examples of trademarks include the Chrysler pentastar, the American Express blue box, and the little RCA dog looking quizzically into the Victrola with the caption "His Master's Voice."

The key to evaluating the strength of a trademark lies in the answer to the question "What association does the trademark generate in a consumer's mind?" If the public associates the pentastar with Chrysler, Chrysler has a protectable trademark. However, if a company gets sloppy and doesn't continually work to associate its trademark with the company itself, it can lose the trademark. This is why Xerox periodically campaigns against use of the word *xerox* as a generic term for the word *photocopy.* If *xerox* becomes the equivalent of *photocopy* in the mind of the public, the term becomes generic and Xerox could lose the trademark. This is exactly what happened with trademarks of old such as *escalator* and *aspirin,* which are now generic terms.

The licensing of trademarks is not all that well suited to the application of DRM technology as described in this book. Trademark licensing doesn't involve content *per se* but more closely resembles rights sales, as discussed in Chapter 2. A license to a trademark typically gives a licensee the right to use the trademark according to a set of guidelines, such as color, size, proximity to other graphics, and so on. Nevertheless, there are opportunities to use the Internet to automate trademark licensing deals to some extent, in the same manner that the online rights exchanges described in Chapter 12 automate some types of content rights sales. One example of a Web-based business that automates the licensing of trademarked material (as well as patents) is the New York-based company ip*network (`www.ipnetwork.com`).

Trade secrets

According to *Black's Law Dictionary*, a trade secret ". . . may consist of any formula, pattern, device of complilation of information which is used in one's business and which gives a person an opportunity to obtain an advantage over competitors who do not know or use it. . . ." To qualify as a trade secret, the company that owns it must take reasonable efforts to protect its secrecy. After a trade secret becomes publicly known, it's no longer protectable as a trade secret.

The best example of a trade secret is the formula for Coca-Cola. The Coca-Cola company could have patented the formula to Coca-Cola; however, had it done so, the formula would have gone off patent years ago, and everyone would be drinking generic coca-cola. The Coca-Cola company would have had to disclose the formula in its patent application. Instead, Coca-Cola chose to keep the formula a trade secret, to which nobody in the world has a right — ever.

Most trade secrets occur within companies (such as Coca-Cola) that are not primarily content providers; therefore DRM vendors haven't considered them to be sales targets; but this philosophy is changing. Trade secrets manifest themselves in documents, e-mail messages, and other forms of digital information within corporate networks. As we discuss in Chapter 11, some DRM vendors have begun to build systems that control access to documents and e-mail within corporate networks and on corporate extranets, so that only those with a need to know can get access to the sensitive information.

Copyright

U.S. copyright law protects ". . . original works of authorship fixed in a tangible medium of expression, now known or later developed, from which they can be perceived, reproduced or otherwise communicated, either directly or with the aid of a machine or device."[1] Let's break this down:

- **Original work of authorship.** The work — a book, song, or movie, for example — must be original. If you take a book, copy it one word at a time, and put your name on it, you do not have a copyright because you did not create anything original. However, it's important to note that copyright law (unlike patent law) doesn't protect against the *independent* creation of a work identical to another copyrighted work – it only protects against copying someone else's work. It's also worth mentioning that only creative expression is protected under copyright; factual information isn't.

- **Fixed in a tangible medium of expression.** You have to write the work down. Why don't they just say that, you ask? The copyright law needs to embrace things like recording a song in a variety of media, such as a record, a CD, a DVD, or on a hard drive. Nothing has been "written" per se, but the song has certainly been "fixed" in a way that is the equivalent of writing words in a book. "Tangible medium of expression" means that you need to fix the work on something that can be accessed, such as the media just mentioned. Significantly, the law provides for media "now known or later developed," so your copyright remains in force even when subsequently fixed on yet-to-be invented platforms.

- **Reproduced or otherwise communicated.** Your work has to be accessible. If you claim that your book is fixed on a particular electron of a hydrogen molecule or inscribed on a tablet on Jupiter's moon Europa, you fail this test. There is no way anyone could access your book. So you don't have a copyright.

Copyrights are central to DRM. All the talk that you hear about stolen music and streaming video being offered on the Internet has to do with the infringement of somebody's copyright. The essence of DRM involves these questions: "Whose copyrights are being abused? Whose may be abused? How can we prevent that? And how can we facilitate the use of such copyrights so that the owner gets paid and the users get access?"

DRM addresses copyrighted works, the ways in which technologies facilitate new uses of copyrighted works, and the ultimate response of law to those technologies and new uses. At the end of the day, DRM determines which uses are legally permissible and which are legally impermissible. DRM is not first and foremost about patents, trademarks, trade secrets, or other types of intellectual property. For the most part, then, two broad bodies of law underpin DRM: copyright law and contract law.

Balance of Interests

Visions of Initial Public Offerings (IPOs) dance in the heads of many seeking to get involved in digital rights management. Although some may indeed eventually become wealthy, such enrichment is, in the law's eye, more a means to an end than an end itself. Copyright law

---

[1] Title 17 United States Code, Section 102

attempts to achieve "progress of the sciences and useful arts"[2] by rewarding creators of works as a means of encouraging them, but it also attempts to balance that with the public's ability to access works. Court decisions that interpret copyright law and legislation that extends it attempt to maintain this balance.

Although Congress provides the owner with certain exclusive rights of copyright, it remains that

> The primary objective in conferring the (copyright) monopoly lies in the general benefit derived by the public from the labors of authors (and their agents). It is said that reward to the author or artist serves to induce release to the public of the products of his creative genius.[3]

The primary intent of copyright is to "increase and not to impede the harvest of knowledge,"[4] and copyright law has long made reward to the owner a secondary consideration. The Supreme Court has regularly reaffirmed that the purpose of copyright is "not to reward the labors of authors" but "to promote the progress of science and the useful arts."[5] Thus, those seeking to profit from DRM systems and applications should remember that their enrichment is not the law's primary consideration.

Benefits of Copyright Law

Copyright law gives you five exclusive rights for a certain number of years for works that you create. Examples of a "work" include a book, an article, a paragraph, a movie, a song, a play, and a software program. Generally, a copyright lasts for the life of the author plus a number of years, but there are a variety of alternatives. The law provides five exclusive rights of copyright. The copyright holder has the right to

- ◆ Reproduce the work
- ◆ Modify the work by creating new work based on the old work (called a "derivative work")
- ◆ Distribute the work (by sale, rental, lease, or loan)
- ◆ Perform the work publicly (play, dance, act, or recite the work in public)
- ◆ Display the work publicly

Given the broad and enduring nature of these rights, the law also stipulates limitations on the rights so that a balance of interests is achieved between the owner and user. If the owner's monopoly were absolute, there would be less incentive to create new works. Similarly, if the limitations on the rights of an author to exploit a creative work were so broad as to vitiate the copyright, there would be no incentive to create at all.

Some argue that people don't need an incentive to create — that individuals will create for other than pecuniary reasons. These views are outside the mainstream of intellectual property

---

[2] Constitution of the United States of America, Article I, Section 8

[3] Sony Corporation v. Universal City Studios, 464 U.S. 416, 428 (1984)

[4] Harper & Row Publishers Inc. and the Reader's Digest Association v Nation Enterprises and Nation Associates, Inc. 417 U.S. 539, 547 (1985)

[5] Feist Publications v Rural Telephone Service Company 111 S.Ct. 1282, 1290 (1991)

thinking, however, and if carried to their logical extreme, they render all rights management obsolete.

Types of Copyrighted Works

Copyright law specifically includes the following types of works, many of which are the subject of various DRM projects and technologies:

♦ Literary works, such as newspapers, magazines, software, manuals and documentation, fiction, nonfiction, poetry, and even advertisements

♦ Musical works, such as songs and instrumentals

♦ Dramatic works, such as plays

♦ Pantomime and choreographic works, such as dance or mime

♦ Pictorial, graphic, and sculptural works, such as photographs, paintings, maps, drawings, graphic art, and fine art

♦ Motion pictures and other audiovisual works

♦ Sound recordings

♦ Architectural works

♦ Audio-visual displays

♦ Software programs

When you consider the multimedia applications pictured by DRM visionaries, the applications they seek to create, and the business they intend to build, all appear to have a solid foundation within the broad scope of copyright law. Certainly the rights provided are broad and, indeed, seemingly monopolistic. How are they balanced? Throughout copyright law, the tension between creating incentives for authors and creators is balanced by the societal goal of promoting progress of the arts and sciences. If either interest were to prevail to the exclusion of the other, the objectives of copyright would not be achieved. Giving away copyrights to promote the arts and sciences would stifle creativity by not providing incentives. Similarly, providing monopolies to authors and creators would inhibit the distribution of information that copyright seeks to foster. This balance recurs throughout copyright law.

Registering Copyrights

Creators should keep in mind two things about registering copyrights with the U.S. Copyright Office: First, registration may be necessary for you to recover monetary damages in any action that you bring against an infringer of your copyright; second, the registration system currently in place is wholly inadequate for automated electronic registrations and is in need of an overhaul. Happily, that process has at least begun.

In the United States, copyright arises upon creation, so why would you register your copyright with the U.S. Copyright Office? Particularly because much of DRM focuses on creating works on the fly, there are legitimate concerns about the feasibility of registering all new works created by DRM systems, given that it is a potentially time-consuming extra step in DRM systems and applications.

Registration of copyrights is not required for a copyright to be considered valid in the United States. Indeed, copyright takes effect upon the creation of the work and doesn't require registration to be effective. However, you receive many benefits by registering your copyright. Here are some reasons why owners should register copyrights that they consider to be commercially valuable:

♦ Registration is the key to the federal courthouse door. Before initiating a suit for copyright infringment, a domestic copyright owner must have registered the copyright. You need not, however, register the copyright before the infringing activities commence.

♦ Copyright law provides recovery that is almost unique in American law. Copyright owners may recover attorneys' fees as well as statutory damages. Statutory damages do not require proof of actual economic harm. Both attorneys' fees and statutory damages are not available without copyright registration.

♦ If you register your work within five years of publication and present a certificate to that effect to the court, it constitites *prima facie* evidence of the validity of your copyright.

Ideally, DRM systems should take into account whether the works they manage have copyrights registered for them and even facilitate registration if appropriate. The Copyright Office is currently working on ways to accept such registrations electronically, and the success of that undertaking will permit automatic deposit by DRM systems.

Beyond Copyright: Fair Use and Licensing

Although copyright law forms the basis of much of the legal and commercial restrictions that lead to the need for DRM solutions, DRM-related concerns spill over into two additional legal areas: fair use and licensing.

Many people have heard of *fair use*, but it's one of the most misunderstood parts of intellectual property law — right up there with broadcasters' quandaries over which words you can't say on radio or television. Licensing, meanwhile, is a branch of contract law that can supersede copyright provisions, or provide additional restrictions beyond those contained in copyright provisions. In many cases, a transaction in content involves a license rather than a sale — and the distinctions between the two are far from obvious.

Fair use

Several years ago, we encountered a cartoon modeled on the Oracle at Delphi, the seat of ancient world prophecy. A disheveled and filthy traveler crawled toward the feet of a most contented-looking oracle. The traveler had apparently come quite a distance, in all likelihood by foot, and although the oracle appeared willing to listen, his interest in the traveler was reluctant — mild at best. Still, the traveler wanted the world's wisdom, and forcing what appeared to be his last breath begged of the oracle to know, "What *is* fair use?"

Fair use is one of the limitations on the exclusive rights of copyright. The law makes clear that "the fair use of a copyrighted work . . . is not an infringement of copyright."[6] Fair use is not a right *per se*. Rather, it's a defense to an allegation of copyright infringement. The following examples may give you a better feel for fair use.

Imagine that three guys publish a book on digital rights management that eventually becomes the bible of the DRM world. Betsy, a law student, knowing that the book is protected by

---

[6] Title 17 United States Code, Section 107

copyright, makes a photocopy of a paragraph from Chapter 3 of the book, which describes examples of fair use. She intends to use the copy for a class outline, and she intentionally makes a second copy for her friend who will use it for the same purpose. The three guys hear about this and then sue Betsy for copyright infringement. Betsy asserts that her use was fair use.

The court would undoubtedly hold for Betsy. Her use was for an educational purpose, the amount of the taking was small, and there is no effect on the market value of the work. This is a classic example of fair use. The three guys hold the copyright, but their right is balanced by fair use considerations. Betsy wins.

Now imagine that Bob, a classmate of Betsy's, knows that the essence of the DRM book is Chapter 3. Bob arranges for the photocopying of 2,000 copies of Chapter 3 so that he can sell the copies to students at his school and other schools. Bob nets $15,000, and the three guys sue for copyright infringement. Bob claims that his use was for an educational purpose because he used the $15,000 to pay tuition bills.

Bob, however, is out of luck. Although Bob is a student, his use was commercial (he made money), the amount of the taking was substantial (the essence of the book), and the effect on the market was measurable (effectively killing book sales at these schools). In this case, the court would rule that Bob's use is not fair use, and fair use would not be available to Bob as a defense in a copyright infringement action by the three guys. The three guys win. (Hooray!)

Courts look to the four fair use factors outlined in the law:

- ◆ The purpose and character of the use
- ◆ The nature of the copyrighted work (for example, fact or fiction)
- ◆ The amount and substantiality of the taking
- ◆ The effect on the market value of the copyrighted work

Because fair use inquiries are so dependent on the facts of a particular case, it's not an easy defense to employ in a copyright infringement case. Furthermore, fair use doesn't eviscerate the copyright owner's exclusive right. Rather, it's an exception to the general rule that copying a work needs to be authorized.

Although fair use is just one of the limitations on the exclusive rights of copyright, it's one of the better illustrations of the balance that copyright seeks to strike between owners and users to ensure that the result is the societal good of "progress of the sciences and useful arts."

DRM and fair use

Much debate is underway as to whether fair use can survive in DRM systems. Why? In the examples cited above, there was no interaction between the copyright owners (the three guys) and the users (Betsy and Bob). Because there was no interaction, there was no possibility of a business arrangement of any kind — no possibility of a contract, for example. The rights of Betsy and Bob rose or fell based on the interpretation of the law.

Let's consider the case of Betsy. Remember that she copied a paragraph and that it was fair use. Suppose, however, that the book was only available as an eBook that was protected by a DRM system and that contained license terms. Suppose that the license said, "This book is the DRM bible. It's only available here in electronic form. You can get a copy by supplying your credit card information and paying us. You agree that any subsequent copying of any kind whatsoever is prohibited." Betsy fills out a form and clicks a button indicating her acceptance of the license, and then the DRM system gives her access to the eBook. Now, suppose that Betsy copies the paragraph, which would normally be considered fair use. Betsy is on firm ground with respect to copyright law because of the Fair Use Doctrine, but she contracted her rights away! The three guys can sue her for breach of contract.

This is the great fear that users, and particularly the library community, have about DRM. Will users in a series of unthinking clicks give away rights that they would otherwise have under copyright law? Opinions are divided on whether fair use is compatible with DRM technology (of the type described in Chapter 5). Some, like Dr. Mark Stefik of Xerox PARC, have expressed the view that DRM systems can support fair use. As explained in the Preface (and in Chapter 6), Stefik invented a programming language designed to describe rights to content, and transactions in those rights, in rich detail. He has said that if such a language is detailed enough, it can capture all possible uses of content and make provisions for those that are fair use.

Others – including the authors of this book – disagree. Fair use is an "I'll know it when I see it" proposition, meaning that it can't be proscriptively defined. Indeed, debate rages continuously among publishers, librarians, lawyers, judges, and others about what constitutes fair use. Just as there is no such thing as a "black box" that determines whether broadcast material is or isn't indecent, there is no such thing as a "black box" that can determine whether a given use of content qualifies as fair use or not. Anything that can't be proscriptively defined can't be represented in a computer system. A content owner could define several possible uses of content that he considers fair and make provisions in his DRM system to allow those uses without requiring payment (or other consideration), but there is no way to objectively define in advance whether those uses are indeed fair uses.

DRM systems impose controls on content that represent contract terms, regardless of whether those terms do or don't conform to copyright law, including fair use. This is a critical point. A related issue within copyright law is something called the *First Sale Doctrine*. You're already familiar with it if you've ever purchased a book. The First Sale Doctrine is so thoroughly ingrained in your understanding of what you buy when you buy a book that you probably never even think about it.

The First Sale Doctrine

Imagine purchasing John Krakauer's *Into Thin Air*. It's a simple, everyday transaction. You pay money, and you get a copy of the book. You own the copy. You can give it to your friend. You can tear out Chapter 6 and give the chapter away. You can donate the book to your library. You can burn it. You have all these rights and more because the First Sale Doctrine — an esoteric theory of copyright law — says that you do. However, you gain no rights whatsoever in the copyright itself, and those rights (reviewed earlier in the section "Rights: Creations of Law") remain Krakauer's. Your first sale rights apply to your copy only. The First Sale Doctrine prevents a copyright owner from restricting the further distribution of a tangible item, such as a book or CD.

Publishers have even fought among themselves about the First Sale Doctrine. Fawcett Publishing, the owner and publisher of *Wow Comics, No. 2 Summer Edition,* discovered that Elliott Publishing purchased secondhand copies and sold them[7]. Fawcett sued but lost. The First Sale Doctrine says that a copyright holder who conveys title to a particular copy of a

---

[7] Fawcett Publications, Inc. v Elliot Publishing Co. 46 F. Supp. 717 (S.D.N.Y 1942)

copyrighted work relinquishes the exclusive right to vend that particular copy. In other words, if you buy a book or a magazine, you can do whatever you want with *that* copy. Congress limited the First Sale Doctrine with respect to record and computer software rentals in 1984 and 1990 respectively, but First Sale largely survives in other contexts.

How can DRM affect First Sale and fair use?

In electronic media, many copyrighted works are not *sold* but are now supplied under *license.* In the earlier examples, you saw how Betsy contracted away her fair use rights by agreeing to a particular license. With First Sale, the effect is even more dramatic: Remember that the rights you got when you bought *Into Thin Air* at the local bookstore rely on the fact that you *bought* it. But guess what? When you agree to a license, you don't *buy* anything. DRM relies on licensing, and whether you are a *licensor* (in the earlier example, the three guys who own the book) or a *licensee* (Betsy), you had better be certain about the terms of the deal.

Consider one familiar example of the effect of licensing. Like most of the computer users in the world, you probably didn't buy your copy of Microsoft Windows — it came loaded on your computer, along with a license agreement found somewhere on the accompanying software package or manual. Therefore, you can't sell or license your copy of Windows to anyone else. If you had purchased Windows as you can purchase *Into Thin Air,* you would be able to sell your copy because of the First Sale Doctrine. The Windows end-user license agreement (EULA) from Microsoft, however, explicitly prohibits such a transfer and any attempt to do so cancels your own license. Even if you buy Windows in a box at your local computer store, you must agree to the same EULA to be able to install the software.

How can this be? Because you agreed to it in the license for Windows. Any rights that you may have had under copyright law have been supplanted by a commercial arrangement between the parties: by a license, a contract that can alter the balance of rights one way or another depending on what the license says. Some lawyers feel that the gradual shift from transactions governed by copyright law to those governed by licenses and contracts enforced by technology will alter the balance of rights between copyright owners and users irrevocably – in particular, because some types of technologically-enforced rights transactions (like superdistribution; see Chapter 2) supersede the limits of fair use and the First Sale Doctrine. Some lawyers also feel that DRM systems are dubious because they can be used to protect material that is not subject to copyright protection, such as copyrighted works for which the copyright has expired or works that are largely fact-based. Yet although these trends may disrupt the balance copyright law seeks to strike, it preserves another principle of law also embodied in the Constitution: freedom of contract. The law allows parties to make choices in contract for good and ill.

Incidentally, we use Microsoft Windows as an example here only because it's a product with which virtually everyone is familiar; but Microsoft is far from unique in its licensing strategy. Most software packages and Web services are licensed through EULAs with limitations similar to those placed on Microsoft Windows. (Notable exceptions are Linux and other so-called *open source* software: They have license agreements, but the terms are almost diametrically opposite those found in licenses for typical commercial software. Instead of *forbidding* the software from being modified and distributed further, open-source licenses specifically *allow* the software to be modified and distributed further, and they *require* licensees to make their modified source code publicly available.)

The focus of DRM systems, however, isn't so much on software as it is on items of digital content. Will content items come to be treated like software under software licensing schemes; if so, what are the implications? We address this question in the remainder of this section.

Purchases versus licenses

The distinction between outright purchases and licensing is not always clear. But you should be absolutely clear as to the arrangement that you are making. If you intend to provide works through a DRM system, consider what licensing terms and rights specification you will use. (For information about rights specifications, see Chapter 4.) Are you thinking about what your business plan should be? Are you offering works for purchase or licensing them? For example, if you go to a site that sells both paper books and electronic books, it may well be that the purchase of the paper book constitutes a sale (giving you one set of rights) and the purchase of an eBook is under license (giving you another set of rights).

How can you tell whether you have the rights of a purchase or a license, particularly if the vendor is not entirely clear? In a business arrangement, you ought to be clear, so let's examine a few factors that clue you in to when a purchase is a license. As you consider these, please remember that this is not unlike what we call the "duck test." If something looks like a duck, quacks like a duck, and walks like a duck, it's probably a duck. So, too, with licensing. The four questions to ask are

- Is there an EULA or similar contract that the user must take affirmative action to agree to, such as clicking or checking a box before gaining access to the content?
- Is there copy-protection technology operating?
- Can you migrate from an obsolete format to a new format?
- Can you break a work into its parts?

The first one of these is rather obvious. If you require the user to accept an EULA, or something similar, you're licensing, not offering for purchase. In the following sections, we examine the other items.

Copy-protection technology

Copy-protection technology, such as encryption, can be built into electronic distribution media such as eBooks. When you purchase a paper book, there is the notion of free transferability. In other words, you can give or loan the paper book to someone else. However, when you purchase an eBook, you don't have the same ease of transferability because of its copy protection. In this way, the copy-protection technology creates a transaction that more closely resembles a license and not a sale. You have to keep this difference in mind when deciding how to implement DRM in your business.

Migration

What happens when the format of an eBook that you purchased becomes obsolete or a particular device manufacturer goes out of business and its format is no longer supported? Do you have the right to migrate the work to a successor format? Or do you have to purchase a new version of the eBook?

Of course, this is not a new issue. When audio CDs came out in the 1980s, owners of LPs didn't have "migration rights" that would allow them to bring their vinyl to a record store and exchange it for CDs. Yet many people bought CDs of music that they already had on LP because of the superiority of the CD format in many respects. It would certainly be possible for some digital content format with built-in DRM technology to be devised with migration rights; for example, an eBook could contain rights to migrate it to some future electronic paper format. In any case, a sale is characterized by continuing access, as is the case with paper. If your access is not continuing and you can't migrate the work, the transaction takes on the characteristics of a license.

Breaking a work into parts

With a paper book, if you consider the whole thing rubbish with the exception of Chapter 6, you can remove Chapter 6 from the book, put it in your filing cabinet, and throw the rest away. Can you do the same with an electronic product? Can you put it in your "e-filing" cabinet? If not, the transaction takes on the characteristics of a license, and not a purchase.

Those are some of the main considerations in determining whether a content transaction is a license or a sale, and therefore whether it falls under contract or copyright law. Remember that the tension between copyright and contract law affects the balance that copyright law seeks to strike. Licenses enable parties to make very clear the extent of their obligations and who bears what risks should certain eventualities arise. Licenses need not directly account for societal goals such as "progress of the sciences and the useful arts," even though their very existence depends on such societal goals.

Whether the increasing impact of contract law with respect to copyrighted works is good or not depends on your own commercial perspective and outlook. You need to understand that what the license says you can do with a work goes to the heart of DRM and how technologies operate. In the future, you should expect epic legal battles that turn on this point. The DRM technologist's dream is indeed of a world in which content not only is subject to EULA-like licensing terms but also in which technology, such as encryption, *enforces* those terms without recourse to the legal system. Such a world, in which all content rights transactions fall under contract instead of copyright law, is one whose existence some would like to prevent — especially because, as we have noted, contract law takes precedence over copyright law when there is a conflict. The Electronic Frontier Foundation (EFF) is an organization that addresses this issue on behalf of users (see `www.eff.org/Intellectual_property`), while the Association of American Publishers has written a document, *Contractual Licensing, Technological Measures and Copyright Law* (see the Bibliography), that represents publishers' point of view.

Important Legislation

In addition to general concerns about copyright, fair use, and licensing, it's helpful to know about a few recent legal developments that will steer the course of DRM-related legislation, affect DRM technologies, and form the legal basis for litigation in the future. Specifically, this section discusses

- ◆ The Uniform Computer Information Transactions Act (UCITA)
- ◆ The Digital Millennium Copyright Act (DMCA)
- ◆ The Electronic Signatures Act
- ◆ The European Copyright Directive

The Uniform Computer Information Transactions Act

The sale of tangible goods (such as toasters or television sets) is generally governed by a set of laws enacted (with some variations) in most of the states of the United States known as the Uniform Commercial Code (UCC). Its basic rules are second nature to people in the business of selling goods. It has been uncertain whether the UCC governs software. Therefore, the success of the UCC has led some to call for UCITA, which stands for the Uniform Computer Information Transactions Act, to clarify this issue. As it was developed, UCITA was expanded to cover other types of transactions in digital information. It is a contract law statute that addresses online information, computer data, and similar products.

In the United States, contract law is state law (as opposed to federal law), and the drafters of UCITA would like to see each state adopt this uniform statute to bring about consistent implementations of computer, software, and information licensing across the country.

The intention of UCITA is to provide commercial certainty similar to the UCC. Its supporters include the software industry through its advocacy group, the Software and Information Industry Association (SIAA). Proponents suggest that UCITA will provide a clear body of law for software and information license transactions. Such clarity is good for everybody, they suggest.

However, 26 state attorneys general and other quite vocal opponents take issue with UCITA, claiming that it is unfair to licensees (consumers) and favors licensors (business). The details of these arguments are too numerous to recount here, but UCITA clearly indicates the growing awareness of the importance of contract with respect to intellectual property uses and how, particularly in electronic environments, contracts are increasingly coming to govern the relationship between businesses and consumers. As of this writing, UCITA has been introduced into the legislatures of six states and is now the law in Maryland and Virginia. UCITA Online (www.ucitaonline.com) is a good source of further information on the Act.

The Digital Millennium Copyright Act

President Clinton signed the Digital Millennium Copyright Act (DMCA) into law on October 28, 1998, partially as a response to requirements in copyright treaties ratified in 1996 by the United Nations–affiliated World Intellectual Property Organization (WIPO) in Geneva. The parts of DMCA of greatest significance to those interested in DRM systems and applications, Sections 1201 and 1202, address technological measures used to protect copyrights.

The most controversial part of Section 1201 is the so-called *anti-circumvention provision*. It specifically prohibits making or selling devices or services that

- ◆ Are primarily designed or produced to circumvent technological measures to protect copyrights
- ◆ Have only limited commercial significant purpose or use other than this kind of circumvention
- ◆ Are marketed for such circumvention

The anti-circumvention provision is a tacit admission that copy protection technologies are not perfect, as we explain in Chapter 5. The controversial aspect of the provision is that while it is intended to prevent illegal activities, such as copyright infringement, it also squelches various benign activities that are protected under copyright law, such as fair use. As a result of intense lobbying effort by various parties, including the EFF, the law contains various carve-outs for exceptional cases. Among others, the exceptional cases include

- Nonprofit libraries and educational institutions circumventing copy protection to help them decide whether they want to include a work in their collections
- Reverse engineering a copy protection scheme as part of an effort to build a system that interoperates with the system that contains the copy protection scheme
- Attempting to break copy protection in a system as a means of testing its strength, as long as the tester has the permission of the system's owner
- Doing research into copy protection technology

Some constituencies are still arguing vociferously against the anti-circumvention provision of the DMCA, including the scope and wording of the exceptions. One of the claims is that it fails to adequately protect research into cryptography, and therefore hampers advancement in the field. As stated in Chapter 5, the only effective way to demonstrate an encryption technique's effectiveness is to turn it loose on the cryptography community to see if anyone can crack it over a period of time.

The way the DMCA is written, the vendor of the encryption technology must give permission to the would-be cracker first. If the vendor refuses permission, anyone who cracks the encryption is running afoul of the DMCA. In the section in Chapter 6 on the Secure Digital Music Initiative (SDMI), we describe how the recording industry invoked the DMCA to muzzle a Princeton University computer science professor.

The anti-circumvention provision of the DMCA has also been invoked on a few other occasions. One involved the magazine *2600*, which published the code for an algorithm that cracked the copy protection of DVDs. The case turned on free speech issues: The defendants claimed that the magazine's publication of the code (or even a link to the code) was protected under the First Amendment, and therefore not subject to the DMCA. Another case involved a Russian programmer named Dmitri Sklyarov, who worked at the software company ElcomSoft. Sklyarov's software broke the encryption of Adobe's eBook format in order to add features to the Adobe eBook reader. He was arrested by the FBI after presenting a paper on eBook security at a conference in Las Vegas in July 2001. Both cases are ongoing at this writing.

Section 1202 of the DMCA addresses Copyright Management Information (CMI), which is essentially identifying information related to the copyrighted work, also called metadata. Section 1202 defines CMI as identifying information about the work, author, owner, performer, writer, director, and terms and conditions for use as well as other information that the Registrar of Copyrights may require by regulation. It not only requires the use of CMI, but it prohibits knowingly providing false CMI for fraudulent purposes and bars the intentional removal of CMI. Happily, for those providing rights management protections of the kind contemplated by the DMCA, Section 1204 provides up to a $500,000 fine or up to five years in prison for a first offense.

Section 104 of the DMCA requires the Registrar of Copyrights to evaluate the effects of the DMCA on certain aspects of copyright law, including the First Sale Doctrine. The Copyright Office should have issued the report by the time this book is published.

The Electronic Signatures Act

No contract can be effective without the assent of both parties. Thus, DRM was enhanced by the addition of an important building block in June of 2000 when President Clinton signed into law the Electronic Signatures Act. This law allows parties to sign checks and apply for loans without a signature on paper and stipulates that no contract can be deemed legally ineffective merely because it is in electronic form.

The Electronic Signatures Act gives most contracts in interstate commerce signed electronically the same legal weight as contracts signed in paper form. The use of electronic signatures is in no way mandated by the act. Certain specialized types of contracts (such as prenuptial agreements) are specifically excluded from the act, but in general, this act sets the stage for nationwide online licensing transactions in the DRM space simply by making online transactions of all types easier. Clearly, the Electronic Signatures Act should provide increased opportunities for those developing copy-protection technologies and systems that authenticate persons as well as digital objects, because it will encourage such technologies' use.

The European Copyright Directive

The countries of Europe have set aside historic rivalries to form the European Union (EU), the largest economy in the world. The EU has more people and a bigger economy than the United States. Thus, the EU Copyright Directive should be of more than a passing interest to those interested in DRM.

After intensive lobbying, the European Parliament approved a draft directive for modernizing copyright law in early 2001. Copyright has been expressly extended in Europe to cover digital works on any medium. Various amendments were attached to ensure that activities such as those by Napster were clearly considered infringements of copyright.

Recent Court Decisions

In addition to the legislation described in the previous section, several recent court decisions will have significant influence on how content providers manage rights in the coming years. Indeed, 2001 has turned out to be a banner year for momentous court decisions in this area. Here we describe a few of them. You should be aware, however, that some of them are working their ways through the appeal process, meaning that the decisions could be overturned by the time you read this.

Napster

The suit against Napster, Inc., was brought by a number of major recording companies and facilitated by the RIAA. The complaint alleged that Napster was infringing on the recording companies' rights to the music hosted on Napster's system because Napster both made illegal copies and encouraged the making of illegal copies of the recordings. The court agreed with the RIAA and found against Napster.

Creators and users of DRM systems should examine the facts and conclusions of the Napster case, in large part because the legal concepts underpinning the decision are not particularly novel; the facts are simply different. The Napster court case concluded that Napster had designed and operated a system that permits the infringing transmission and retention of sound recordings employing digital technology.

Napster's sins revolved around an audio file format called MPEG-2 Group 3, better known as *MP3*. MP3 files may be readily copied onto CDs or hard drives and, when compressed, may be shared with other computer users either by e-mail or file transfer protocol (FTP). Napster facilitated the transmission of MP3 files among its users through a process commonly called *peer-to-peer file sharing*. As the court observed, Napster allowed its users to

- Create MP3 music files and store them on individual computer hard drives
- Search for MP3 music files stored on other users' computers
- Transfer exact copies of the contents of other users' MP3 files from one computer to another via the Internet

These functions were made possible by Napster's MusicShare software, available free of charge from Napster's Internet site, and Napster's network servers and server-side software. Napster also provided technical support for the indexing and searching of MP3 files.

Napster argued that its use of the copyrighted works was a fair use. Not surprisingly, given the facts of the case, the court reviewed each of the four fair use factors in detail and concluded that Napster did not have a fair use defense. In particular, the court noted Napster's stated intent to put the recording companies out of business, which goes against the fourth fair use factor (effect on the market value of the copyrighted work). Napster argued as part of its fair use defense that it did not directly benefit financially from the sharing of copyrighted works, but such a finding, even when true, does not ensure that a fair use defense will prevail. The Napster case and cases like it are by no means settled, but the court's current ruling is within the bounds of traditional copyright law. The law does not prohibit the peer-to-peer distribution that Napster facilitates as long as adequate safeguards are in place to protect copyright owners' rights. Such safeguards represent an opportunity for DRM vendors, users, and copyright owners. Indeed, as explained in Chapter 2, Bertelsmann is working with Napster, through Bertelsmann's DRM service provider, Digital World Services, to bring some measure of rights protection to the system.

Random House versus RosettaBooks

In February 2001, RosettaBooks (www.rosettabooks.com) offered for sale eBooks of works by authors including William Styron, Kurt Vonnegut, and Robert B. Parker. These authors had granted Random House, the major book publisher now owned by Bertelsmann, the right to publish these books during the 1960s and 1970s. Random House brought suit in District Court of the Southern Circuit of New York seeking a preliminary injunction against RosettaBooks, which would have required Rosetta to immediately stop selling the eBooks in question pending the outcome of the full trial on the merits of the case. Random House's motion was denied because the court concluded that Random House was unlikely to prevail in a full trial.

The authors originally granted to Random House the right to "print, publish and sell the works in book form." The court found that this language does not convey to Random House any rights with respect to eBooks. Ironically, the court cited, among numerous other sources, the *Random House Dictionary of the English Language*, which defines "book" as "a written piece of fiction or nonfiction, usually on sheets of paper fastened or bound together with covers." The contracts, drafted at a time when eBooks had not yet come into being, specifically reserved certain rights to the author and specified that "in book form" included the right to publish book club editions, reprint editions, abridged editions, and Braille editions. Thus, the court concluded that the phrase "in book form" does not encompass every conceivable right to written content, and in particular, did not encompass eBooks.

Some of the contracts included non-compete clauses that restricted the authors from competing against Random House. Random House sought to use these clauses against RosettaBooks, but the court noted that any legal issue regarding the non-compete clauses is not an issue for RosettaBooks but, if anything, for the authors.

The court concluded that Random House does not possess rights to the copyrights in the books in question to the extent of controlling the rights to publish the books in question as eBooks. Accordingly, Random House was unable to show that it would suffer irreparable harm, so on July 11, 2001, its request for a preliminary injunction was denied. Random House has appealed this decision.

Tasini versus New York Times

The case of *Tasini, et. al. v. The New York Times, et. al.* is another example of recent court decisions that limit the rights of publishers to reuse content in a new medium without an express contract that gives such rights to the publishers. The suit was brought by several members of the National Writers' Union (NWU), led by its president, Jonathan Tasini, against the New York Times Co., Newsday, Inc. (now a unit of Tribune Co.), Time Inc., Lexis/Nexis, and University Microfilms International (now ProQuest Information and Learning; see Chapter 12).

The case concerned publication of articles written by freelancers for print publication in papers such as the *New York Times* and *Newsday,* and magazines such as *Sports Illustrated* (owned by Time Inc.). The publishers later made these articles available online (and on CD-ROM) in digital archives such as those operated by Lexis/Nexis and ProQuest. The complaint alleged that the writers deserved additional compensation for their work from its online publication because the writers either had never signed contracts with the publishers or signed contracts that did not give the publishers specific rights to sell the content in online database form.

In particular, the writers claimed that they sold publishers only First North American Serial rights, which allowed them to publish the articles in print one time. The basic rule under copyright law is that any rights not expressly granted by the owner of a copyright are retained by the copyright owner and not granted to the licensee — in this case, the publishers. Yet the publishers claimed that their purchase of First North American Serial rights implied electronic republication rights as well.

In August 1997, a district court ruled for the publishers. The decision turned on a very technical provision of copyright law that gives publishers limited rights to publish revisions of a collective work (such as a newspaper or magazine). The district court judge held that an online database constitutes such a revision, and therefore publishers were within their rights to sell articles in online databases without further compensation to the authors.

The NWU appealed, and the federal appeals court for the Second Circuit overturned the decision in September 1999, disagreeing with the district court judge's interpretation of the revision right as it applied to online databases in which the articles were made available individually. The appeals court held that online publication rights are different from print rights and, therefore, that contracts that sell print rights cannot be interpreted to include online rights as well. The publishers requested a rehearing, were denied, and promptly appealed the decision to the United States Supreme Court.

For the Supreme Court appeal, the publishers brought out the heavy artillery, enlisting attorneys Kenneth Starr of Whitewater fame and Harvard Law School Professor Laurence Tribe (who argued Al Gore's case before the Supreme Court in the 2000 presidential election recount), and accepting amicus briefs from over 50 publishers and database operators, as well as an assortment of writers, historians, and filmmakers. On June 25, 2001, in a decision written by Justice Ruth Bader Ginsburg, the Supreme Court upheld the appeals court decision in favor of the writers by 7 to 2. Soon afterward, the NWU, emboldened by the precedent of the decision, commenced a series of class action lawsuits, with one against the *New York Times*.

The effect of the decision is, at this writing, yet to be fully determined. It should go without saying that publishers aren't happy about it. The decision mainly concerns contracts written more than a few years ago because more recent contracts tend to have language in them that specify terms for distribution in any format, current or yet to be invented, anywhere in the world.

Certainly, the decision is pro-author, and it's likely to result in some sort of retroactive financial settlement from publishers to many authors. Very few publishers have the capability to track the kind of information about authors and content access that would be necessary to compensate authors accurately. So it's likely that a settlement will be the result or a third party will emerge that can track usage and determine payments. The NWU is pushing for the latter approach via the Publication Rights Clearinghouse (PRC).

Some people feel that it's likely that the decision will have a chilling effect on publishers' willingness to make their archives available online, thus potentially deleting major portions of the historical record from the Web. Justice Ginsburg's decision refuted this contention, as does the NWU. Yet already, some publishers, such as the *San Jose Mercury News*, as well as online search services such as DIALOG, have been pulling content from their archives while the ramifications of *Tasini* are played out.

The *Tasini* case has already begun to influence other legal decisions. In September 2001, for example, a federal judge in New York found that Universal Music Group, one of the major recording companies, violated the terms of licenses from music publishers by streaming songs on the Web site Farmclub.com without compensating the publishers. Universal claimed that its right to stream the music on the Internet was implicit in its right to record music for sale on albums.

Although Universal is appealing the case, the theme of the decision is the same as for *RosettaBooks* and *Tasini*: A new type of use of content isn't specifically provided for in license terms, and the courts are ruling that if it isn't included, the licensee must compensate the licensor. This trend, if upheld, is likely to give the recording companies fits in their efforts to launch their online subscription services, pressplay and MusicNet.

Advice for Stakeholders

This chapter concludes with some advice for the various stakeholders in the DRM market. Although we hope this book provides you with useful information, remember that it doesn't constitute any sort of official legal advice. Consult your attorney for that.

Copyright owners: Know what you have

Movie producers, recording companies, and publishers enjoy the exclusive rights of copyright, whether directly or by license from authors. DRM doesn't change the nature of these exclusive rights. So why all the fuss about DRM? It may well be that for rights holders to successfully exploit their copyrighted works in the future, they will need to avail themselves of DRM applications and technology. This is a change in how copyrighted works are vended, in that the reliance on DRM technology vendors may prove to be far more substantial than the reliance that publishers, for example, came to have on printing companies, whose offerings became very much a commodity.

As we point out earlier in this chapter, commercial arrangements with DRM vendors are fraught with consequences, both for good and ill. Without realizing it, you can easily contract away even small rights. The most fundamental thing you need to do as a copyright owner is to know what rights you have. Are your hard-copy contracts readily available and organized? Do you have a database that contains your rights information? Is it kept up to date?

After you know your rights, you need to understand your business objectives before you can determine which rights you want to sell or license. Understand what your rights are under the law, and consult your lawyer before you sign anything. Under the law, copyright owners have great advantages that can be contracted away. This sounds like simple advice, and it is; but the anxiety arising as a result of cases such as the ones described in the previous section causes people to take ill-considered steps occasionally.

If you're thinking of doing anything with your copyrighted works, you need to consider more than the technology. The license that you sign for a "technology deal" may well have consequences beyond what you intend. In particular, it's important to account for types of digital content repackaging and distribution that are both known and yet to be invented.

Users of copyrighted works: Can you bargain?

Remember the Microsoft Windows license? What happens if, as a user, you don't like what the arrangement DRM system offers? Institutional users can bargain. In Ohio, an organization called Ohiolink formed a consortium, and its collective bargaining power became more substantial than that of an individual user.

In some cases, individual users may have no choice but to adhere to the terms of the contract or seek an alternative if one is available. The likelihood of an individual user working out a special arrangement in a DRM system to preserve rights she would have had under law is low. In fact, some legal authorities consider typical commercial EULAs to be unenforceable, mainly because they are "adhesion contracts" that are not negotiable: You either click to agree, or you can't install the software or sign up for the service. The UCITA addresses this issue by providing certain protections for consumers that go beyond existing state law.

DRM systems of the future may well make negotiation at least possible; in fact, as discussed in Chapter 6, the Information and Content Exchange (ICE) standard for business-to-business content syndication has a framework for automated negotiation of deal terms, although it's doubtful that anyone has used it to negotiate rights-related terms in contracts.

DRM vendors: It's not just the technology

Technology continues to enable content use that was not previously possible. DRM technology enables publishers to extend more control over the use of content than the five exclusive copyright rights, as listed in the subsection "Benefits of copyright law" earlier in this chapter, and as mitigated by defenses such as fair use and First Sale.

Yet the excitement that DRM technologies generate tends to obscure the facts that technology does not solve every problem. Indeed, it is orthogonal to many issues, even in the DRM space. As covered in Chapter 4, rights models inherent in DRM solutions cannot cover many types of rights that appear in the real world (for example, fair use) or even that are represented in written contracts.

Being sensitive to this only heightens your commercial appeal. The failure of many DRM companies in 2001 is not a bellwether for the industry. Opportunity abounds, and those DRM vendors who went under in 2001, in many instances, were early to market, lacked credible business plans, thought that technology solves all problems, or did not address the business needs of their would-be customers whose rights are rooted in copyright and contract law. What need of these customers does your technology address?

DRM business opportunities rely on certain rights that are creatures of law. Without foundations in copyright and contract law, there would be no such opportunities whatsoever for rights holders, vendors, or intermediaries. The need to invest in, or even contemplate, building DRM technologies would not exist. Much DRM technology is really about complying with contracts, and all parties need to remember the old adage: What the large print giveth, the small print taketh away. Know your rights. Be vigilant in exploiting them, and by all means negotiate them away when it is in your commercial interest to do so. DRM does not change the basics of law or commercial arrangements or what is in your particular business interest.

Part II

The Technology of DRM

Chapter 4

Rights Models: Representing Rights as Bits

At the core of any system for managing content rights is a rights model. A *rights model* is a specification of the types of rights that the system can keep track of and what the system can do to or with those rights. In this chapter, we're really talking about *digital rights models,* which are models of rights that a computerized device can represent.

It's important to understand rights models so that you can understand what sorts of business models a digital rights management system can support. You should understand to what degree digital rights models are capable of supporting traditional content business models, as well as the new types of business models that digital rights models can enable.

Any kind of software system that deals with objects from the real world contains models of those objects. For example, a traffic simulation system used by urban planners contains models of cars, trucks, intersections, and traffic lights in order to predict throughput. Another example is a phone company's system for detecting calling card fraud, which has models of users (cardholders) and the calls they make.

Computer models of physical objects such as cars, traffic lights, and calling cards are never precise; thus the software that's based on those models can never be 100 percent accurate either. For example, traffic simulation systems can account only for driving behavior that's predicted in advance: If someone builds a road system, it's highly unlikely that the computer simulations determine what happens if the Army decides to send a convoy of tanks down the road every afternoon or if a new set of zoning laws forces the speed limit down from 50 to 25 miles per hour.

Analogously, real-world content distribution models often contain subtleties that are hard to model digitally with precision. They are heavily dependent on two kinds of man-made things that weren't designed with digital representation in mind: legal documents, including contracts and intellectual property law, and the physical technologies of content distribution, including books, magazines, videotapes, distributors, retailers, and so on. As you read this chapter, you will see that digital rights models can't be 100 percent accurate in modeling legacy content distribution paradigms, although they can come fairly close. You should be familiar with the limitations as well as the capabilities of these models so that you can determine when and how to apply them.

You should also bear in mind that rights models do not necessarily have to represent the rights that are covered (or not covered) by the transfer of copyrights. As we explained in Chapter 3, many types of content commerce involve license agreements, not copyrights; a license agreement can transfer virtually any set of rights that the rightsholder wishes. Rights models are meant to help automate those transfers by specifying the exact rights that the licensor wants to make available. It turns out that you have to think harder than you may initially suspect about how to model rights in a DRM system. We hope that this chapter helps you understand this and plan accordingly.

Content Rights Transactions

We start by looking at content rights transactions that underlie some traditional business models and taking them apart, reducing them to the essentials.

Content rights transactions are the heart of content distribution. No matter what format the content is in, when you sell it to someone — even though you may be selling him a product such as a book or videotape — you are really selling him *rights to content* under a certain set of conditions. Products such as books and videotapes are merely vessels for the content that embody certain rights to it, which are legally and technologically circumscribed.

Buying a book

The simplest example of a content rights transaction is your buying this book in print format from its publisher, Hungry Minds, Inc. (Let's forget for the moment that people rarely buy books directly from publishers nowadays.) What are you actually buying? Of course, you're buying the physical book. But in terms of intellectual property rights, here is what you're buying:

♦ The right to read one copy of the physical book as often as you like, for as long as it lasts (effectively forever)

♦ The right to sell or give the book to someone else to read, after which you can no longer read it

There are many possible rights to the book's content that you are *not* getting with your purchase, such as

♦ Rights that are excluded by the printed book's technology, such as the right to view it on your PalmPilot or listen to a spoken-word version

♦ Rights that are excluded by copyright law (refer to Chapter 3), such as the right to make copies for resale or quote from it in another work without permission or without adhering to fair use principles

For the rights that you do get, you pay the price of the book. That money goes to the publisher, who typically pays a percentage of it to the authors as royalty.

Seeing a movie

When you buy a ticket to your local megaplex, you are once again engaging in an intellectual property rights transaction. Specifically, you are getting

♦ The right to see the movie once

♦ In some theaters, the right to see the movie again and again until the theater closes that day

You don't get the right to see the movie another day, to let a friend see it without buying another ticket, to make or sell a copy of it, to use a clip from it in your own film, to print the transcript, and so on.

Listening to a song on the radio

You don't pay anything to listen to songs on the radio (other than the cost of the radio itself), but you still engage in a rights transaction. You get

♦ The right to listen to the song

♦ The right to record it for your personal use

The latter right was essentially established in the 1984 Supreme Court decision –in *Sony Corp. v. Universal City Studios* regarding home taping of movies on television; before that, it was considered a breach of copyright to tape from broadcast media. Beyond that, you don't get the right to make copies of your recording for anyone else.

Viewing a Web site

Your rights to content that you view on Web sites differ considerably from those that you get with printed material. Web technology enables you to copy content much more easily, and the copies are in digital form and thus are "perfect," as opposed to the flawed copies you can make of hardcopy or videotapes. To deal with this problem, some Web publishers are adopting DRM technologies that offset the loose, unrestrictive nature of Web technologies. Others have tried to offset the permissive technology with end user license agreements (EULAs) that contractually restrict what users can do with the content. But many more have effectively thrown up their hands and made the content available for free.

As a result, on many content-rich Web sites, you get

♦ The right to view the content on your Web browser and to print it on your printer

♦ The right to make copies of the content by e-mailing it to others, either by using your browser's Send Page by E-mail command or by an explicit E-mail This Page button on the Web site

♦ The right to save it on your computer's hard drive

You still don't get various other rights, such as the right to embed the Web site content in other works without permission, to plagiarize, to sell the content to others, to play a spoken-word version, and so on.

Components of Rights Models

Rights models describe types of rights (what does the consumer want to do to or with the content?) and attributes of those rights (how many times, for how long, by whom, for how much money, and so on). This section discusses these in detail.

Types of rights

The examples in the preceding section help illustrate the fundamental types of rights to content that can exist. These were enumerated in the paper "Letting Loose the Light" by Dr. Mark Stefik of Xerox PARC research labs, as mentioned in the Introduction.

Figure 4-1 shows the fundamental types of content rights: render rights, transport rights, and derivative work rights.

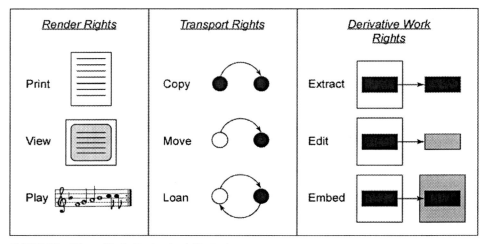

© 2000 GiantSteps Media Technology Strategies

Figure 4-1: Examples of fundamental types of content rights.

Render rights are the rights to render the content or represent it on some specific output medium. Here are three important examples of render rights:

- ♦ **Print:** Render as permanent hardcopy
- ♦ **View:** On a dynamic display, such as a computer screen
- ♦ **Play:** Render the content in sequence from beginning to end, after which time the rendering is over

Transport rights are the rights to move or copy content from one place to another. The differences among the three examples shown in Figure 4-1 have to do with which users have access to the content at any given time. In the first instance (copy), both users have access simultaneously. In the second (move), the first user gives up access after she moves it to the second user. In the third (loan), the first user cedes access to the second, but only temporarily; when the second user gives the rights to the content back, she no longer has access to it, but the first user does again.

Derivative work rights have to do with manipulation of the content to create additional (derivative) works. Of the examples shown in Figure 4-1, *extract rights* are the rights to use pieces of the content on their own, such as a chapter of a book or a few paragraphs from a magazine article. *Edit rights* are the rights to change some of the content to something else. *Embed rights* are the rights to take a piece of the content and use it in a different content item entirely, such as taking an image from a stock photo agency and using it in a layout for an advertisement.

The examples offered in Figure 4-1 are not meant to be exhaustive. There are other examples, such as the right to translate content into another language, which is a derivative work right. But the three fundamental types of rights — render rights, transport rights, and derivative work rights — are comprehensive. Stefik contends that most types of content rights transactions can be broken down into these three types. When you examine any DRM system, you should be able to deconstruct its rights model into rights that fall into these three categories.

In his paper, Stefik also refers to the right to make a backup copy of content. This can be considered as one of another type of rights, *utility rights,* which exist out of technological necessity rather than to explicitly support publishers' business models. Utility rights include

♦ **Backup rights:** Allow a copy of the content to be made for the sole purpose of restoring the primary copy if something happens to it.

♦ **Caching rights:** Permit things such as database caches and proxy servers to make local copies of content to improve system performance. (On more than one occasion, legislators have proposed reproduction rights laws that unintentionally jeopardized this type of right.)

♦ **Data integrity rights:** Include the right to create error-correcting codes, checksums, and other low-level means of ensuring that data does not get corrupted.

Rights attributes

The other important parts of rights models are referred to as *rights attributes.* Rights attributes are the particulars attached to each of the fundamental rights. Three important kinds of rights attributes are consideration, extents, and types of users, as illustrated in Figure 4-2.

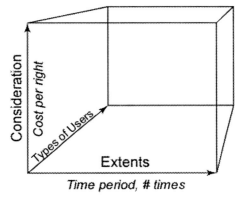

© 2001 GiantSteps Media Technology Strategies

Figure 4-2: Attributes of content rights.

Perhaps the most important rights attribute is *consideration,* which is whatever the user has to give in return for the rights. The most obvious type of consideration is money, but it can be anything that's useful to the publisher, such as the user's willingness to fill out a registration form or to have her usage of the content monitored (see Chapter 2). When one publisher confers rights on another, it may do so in return, not for money, but instead for an appropriate copyright notice in the other publisher's work.

Rights *extents* tell how long, how many times, or in what places the right applies. The following are some examples of extents that you have probably seen (and can do):

♦ Get 500 reprints of a magazine article.

♦ Watch a videotape as many times as you want for up to two days and then return it.

♦ Use a product for a 30-day free trial.

♦ Use the software up to 25 times before being forced to register.

♦ Play up to seven selections from a jukebox.

♦ Use the software in the United States and Canada only.

Finally, the *types of users* attribute enables you to specify different sets of rights and rights attributes for various classes of users. For example, you may have content on your Web site for which you charge money to ad hoc users but give away free to subscribers to your print product. Or you may make your content available at a lower cost to students or senior citizens. As discussed in Chapter 5, a DRM system determines the type of user by means of authentication.

Each right that you confer on content can have its own set of attributes attached to it. For example, a view render right may be one price and good for a certain length of time; a print render right may be another price and good for a certain number of copies; an embed derivative right may be available for no charge but with the requirement that the other party include a certain copyright notice or credit line, such as "© 2001 GiantSteps Media Technology Strategies, Used by Permission."

Rights Models and Traditional Media

It's possible to take the examples of the rights transactions discussed at the beginning of this chapter and express them in terms of fundamental rights and rights attributes. In doing so, we use a rudimentary form of a *rights language,* which is a way of expressing rights explicitly. The most sophisticated DRM solutions contain flexible ways of expressing rights. Some use a *rights specification language* such as XrML (Extensible Rights Markup Language; see Chapter 6), and some use sets of routines in a programming language such as C++ or Java.

A rights specification is a list of the rights that a *rights holder,* the owner of the content rights, can confer on a *consumer,* or user.

Buying a book

In the case of buying a book from a publisher, the consumer is purchasing the following rights and attributes:

♦ **Render rights:** Print

  • Consideration: the price of the book

  • Extent: forever

  • Type of user: only one type

♦ **Transport rights:** Sell, give away, and loan

  • Attributes defined by the user

♦ **Derivative rights:** None

Seeing a movie

♦ **Render rights:** Play

  • Consideration: the price of the movie ticket (adult or child, matinee or evening)

  • Extent: once or the rest of the day

  • Type of user: adult or child

♦ **Transport rights** : None

♦ **Derivative rights** : None

The first two examples are straightforward. But for the examples after this, it gets hairier. Consider the following cases.

Listening to a song on the radio

♦ **Render rights:** Play

- Consideration: none

- Extent: once for each radio you have turned on

- Type of user: one type

♦ **Transport rights** : Copy for personal use

- Consideration:

  o Analog media (for example, cassette tapes): none

  o Digital media (for example, DAT): a percentage of the cost of the tape

- Extent: arbitrary, as long as it's for personal use

- Type of user: one type

♦ **Derivative rights:** None

In this example, your listening to a song on the radio is actually one step in a chain of rights transactions. (For more information on chains of rights transactions, see the section "Superdistribution," a little later in this chapter.) The rights in the preceding list may seem clear, but there are subtleties involved. First, notice that your consideration for making a recording varies with the type of recording media that you use. The Audio Home Recording Act of 1992 resulted in a "tax" that makers of digital recording media, such as Digital Audio Tapes (DATs), had to pay to record companies in compensation for lost revenue. The act didn't cover analog media such as standard cassettes because copies made on analog media aren't perfect representations of the original. Of course, the makers of digital recording media pass the tax they must pay along to consumers in the form of higher prices.

Another complexity in this example has to do with the fact that broadcast content and recorded content have different properties: You are able to do many more types of things with the latter than with the former. In other words, if you tape the song, you have a different set of rights to the taped version than you do to the version that you originally heard on the radio — specifically these:

♦ **Render:** Play

- Consideration: none

- Extent: forever

- Type of user: one type

♦ **Transport:** Copy for personal use

- Consideration:

  o Analog media (for example, cassette tapes): none

  o Digital media (for example, DAT): a percentage of the cost of the tape

- Extent: arbitrary, as long as it's for personal use
- Type of user: one type

♦ **Derivative:** Any, as long as it's for personal use; extract and embed rights to samples of 30 seconds or less for commercial use
- Consideration: none in either case
- Extent: arbitrary in either case
- Type of user: personal or commercial

A further problem with this example is that these derivative rights really don't depend on the type of *user;* they depend on the type of *use.* We discuss the implications of this in the section "Users versus Uses," at the end of this chapter. The 30-second sampling rule became well known in the 1980s with the rise of hip-hop music, which made liberal use of samples for commercial purposes.

Viewing a Web site

♦ **Render:** View and print
- Consideration: varies (money, registration form, and so on)
- Extent: arbitrary
- Type of user: varies with consideration

♦ **Transport:** Copy for personal use and copy via e-mail
- Consideration: none
- Extent: arbitrary
- Type of user: one type

♦ **Derivative:** Varies

In the world of the Web, publishers must create their own rights specifications; as mentioned earlier, they can do this through technological (using DRM technologies) or legal (through contracts or EULAs) means. Because standard Web-browsing platforms are like sieves as far as copyright protection is concerned, the default rights specification for Web content is broad indeed. More restrictive rights specifications for Web content, such as the preceding list, really depend on the legal and technical frameworks that the publisher puts in place.

Contracts between publishers and content sources

Perhaps the most complex types of rights specifications are those that exist between publishers and their sources of content, which include authors, agents, and other publishers. For example, a textbook can contain illustrations, tables, charts, or formulae that are licensed from other publishers. A work of fiction can be written under a contract between the publisher and the author's agent.

Publishing contracts contain rights clauses that can be quite detailed and can vary widely. For example, a book author may receive different royalties (consideration) for many different rights in a single contract, such as

- ◆ **Render rights**: Standard print, Braille, eBook, and other electronic versions
- ◆ **Render rights extents:** Domestic direct sales, domestic sales through distributors, foreign sales, and sales through book clubs
- ◆ **Derivative rights:** Foreign language translation, anthologies, and excerpts

A publishing contract is a pile of legalese that may or may not be neatly translatable into a digital rights model. In many cases, publishing contracts use boilerplate language that is straightforward to represent in a formal rights specification. But sometimes publishers negotiate contracts with authors who are celebrities or world-renowned experts on their subject matter. In these cases, publishers have less leverage over the authors, and terms become more negotiable. The resulting contracts can be messy indeed, containing rights clauses that are ambiguous or conflicting. The same goes for contracts that record labels negotiate with major pop music stars.

The messiest rights specifications of all are for those works that bundle rights from multiple pieces of content — such as textbooks, which license illustrations, tables, or quotations from other publishers, or television documentaries, which often license film and video footage from various sources. (Think about the number of sources used in a sprawling work such as Geoffrey C. Ward's *Baseball: An Illustrated History* or *Jazz: A History of America's Music*, produced by Ken Burns.) Producers of these types of works spend incredible time and effort in securing the rights to each snippet that they need to complete the work. Textbook publishers and cable TV programmers such as the History Channel have entire departments devoted to nothing but this task, which is often done using paperwork and spreadsheets on PCs.

Think of a textbook or TV documentary as a big collection of rights specifications, and assume for the moment that each rights specification is expressible in a rights specification language like the one we use in this chapter. Now imagine trying to determine the rights of the work taken as a whole, for the purpose of distributing the work in a way other than that for which it was originally intended: for example, taking Ward's and Burns' *Jazz* and streaming it over the Internet.

In reality, Burns' production staff would try to specify in advance the various distribution channels over which the documentary would flow, and they would secure the appropriate rights to all the video and audio clips that they need. Certainly, for example, they would clear the rights to make videocassettes of the documentaries that they can sell. But imagine that they wanted to distribute it in some unforeseen way — for example, to license it in QuickTime format to a large educational institution's campus network. In an ideal world, they could take the whole collection of rights specifications, throw them into a "rights machine," and turn the proverbial crank. The machine would come out with a list of all the consideration due to each content source in return for the right to distribute the work in this new way, or issue an indication that some legal constraint makes this new form of distribution impossible.

Unfortunately, such a "rights machine" is not feasible in general because the legalese involved in each of several dozen (or several hundred) contracts would be too complex and varied to analyze and compare with complete certainty. Nevertheless, a system that records all the rights using a consistent rights specification language is useful in itself because it can make the manual rights clearance processes more efficient. That's why certain publishers and film studios are implementing internal rights management systems, even though they are expensive and complex to build. In Chapter 12, we look at vendors that supply internal rights management systems.

Rights Models and Digital Media

From the preceding section, you should get the idea that business models from traditional media can be difficult to represent in digital rights models with complete accuracy. This begs the question, why bother?

The answer is that many publishers have long-standing relationships with their customers that they are loath to change. Publishers' first forays into every form of digital media were to produce "shovelware," meaning that they took existing products and simply translated them into the new media. Early products on compact disc, CD-ROM, the Internet, DVD, and other media were done before publishers understood how best to exploit these new media: We got things like reference works on CD-ROMs or the Web with only minimal searching and indexing features, linear movies on DVD, and 45-minute music albums on compact disc.

Similarly, publishers attempted to implement the same rights models in the new digital formats as they did for the older ones. As mentioned in the Introduction, digital rights management started out as a way of protecting against piracy in a manner that approximated analog media. Now publishers have begun to realize the potential of digital rights models beyond emulating legacy rights models. The sky's the limit. In Chapter 2, we discuss many possibilities for new business models. At the heart of these business models are new rights models.

If you try to model rights associated with DRM-enabled business models, you find that they map neatly to our rights modeling scheme. This should not be surprising because, as we mentioned at the beginning of this chapter, DRM-enabled distribution models are based on software systems.

Consider the original DRM business model: the paid download. Early DRM systems typically had their own rendering applications, which enabled you to view content on-screen, but that's it – you couldn't print the content, copy and paste it to another application, or save it to your hard drive. Furthermore, you could send the downloaded file to someone else, but he couldn't access the content because his authentication credentials (for example, password or CPU ID) would not match those with which you purchased the content. The rights model for this type of paid download is very simple, as follows:

- ◆ **Render rights:** View
  - Consideration: the price of the download
  - Extent: forever
  - Type of user: only one type
- ◆ **Transport rights:** None
- ◆ **Derivative rights:** None

This would be easy to extend to a subscription-based scheme, such as PressPlay or MusicNet (see Chapter 2), in which users pay subscription fees and download tracks in a DRM format. The user can listen to the track as often as she wants until the subscription expires. To make it more interesting, assume that the subscription service supports lending and giving away music tracks to friends. (Access during the loan period or after the giveaway is denied.) The rights model looks as follows:

- ◆ **Render rights:** Play
  - Consideration: presentation of subscription license

- Extent: until subscription expires
- Type of user: subscriber
- **Transport rights:** Lend, give
- **Derivative rights:** None

In this example, the consideration is simply evidence of a paid subscription. In practice, the DRM software would look for an encrypted *license* that shows the rights that the user paid for. The license acts like a ticket, analogous to a monthly commuter ticket on a railroad. You see more about licenses in the next chapter.

Suppose that we extend this example to show what happens when the subscription service decides to allow nonsubscribers to listen to the first 30 seconds of a track (which is common on physical music purchase sites such as Amazon and CDNow). The result is as follows:

- **Render rights:** Play
  - Consideration: presentation of subscription license
  - Extent: until subscription expires
  - Type of user: subscriber
- **Render rights:** Play first 30 seconds
  - Consideration: none
  - Extent: forever
  - Type of user: nonsubscriber
- **Transport rights:** Lend, give
- **Derivative rights:** None

Finally, imagine a scenario in which the subscription service enables users to choose between paying for their subscriptions, listening to the first 30 seconds for free, or getting a free subscription in exchange for having their usage monitored, as follows:

- **Render rights:** Play
  - Consideration: presentation of paid subscription license
  - Extent: until subscription expires
  - Type of user: paid subscriber
- **Render rights:** Play first 30 seconds
  - Consideration: none
  - Extent: forever
  - Type of user: nonsubscriber
- **Render rights:** Play with monitoring
  - Consideration: presentation of monitored subscription license
  - Extent: until subscription expires
  - Type of user: monitored subscriber
- **Transport rights:** Lend, give
- **Derivative rights:** None

In the case of "Play with monitoring," the license is a different one – one that shows evidence that the user agreed to have her usage monitored.

Superdistribution

Publishing contracts, such as the one mentioned earlier, represent rights transactions between content creators and publishers. Then when you buy books from publishers, they engage in rights transactions with you. (More typically, you buy books from bookstores, which buy them from distributors, which in turn buy them from publishers.) If you subsequently sell your book to a used bookstore, you engage in yet another rights transaction. Figure 4-3 shows these rights transactions with the consideration in each case.

Analogously for music, recall our example of listening to a song on the radio. A musician records an album under contract to a record company. The label provides a copy of the album to a radio station, which pays the record company through license fees to the collecting agencies, such as ASCAP and BMI. The radio station plays the song, you hear it, and you can record it for your own personal use. Figure 4-4 shows this sequence of rights transactions and their respective considerations.

These chains of rights transactions are ad hoc examples of *superdistribution,* or multilevel distribution. Superdistribution was formalized by Brad Cox, a former computer science professor at George Mason University, in a 1994 article in *Wired* magazine and the 1996 book *Superdistribution: Objects as Property on the Electronic Frontier.*

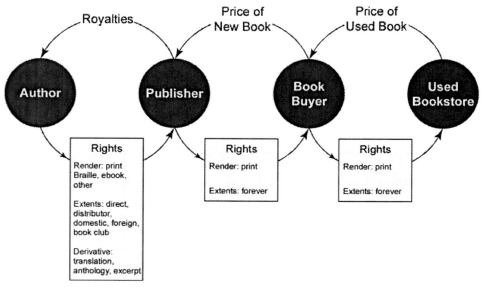

Figure 4-3: Rights transactions on a book.

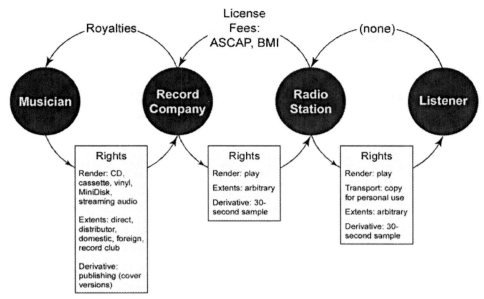

Figure 4-4: Rights transactions on a song.

Like Mark Stefik, Cox was a pioneer in the field of object-oriented programming, which came to prominence in the late 1970s through early 1980s and exists today in such popular programming languages as C++ and Java. The connection between digital rights models and object-oriented programming is not coincidental. In object-oriented programming, a programmer creates models of things, called *objects,* which have precise descriptions of things that can be done to or with them. (For example, a traffic simulation system may have a simple object called TrafficLight that can turn green, red, or yellow, but not purple, orange, or blue.) Digital rights models are essentially object models for digital media — or as Stefik and Cox have both called it, *digital property.*

Superdistribution extends the idea of rights models a step further. In a superdistribution scheme, you model two things:

♦ The rights that you define for an object, along with attributes such as consideration, extents, and types of users

♦ The rights that you allow the user to pass along to others, for those others to pass along to yet other users, and so on

Cox intended superdistribution to apply to any type of object modeled in software, but some digital rights technology vendors have used it specifically for intellectual property — the first notable case being IBM with its Cryptolope technology of the mid-1990s.

Superdistribution lets a publisher formalize what a consumer can do with content after she has bought it — that is, after she has become a rights holder herself. For example, think back to the simple "buy a book" example used earlier in this chapter.

Recall that when you buy a book, you get

- The right to read one copy of the physical book as often as you like, for as long as it lasts.
- The right to sell or give the book to someone else to read, after which time you can no longer read it.

In rights model terms, you get these rights:

- **Render rights:** Print
  - Consideration: the price of the book
  - Extent: forever
  - Type of user: only one type
- **Transport rights:** Sell, give away, and loan
  - Attributes defined by user
- **Derivative rights:** None

The de facto transport rights that you get are like rudimentary cases of superdistribution: You can give away, loan, or sell the book under whatever terms you can command. True superdistribution replaces transport rights with descriptions of the subset of rights that the user can pass along to the next person and any specifications of or limitations on attributes of those rights.

For example, let's say that instead of distributing books through traditional print, our book publisher does so in digital form through a DRM scheme that supports superdistribution. The book can be viewable on some digital display device (Web browser, eBook, PDA, and so on), and it can be printed. Let's say that the publisher lets the first consumer exercise the print right but not pass it along to consumers further down the chain. In this case, it can publish a book with a rights model like this:

- **Render rights:** Display on output device and print
  - Consideration: the price of the book
  - Extent: forever
  - Type of user: only one type
- **Superdistribution rights:**
  - Render: display on output device
  - Consideration: same as the selling price
  - Extent: arbitrary
  - Type of user: only one type

The preceding specifies that the book consumer can resell the book as many times as she wants but must charge the same as the original selling price and that those buyers can view the book only on its display device and cannot print it. Furthermore, whoever buys the book from the original consumer can sell it again, and those consumers can sell it again, and so on, and so on. The publisher can usually set it up so that with each sale, no matter how far removed from the original sale, the publisher can get a percentage of the price. Figure 4-5 shows this. The transaction in the superdistribution oval can happen any number of times.

The basic superdistribution scheme depicted in Figure 4-5 can be extended in various ways. For example, say that the publisher wants to build readership by allowing consumers to sell copies of the book to their friends at a reduced cost. In that case, the publisher will want to limit the number of copies that consumers can distribute so that the consumers don't end up competing with the publishers. That implies a rights model like this:

♦ **Render rights:** Display on output device and print
  - Consideration: the price of the book
  - Extent: forever
  - Type of user: only one type
♦ **Superdistribution rights:**
  - Render: display on output device
  - Consideration: half the selling price
  - Extent: up to 10 copies
  - Type of user: only one type

This rights model specifies that the book's buyers can resell the book at half the original selling price to up to 10 other people.

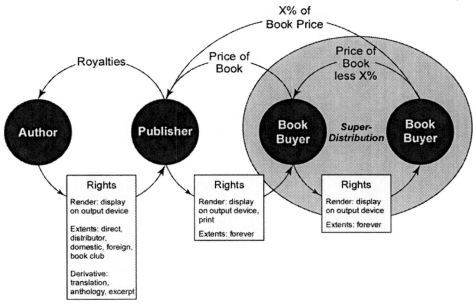

Figure 4-5: Superdistribution of book content.

Rights Models in Practice

Rights models underlie all DRM implementations in one form or another. The ultimate in rights model technology is the Digital Property Rights Language (DPRL), which Mark Stefik invented in the mid-1990s and which is covered in his paper "Letting Loose the Light." As discussed in Chapter 6, the Xerox spin-off company ContentGuard, Inc., has transformed DPRL into XrML, for Extensible Rights Management Language. XrML enables highly detailed and complex rights models to be defined so that they can be understood by DRM systems and media players. Microsoft's Unified DRM solution uses XrML.

Rights models in DRM solutions

Rights models built into DRM solutions that don't use a language such as XrML tend to be focused on defining business models that are only possible in the online digital world, as opposed to replicating legacy business models. For example, SealedMedia's SoftSeal technology (see Chapter 11), which works with several different types of media, enables publishers to specify content rights in three ways:

1. Through a user interface, which must be invoked on content items one at a time.

2. Through a scripting language that enables batch import of content into SealedMedia's system together with its licensing rules, enabling rights to be defined on multiple content items in one go.

3. Through a programming interface for the C++ language, enabling other pieces of software, such as customized content delivery services, to define rights for content automatically.

Figures 4-6a and 4-6b show the first of these three options — part of SealedMedia's user interface.

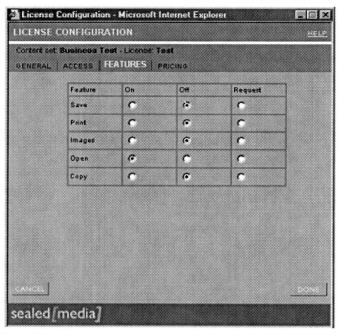

Figure 4-6a.

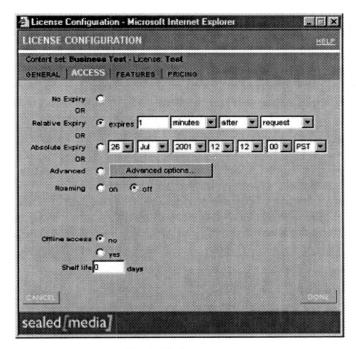

Screen shots courtesy of SealedMedia

Figure 4-6b: SealedMedia's user interface for entering rights extents.

As Figures 4-6a and 4-6b show, the rights model accessible through SealedMedia's user interface consists of the following:

- ♦ **Render rights:**
  - Save (to the consumer's hard drive)
  - Print
  - Images (shown when the file is opened)
  - Open (the file in its viewer or player application)
  - Pause (during playback)
- ♦ **Consideration:** to be defined by publisher
- ♦ **Extents:**
  - Relative: time period after purchase date/time
  - Absolute: until specific date/time

SealedMedia's rights model also includes some utility rights for features such as moving content from one machine to another (Roaming) and access when not connected to the SealedMedia server (Offline Access).

SealedMedia's user interface is typical of many full-featured DRM implementations, as are its scripting language for batch import and its C++ programming interface (although other vendors may use Java or some other language instead of C++). It's often the case that the user interface presents only a subset of the rights that one can define using a given DRM technology;

sometimes even the scripting language limits options and leaves the programming interface as the only way to access the full range of features in the vendor's rights model.

As we imply in Chapter 8, it's important to gather your requirements for rights that are inherent in the business models that you intend to implement *now and in the foreseeable future*. Only then can you really judge the efficacy of the rights modeling power of DRM solutions that you are considering. You can use the rights specification syntax presented in this chapter as a guide for writing down your requirements.

Users versus Uses

There are two important limitations in digital rights models' capabilities to implement arbitrary business models for publishers. First is one that we've seen before: the lack of ability to represent the subtleties and complexities of content business models from the real world. That's not a showstopper, however, because digital rights models can support plenty of new-media business models, both known and yet to be discovered.

The second limitation in digital rights models may be more insidious: They don't do a great job of modeling the actual *uses* of content.

Render, transport, and derivative work rights are all really narrow cases of rights to use content in certain ways: to send it to a printer, to make a copy of it, or to embed a section of it in another work. But if we think about it, we find that there are many types of uses about which rightsholders ought to be concerned that these rights don't cover.

A classic example is the commercial-versus-noncommercial use of content. Say that a graphic artist at an advertising agency is using Adobe Photoshop to lay out a magazine ad for a carmaker — clearly a commercial task. He wants an image of an eagle soaring in flight to be used in a Rocky Mountain landscape with a winding road and the latest sport-utility vehicle. Typically, he will go to an online stock image agency, such as Getty Images or Corbis, whose Web sites allow users to download image files. Now let's say that you want the same type of eagle image for inclusion in a PowerPoint presentation that you are making to your company's management about how your business plan will result in "soaring" sales in the coming year. This is considered a noncommercial use because the content that you are producing isn't for sale. You can also go to Getty or Corbis to get your eagle image.

Stock image agencies price their images quite differently for commercial and noncommercial use. Many commercial uses of images require that the user pay a royalty to the source of the image for each use, in addition to any fee for downloading. Some agencies also maintain libraries of images that users can download for free (such as Microsoft's online clip art gallery) or as part of an annual subscription fee (such as ArtToday.com); these sites often make you attest, by registration form, that you are using their images within certain guidelines.

The problem is that there is no technological means of ensuring that the *actual* use of the content conforms to the *claimed* use. The graphic designer in our car magazine ad example can claim noncommercial use and purchase the eagle image for a lower price. Let's even assume that the image is protected within an encryption-based DRM scheme. The designer can unlock the image and read it into his Photoshop layout. When the Photoshop layout is complete, he can output it in some common graphics format, such as TIFF, and send it to a prepress house, to the advertising client, or wherever it needs to go.

It is possible to imagine some measure of protection against this type of fraud through DRM technology: The image agency could make the dubious assumption that all uses of Photoshop are commercial, and all uses of PowerPoint are not. In this case, the DRM technology would not release the image into Photoshop unless the designer paid the commercial-use download fee. But there are many reasons why this wouldn't work. First of all, the scheme would be child's play to circumvent: Just load the image into PowerPoint (after paying the lower noncommercial-use fee) and export it to a format that Photoshop can load. Furthermore, this scheme doesn't cover the usage tracking necessary to enforce the generation of royalty payments.

In general, the only way that the rightsholders (the stock image agency or the original source of the image, such as the photographer) would know that the image was used for a commercial purpose would be to actually see the magazine ad. In that case, the rightsholders could take legal action against the ad agency if it did not pay the commercial fees.

Another example of commercial-versus-noncommercial use of content is the reference earlier in this chapter to listening to a song on the radio. It's okay to record a song from the radio to play on tape at home or in your car. It's not okay to include the song in a collection of your favorite dance hits and sell copies of the collection on the street — as you see all the time on the streets in most major cities. It doesn't matter whether the medium is analog cassette, DAT, or a digital file format such as MP3: This is a legal restriction, not a technological one.

Another important example of the difficulties of tracking uses of content is fair use. A mainstay of critics and academics for decades, fair use allows content creators to use copyrighted material without permission or consideration for certain specific purposes, such as for commentary, criticism, or parody. Many hours have undoubtedly been spent in courtrooms arguing over what constitutes commentary or criticism. Representing this type of use in a rights model may be straightforward: You could simply identify a type of rights associated with fair use and perhaps a type of user called a fair use user.

But actually tracking fair use is even harder than tracking the commercial or noncommercial use of an image. You could argue, as suggested previously, that the professional graphic designer and the corporate presentation developer use clearly different tools and file formats to do their work. But both the fair use user (for example, a book reviewer) and the content pirate may use the same tools to do their work: Both are creating commercial publications.

Despite these limitations, rights models are both important and powerful in the field of digital rights management. Throughout the remainder of this book, you'll see explicit and implicit references to rights models as we discuss DRM technologies and solutions.

Chapter 5

DRM Building Blocks:
Protecting and Tracking Content

Many types of technology components fall under the rubric of "DRM." These include subscription systems such as those found on *The Wall Street Journal* and *Consumer Reports* Web sites, paid download services like QPass and ProQuest; business-to-business (B-to-B) content syndication technologies from vendors such as Vignette and Kinecta and services such as YellowBrix and Screaming Media, and various types of print-on-demand services. However, none of these technologies actually enforces rights models. They may describe rights or leave them to written license agreements, but otherwise they implement fairly standard components such as file transfer protocols, user registration databases, and e-commerce payment processing.

In this chapter, however, we concentrate on the components of systems that use technology to control distribution — to enforce rights models. It turns out that most DRM solutions are variations on a common theme — a DRM reference architecture. In this chapter, we present a DRM reference architecture and examine each of its components. We also discuss the two most prevalent core technologies involved in DRM implementation: encryption and watermarking.

We don't say much here about specific vendors' offerings; see Chapters 7, 11, and 12 for those details. Our intent in this chapter is to give you a solid understanding of the general principles of DRM technology to help you evaluate solutions that you may want to adopt. Vendors come and go, but these principles should remain for the foreseeable future.

A DRM Reference Architecture

The components of the DRM reference architecture range from those that must be behind the content provider's firewall to those that may be elsewhere — on the consumer's hardware or on a server at a DRM service provider. There are three major components: the content server, the license server, and the client.

The content server

The content server component of the DRM architecture is the one that is most likely to sit behind the content provider's firewall. It consists of the actual content, information about products (or services) that the content provider wants to distribute, and functionality to prepare content for DRM-based distribution.

Content repository

A content provider who implements a DRM solution has a *repository* of content, which is a collection of content that's either in a suitable format for distribution through the DRM system or (as depicted in Figure 5-1) can be put into the correct format on demand. The repository is often built into the DRM solution, or sometimes the DRM solution interfaces to a content management system that serves multiple purposes (see Chapter 10). Some publishers are building content management systems that serve several distribution channels simultaneously, such as print, Web, syndication (see Chapter 6), and controlled consumer distribution via DRM. From a purely pragmatic standpoint, the repository is a file server or a database system. In either case, it contains content as well as *metadata*, or information about the content.

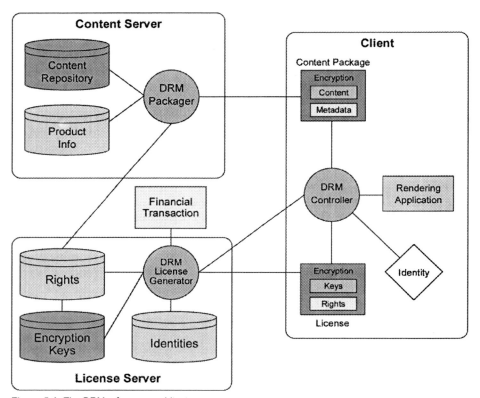

Figure 5-1: The DRM reference architecture.

Product info

Content providers typically have catalogs of product information for their products in physical media. These contain metadata about products, such as price, marketing information, format, physical dimensions, and so on. In implementing DRM, content providers also need to create databases of information about products they intend to sell. If the DRM system is integrated with an e-commerce storefront, the product info is inserted into the storefront system's product catalog.

Notice that both the content repository and the product info database contain metadata. There is a subtle yet important difference between content and product metadata: Price is clearly product metadata, for example, whereas an internal revision number would be content metadata. Other elements of metadata, such as title, author, number of pages, and file format could be either.

DRM packager

Every encryption-based DRM system contains functionality for preparing content for distribution through the system. We call this functionality the *DRM packager* or *content packager*. The packager does its job either before putting the content into the repository, or (as Figure 5-1 shows) on-the-fly before distribution. Various vendors have trademarked names for content packages, such as InterTrust's DocBox for PDF files and SealedMedia's SoftSeal.

In addition to the content itself, the content package contains metadata. There are various kinds of metadata, but two in particular are prevalent in DRM content packages:

♦ **Identification:** A unique number that the publisher can use as a reference for various purposes, such as getting up-to-date pricing information and tracking content usage remotely

♦ **Discovery:** Information that can help users locate the content, such as keywords, title, and author

In some DRM systems, the content packages also include metadata on content usage. This is especially common in DRM systems meant to be used offline. In these systems, usage can be tracked locally to the content package and periodically reported back to a server.

Both the content and the metadata in a package are usually encrypted. We discuss encryption in more detail later in this chapter, in the section "Encryption." The metadata does not need to be encrypted, but it must at least be tamperproof (unable to be changed) and inextricably tied to the content. The content package can exist as an indivisible unit; alternatively, the package can simply contain metadata and a link to the content through the identification metadata. The latter is the usual case for streaming media formats (see the "Streaming media" section a little later in the chapter).

The other important task of the packager is to create descriptions of the rights that the content provider wants to allow the user to exercise on the content. As we saw in Chapter 4, DRM solutions enable content providers to specify rights through a user interface (one content item at a time), through a batch process, or through a programming interface for a language such as C++ or Java. This is part of the packaging process.

What happens after rights are specified varies with different DRM technologies. In the older technologies, such as InterTrust's DigiBox (see Chapter 7), rights were bundled in with the content package and sent to the user. Although this scheme is the most straightforward to implement, it has some major shortcomings, such as the following:

♦ You may want to specify multiple sets of rights for a given piece of content, such as for different types of users. It is more cumbersome to implement this if rights are packaged along with the content.

♦ Conversely, you may want to offer a set of rights that applies to more than one piece of content, such as a subscription service to a body of content. Bundling rights with individual content items makes this difficult to implement.

♦ Certain types of content, such as streaming media, must reside on servers rather than on the user's device or hard drive. In that case, you can't distribute the content to users, but you still must distribute information about their access rights.

Therefore, more modern DRM implementations separate rights information from content packages by encapsulating the former in *licenses* (also called *permits* or *tickets*).

The license server

Licenses contain information about the identity of the user or device that wants to exercise rights to content, identification of the content to which the rights apply, and specifications of those rights, which conceptually resemble those we saw in Chapter 4.

A reasonable analogy to DRM licenses in the real world is tickets for planes and trains. When you buy a ticket on the 6 p.m. American Airlines flight from LaGuardia in New York to O'Hare in Chicago, you must show a photo ID to get a boarding pass and get on the plane. The ticket and boarding pass give you (and only you) the right to board that plane (and only that plane). Or if you're a train commuter, you may buy a monthly pass on the New Jersey Transit between Princeton Junction and New York. In that case, you (and only you) get the right to ride certain trains (trains from Princeton Junction to Penn Station and back) every day for a month. Analogously, you may get a DRM license that gives you access to one specific piece of content, or you may get a license to access any item in a collection of content over a certain period of time.

There are several ways to implement licenses; the one we depict in the DRM reference architecture is fairly typical. The DRM packager creates specifications of rights and hands them off to a second set of server components, which we call the license server. In addition, the DRM packaging process creates a set of *encryption keys* that are used to authenticate users and decrypt content. Rights specifications and keys are stored in separate databases. It is, of course, particularly important that the latter be tightly secured. Each of these databases contains unique identifiers – the identification metadata mentioned previously – that link rights and key information to particular content items.

The license server also stores *identities*, which are information about users who exercise rights to content. As we see later in the section "Identification," the identities of users can take different forms, such as usernames, device information, or biometrics. In our train example, the identification takes the form of the rider's signature. Taken together, identities, rights specifications, and encryption keys constitute sufficient information for the *license generator* to create licenses and send them to users. We see how this is done shortly.

The client

Components of the DRM reference architecture that reside on the user's side are the DRM controller, the rendering application, and the user's identification mechanism. We use the term *client* not only because it is analogous to *server*, but also because the client is really a combination of the user and the device that the user is using.

The DRM controller

The client side contains a collection of functionality that we call the *DRM controller*. Vendors' names for this type of component include Microsoft's Black Box and the Secure Digital Music Initiative's (see Chapter 6) Licensed Compliant Module. The DRM controller is the real nerve center of the DRM system. Figure 5-1 (earlier in this chapter) depicts the DRM controller as an independent piece of software, but it can also reside within a rendering application (player, viewer, and so on), or it can be a piece of dedicated hardware.

The DRM controller does several things:

- ◆ Receives the user's request to exercise rights on a content package.
- ◆ Gathers the user's identity information and obtains a license from the license server.
- ◆ Authenticates the application that performs the rights exercise, such as a rendering application.
- ◆ Retrieves encryption keys from the license, decrypts the content, and releases it to the rendering application.

A typical sequence of events inherent in DRM use on the client side is shown in Figure 5-2.

The first thing that happens is that the user obtains a content package (number 1 in the figure). This could happen in several ways, such as by downloading it from a Web site or FTP server, detaching it from an e-mail message, or reading it from physical media such as a CD-ROM. At some point after the user gets the content package, she makes a request to exercise rights on it (2). The user may do this by choosing a menu item in a rendering application, executing an operating system command, double-clicking a file, or whatever — we say generically that she "activates a DRM controller."

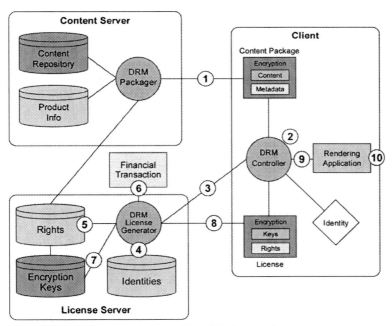

Figure 5-2: Sequence of events in exercising rights to content.

For the remainder of this discussion, assume for the sake of concreteness that the right being exercised is a render right. Thus, a rendering application is necessary to exercise the right. However, it's worth noting that for some transport rights, such as copy and lend, the DRM controller could conceivably perform the job itself. Exercising a copy or lend right involves constructing another content package, which can involve nontrivial tasks such as encryption and registration with content and/or license servers.

Once activated, the DRM controller gathers information necessary for generating a license. In addition to the information the user has already specified about which rights she wants to exercise, this includes obtaining identity information for the user and/or client device and information from the content package, including the content identifier. If the user hasn't used this DRM system before, the DRM controller must create the identity. This may entail getting the user to fill out a registration form (possibly containing a credit card number) or clicking to accept an end-user license agreement. After it's created, the identity is passed to the license server for insertion into the database of identities.

The DRM controller then sends the identity and content information in a request to the license server (3). The license generator authenticates the client's identity against its identities database (4) and uses the content identifier to look up rights information about the content (5). Then it gathers rights information from the user's license request. If necessary, it kicks off a financial transaction at this point (6). (In some DRM systems, the transaction takes place earlier in the process – sometimes even before the user obtains the content package in the first place.) Or, if the consideration specified in the license is something other than financial, that consideration can be given – the user fills out a demographic survey, gives up some of her Frequent Reader points, or whatever. Finally, the license generator pulls together rights information, client identity information, and encryption keys (7), and creates a license – which is itself encrypted or at least tamperproofed. It sends the license back to the client (8).

At some point in this process, the DRM controller on the client side may take steps to authenticate the rendering application to make sure that it is authorized to view the content.

There are two main reasons why it may be necessary to do this. First, if the DRM controller is separate from the rendering application, the vendor may have an established offline process for certifying rendering applications to ensure that they behave properly and don't do naughty things like make unencrypted copies of content on the sly. Second, the rights model may require that the rendering application be tied to the individual user or client device, instead of just being some generic rendering application. In that case, the DRM controller has to check the client's identity against registration information in the rendering application.

After the license is generated and any authentication steps are complete, the DRM controller can decrypt the content and release it to the rendering application (9). Finally, the rendering application plays or shows the content to the user (10).

Rendering applications

Two types of rendering applications are prevalent in DRM systems: those built specifically for the DRM system and general-purpose applications that the DRM system modifies in order to restrict their behavior.

Standalone rendering applications

Early DRM systems incorporated their own standalone rendering applications with DRM controllers built in. The great advantage of this approach is that the purpose-built rendering application can be made airtight: It can allow only the specific functions that the user is authorized to perform. But this approach has bigger disadvantages. First, the vendor has to distribute the application to its users — which can be done over the Internet or even through floppies or CD-ROMs. Then, the user has to install and learn how to use the new application.

All this is a major hassle. InterTrust's DigiBox, which originally included a standalone viewer, suffered from this problem. The application was several megabytes in size, making it virtually impossible to download over the Internet for users with dial-up connections. InterTrust tried easing the distribution problem by cutting deals with major software vendors; for example, they got the software included with the CD-ROM for America Online. The only successful standalone rendering applications with DRM built in nowadays are those for popular new formats or devices, such as Microsoft Reader for the eBook format on PCs and handhelds. In other words, obviously, good file formats and rendering applications are far more important to users than are DRM controllers. Yet even in those cases, users must still download DRM controller functionality unless it is bundled in with their devices (as it is, for example, with Microsoft Windows Media Player on PCs).

Plug-ins

The second approach, more common for PC platforms nowadays, is to start with general-purpose playing or viewing applications and modify their behavior. These applications tend to do lots of things that DRM systems don't want them to. Common applications such as Adobe Acrobat Reader have functions like Print, Save As, and Copy to Clipboard, which let the user do things with the content that the DRM system may not want done. The underlying operating system also has functions that are accessible within general-purpose applications that let users do things that they shouldn't, such as the Alt+Prnt Scrn function in Microsoft Windows that lets you to make a bitmap copy of the window open on your screen.

Adobe Acrobat Reader in particular has an architecture that allows for *plug-ins,* which are pieces of code that act as DRM controllers and change the Reader's behavior. Several DRM vendors have implemented Acrobat plug-ins that perform tasks such as prompt the user for a password or collect payment. Plug-ins can also turn off functions such as Print and Save As, but they generally can't override operating system–level functions like Alt+Prnt Scrn. The Netscape Web browser also has a plug-in architecture. Microsoft applications such as Internet Explorer achieve similar results through ActiveX controls.

The plug-in approach has a few advantages: It's likely that users either have the base application already or at least will be motivated to get it for reasons other than viewing one specific piece of content that happens to be protected by some DRM mechanism. Also, the plug-in code is usually smaller in size than a full application would be, which makes distribution less problematic. The disadvantage is that, as implied earlier, it's generally not possible to make an existing application with a plug-in as secure as one that's purpose-built.

Java technology

The plug-in approach still has the disadvantage of requiring users to download and install a piece of software. Some users are afraid to do this; others just don't want to. In the late 1990s, a third approach suggested itself that would virtually eliminate this problem. The silver bullet was Sun Microsystems' Java technology.

Programs written in the Java programming language are supposed to be able to run on any platform that has a core piece of software called a *Java Virtual Machine,* or JVM. JVMs have been implemented for many different platforms, including PCs, Macintoshes, UNIX systems, cell phones, PDAs, and the major Web browsers. The idea is that you can download any piece of Java code (called an *applet*) into your environment and have it run without needing to go through an installation process, as would be necessary with plug-ins or other types of software.

It was thought that you could implement a DRM controller in Java that ran inside a Web browser or standalone on a PC or Mac. You would find a piece of content that you wanted to view or play. You would click the URL, and some Java code would download to your machine; this would be the DRM controller. You would need to download it only once, and it would install automatically and then run. No muss, no fuss.

That was the theory, anyway. The problem was that the "write once, run anywhere" promise of Java was never quite delivered. There were version incompatibilities, performance problems (particularly on the Macintosh platform), and various issues relating to Sun's lawsuit against Microsoft over the technology. Many thousands of Java applets do exist all over the Web, but no one has been able to successfully implement a DRM controller in Java that has acceptable performance and wide enough platform compatibility. Sun took steps toward building its own DRM controller as part of an e-commerce component called the Java Wallet, but the product was never completed.

In Chapter 7, we outline Microsoft's approach to rendering application and DRM controller architecture. Briefly, Microsoft solves the problem by separating the DRM controller into its own application and developing a series of rendering applications designed to be compatible with it. Unless someone figures out how to do something similar in Java, this may be the most effective approach to integrating DRM functionality with rendering applications.

Identification

A user has to establish an identity in order to be cleared to exercise a right on content. Authentication of identities is one of the classic problems in the security field. The first thing to worry about is what you're identifying – the user or the device? This is not a trivial matter. A user may want to view or play content on multiple devices that he owns; for example, he may want to read an eBook on both a PC and a PDA. He may think that he shouldn't need to pay for separate versions of the eBook for those platforms. Analogously, if a user buys a music CD and wants to listen to it on the cassette player in his car, he feels free to make a cassette copy of the music (and, indeed, is legally in the clear if he does so).

Conversely, there may be a device that more than one person uses regularly, such as a shared PC in an office or the family Internet music player. Should each person who uses the device pay separately? Before the Internet, content providers never seriously considered these questions, because of the limited capability to copy physical media and the limited numbers of people who can pragmatically use a single device. But DRM vendors are now grappling with this issue.

User identification

A user's identity can be

+ A piece of information that you supply, such as a name, an e-mail address, a phone number, a Social Security number, an account number, a user ID, or a password

+ A piece of information inherent to you, such as a biometric (fingerprint, retina scan, and so on)

+ A set of information that a trusted third party holds about you, such as a digital certificate

Each type of identity has pros and cons. The first of type is the most common: The system prompts you for one of these pieces of information. All are things that others can find out about you. Passwords are somewhat different because they supposedly aren't used for any purpose other than to get access to a certain system, and they are kept in some place that has greater or lesser degrees of inaccessibility, ranging from highly encrypted password files to cookies on your hard drive to yellow sticky notes on your PC monitor. In general, though, these pieces of information are easily transferable from one person to another, which means that their value for authentication purposes is only approximate.

User identity information is often stored on the machine. The most common way to do this in the world of Web browsers is a *cookie,* which is a text string within a file or a file unto itself. In addition to containing information about your identity, a cookie can contain things about what pages on a site you visited, the status of your shopping cart, and so on. Cookies can also contain usernames and passwords. One problem with cookies is that they are tied to machines, not people. Someone can walk up to your machine and assume your identity by going to Web sites that use cookies that are stored on your machine.

Unique pieces of information about you, such as biometrics, are the surest method of personal identification. However, they are expensive to implement — no one wants to have a retina scanner or palm reader next to his PC — which is why their use in consumer content distribution is rare, although at least one DRM vendor, Musicrypt (see Chapter 11), uses them.

Digital certificates, the third type of personal identification, are supplied and maintained by third parties called certificate authorities (CAs). You apply for a digital certificate through a CA, which collects various pieces of information about you. The CA, to uphold its reputation as trustworthy, takes steps to verify that you are who you say you are.

There are several commercial CAs, such as Verisign and RSA Security. Verisign issues certificates for businesses that want to do e-commerce on the Web using the standard Secure Socket Layer (SSL) protocol. To apply for an SSL certificate, you have to supply information such as your business's taxpayer ID, DUNS (Dun & Bradstreet) number, and so on — all information that can be verified. Microsoft has a sort of lightweight certificate authority called Passport, which we discuss in more detail in Chapter 7. Some institutions, such as large companies and universities, maintain their own CAs.

CAs store digital certificates in encrypted, secure formats in certificate repositories. They are integrated into certain DRM systems so that when the DRM controller wants to verify a user's identity, it requests a digital certificate from a CA.

Device identification

Authenticating the identities of devices, rather than people, is another matter. The simplest way to identify a device is by putting a unique serial number in it that software can read. Intel tried doing this with some of its microprocessors, only to be met with howls of protest from privacy advocates. Nevertheless, several DRM vendors have figured out ways to extract ID information from PCs that is unique or nearly so. One way is to read serial numbers that are stored on hard disk drives. Disk manufacturers put software-readable serial numbers on their drives starting long before anyone thought about Internet privacy.

Another technique is to authenticate devices based on their IP addresses, which are the basic numerical addresses of every device attached to the Internet (an IP address is a group of four numbers from 0 to 255). This is sometimes used to authenticate users of content in an institutional setting, such as a corporate site license to an expensive market research service. However, as networking technology gets more and more sophisticated, this technique becomes less feasible. For example:

♦ It used to be that all devices had IP addresses that were permanently assigned. Nowadays, some network management techniques assign IP addresses dynamically, meaning that a given device might have a different IP address every now and then.

♦ It also used to be that all IP addresses were globally unique. There are some increasingly popular networking technologies that assign IP addresses which are only unique within a subnet (a single office, for example). Modern SOHO (small office/home office) networking equipment often works this way. If IP addresses are not universally unique, it's not possible to identify devices by their IP addresses.

Some DRM vendors, like Microsoft, have tried combining personal and machine IDs into schemes that approximate the situations mentioned at the beginning of this subsection, such as one person owning multiple devices. However, none of the schemes we have seen so far are entirely satisfactory. As we said in this book's Introduction, the original intent of DRM was to replicate aspects of physical media distribution paradigms in the online digital world; identity authentication turns out to be one of those aspects that are hard to emulate correctly.

Service providers

A number of vendors have established themselves as DRM service providers, also called *clearinghouses.* These take much of the complexity of DRM implementation away from publishers by outsourcing it.

Service providers can perform several of the functions shown in the Content Server and License Server boxes in Figure 5-1. Often they perform license server functions, including storage of identities, encryption keys and content rights information, and generation of licenses. Sometimes they also host the actual packaged content and distribute it themselves. And some service providers even outsource the packaging function; just send them your content and metadata, and they take care of everything else – and send you a check and an activity report at the end of each month.

The function of a service provider is to ease the DRM implementation burden for content providers. Some vendors, such as Reciprocal (see Chapter 7) and Digital World Services (see Chapter 11), do nothing but outsource DRM solutions that come from multiple DRM technology vendors. A larger number of vendors outsource DRM solutions based on a single system from a vendor that built its technology specifically with service providers in mind. These service providers sometimes act as CAs, as described earlier, although they usually work with an established commercial CA rather than build their own. Other DRM vendors let content providers choose between licensing their software for implementation in-house and having the vendor outsource the implementation.

Streaming media

We conclude the discussion of the DRM reference architecture with a few thoughts on how DRM works for streaming media formats, such as RealAudio, RealVideo, Windows Media, or QuickTime 4.

Streaming formats differ from standard formats in that they aren't delivered to the user as entire files, as would be the case for text and (most) still image formats, as well as certain audio and video formats such as WAV and MP3. Instead, a server delivers streaming media to the user on demand (that is, when the user initiates playback), a bit at a time, in increments called *packets.*

There is nothing about the DRM reference architecture that doesn't apply to streaming media. Instead of moving the file from the content repository to the packager and then to the client in discrete steps, it happens a packet at a time — including encryption, if used. On the client side, packets can be decrypted and then rendered one at a time as well.

Certain DRM vendors have begun to come out with solutions for streaming formats. DRM solutions that measure data about viewership are useful in the world of streaming media, but those that mainly exist to protect against piracy are of marginal relevance because there is little reason at this time to worry about the piracy of streaming media. Capturing a video or audio stream in order to make unauthorized copies of it is considerably more trouble than obtaining a file. You would have to set up a bogus player application that captures the stream as it is delivered, packet-by-packet, from the server, and saves the data in a file — often a *very large* file. Furthermore, streaming media often reaches users in poor quality because of missed packets, dropped connections, and so on.

In the future, when broadband delivery of streaming media is not only much more ubiquitous but also much more reliable, the piracy of streaming media will be of concern to content owners. But for now, the streaming media infrastructure is just too unreliable to worry much about piracy. Nevertheless, major record labels and movie studios are taking piracy seriously and embracing DRM solutions for streaming media from vendors like Microsoft, RealNetworks, and InterTrust.

In Chapters 7, 11, and 12, we look at examples of vendors' DRM solutions and see how they match up with the DRM reference architecture.

Encryption

Not all the systems that we classify as DRM use encryption, but it is the most common means of copy protection, and it is the core technology most closely associated with DRM. Much of the constant discussion about the efficacy of DRM systems for copy protection focuses on the power of encryption, even though most instances of DRM systems being cracked have not involved breaking the actual encryption but instead have involved some other security hole. Although everyone has heard of encryption, few people really understand it. Therefore, it's worthwhile to delve into the mysteries of this field.

The field of cryptography is sort of like a black hole. If you took physics, you may recall that black holes are objects of virtually infinite gravity. If you stay far enough away from one, you can observe it but not get much detail about it, but if you get too close, you cross an event horizon and then get sucked into its gravitational field — from which there is no escape. Analogously, black hole subjects, such as cryptography, are those about which you can either learn a superficial amount or get sucked inexorably into the gory details.

In the case of cryptography, the gory details concern things like encryption algorithms and government cryptography policy. This section is an attempt to bring you across the event horizon just enough to give you the information about encryption that you need to evaluate digital rights management solutions — and then bring you back to the safety of normal gravity. If you are interested in crossing the event horizon, the best book on the subject — although slightly out of date by now — is Bruce Schneier's *Applied Cryptography*. A briefer but more up-to-date source of information is the Crypto FAQ on RSA Security's Web site, at `www.rsa.com/rsalabs/faq/index.html`. For those who would like to read a fascinating recent history of the subject, we highly recommend Steven Levy's book *Crypto*.

The overall goal of cryptography in the digital world is really not so much to protect secrets as it is to emulate physical-world human behavior toward information. The problem with online digital information is that it's far easier for people to access, copy, analyze, and manipulate it than it is in physical analog form. Think of digital cryptography as a set of techniques that restrict access, analysis, and manipulation so that online information exchanges resemble their old-fashioned, real-world counterparts.

For example, one application of cryptography is ensuring that the contents of a message in transit aren't changed. In the physical world, you can take simple steps to make sure that a message doesn't get changed on its way from the sender to the receiver, such as sealing it in an envelope. It is possible to alter the contents of a hard copy message in such a way that the receiver doesn't realize that it has been tampered with, but not easy. In the networked digital world, in contrast, it can be easy to alter a message in transit — or alter the identity of the sender. Cryptography steps in to re-establish the difficulty of that which is easy in the networked digital domain.

The primary goal of cryptography in DRM is to prevent content from being accessible in its native format at all times except when the DRM controller permits it. As mentioned earlier, it is also the responsibility of the rendering application to allow users to do only what the DRM controller permits.

The question most likely to go through the minds of people who evaluate DRM technologies is, "How good is the encryption?" For better or worse, the answer is usually, "Good enough." There is no truly reliable way of measuring the efficacy of encryption systems. However, we can give you a bit of background and some parameters to look at, in order to justify and help you understand this admittedly weak answer.

The strength of encryption algorithms

Cryptography has been around for thousands of years. Encryption algorithms — procedures for doing encryption — have come a very long way since the early days, when they generally consisted of simple things like substitution ciphers. (For example, take a message and substitute H for A, Y for B, E for C, and so on.) Nowadays, encryption algorithms have their bases in advanced mathematical concepts.

Some algorithms are stronger — more impervious to cracking — than others, but one absolute truth remains: There is *absolutely no such thing* as an encryption algorithm that is both provably unbreakable and practical to implement. There is a provably unbreakable algorithm known as a *one-time pad*, but it has no practical implementation on the Internet. In a one-time pad, you encrypt a message with a key that is completely random, has no relationship whatsoever with the keys you generated for previous messages, and is only used once. Furthermore, the key is at least as long as the message it encrypts. The recipient needs the key to decrypt the message. The problem is how to get the key to the recipient without compromising security. In the real world, this was done by sending agents out into the field with keys written down on pads (hence the name), which they would use later when they received messages. But you can't do something similar on the Internet.

In general, there are trade-offs between an algorithm's strength and its implementation practicality: Stronger algorithms take longer to encrypt and decrypt content. You want an algorithm that is strong, but you don't want your users waiting a long time while the DRM system's client decrypts the content. At the same time, because computers get faster and faster, that which takes a long time now may not after a few years.

In other words, you can think of cryptosystems as analogous to antitheft devices for your car (with the difference that the car thieves get faster every year). When you purchase a device such as an ignition cutoff switch or a steering wheel lock (like the Club), you're *deterring* theft, not preventing it on any absolute basis. And you choose which antitheft device to purchase based, in part, on how annoying it is to use.

The strength of a cryptosystem derives from several factors, including

♦ The length of time it would take for a cracker to break it using a *brute-force attack*

♦ The algorithm's susceptibility to various clever forms of *cryptanalysis,* which can make brute-force attacks unnecessary

As a very simple example, consider the combination locks commonly used on luggage. They have three dials with settings from 0 to 9 each. A brute-force attack is one that starts at 000 and works its way up to 999 until the briefcase opens. One form of cryptanalysis for a suitcase lock is to find pieces of information about the suitcase's owner that she may use as a combination, such as her birthday, her age, or the last three digits of her phone number. (Another may be that most people are too lazy to reset the combination to something other than the usual factory default of 000.)

Of course, by most measures, three-digit combination locks on suitcases are not very effective. An experienced burglar can open one in well under an hour, and it would be easy to do so without being detected after the fact. The suitcase owner may find this acceptable. But if this were digital cryptography, she would have to take into account that an algorithm that takes an hour to break today may take a few minutes in a couple of years. This would be tantamount to the three-digit combination magically shrinking to two digits.

As another (and more germane) example, consider the security of your e-mail account. Whenever you log in to read your e-mail, you enter a username and password. Most e-mail servers store passwords in a file in encrypted form. Therefore, a would-be cracker has two avenues: an attack on the password itself or an attack on the encryption of the password file.

As in the suitcase example, the cracker can try guessing the password by brute force. The length of time it would take a cracker to guess your password through brute force is a function of the number of possible characters in the password and the universe of characters from which users can choose (such as uppercase letters, lowercase letters, numbers, and punctuation). For passwords of up to ten characters that allow upper- and lowercase letters and numerals, there are 839,299,365,868,340,224 possibilities. That makes brute force pretty unlikely. A better possibility may be to guess a particular user's password through knowledge of the user. Many people use personal information such as names of family members, nicknames, and makes of their cars for their passwords. If a cracker were to try breaking the encryption of the password file itself, it becomes an issue of how secure the password file is.

Key length

In cryptography, the most basic measure of an algorithm's strength is the key length. A key is the secret number necessary to decrypt the message; thus, the objective of a cracker is to find the right key. In the preceding examples, the suitcase's combination and the password to your e-mail account are keys. The length of a key is an expression of the number of possible keys in a cryptosystem. Specifically, it's the maximum number of digits in the binary number that makes up the key. If the key can be up to N digits, the number of possible keys is 2 to the nth power. So, for example, a key length of 20 gives you 2 to the 20th power, or 1,048,576 (about a million) possible keys. A key length of 30 gives you 2 to the 30th power, or 1,073,741,824 (roughly a billion) possible keys. In fact, a good rule of thumb is that each 10 of key length multiplies the number of keys by 1000, or adds three decimal digits or an "-illion" to the number of possible keys.

In the earlier two examples, the suitcase combination lock has 1000 possible keys, which is roughly equivalent to a binary key length of 10. The password string, in contrast, has a binary key length of about 60. In Figure 5-3, *Avg. time to brute force crack* assumes that each try takes one second, just for comparison purposes. As you can see, a ten-character alphanumeric password is nominally *much* more immune to brute-force attacks than a three-digit numeric suitcase lock. Even if you had a computer that could crunch a million keys per second, the e-mail password would still take more than 13,000 years to crack by brute force.

Suitcase lock
Decimal key length: 3
Number of digits per character: 10
Number of possible keys: 1000
Binary key length: ~10
Avg. time to brute force crack: **8.33 minutes**

Email password
Alphanumeric key length: up to 10
Number of digits per character: 62
Number of possible keys: 839,299,365,868,340,224
Binary key length: ~60
Avg. time to brute force crack: **13,307,004,152 years**

Figure 5-3: Different key lengths determine the strength of a cryptosystem.

Key lengths make a significant difference in the strength of a cryptosystem. For example, most Web browsers offer the SSL protocol to facilitate secure e-commerce transactions so that people can send their credit card numbers and other personal information over the Internet without worrying (too much) about placing that information into the wrong hands. In North America, Web browsers now use a key length of 128 bits, which is considered very high indeed — not likely to be brute-force crackable by the most powerful computers for many years to come.

It's so good, in fact, that the U.S. government considers the technology that supports 128-bit SSL encryption to be "weapons technology " — unexportable for national security reasons — so Web browsers outside North America must support weaker 40-bit encryption. 128-bit encryption is nominally 309,485,009,821,345,068,724,781,056 (2 to the 88th power) times harder than the 40-bit version to crack by brute force. There are rumors that the National Security Agency (NSA) has computers that can crack 40-bit encryption in a reasonable amount of time.

Factors other than key length

It's important to understand that key lengths are not the only criteria to use in judging encryption systems — just as you shouldn't judge the true power of a car just by its engine's displacement or number of cylinders. Nor are key lengths comparable across different algorithms: You can't say that Algorithm A is stronger than Algorithm B just because Algorithm A has double the key length of Algorithm B.

There are many other factors in considering encryption strength. One is the imperviousness of the cryptosystem to attacks that are more sophisticated than brute force — as are most serious attacks anyway. Some involve heuristics (educated guesses) of the type discussed earlier. Others involve exploiting weaknesses in the system that allow crackers to detect patterns. For example, many cryptosystems involve random number generators; random number generators sometimes exhibit patterns, so after a while it's possible to predict (or at least narrow down) the next number that a random number generator will generate. Code breakers at organizations such as the NSA have been known to spend years finding the tiniest weaknesses in an encryption scheme in order to crack it.

Still other attacks on cryptosystems involve techniques that have nothing whatsoever to do with finding the key. The algorithm may be sound, but the system of which the algorithm is a part may have holes in it. As it has been said, you can put as many deadbolts on your front door as you like, but if your side window opens from the outside, it doesn't make any difference. This is the most common avenue for crackers.

It's even possible to go beyond the hardware or software of a cryptosystem to break it, through plain old human fallibility. In the early days of the Cold War, the progenitor of the NSA achieved an important breakthrough in cracking Soviet codes because the Soviets reused keys in their supposedly uncrackable one-time pad system. (They did this by discovering that the Soviets were reusing pads with encryption keys on them, either out of laziness or to conserve paper.) It may even be more expedient to bribe someone to divulge a key than to try to crack a cryptosystem at all.

Published versus proprietary cryptosystems

Many cryptography experts feel that the only truly valid way of judging the strength of a cryptosystem is public scrutiny. Only when a cryptosystem is out there in the real world, with real crackers banging on it for an extended period of time, does the public gain confidence in it. Neither pure mathematical analysis nor any expert testimonials, let alone vendors' claims, are good enough anymore.

Unfortunately, the need for public scrutiny clashes with three other factors: the past history of cryptography, the newness of the DRM market, and plain old paranoia.

Throughout cryptography history, it was considered necessary to keep secret the details of the encryption algorithm as well as the key itself. Older algorithms weren't that sophisticated, so if you knew how they worked, you were halfway to breaking them. Furthermore, the information that encryption protected was the stuff of life and death, of political systems, dynasties, and nationhood — slightly more important, you have to admit, than someone's journal article or hit single. In particular, cryptography was the virtually exclusive province of the government.

It wasn't until the 1960s that digital cryptography became common in private industry. Around that time, IBM researchers invented an algorithm that the NSA eventually co-opted as a government standard: the Data Encryption Standard, or DES. DES is quite powerful as an encryption algorithm, as long as the key length is sufficient. The details of DES were published within the United States after a long series of legal and political battles. It was necessary to do so because the private sector was not about to take the government's word on the power of the algorithm for granted: In particular, the private sector didn't trust that the NSA would let private industry keep secrets from *it*.

The same lack of trust has attended all major encryption algorithms since DES. The cryptographic community has a habit of hounding out of the marketplace any vendor that tries to keep the details of its algorithm secret. There are many examples of this:

♦ A startup company called Tri-Strata claimed to have a practical implementation of the one-time pad but refused to divulge the details, citing competition; subsequent forced scrutiny by leading cryptographers revealed that the solution wasn't really a one-time pad.

- Chapter 6 describes the RIAA's panicked refusal to let a researcher give a paper at a conference that explained how he broke the Secure Digital Music Initiative's proposed secure watermarking scheme. The crypto community and other factions eventually shamed the RIAA into backing off and letting the researcher deliver his paper.

- A group of crackers recently managed to break the proprietary encryption of Gemstar's eBook platform. They threatened to expose the weaknesses that they found in Gemstar's algorithm unless the vendor agreed to do certain things, which included publishing the details of the algorithm.

The only way for a cryptosystem to really take off in the marketplace is if its inventor is willing to invest the time and money — and adopt the attitude — necessary to subject its algorithm to the rigors of scrutiny by an industry full of cryptographic experts who live for opportunities to break yet another encryption scheme.

One published algorithm that has become prominent is the RSA algorithm, named for its inventors, Ronald Rivest, Adi Shamir, and Leonard Adleman, all of MIT. They implemented a specific form of a mathematical technique known as public-key encryption.

In traditional encryption schemes such as DES, two parties have to give each other their keys in order to read messages from each other. (For this reason, this type of encryption scheme is often called *symmetric-key* encryption.) This presents a problem because the two parties have to meet in advance to do this. Whitfield Diffie (now of Sun Microsystems), Martin Hellman of Stanford University, and Ralph Merkle of Berkeley achieved a breakthrough in which they figured out a way around this. (At around the same time, James Ellis, Clifford Cocks, and Malcom Williamson made a similar discovery in the U.K., but it was done for British Intelligence and so was not made public.)

Here's how public-key encryption works: Each party has two keys, a public key and a private key. You can combine the two keys into one larger key; you do this in a way that makes it possible to recover one of the original keys if you know the other one, but practically impossible if you know neither. In mathematical terms, you need a way of combining the numerical values of the two keys into a third number from which it's virtually impossible to extract the original two numbers. (Think of this as pouring two piles of sand into a bigger pile and trying to determine the number of grains of sand in each of the two original piles — only harder.)

The mathematical name for this is a *one-way function.* Diffie, Hellman, and Merkle found a type of one-way function that has enough different possible inputs to make it worthwhile for cryptography: the multiplication of two large prime numbers. If you take two large primes and multiply them together, you get a larger number; but if you only know that larger number, it's very hard to reconstruct the two primes that generated it. However, if you know the larger number and one of the smaller ones, it's very easy to generate the other smaller number: Just divide one into the other.

In public-key encryption, if I want to send you a message, I ask you for your public key. You can send your public key to me without fear of eavesdropping, because your public key is useless without your private key. I can use my private key in conjunction with your public key to encrypt the message. When you get the encrypted message, you can use your private key to decode it.

The RSA implementation of public-key encryption has a variable key length; most commercial implementations now use a staggering 1024 bits (that's roughly equal to a 2 with 308 zeroes after it), with some especially sensitive implementations using 2048 bits (or about 2 with 609 zeroes after it). How does this compare to the 128-bit encryption used in U.S. and Canadian SSL? Remember that comparing key lengths in different algorithms is like comparing apples to oranges. 1024-bit RSA is not 8 times stronger than 128-bit SSL. It's necessary to use key lengths that long in RSA because of the mathematics involved. No one would ever use brute force (that is, try all 2^{1024} keys until one works) with RSA because there are well-known techniques for reducing the size of the problem substantially — meaning that in the worst case, the number of attempts necessary to crack the algorithm would be much less than 2^{1024}.

RSA is used in many popular software products, including operating systems from Sun, Microsoft, Apple, and Novell, as well as major Web browsers, e-mail programs, and groupware packages. It is the closest thing there is to a de facto standard. So why doesn't every vendor use it in their encryption implementations? One reason is that it is inefficient to implement, especially with the longest key lengths. Another is that cryptographic research is always advancing, and there are always new algorithms that their inventors optimistically feel will improve upon RSA and other popular algorithms.

More importantly, although the details of the RSA algorithm are publicly available (at least in the United States), it's been covered under a patent owned by RSA Security, Inc., until the patent expired in September 2000. This meant that if you wanted to use the algorithm, you had to pay a license fee to that company or risk probable lawsuit for patent infringement. For a DRM solution vendor, using RSA encryption thus added to the cost of the technology.

Encryption in DRM solutions

So where does this leave you if you need to choose a DRM solution based on its encryption? Unfortunately, some of the encryption schemes used in DRM solutions are both new and proprietary. When you ask a vendor to vouch for the strength of such a cryptosystem, it will usually point out the impressive credentials of the designer or the number of patents it has pending. Our point of view is that if you're really worried about encryption strength, this isn't good enough.

Two things can happen with a vendor like this: If the vendor remains obscure, it's likely that the cryptography community will leave it alone. This may be okay if the vendor is committed to a niche market, but otherwise, the vendor could go out of business. On the other hand, if the vendor becomes big and popular, it becomes a target for cracking. If you're lucky, the cryptosystem is strong, but if not . . . . Those who have responsibility for very large-scale deployments of encryption-based DRM technology — such as the heads of online initiatives within major record labels, or eBook product designers — have reason to worry.

DRM technology vendors have finally begun to realize this and are now basing their technologies on trusted public encryption algorithms. Symmetric-key algorithms that came out after DES are now popular for encrypting content: Examples include RC5 and RC6 from RSA Security; BlowFish and TwoFish from Counterpane Labs; and AES (Advanced Encryption Standard), the government's new successor to DES, which is based on a Belgian algorithm called Rijndael (pronounced *RAIN-doll* and meaning "Rhine Valley").

Public-key algorithms aren't used to encrypt content, because they are too inefficient. However, they are used for other purposes, such as generating digital signatures (see below) and encrypting the keys used for symmetric-key algorithms, thereby adding an extra layer of security.

Recent history is rife with tales of cryptosystems designed to protect content that have been broken. This happens despite the strength of the algorithm used because crackers can often find security holes in a system that do not depend on the actual cryptographic algorithm. Although the recently passed Digital Millennium Copyright Act (DMCA; see Chapter 3) provides a legal shield to publishers for certain types of code breaking, you should consider it likely that any encryption scheme popular enough to be in widespread use is also a prime target for crackers. In fact, you should *assume* that a new, proprietary cryptosystem will eventually be cracked. You shouldn't assume otherwise for years. While this book was being written, the security for Adobe and Microsoft eBook DRM systems were both cracked.

Does this mean that encryption is useless? No. If someone cracks an encryption scheme, it doesn't necessarily imply that everyone who receives content in that encrypted format is suddenly going to get it for free. Analogously, just because someone figures out how to pick Master brand combination locks doesn't mean that every high school student's locker is now unlocked. As a more germane example, consider DeCSS, a piece of software written for the Linux operating system that decrypts DVDs. DeCSS was written so that Linux users would have a way of playing DVDs on their machines because the only commercial player software available was for the PC and Macintosh platforms. DeCSS allows decrypted digital files of DVD content to be created; such files can then be used to create pirated DVDs with perfect quality.

DeCSS is the subject of a lawsuit by the major movie studios, who hope to stifle it via DMCA. (At this writing, the case is being heard in a federal appeals court.) The descrambling algorithm within DeCSS has been ported to the PC and Macintosh, but very few people have it. No computers have been distributed with DeCSS preinstalled. No major software vendor is marketing it. In other words, the average computer user is highly unlikely to have DeCSS on his or her machine.

As with many such issues, this ends up being a business decision. How much risk of "bleed" (loss of revenue due to piracy) are you willing to live with? Who are your enemies, and to what lengths are they willing to or can they go to persecute you? And by the same token, as we say several times in this book, who are your friends (customers), and how much inconvenience do you think they are willing to endure?

We conclude this section by noting that encryption in DRM solutions isn't confined to copy-protecting content, although that is certainly the most important use. Some other uses are to verify the contents of a file and the identity of its creator or rightsholder.

Verifying content: digests

Encryption-related technology can be used to ensure that the contents of a file aren't tampered with, just like the example at the beginning of this section with the written message and the envelope. An algorithm that involves a secret key can be used to create a *digest* for a file, which is a unique number that represents the contents of the file in shorthand form.

Say that the digest (sometimes also called a *hash value*) is 128 bits long, meaning that it can be represented in 16 characters appended to the end of a file. (Each character contains 8 bits.) This means that there are 2 to the 128th power possible digests — a number roughly equal to a 3 followed by 38 zeroes. In other words, it is possible that two different files can have the same digest, but *highly* unlikely.

Figure 5-4 shows how this works. In this case, two text files are identical except for one word. Despite this, the digest algorithm generates completely different digests for the two files.

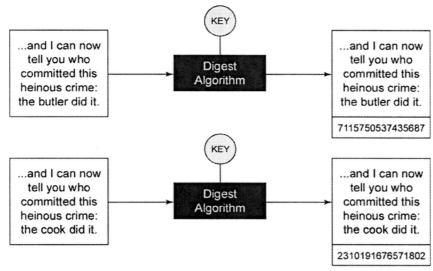

Figure 5-4: Generating unique digest numbers from files.

A rendering application for this type of file can compute the digest before rendering it. If the digest that it computes doesn't match the digest in the file, it means that the file was changed, and the application can refuse to render it. This scheme makes the file tamper-resistant, even if it isn't copy protected. Only those who can crack the digest generation algorithm can change the content without being detected.

This type of tamper resistance scheme is one way to enforce edit rights.

CROSS REFERENCE: Edit rights are discussed in Chapter 4.

Verifying identities: digital certificates

As mentioned earlier in this chapter, certificates are important ways of establishing the identities of both users and organizations. CAs, the organizations that create, store, and manage digital certificates, have businesses that fundamentally depend on their being trustworthy — that is, doing everything possible to guarantee both the validity of the data inside the digital certificates and that they are protected from tampering, theft, and privacy violations. A CA will lose its franchise the minute any of these things happen:

- It allows a user to create a certificate under false circumstances, such as a fraudulent business.
- It allows the data inside a certificate to be tampered with.
- It makes the information inside the certificates that it manages available to third parties or otherwise allows it to be used for any purpose other than the exact ones for which it was intended.

Digital certificates use encryption to accomplish all these goals.

Verifying content and identities: digital signatures

An important variation on the themes of both digests and certificates is the *digital signature*. A digital signature ensures both the contents of a message and the identity of the person who signs it. Digital signatures are now legally acceptable replacements for handwritten signatures, thanks to the Electronic Signatures Act that President Clinton signed into law in 2000 (see Chapter 3). They are useful in DRM implementations for establishing the identity of the rightsholder of a piece of content, verifying the content itself, and binding the rightsholder to the content. In other words, if *either* the identity of the rightsholder *or* the content itself were altered, the digital signature would not match.

Furthermore, it's not possible to take the signature part of a message with a digital signature and graft it onto another message: Because a digital signature depends on both the message and the signature, the signature on the new document would be exposed as fraudulent.

Because digital signatures take up relatively small amounts of data, DRM implementations usually use public-key encryption algorithms to generate them.

Watermarking

Watermarking is the other core technology most closely associated with digital rights management. Historically, the term *watermark* applied to marks that paper manufacturers embedded in their papers to show their identities and that printers of important documents such as paper money and stock certificates used to prove authenticity.

Generically speaking, watermarks were meant to convey some information about a document in a way that

♦ Didn't interfere with the appearance or readability of the document

♦ Was inextricably bound together with the document

Fine-quality stationery, of the type you may use to print your resume, has watermarks in it.

If you fast-forward to the digital age, you find that watermarking — called *information hiding, data embedding,* or *steganography* by specialists in the field — is used for a variety of purposes with audio, image, and video content. Watermarking is a separate field from encryption, although there is some overlap: For example, some watermarking schemes incorporate encryption, as we discuss later in this chapter in the section "Encrypted watermarks."

The body of literature on watermarking is much smaller than that of encryption. Encryption is not only the stuff of recondite academic treatises; it's also fodder for popular writings that have to do with subjects such as spying, security, and privacy. Watermarking hasn't captured the broader public's imagination thus far. The only book-length writing on the subject at this point is a collection of technical papers called *Information Hiding Techniques for Steganography and Digital Watermarking,* edited by Stefan Katzenbeisser and Fabien Petitcolas, researchers at the University of Vienna and Microsoft, respectively.

As with paper watermarks, digital watermarks are used to associate metadata with content in a (mostly) permanent way without having to format the content in a special package and use encryption, as discussed earlier in this chapter. Put simply, a watermark is a way to make metadata become *part* of the content, instead of sitting alongside it.

How you do this depends, of course, on the medium of the content. In an image, watermarking software selects a region of the image and varies the colors and light intensities in a certain way. Video watermarking involves similar techniques. In an audio clip, watermarking software inserts ultrasonic information. Images, video, and sound are all "continuous" media with a resolution depth that can be deeper than humans can perceive; watermarking takes advantage of the medium's ability to go "under the radar" of human perception. For this reason, it's not really possible to watermark a text file: Humans perceive each character of text discretely, so there's nowhere to put information that isn't detectable. (However, a related and very old technique of text steganography is to hide one message in another – for example, by using every third or fifth word for the hidden message.)

Watermark characteristics

Digital watermarks have the following characteristics:

- ♦ **Undetectability:** The watermark doesn't detract from the visual or audible experience of the content.
- ♦ **Robustness:** The watermark survives copying to lower-resolution formats or from digital to analog formats.
- ♦ **Capacity:** The watermark should be able to contain as much data as possible.
- ♦ **Security:** The watermark resists attempts to erase or alter it.
- ♦ **Efficiency:** The length of time it takes to insert and extract the watermark isn't excessive.

As you might imagine, there are trade-offs among these criteria.

Making watermarks undetectable by humans involves finding places in the content where they can go unnoticed. The key to creating a watermark is finding some part of the content where there's a lot of variation in sound frequencies, colors, light intensity, or whatever the medium conveys. Think of it this way: It's much easier to conceal an object in a clump of plants and bushes than in the clear blue sky; similarly, it's easier to conceal an ultrasonic sound in a complex piece of music than in a one-kilohertz sine wave.

However, the watermark must also be robust enough to survive copying and digital-to-analog conversion. If you make a copy of a photo in some low-resolution format (for example, if you copy a TIFF image, of the type that graphics professionals use, to the GIF format common on Web sites), the watermark may be lost. Making a watermark that survives copying requires a maximum amount of space on the image or in the audio or video clip. Thus there is a direct trade-off between robustness and undetectability.

Another dimension to the trade-off involves capacity — the amount of useful information that a watermark can contain. Obviously, more space is needed to contain more useful information. Various PhD dissertations have been written on how to shoehorn the maximum amount of data into a piece of content while preserving undetectability: Techniques involve the detailed analysis of the psychology of how humans perceive images or audio. Some watermarking schemes actually measure the amount of data that they can include in a particular file and only include up to that much.

If watermarks are used to embed copyright information in files, it's important that they be secure in addition to robust. The information contained in watermarks is often encrypted in such a way as to be tamperproof (as discussed earlier). They can also be created in a way that makes it impossible to remove the watermark without visibly or audibly marring the file.

Finally, it's especially important for watermark extraction to be efficient if watermarks are being used for DRM. You'll see shortly how this works.

Watermarks and DRM

Some people get confused about how watermarks relate to encryption and other elements of digital rights management — because vendors are out there making various claims for the two technologies that need to be put into perspective.

Here are some principles to bear in mind:

♦ Encryption requires a special application to decrypt and render content; watermarking does not.

♦ Watermarking binds metadata (semi)permanently with content; encryption does not.

Because watermarking does not require a special application to render content, it is fundamentally not suited to the task of copy protection by itself.

Figure 5-5 shows the difference between encryption and watermarking with a music example, although it would apply equally to image or video. With encryption (A), you need to decrypt the content (with a DRM controller, as explained in the section "A DRM Reference Architecture") before it can be played. Furthermore, the metadata exists separately from the content; after you decrypt the content, the metadata is gone. Contrast this with watermarking (B): After you insert the watermark, the metadata is inextricably bound together with the content. The watermark extractor can pull out the metadata and use it separately, but it's still there, even when the music is played. (Look closely at the figure, and you'll see it.)

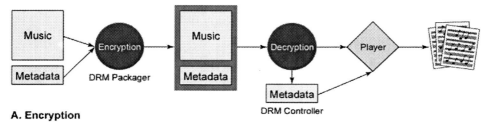

A. Encryption

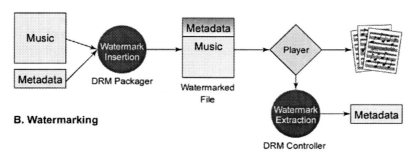

B. Watermarking

Figure 5-5: Encryption versus watermarking. Encryption requires a special application to decrypt the content for rendering, whereas watermarking requires a special application to extract metadata from the content.

Visible source identification

The most basic use of watermarks in DRM is akin to the original definition of watermarking: The watermark simply — and often visually or audibly — identifies the source of the image. For example, various stock image sites on the Web (such as PhotoDisc) display images for browsing purposes; these have logos plainly visible on them to prevent people from copying them from their Web browsers and using them unscrupulously. Clearly these watermarks are meant to disrupt images, and they would be difficult to remove without damaging the image. Some don't consider this scenario true watermarking because the marks are not hidden.

Invisible source identification

The second use of watermarks is to establish the ownership of the file but keep the watermark undetectable. The idea is to leave information about the file's ownership, and any other relevant metadata, embedded permanently and invisibly (or inaudibly) as an "audit trail" so that pirated copies can be discovered and, presumably, copyright infringement claimed.

This is the classic application of watermarking in DRM. It is clearly an improvement on things such as plain-text copyright notices, which can be removed. However, it's generally not possible to "discover" pirated copies, especially if they have been printed to hard copy or are sitting on random hard drives. Digimarc, the leading vendor of image watermarking technology, created a program called MarcSpider that purports to search the *entire Internet* for watermarked images and report usage to the owner. This is not an effective way of tracking usage. This second use of watermarks has largely been abandoned.

A more appropriate use of putting ownership information in content watermarks is usage tracking. An application on the client side can read identification and ownership metadata from a watermark and report it back to a server that collects such data. In Chapter 7, we discuss the use of watermarking in broadcast monitoring, which is an example of usage tracking in radio and television. Using watermarks to track content usage is also becoming popular for digital content distributed on the Internet; for example, Minneapolis-based Cognicity, Inc. (www.cognicity.com) makes technology that does this for digital music.

Metadata conveyance

A third use of watermarks is one in which the watermark is visible or audible but does not disturb the image or sound quality and is just there as a convenient way of conveying metadata. Think of a bar code on a jar of jam in the supermarket: The bar code is plainly visible, but it doesn't detract from the jam company's logo, nor from the jam itself. However, it does allow the cashier to scan the price at checkout time.

Xerox' Glyph technology, in which tiny dots sprayed on paper convey lots of meaning in very little space, fits this category. Similar technology is used by the U.S. Postal Service for a handy way of encoding information on bulk mailings.

Encrypted watermarks

Nowadays, watermarking often works in conjunction with encryption as part of end-to-end secure content distribution solutions. In this case, watermarking serves as both a metadata vehicle and as a barrier to rendering.

There are two ways of combining watermarking with encryption. The first is to encrypt the watermark, but not the file. There are two reasons for doing this. The first is to make the watermark tamperproof, as described earlier in this chapter. Watermarks used in usage-tracking schemes, as previously described, contain data about content ownership that must be protected against alteration. A variation on this theme is tamperproof watermarks that contain timestamps, which indicate when the document was created. It's desirable in certain cases to be able to definitively establish the creation time of a document. For example, if two parties created similar intellectual property and are disputing claim to a patent, the winner will be the one who can say that he or she created the intellectual property first. Surety, Inc.'s Digital Notary technology (www.surety.com) does this.

The other reason for encrypting watermarks is to keep the metadata in the watermark secure, even if the content is not. Digimarc's scheme for discovering pirated files depends on this.

Encrypted files with watermarks

The other way of combining watermarks with encryption is to watermark a file and then encrypt it, as shown in Figure 5-6. This is the general type of approach taken in Phase II of SDMI (see Chapter 6) and used in products by vendors such as Liquid Audio. Assuming that the encryption is effective, this is really the ultimate in secure content distribution because it not only protects copy but also binds content with metadata — which can include rights metadata.

The result is the best of both worlds. Even if someone were to crack the encryption, the metadata would remain with the content — presumably in a tamperproof form — allowing rights and ownership information to be permanently trackable. This allows the DRM controller and the rendering application to be tightly integrated: The controller can decrypt and feed to the player only as much content as necessary to decode the watermark and get the metadata. Then the player can extract the metadata from the watermark and pass it back to the DRM controller for processing — for authentication, payment processing, usage metering, and so on. If the DRM controller doesn't get the feedback that it wants from the player (that is, the player isn't sending back data from the watermark), the controller can suspect a bogus player and shut it off. Thus, would-be crackers have to decode watermarks in addition to breaking the encryption.

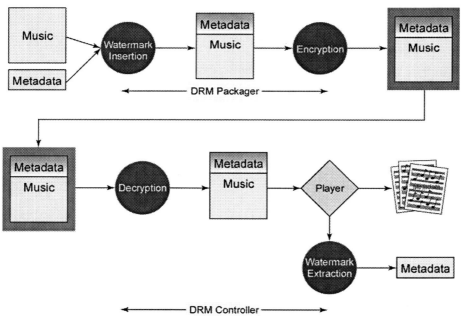

Figure 5-6: Watermarking combined with encryption.

A scheme that incorporates both encryption and watermarking is not foolproof, but (all else being equal) it's the best DRM scheme available. Watermarking applies only to image, audio, and video data types — not to text. But it's likely that the most successful DRM solutions in the years to come will combine encryption and watermarking in this way.

Chapter 6

Technology Standards:
Leveling the Playing Field

Digital Rights Management is an emerging technology market. At this writing, there are no dominant vendors in the DRM space — no standard choices to make when you're in the market for solutions, à la Microsoft for PC software or Oracle for databases. Eventually, some leading technologies will emerge. The question is whether they will be proprietary technologies, controlled by one or a small number of vendors, or based on open standards.

In the olden days of computerdom, single vendors (such as IBM) created large, monolithic information system architectures that customers had to adopt in their entireties. Since then, the industry has been moving more toward a "network economy" in which technology paradigms result from synergies among several individual components. Those synergies tend to spread farthest, and the resulting markets expand most rapidly, if the right standards are in place on which to base all the components. A standard is *open* if anyone who wants to use it can get access to it in its entirety, if it is controlled by a publicly accessible authoring process rather than by a single vendor, and if it is complete and unambiguous enough to serve as the basis for implementations.

The Internet industry is the ultimate example of a successful technology paradigm mostly based on open standards. The two primary standards, HTML and HTTP, form the basis of lots of different products, including Web servers, Web browsers, Web page authoring tools, site traffic analysis packages, and so on. Open standards promote markets in which multiple vendors put out products that are competitive yet compatible. When this is done right, customers end up with products that perform better and are more likely to satisfy their requirements. Contrast this with the PC industry, which is controlled by proprietary standards for microprocessors (Intel) and operating system software (Microsoft). Many people feel that PCs would be faster and more reliable if they were based on open standards.

The Role of Open Standards in DRM

For the Digital Rights Management market to take off, it must also settle on a set of technology standards that apply to the types of components discussed in Chapter 5: authentication, player formats, encryption, and so on. Most of the players in the DRM industry would prefer open standards. Certainly publishers would prefer to have a choice of vendors to work with to manage and serve up content, and consumers would similarly like to choose the best way of viewing or playing that content.

The only entities who may not favor open standards are deep-pocketed vendors who have the potential to monopolize the market and technology startups with dreams of becoming the monopolists (as well as the investors who back both).

There are also legal reasons why open standards are a good idea. As discussed in this chapter, some open standards have resulted from publishers, or their equivalents in related industries, getting together in trade association working groups and defining standards. It would be very efficient for such a group to convene, put out a request for proposals (RFP) to vendors, and have vendors bid on the right to be chosen as the preferred vendor for the industry. The vendor could build a solution (or offer one already built), and that would be the end of it. Yet antitrust law makes this illegal; it's analogous to price fixing in an industry such as petroleum or air travel. To pass legal muster, a standard must be *procompetitive,* meaning that it promotes competition among vendors rather than prevents it.

Types of standards relevant to DRM

Which aspects of the technology should DRM vendors standardize? Two principles are relevant here. First, because virtually all activity in the DRM world now takes place over the Internet in one form or another, DRM-related standards should work in conjunction with existing Internet standards. Second, standards should cover those aspects of content providers' businesses on which they will want to standardize; standards should not cover aspects that constitute a competitive advantage for individual content providers because they will want to keep those elements to themselves.

We will examine which aspects of content providers' businesses are proprietary and which are standardizable. Refer to the DRM reference architecture from Chapter 5. The primary categories of technology from the architecture are

- ♦ Components, such as content packagers and DRM controllers
- ♦ Protocols, or methods of communication between components.
- ♦ File formats
- ♦ Metadata, or information about content.
- ♦ Encryption and watermarking schemes

Technology components such as content packages and DRM controllers are not good candidates for standardization because publishers need a competitive market for these things. File formats are not good candidates both because there are already a few well-established standard formats (HTML, PDF, RTF, GIF, TIFF, JPEG, MPEG-1, MPEG-2, and so on) and because most decisions about file format standards are made well outside the purview of the DRM field.

Metadata is the most promising area for standardization. Protocols, which depend heavily on metadata, are also good candidates.

It would also be nice to standardize on encryption and watermarking schemes. As we see in Chapter 7, there are de facto standards for watermarking of images and audio.

Encryption is another matter. The U.S. government has advanced encryption standards such as DES and AES (see Chapter 5), but the cryptographic community tends to shy away from them for several reasons. First, some in that community don't trust the government to promote a standard algorithm that is truly strong (that is, impervious to cracking by government agencies such as the NSA). Second, cryptographers constantly tinker with algorithms and invent new ones that are allegedly more secure, and some of these have patents on them (or patents pending). Furthermore, different encryption algorithms are designed for different purposes. The result has been a profusion of encryption algorithms that is confusing and only understood by experts in the field.

You may expect there to be some open source standards for these technologies that work "well enough" and that everyone could adopt. Certainly the open source community has produced some popular and effective encryption-related standards, such as PGP (Pretty Good Privacy) for securing e-mail messages. However, copy protection is slightly different; it's something that the open source community frowns on in general. In particular, some in the open source community have been openly hostile to some of the standards discussed in this chapter that depend on strong encryption, such as the Secure Digital Music Initiative (SDMI).

Because metadata is a highly promising area for standardization, we will look at it more closely. Recall the types of metadata common to most content packages, as described in the DRM reference architecture in Chapter 5: identification, discovery, and rights.

Identification

Content identification is the most basic element of any DRM system. Just as SKU (stock keeping unit) numbers are necessary in the world of retail, each content item must be uniquely identifiable. Various segments of the content industries have invented their own identification schemes, most of which are tied to particular publication types — a veritable alphabet soup of identification schemes. Here are just a few examples:

- **ISBN (International Standard Book Number):** used for hard-copy books and related products, such as spoken-word editions
- **ISSN (International Standard Serial Number):** used for hard-copy serials, such as magazines and journals
- **LOC (Library of Congress) number:** used for books published in the United States
- **ISWC (International Standard Musical Work Code):** an emerging standard for musical works

None of these identification schemes was ever intended to be used for online content. The Internet, of course, uses uniform resource locators (URLs). URLs are very widely used, of course, but as discussed in the section "The Digital Object Identifier (DOI)," they have limitations when used to identify pieces of intellectual property. Another type of identifier that was developed with the online world in mind is the Publisher Item Identifier (PII), which has been fairly well established among scientific publishers such as the American Institute of Physics and the American Chemical Society, but is being phased out in favor of the more comprehensive DOI.

The Internet Engineering Task Force (IETF) has also been considering constructs called the uniform resource name (URN) and persistent uniform resource locator (PURL), which are both similar to the DOI. Work on the URN has been going on for several years, but at this writing it has not become an official Internet standard.

Therefore, the DOI has the highest potential as an open standard for content identification in DRM.

Discovery metadata

The most essential type of metadata beyond identification is *discovery metadata*, also called *descriptive metadata*, meaning metadata that enables the content to be found within a collection of content, such as a library or the Internet, if the unique identifier isn't known. For published works, discovery metadata would be likely to include bibliographic information, such as the title, author, publisher, publication date, and number of pages. It could also include a set of keywords that describe the book's subject matter.

It has been difficult to get publishers to agree on metadata sets because they can be used for so many different purposes. But one standard for bibliographic metadata has been gaining in popularity: Dublin Core. *Dublin* in this case refers not to the capital of Ireland but to the city in Ohio where the Ohio College Library Center (OCLC — now known as the Online Computer Library Center) is. The Dublin Core metadata set was developed at an OCLC workshop. It was originally intended for the library community, but it has been incorporated into standards used by other types of institutions concerned with content, such as educational institutions and magazine publishers.

Dublin Core is quite general in its scope and therefore widely applicable, but it's not considered comprehensive enough for any one publication type in particular. A few other discovery metadata standards have arisen that are more specific to certain publication types:

- **Magazines:** PRISM (Publishing Requirements for Industry Standard Metadata) centers on magazine publishers and their online operations. It uses the Dublin Core bibliographic metadata set and builds on top of it. Version 1.0 of PRISM was released in April 2001; see `www.prismstandard.org` for details.

- **Books:** ONIX (Online Information Exchange) is being widely adopted among book publishers and retailers such as Amazon and Barnes & Noble. ONIX describes physical books; it includes fields for such things as the cover image, number of pages, and physical size of the book. ONIX does not apply to online content, although eBook extensions to ONIX are currently in the works. ONIX was originally unveiled in January 2000; see `www.editeur.org/onix.html`.

- **Scientific journals:** CrossRef (`www.crossref.org`) is increasingly used in the scientific journal community for reference linking in online journals. It specifies a set of bibliographic metadata for journal articles that includes DOIs. Researchers can click CrossRef links in online journal articles to look up full bibliographic citations of other articles; then they can use DOIs to get to the articles themselves. The CrossRef system went live in June 2000.

- **Educational materials:** The Learning Objects Metadata (LOM) scheme, overseen by the IEEE (Institute of Electrical and Electronic Engineers) Learning Technology Standards Committee, covers educational materials, ranging from lecture notes to entire courses. LOM also builds on Dublin Core for bibliographic metadata; see `ltsc.ieee.org/wg12/index.html`.

- **Music:** Two vendors, Schwann (`www.schwann.com`) and MUZE (`www.muze.com`), control competing proprietary metadata schemes for information about recorded music, such as artists, song and album titles, and release dates.

- **News stories:** NewsML is an emerging standard for exchanging news content items — including stories, illustrations, photos, sound clips and video — that is expected to be adopted by wire services worldwide (such as the Associated Press and Agence France Presse). Developed by the International Press Telecommunications Council (IPTC), NewsML replaces the ANPA 1312 header format for wire stories that has been in use at newspapers and broadcast news stations for decades. Because of the high volume and widespread distribution of wire-service news feeds, NewsML is poised to become an important metadata standard for news items. It was released in October 2000; see `www.xmlnews.org/NewsML/`.

- ◆ **Multimedia:** MPEG-4 is a standard for multimedia content from the Moving Picture Experts Group, which has already given us important standards for audio and video compression. MPEG-4 is intended to include all sorts of metadata about multimedia objects. MPEG-4 allows rights information to be specified by means of generic metadata definition capabilities, and it allows DRM tools to be integrated with playback functionality by means of the Intellectual Property Management Protocol (IPMP) interface. Some DRM vendors have implemented their technologies so that they work with the MPEG-4 IPMP interface. See `www.cselt.it/mpeg/standards/mpeg-4/mpeg-4.htm` for details. Future MPEG standards, MPEG-7 (whose specification should be released by the end of 2001) and MPEG-21 (discussed in Chapter 3), also contain potentially important metadata standards for multimedia content.

Overall, it's hard to imagine a content description standard that is comprehensive enough to meet the needs of all content industries without being impractically complex. Nevertheless, one such project called *<indecs>*, for Interoperability of Data in E-commerce Systems, was released in March 2000. The <indecs> creator is Godfrey Rust of MUZE in the UK (see `www.indecs.org/` for details).

Rights

Rights metadata schemes can be standardized by adopting a rights model, as discussed in Chapter 4. But as we mention in Chapter 4, real-world rights specifications are often hard to pin down in a formal rights model, and many uses of content (such as fair use) cannot be accurately represented by a rights model.

This implies that a truly comprehensive rights model would have to be large and powerful in order to be useful. The most comprehensive open standard rights model available now is XrML, which is discussed in detail later in this chapter in the section "Extensible Rights Markup Language." A useful subset rights model is embodied in the Information and Content Exchange (ICE) protocol, which deals with business-to-business content syndication. ICE is also covered in detail later in this chapter, in the section "Information and Content Exchange."

A lightweight rights model is also included in the PRISM standard for magazines. The standard includes a set of rights description fields designed to be read and understood by humans rather than machines — that is, they are really just text descriptions of the rights available on a given piece of content (for example, a magazine article).

The more recent MPEG standards for audio, video, and multimedia include hooks for rights models and rights management tools, although they do not specify rights information per se. MPEG-7 also includes rights information, but not in detail — its content management model includes pointers to detailed rights info, which are outside the scope of the standard (and possibly intended to be the domain of a language such as XrML).

Functions without standards

As implied earlier, a few additional aspects of DRM do not invite standardization because they are unique to each publisher or a source of competitive advantage. These areas are

- ◆ **Content management:** As covered in Chapter 10, it's vitally important for publishers to deploy repositories of content in digital form that are accessible to DRM systems through APIs or other interfaces, enabling the DRM systems to get the content that they need automatically. Content management schemas and system implementations are unique to each publisher because they reflect the publisher's brands, organizational structure, and internal operations.

♦ **Rights and rightsholder management:** As implied in Chapter 4, relationships between publishers and other rightsholders — authors, agencies, and other publishers — are quite complex and hard to model. Furthermore, each publisher has a different way of processing rights and rightsholder information and transactions. Attempts to standardize on schemes for rightsholder management among publishers have largely failed (see Bill Rosenblatt's presentation, "Two Sides of the Coin: Publishers' Requirements for Digital Intellectual Property Management," in the bibliography), simply because the task is too complex — even more complex than content management.

♦ **Business models:** Of course, each publisher derives competitive advantage from the business models that it creates and implements. Publishers will never want to standardize on business models.

The DRM standards hierarchy

Figure 6-1 summarizes the preceding discussion by showing various layers of DRM-related standardization and how they relate to the basic standards of the Internet. The lowest layer shows the bedrock Internet standards, HTTP, HTML, and XML. The XML metalanguage forms the basis for many of the DRM-related standards at higher levels, including XrML, ICE, PRISM, and NewsML. The next layer up shows components of DRM that are necessary but not unique to DRM or to the media/publishing industries. These are mostly e-commerce elements, such as transaction processing, encryption, and authentication.

The third layer (second from the top) is where most of the action is. These are standards that are specific to the content industries, and they are as we just specified. Some are pure metadata standards, whereas others are protocol standards that contain metadata models. The principal ones are DOI for content identification, XrML and ICE for rights metadata, industry-specific discovery metadata standards, and the various popular content formats. The top layer of the diagram shows those elements that are unlikely to ever become standardized.

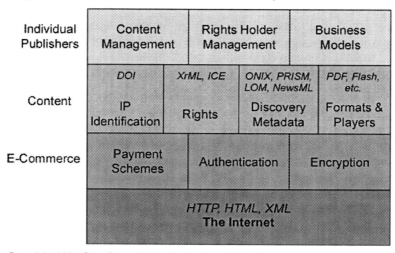

Copyright 2001 GiantSteps Media Technology Strategies

Figure 6-1: The hierarchy of DRM standards.

In the remainder of this chapter, we look at the most important of these standards initiatives in detail.

The Digital Object Identifier

The Digital Object Identifier (DOI) began in 1994 as part of a general online copyright management initiative within the Association of American Publishers (AAP) — the U.S. trade association for book and journal publishers. The initiative began as an attempt to find standard ways of solving the problem of online copyright management. At that time, the problem was focused on copyright protection on the Internet, as opposed to the broader problem of rights management that this book addresses. Nevertheless, DOI applies just as well to the latter as to the former.

After commissioning a study by the consultant Christopher Burns on publishers' attitudes towards online copyright issues (see Burns in the bibliography), the AAP's Enabling Technologies Committee broke the online copyright management problem down into layers similar to those discussed in the section "Types of standards relevant to DRM" earlier in this chapter.

The AAP's Enabling Technologies Committee decided to concentrate initially on the problem of content identification because the rest of the potential areas of standardization were too complex or varied too much from one type of publisher to another (for example, elementary through high school education versus scientific journals). The committee listed a number of requirements for online content identifiers. These are adapted from Bill Rosenblatt's December 1997 paper, "The Digital Object Identifier: Solving the Dilemma of Copyright Protection Online" (`www.press.umich.edu/jep/03-02/doi.html`), which gives more detail about the early history of the DOI project:

- The identifiers must be as "dumb" as possible; that is, they will have no intrinsic meaning.
- Identifiers must uniquely identify content items; there can be no duplication.
- There can be an infinite number of identifiers, with no limitation. Publishers will want to assign identifiers to individualized, potentially ephemeral products created on-the-fly.
- The identifying scheme must be a *metascheme* that will subsume any existing scheme that publishers may be using already, such as ISBN, ISSN, and so on, as well as Web URLs.
- Unlike the schemes mentioned in the section "Identification," earlier in this chapter, the identifying scheme can be used for content of any type, including static print-like material, services (for example, subscriptions or time-based access to content), software, audio, video, and so on.
- The scheme can also apply to objects of any granularity, ranging from the online equivalents of multivolume sets down to individual paragraphs or illustrations. Granularity decisions will be left entirely up to the publisher. Furthermore, an identifier can apply to a large object composed of smaller objects, each of which has its own identifier.
- An identifier must persistently refer to a content item regardless of its physical location or ownership, even if either are transferred to another publisher.

The committee created a specification for an identification scheme that met all these characteristics — the Digital Object Identifier.

DOI technology

The easiest way to understand DOIs technologically is to think of them as URLs that are permanent and location independent. The problem with using URLs as identifiers of intellectual property is that they point to locations of specific files on specific computers, which can change over time. If a publisher reorganizes its Web servers or (as happens regularly) sells a line of content to another publisher, the URLs are no longer valid, and anyone trying to browse to them gets the dreaded HTTP 404 (`File not found`) error.

DOIs, in contrast, point to entries in a huge table called a *DOI directory.* The table entry for a DOI specifies a URL to which the user will be referred; the publisher can change the URL at any time. So if a publisher changes its Web server architecture or sells an imprint to another publisher, it simply needs to change the URLs in the DOI directory entries for its DOIs.

The syntax of a DOI is shown in Figure 6-2, which shows an actual DOI for an article in the February 2000 issue of the journal *Growth Hormone and IGR Research,* published by Churchill Livingstone, a medical imprint of the publishing company Harcourt International.

A DOI has two components: a prefix and a suffix, separated by a forward slash (`/`). The prefix starts with `10`, which denotes the number of the DOI directory used to look up this DOI. (Currently there is only one directory, but this allows for future expansion.) The second part of the prefix is a number that identifies the publisher who created and registered the DOI. A publisher can have one or more prefixes, perhaps one for each brand or product line. In the case of Figure 6-2, the second part of the prefix is `1054`, denoting Churchill Livingstone; other Harcourt imprints have other DOI prefixes. Note that if the content changed hands — say, if Harcourt sold Churchill Livingstone to John Wiley & Sons — the prefix would stay the same; it would not change to `1002`, which is Wiley's prefix. The prefix stays the same to guarantee uniqueness of the overall DOI; if the prefix were to change, the overall DOI could change to something that already exists.

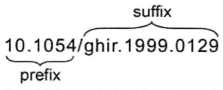

Figure 6-2: An example of a Digital Object Identifier. The prefix identifies the publisher that registered it, whereas the suffix is a character string of the publisher's choosing.

The suffix is a character string of the publisher's choosing; it has no special meaning to the software that processes DOIs. The string can contain letters, numbers, and most punctuation characters. The only requirement is that it be unique. The combination of a unique publisher prefix and suffix ensures overall uniqueness of DOIs across all publishers. In Figure 6-2, the suffix is `ghir.1999.0129`, which is mnemonic for *Growth Hormone and IGR Research* (the name of the journal), 1999 (year), and 0129, a number that is meaningful only to the publisher.

Many publishers have converted their existing numbering schemes, such as ISBNs and ISSNs, into DOIs simply by prepending their publishers' prefixes. DOIs can also be used at any granularity of content that the publisher wants, from complete works down to individual paragraphs or sentences if desired. (Pragmatically, most publishers are assigning DOIs at the levels of book, chapter, or journal article.)

A publisher starts the DOI process by paying a fee and obtaining a prefix for itself through a DOI *registration agency*. (Registration agencies are discussed later in this section.) After the International DOI Foundation (IDF, the organization that governs DOI — see www.doi.org/) grants the prefix, the publisher can start registering DOIs, which it can also do through a registration agency. For each DOI that the publisher wants to register, it submits a suffix to the registration agency along with the URL to which the publisher wants the DOI to point. The registration agency installs the DOI along with its corresponding URL in a central DOI directory and charges the publisher a fee for doing so. The publisher can subsequently change the URL associated with the DOI. (DOIs can't be deleted; they are considered to be permanent.)

It's important to remember that the URL need not point to actual content: It can also point to some software code that does various things, such as the following:

♦ Requires the user to log in, pay, or register before she can see the content

♦ Downloads a secure container that has the content in encrypted form

♦ Executes a database query, the result of which is the content requested

♦ Offers the user a subscription to the content

♦ Informs the user that the content is no longer available

After the publisher has registered DOIs, it can use them in a number of ways. Figure 6-3 shows one of them, in which the DOI directory server dx.doi.org is used to look up a DOI and then redirect the user's browser to the URL to which the DOI points. This process is called DOI *resolution.*

In step 1, the user is using a Web browser and clicks a link to the (hypothetical) URL http://dx.doi.org/10.1346/ejournal-09-97, denoting the September 1997 issue of *EJournal.* This syntax leads to a server, dx.doi.org, which treats everything after the .org/ as a DOI and does a directory lookup.

In step 2, the DOI directory lookup finds the DOI 10.1346/ejournal-09-97 and retrieves the corresponding URL, http://www.giantsteps.com/ejournal/purchreq?09-97. Step 3 shows the DOI directory going to the www.giantsteps.com Web server and retrieving the URL, which turns out to be not the actual journal article but a CGI program that presents the user with an offer to purchase the content (step 4).

The technology underlying the DOI directory and DOI resolution is an existing system called the handle system, which was developed by the Corporation for National Research Initiatives (CNRI), a nonprofit research organization dedicated to inventing new technologies that enhance the Internet. CNRI is led by Dr. Robert Kahn, one of the two inventors of the TCP/IP protocol that forms the basis for the Internet. During the process of defining the DOI and determining how the technology was going to be implemented, the AAP committee members found that CNRI's handle system provided a very close match — a superset, in fact — to the desired functionality.

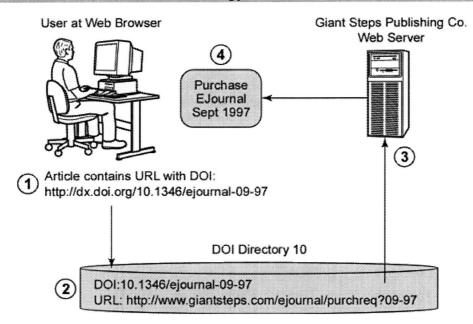

Figure 6-3: An example of the use of a DOI. The DOI Directory looks up the DOI and returns a URL.

CNRI operates the DOI directory and initially served as the only DOI registration agency available to publishers who wanted to register DOIs. At this writing, there are three others:

- CrossRef (see the section "Discovery metadata," earlier in this chapter), a nonprofit organization that uses DOIs to promote the linking of article references in scientific journals (`www.crossref.org/`).

- Content Directions, Inc. (`www.contentdirections.com/`), a New York–based startup company that offers DOI-related consulting as well as registration agency services.

- Enpia Systems Co., Ltd. (`www.enpia.com/`), an Asian digital content distributor based in Korea.

A company that wants to become a DOI registration agency must obtain certification from IDF. Publishers can set up their own registration agencies if they want to.

The example in Figure 6-3 shows how a DOI can be embedded in a standard URL on a Web page, but there are other ways to use DOIs. At worst, someone who knows a particular DOI can go to the site `http://dx.doi.org/` and type or cut and paste the DOI in — just as someone can type a URL in to a Web browser's Address bar. Beyond that, CNRI's handle system includes a *handle resolver,* which is a free piece of software available for download at `www.handle.net/resolver/index.html`. The handle resolver is a browser plug-in for Netscape and Microsoft browsers that implements the Web browser protocol `doi:` so that the browser can process URLs of the form `doi:`*prefix*`/`*suffix* (for example, `doi:10.1346/ejournal-09-97`) as opposed to `http://dx.doi.org/10.1346/ejournal-09-97`. The former is more efficient. CNRI has also created a handle resolver for wireless Internet connections through Palm handheld devices such as the Palm VII.

Another likely use of DOIs is embedding them into DRM software. Every DRM solution has some sort of field denoting an identification code for the content. Various vendors of DRM container and rights clearinghouse technologies have made it clear that it would be easy to use DOIs for this field. Therefore, in complete DRM solutions, a user could download some metadata that includes a DOI, which could be used to communicate with a secure server to get the content. Various vendors are reputedly working on DRM systems that include DOI registration agency functionality, but none have come out on the market yet. (One of them, Digital Goods, ceased operations in May 2001.)

Another possibility that has been discussed, but not yet implemented, is to build DOIs into metadata services that help users locate content. Users could search libraries in specific subject areas and get search results that include, say, abstracts of articles. DOIs would then link to the actual content. The CrossRef initiative is a simpler version of this: In the online journals of publishers participating in CrossRef, DOIs are used along with reference citations. These make it much easier for researchers than simply citing the usual bibliographic information, such as volume, issue, and page numbers.

DOI status

As mentioned previously, DOI is under the jurisdiction of the International DOI Foundation, a nonprofit organization founded in 1998. IDF has about 50 members, spanning educational and professional publishers, technology vendors, trade associations, and scholarly organizations. The DOI syntax has been accepted as a standard by ANSI and NISO (ANSI/NISO Z39.84-2000).

IDF has been working closely with CNRI and others to further the development of the DOI system along several fronts. CNRI's original handle system, on which DOI is based, has the capability of resolving handles (its name for DOIs) to multiple URLs, not just single URLs. IDF is currently expanding the DOI system's functionality to take advantage of this feature.

The vast majority of the early adopters of DOI have been scientific and educational publishers. DOI can certainly apply to all kinds of other media — indeed, to all other content on the Internet. IDF and other organizations have been evangelizing DOI to audio and video producers, financial research publishers, and so on, but the interest in those communities remains to be seen. IDF is also looking into ways of extending the reach of DOI into metadata schemes.

The eBook industry is looking seriously at DOIs in various ways. The AAP commissioned a study in 2000 that recommended the use of DOIs as the primary means of associating metadata with eBook content, and an initiative called DOI-EB (chaired by Steve Mooney) has been launched to foster the development of DOI applications for eBooks.

DOI is a simple yet powerful idea, and it is vitally important in the process of helping the DRM industry grow through open standards. There is a real need for what IDF calls an "actionable identifier," that is, an identifier for content that is not only unique but also allows content to be found, subscribed to, purchased, and so on online and that can identify any type of content. It was clear to the AAP committee that created DOI that no existing type of identifier would satisfy all those requirements.

The sheer numbers of organizations adopting DOIs and becoming members of IDF suggest that DOI has a bright future — at least in publishing, if not across all content industries. And with companies such as Microsoft, Hewlett-Packard, and several DRM vendors as IDF members,

DOIs are bound to make their way into the next generation of DRM-related technology solutions.

Extensible Rights Markup Language

Extensible Rights Markup Language (XrML) is a language for building rights specifications, as defined in Chapter 4. XrML has its origins in the work that Dr. Mark Stefik did at Xerox PARC research labs in the mid-1990s. As discussed in the Introduction, Stefik's work focused on his concept of trusted systems. *Trusted systems* are conceptual "black boxes" that can render content but only according to a precise definition of the conditions under which it should be rendered. Stefik decided that a trusted system needed a formal, standardized way to specify those conditions, which include the rights model issues discussed in Chapter 4. So he invented a language for doing so — the Digital Property Rights Language, or DPRL.

Stefik's idea is that any type of trusted system can be built so that it can read specifications written in a certain language and act on them accordingly. He originally imagined trusted systems to be hardware devices, but in reality, trusted systems can be DRM software on PCs, as well as hardware devices such as eBooks, digital music players, PDAs, smart cards, and so on.

Another important concept in Stefik's research is that of a *digital repository,* which is a collection of *documents,* which in turn include both content (presumably in encrypted form) and rights specifications. A digital repository can be a file system on a computer, the memory in a PDA, or a digital memory card such as those used in digital cameras and some music players.

As mentioned in Chapter 4, Stefik's background included research in object-oriented languages; he had designed an object-oriented version of the LISP programming language. Therefore, it's no surprise that DPRL originally resembled LISP in its syntax.

Xerox Corp. patented DPRL. As Xerox has done with many technologies from its renowned research lab, Xerox attempted to commercialize DPRL, forming a business unit called Xerox Rights Management to take it to market. Xerox Rights Management developed commercial DRM technology around DPRL and attempted to sell it to publishers with mixed success. It also created a second version of DPRL with an XML syntax instead of one derived from LISP.

In early 2000, Xerox spun Xerox Rights Management off into a separate company called ContentGuard, Inc. Xerox took a large stake in the new company; Microsoft also became a significant minority investor. ContentGuard took over all the intellectual property of Xerox Rights Management, including the patents on DPRL — which it modified and renamed XrML to reflect its XML foundation.

In sharp contrast with DOI, which is simple conceptually and syntactically, XrML is a large, rich language, with complexity roughly equivalent to the SQL programming language for databases or perhaps the PostScript language for print page description. But XrML is not quite a programming language; it is a *specification* language. That is, its intent is to allow programmers to specify the form or structure of something in detail without having to specify how that form or structure is actually implemented. This is true to the principles of XML, which is supposed to allow the structure of content to be specified without saying anything about how that content is rendered on a specific output device.

XrML enables programmers to specify how trusted systems communicate with other trusted systems, or with the "outside world" (for example, output devices), in terms of the exercise of rights. The language is meant to do so in enough detail that media companies, software vendors, and device manufacturers can create content, software, or hardware that implements the specifications accurately and unambiguously — just as it is up to printer makers to implement PostScript drivers or up to database vendors to implement SQL interpreters.

Those who want to implement XrML need to develop an *interpreter* for the language, which is a piece of software that takes commands in XrML and makes them run on the device in question, such as a PC, music player, PDA, eBook, or whatever. An XrML-enabled device can accept files (documents) written in the language and understand how to handle them, just as a PostScript printing device can interpret PostScript files.

For example, XrML has ways of defining rights on content, such as PLAY and COPY. An XrML interpreter must translate the PLAY right into code that actually plays the content on the device when the right is invoked. That's a straightforward example, but in order to make it work, XrML includes the definition of protocols between trusted systems that involve such "ugly" things as public-key cryptography, levels of security, and the details of file systems. Implementations of XrML must address these ugly aspects because without them, trusted systems would not have the security that they need.

All this is a way of saying that XrML has a lot of grungy details that won't be of interest to the reader who wants to understand what the language does and where it applies, without wanting or having to program in it. XrML code, though readable to anyone familiar with both XML and the ideas in this book, is intended to be read by machines, not humans.

Therefore, this section covers most of XrML's capabilities without getting into those ugly details. It would take an entire textbook to do justice to the language and provide a wide range of sample code. Anyone who wants to dig deeper can look at the XrML specification, version 1.03 at this writing, which is available at www.xrml.org/ and which has plenty of examples in it. We provide a high-level overview of the language's capabilities here and refer the reader to the specification for further information.

XrML technology

A specification written in XrML is called a *document*. Don't confuse this with the actual content; it's really a bunch of metadata. The most important part of an XrML document is the WORK component.

The WORK component

The WORK component includes the content item's rights information and other metadata. It contains the following subcomponents:

- ◆ OBJECT
- ◆ DESCRIPTION
- ◆ CREATOR
- ◆ OWNER
- ◆ DIGEST
- ◆ PARTS
- ◆ CONTENTS
- ◆ COPIES
- ◆ COMMENT

+ SKU

+ RIGHTSGROUP (or REFERENCEDRIGHTSGROUP)

Of these, RIGHTSGROUP is the most interesting.

CROSS REFERENCE: We cover this topic shortly in the subsection, "Rights specifications."

OBJECT is the name of the work (for example, *Digital Rights Management: Business and Technology*) and an ID, which can be a DOI, ISBN, or other type of identifier. DESCRIPTION is an optional description of the work, mainly meant for human readability. CREATOR is a description of the work's creator, who can be an author, composer, or photographer. OWNER allows the creator of the XrML document to optionally specify a principal who is authorized to make changes to the rights of the content.

DIGEST is a cryptographic value, similar to a digital signature, that allows the creator to verify the integrity of the actual content — as opposed to SIGNATURE, which helps verify the integrity of the overall XrML document.

PARTS allows the XrML document creator to specify that other works are included as parts of the work that this XrML document describes. Conversely, CONTENTS describes the part of the actual content to which the rights specification applies. The way CONTENTS is described depends on the type of content it is; it can be expressed in bytes, SMPTE (Society of Motion Picture and Television Engineers) time codes, and so on.

COPIES describes the number of copies of the content to which the rights apply; if COPIES is omitted, the number is assumed to be one. This can be important because it influences transport rights (see the subsection "Types of rights"). If there are two copies of the content and the user exercises a LOAN right to lend a copy to another user, a second copy remains for the first user to use while the first one is lent out.

COMMENT is a text field reserved for comments, typically written by the person or application that created (or edited) the XrML document. As with comments in other programming languages, the comments aren't intended to be meaningful to any system that reads the document — just to the humans that read it.

Finally, SKU (a term borrowed from the retail world) is useful for retailers or distributors of digital content. It helps them relate the content to other things needed to sell it, such as cryptographic keys or discount coupons.

Rights specifications

RIGHTSGROUP specifies rights to the work. There can be several of them per document. RIGHTSGROUPS can have names, for example, "standard," "subscriber," "student," and so on. The main component of a RIGHTSGROUP is a RIGHTSLIST.

The RIGHTSLIST embodies the rights modeling power of XrML. The following rights are supported:

+ **Render rights:** PLAY, PRINT, EXPORT, and VIEW

+ **Transport rights:** COPY, TRANSFER, and LOAN

+ **Derivative work rights:** EDIT, EXTRACT, and EMBED

The preceding rights map to the types of rights discussed in Chapter 4. In addition, XrML supports several types of rights that are called *utility rights* in Chapter 4:

- **File management rights:** BACKUP, RESTORE, VERIFY, FOLDER, DIRECTORY, and DELETE
- **Configuration rights:** INSTALL and UNINSTALL

Each right in a RIGHTSLIST has a set of terms and conditions associated with it, consisting of access controls, time periods, geographies, and considerations associated with exercising the right. In the following subsections, we examine the types of rights that XrML supports and then take a look at how terms and conditions are specified.

Types of rights

Mark Stefik's research identified fundamental differences between the types of render rights supported by XrML. PLAY means to create an *ephemeral* rendering of the content, one that goes away when the content is finished. (For example, the song or video is over.) VIEW is merely a synonym for PLAY, but it can apply to media to which the term *play* isn't particularly meaningful, such as still images. PRINT means to create a *permanent* rendering of the content on some output medium, such as hard copy. EXPORT means to pass the content out of the trusted system in plain, unencumbered digital form.

Transport rights in XrML refer to the same set of transport rights discussed in Chapter 4: COPY, meaning to create another copy of the XrML document; TRANSFER, meaning to move the XrML document from one digital repository to another; and LOAN, meaning to create a temporary copy of the document and move it to another digital repository for a specified period of time during which the original copy is inoperative (although, as explained earlier, if the XrML document specifies more than one copy, the other copies can still be operative, unless they too are loaned out).

Each of the transport rights has an optional clause called NEXTRIGHTS, which enables superdistribution. NEXTRIGHTS describes the rights to be added to or deleted from the new copy of the content; for example, the new copy may have its COPY right deleted, or its rendering fees can be marked up (a new PLAY right added). If NEXTRIGHTS isn't specified, the new copies of the content have the same rights as the original copy. The LOAN right also has a REMAININGRIGHTS clause, which is a convenience for specifying the (reduced) rights that the loaned copy of the work has.

Derivative work rights, as discussed in Chapter 4, are for using pieces of the work in another work. As mentioned before, it is not possible for any rights language to model all possible uses of content items. The designers of XrML admit this and suggest that the derivative work rights included in the language are meant only to cover the types of rights that are easiest to automate.

EXTRACT gives the user the right to take a portion of the work and create a new work, which in turn can be incorporated into a larger work. The new work that the EXTRACT right creates is represented in another XrML document. EXTRACT has an option, EDITOR, that lets you specify the type of editing software that you will allow to do the actual extraction. Ideally, EDITOR is another trusted system that knows how to create XrML documents. If EDITOR is omitted, as would be the case in most real-world applications, you can use any program to do the extraction; for example, you can use a Perl script to extract a certain section of a text document automatically or Microsoft Word to do it manually. However, the ideal world to which XrML applies is one in which every process that operates on content is a trusted system – which Perl and Microsoft Word are not.

The EDIT and EMBED rights are variations of EXTRACT. EDIT allows for extraction plus the option to change the content. EMBED allows extractions that explicitly insert the new work inside a new composite work. All three types of derivative work rights include an optional NEXTRIGHTS clause, as with transport rights, supporting superdistribution of portions of the original work.

Of the file management rights, FOLDER and DIRECTORY are ways of manipulating hierarchical folders of works, allowing XrML's notion of a repository to map onto hierarchical file systems, such as those found in Windows, Macintosh OS, UNIX, and other operating systems. The FOLDER right lets you specify rights that span an entire folder; these rights add to or override the rights that each document specifies. For example, you can use a FOLDER rights specification to disallow EXPORT rights on any of the documents in the folder, even if some of them specify EXPORT rights. If you are familiar with UNIX or other multiuser operating systems, you can think of FOLDER rights as a more sophisticated version of directory permissions.

DIRECTORY rights allow the user to list contents of a folder and their characteristics, similarly to the DIRECTORY command in DOS or the ls command in UNIX. DELETE rights are self-explanatory, but note that (as with any right) you can attach terms and conditions, such as fees charged.

BACKUP and RESTORE allow you to make backups of documents for the explicit purpose of restoring them if the original document has a problem. You can specify terms and conditions to the restore, such as to limit the number of restores possible or to charge a fee for each restore.

VERIFY rights allow users to run a program (a verifier) on the work that verifies its contents, according to some sort of security scheme. Such a program can verify a hash value or that the content is encrypted correctly.

Finally, the configuration rights INSTALL and UNINSTALL are necessary when dealing with secure repositories of works. They don't apply to platforms such as PCs and Macs, where no special permissions are necessary to install software.

Terms and conditions

Four types of terms and conditions can be attached to all types of rights in XrML:

- **Times:** At what times are the rights valid?
- **Consideration:** What sort of transaction takes place when the right is exercised?
- **Access controls:** Who can exercise the right, and what credentials do they need?
- **Territory:** Where, in geographic or digital space, is the right valid?

Time specifications in XrML are quite flexible. They allow for three kinds of time intervals: fixed, sliding, and metered. Fixed intervals are specified as FROM and UNTIL. Sliding intervals specify blocks of time from the time when the right is first exercised until a certain deadline — for example, any six-hour block until the end of December 2001. Metered intervals are like fixed intervals except that the time is cumulative, not in a single block — for example, a *total* of six hours through the end of December 2001. Time units in XrML time specifications are stated in units from years down to seconds.

XrML refers to consideration, as defined in Chapter 4, as "fees and incentives." You can specify these in two basic ways: as currency (any ISO-defined world currency, with U.S. dollars as the default) or as *tickets*. Tickets are a way to create a sort of private currency for publishers who want to support other forms of consideration. They are a kind of digital work in themselves, in that they have rights associated with them and they are meant to be stored in trusted system repositories. When you "play" a ticket, you use it according to some rules; for example, you render it invalid, or you decrement some value stored in it.

Tickets can be used for many purposes. The most obvious example is to use tickets as coupons that are exchangeable for "merchandise," that is, rights to digital works. You can issue tickets to premium subscribers that they can use to access content; those who are not premium subscribers must pay cash. You can also use tickets as frequent flyer–style credits for users who spend a lot of time on your Web site or are otherwise loyal customers. Tickets can be shared among a number of publishers, similar to Flooz or other electronic incentive programs.

Tickets in XrML can have expiration dates, and they can be metered, with the same meaning as for time specifications. It is also possible to invoke transport rights on tickets, that is, to copy and transfer them to other users.

XrML handles currency transactions by including information about users' financial accounts, which can be exported to transaction processing systems. This makes it possible to do several useful things, such as verifying credit card transactions on the fly and allowing users to be credited (given incentive) for viewing content instead of being charged fees. (For example, a publisher may offer credits for viewing advertisements.)

Several types of pricing are supported in XrML:

- ♦ PERUSE
- ♦ METEREDFEE
- ♦ BESTPRICEUNDER
- ♦ CALLFORPRICE
- ♦ MARKUP

Per-use pricing is straightforward: It's charged each time the user exercises a right. Metered-fee pricing is used with time interval specifications that call for a time limit on exercising the right, such as sliding or metered intervals. With metered-fee pricing, you can specify the time increment (for example, minutes or seconds) as well as the time unit used for computing the time actually used. For example, you can charge a dollar a minute for use of some content, but actually charge to the nearest second.

A best-price-under scheme allows you to charge a price that isn't determined exactly until the account is settled with a user. To use best-price-under pricing in an XrML document, you specify a maximum price that the user can expect to pay. This allows publishers to implement such things as rebates and situations where the exact price isn't immediately known. For example, say that best-price-under pricing is used in a trusted system, such as a portable music player, that isn't normally connected to the Internet and the user is purchasing content in a foreign currency. The exact purchase price won't be known until the device connects to the Internet and does a currency conversion. Best-price-under schemes cover this eventuality while giving the user some idea of what she will be paying.

Call-for-price pricing is similar to best-price-under, except that the price must be settled *before* the right is granted, not later when the account is settled. A price ceiling isn't necessary in call-for-price pricing.

Markup pricing is used in composite works in which each component of the work has its own pricing. You can use it to specify a percentage that is added to the aggregate price of the components. For example, consider a secondary publisher that produces a monthly digest of articles for a subscriber that is chosen according to her interest profile. The secondary publisher can impose a 10 percent markup for the convenience of having all those interesting articles delivered in one package. Using markup pricing in XrML, the secondary publisher can take just its 10 percent and leave the transactions for each of the articles to their original publishers to process.

You can specify minimum and maximum charges to each of these types of pricing. This makes it possible to charge tiny amounts for viewing small units of content while ensuring that the value of the transaction isn't less than the cost of processing it. It also allows pricing schemes such as "A dollar per play for the first ten plays; subsequent plays are free" (that is, setting a maximum price of $10). There is no direct way in XrML to support tiered pricing schemes such as "Copies 1 to 100 are 10 cents each, copies 101 to 1000 are 8 cents each, and copies 1001 and up are 5 cents each."

Access controls in XrML are used to put limits on the users that can exercise the specified rights. Without them, anyone could access content, as long as she had the proper consideration — for example, as long as she paid fees or possessed tickets. Some examples of cases in which a publisher would want to limit access to specified classes of users are

♦ Adult material — no one under age 18

♦ Material available to paid subscribers only

♦ Material intended for registered students of XYZ University (or employees of XYZ Corporation) only

♦ Classified material — secret clearance required

♦ Material playable only by devices made by XYZ manufacturer

♦ Material playable only on a player owned by the same person who owns the trusted system repository

The access control feature in XrML lets you specify electronic credentials (certificates, licenses, and so on) for both the source and the destination of the work. The source is the trusted repository where the work is currently stored; the destination is the trusted system to which it's going, whether that's a file system, an output device, or some other piece of software. (For example, the destination can be a media player that confirms the ID of its user via a password, a smart card, or a biometric device such as an iris scanner.)

XrML's access control scheme also lets you specify relative strengths of security, enabling you to stipulate that users or devices wanting access to a work have *at least* a certain level of security. Using the SECURITYLEVEL feature, you can specify different security criteria and require that devices wanting to access the work meet or exceed them. For example, you can use SECURITYLEVEL to define security attributes such as "password strength," "physical security," "government security clearance level," "virus checking enabled," and so on. Then you can assign level numbers to those attributes so that they can be compared.

Of course, getting the SECURITYLEVEL feature to work requires inventing standards for several types of security and levels within those types and implementing those standards across many different devices and pieces of software. A good example of such a scheme already in place is the security levels that the U.S. government assigns to computing facilities that handle classified data, which are designations such as C2 and B1. (Lower letters and numbers mean higher security.) Standardizing on security levels in the consumer sector is another matter — a monumental task, but XrML has the capability to handle it after it is done.

The final type of term and condition element in XrML rights specifications is the TERRITORY. This allows you to further limit the applicability of a right to a geographic range or a digital domain. You can specify physical (country, state, city, zip code, and street) or digital (IP addresses and other network domain identifiers) addresses with TERRITORY clauses.

Watermarks and tracking

Chapter 5 describes a watermark as a marking that can be inserted into a piece of content in such a way as to be both impervious to removal and minimally intrusive to the content's rendering. XrML provides support for watermarking — not by actually doing the watermarking, but by being able to provide information to a watermarking function that it may need.

Watermarks typically provide ways of identifying content for the purpose of tracking its use. Many types of information can be useful in such an identifier, such as the name of the content, the name of the publisher, the time and date of publication or of rendering (playing or printing), the name of the user for whom it is being rendered, and so on.

XrML's WATERMARK feature allows two types of information to be passed to an actual watermarking program:

♦ Data that is known at the time of publishing, which can be a text string (for example, the title of the work and name of the publisher) or binary data (for example, some audio material to be embedded into an audio clip)

♦ Data describing the actual rendering of the content, which can include

- The list of rights defined on the work
- Information about the user who is rendering the content
- Information about the device doing the rendering
- Information about the institution that owns the rendering device
- The time of the rendering
- The number of copies being rendered

You can include WATERMARK specifications in rights specifications in XrML. If a right has a watermark specification, the specified information is passed to a watermarking program when the right is exercised. Normally, this applies only to render rights, but it's easy to see how watermarking can also be applied to some transport and derivative work rights as well.

Related to watermarking is the capability of tracking each use of content. XrML has a TRACK feature, which lets you specify an entity that does the tracking, such as a logging program, and what information to feed it. You can specify TRACK with any right so that the exercise of that right can be tracked.

XrML status

As implied earlier in this section, XrML is a complex and impressive piece of technology. The result of meticulous research, XrML is the only comprehensive rights language available. It is not too much to say that the field of DRM came into existence with the publication of Mark

Stefik's paper on the original DPRL language. There are many advantages to standardizing on a rights specification language such as XrML throughout the media industry.

However, it would also be fair to say that ContentGuard has some work to do to achieve such standardization. Although over 20 companies — including DRM vendors, publishers, clearinghouses, and powerhouse vendors such as Adobe and Hewlett-Packard — have endorsed XrML, at this writing only one vendor other than ContentGuard has actually been implementing it . . . although it's not just any vendor; it's Microsoft.

The first issue that ContentGuard must address is that of the openness of XrML. ContentGuard controls XrML through several patents that it holds on the technology. That makes it fundamentally different from standards such as PRISM, ONIX, ICE, or even XML itself, which are not under patent protection. Some DRM technology vendors are not comfortable using a technology that's ultimately under the control of a company that may be a competitor.

ContentGuard has positioned XrML as analogous to the Java programming language from Sun Microsystems. As Sun did with Java, ContentGuard wants to appear as a thought leader for the industry, making a key enabling technology available to all, while offering products based on the technology that may be direct competitors to products from other vendors who license it. This was a good position to take a few years ago, when Java's openness was viewed in a positive light. But more recently, there has been something of a backlash against Java, as Sun has fought to control its definition and evolution against competitors such as Microsoft and HP. The general consensus now is that regardless of how "standard" Java is — what standards bodies have it registered, what authoring process it has, or whether the source code is under an open-source license — Sun remains in control of the language, to the annoyance of certain other vendors.

The good news is that ContentGuard is licensing XrML freely. It is possible for anyone to get the XrML specification simply by registering for it on the `www.xrml.org` Web site, and anyone can implement the language without paying royalties. However, ContentGuard has not established an open authoring group for the evolution of the language (as all the other standards mentioned earlier have done), although it intends to do so.

The complexity of the language is another issue. XrML has lots of features, some of which overlap — meaning that there may be several ways to implement a certain business model in XrML. This isn't meant to be a criticism, though: The same is true of virtually all programming languages. Mark Stefik and his team at PARC talked to a wide variety of publishers and device makers in order to gather requirements for the original DPRL language, and they wanted to ensure that all the requirements were met. ContentGuard has done more of the same.

Yet XrML is so full-featured that an interpreter for the language has to be a large piece of software, one that takes up lots of expensive memory (for example, in a portable music player) or software download time. Furthermore, the language embraces several software elements with deep implications for the inner workings of the systems that implement it, such as public-key encryption and multidimensional security levels, which may conflict with features already built into (or intentionally omitted from) those systems. This also adds to the complexity of implementing the language, although such features are necessary to enforce rights. XrML was originally intended to support the entire trusted systems concept, not some lightweight subset thereof, and it's unclear whether it can be used successfully for the latter.

These are all problems that ContentGuard can fix, and indeed intends to fix. ContentGuard can evangelize XrML to the industry by creating an open authoring group, offering training and implementation assistance to vendors, holding developers' conferences, touting its benefits at other conferences, and so on. Remember that despite the minor backlash against Java, Sun evangelized it to the entire computer industry, and it's an undeniable success.

With so many DRM vendors having introduced incompatible, proprietary rights models, the need for XrML to succeed is great — but the industry has to be properly motivated for it to happen. We hope that ContentGuard is up to the challenge as it also builds the revenue-generating portion of its business.

Information and Content Exchange

The Information and Content Exchange (ICE) is a protocol for supporting content syndication relationships. It began as an effort within Vignette Corp., the makers of the popular StoryServer Web publishing system, to create technology that enabled Vignette's customers to exchange content. Instead of building a proprietary product within the company, Vignette decided to create an open standard in collaboration with some customers.

One of those customers was News Internet Services, the Internet arm of Rupert Murdoch's News Corp., whose vice president of engineering, Laird Popkin, ended up coauthoring the original ICE specification along with Vignette's Brad Husick. The first version of the specification appeared in October 1998.

ICE is concerned with the business-to-business (B-to-B) side of digital rights management. Throughout this book, we point out that although the media has paid the most attention to the business-to-consumer (B-to-C) side of DRM (covering the controlled distribution of content from publishers to consumers), B-to-B side is just as important, if not more so. The B-to-B side of DRM covers cases of publishers wanting to get content from each other. In Chapters 2 and 4, we include examples of book publishers using each other's content, particularly in the textbook area where publishers routinely license illustrations, tables, equations, and other small pieces of content from one another.

Another important example of B-to-B content transactions is among Web sites. A content Web site devoted to a particular area of interest may want to get some of its content from other sources. For example, a travel Web site may want to get restaurant reviews from a food Web site to augment its information about vacation destinations. A reseller of computer software may want to get documentation updates from the vendor whose wares it resells and put them up on its site. One of the great things about the Web is that it's so easy to include content from Site A on Site B: Just copy it or hyperlink it.

Yet doing this kind of thing on a regular basis has its logistical problems. Site B needs information such as where to get Site A's content, what format the content is in, when it is updated, what content items Site A has from which Site B can choose, and of course, what rights it has to display and redistribute Site A's content. These are some of the main elements in what we call a *syndication* relationship.

Historically, the term *syndication* has been most often associated with radio and TV programs, news stories, and cartoons. Major newspapers such as the *New York Times* and *Los Angeles Times* have their own syndicates. If the *Times* (either one) has a news story that it thinks may be of national interest, it puts the story up on its own syndication network. Subscribers to that network pick the story up and run it in their own newspapers if they choose. Companies such as King Features syndicate cartoons (such as "Beetle Bailey" and "Blondie") and columns (such as those written by Dr. Joyce Brothers and Dan Rather). In the world of television, the big studios have divisions that syndicate their programming to TV stations; for example, Buena Vista is Disney's syndication division.

Major content brands have begun to syndicate their content to other sites on the Web. They have discovered that the best way to increase brand recognition is not to try to draw the most users to a single Web site but to get their branded content to as many other sites as possible that attract the right kind of user. For example, *Business Week* magazine maintains its own Web site, *Business Week* Online, but also syndicates its content to several different places, ranging from general Web portals such as Lycos to business destinations such as Staples.com, the online store of the office supply retailing giant. *Business Week* also syndicates its content to traditional, pre-Internet online services such as Dialog and Lexis-Nexis.

If a publisher wants to syndicate its content to a certain number of different sites, it has to set up the same number of different logistical schemes for getting the content to them. Typically, such schemes have been set up with FTP (the standard File Transfer Protocol on the Internet) and a collection of ad hoc file formats. Such schemes require fairly major programming efforts every time the publisher wants to add another syndication partner. Clearly this is not a scalable activity.

ICE was invented to create a standard way of handling the logistics of content syndication. It does *not* handle two kinds of things that are common to consumer-oriented DRM solutions: business terms and copy protection. Terms of business relationships, such as pricing and legal liabilities, are assumed to be negotiated by humans and represented in contracts — and the parties in the contracts are assumed to trust each other to carry out their parts of the relationships appropriately. It's taken for granted that the subscriber to the content will pay for it (if necessary) and will not distribute unauthorized copies of it.

Nevertheless, ICE has a lightweight way of describing content rights, and it can interoperate with DRM solutions that specify rights in detail and that enforce copy protection. The authors of ICE didn't expect most B-to-B content syndication relationships to need heavy-duty rights protection, so they didn't build it in.

ICE technology

The ICE standard is currently being developed under the umbrella of IDEAlliance, a group within the Graphics Communication Association (GCA) that promotes open standards and oversees the PRISM standard for magazines and their Web sites. The definitive document on ICE is the ICE specification, currently version 1.1, available on the `www.icestandard.org` Web site. Another very useful document on the same Web site is the ICE Implementation Cookbook, which provides step-by-step examples of ICE-compliant implementations.

ICE is a communications protocol. Like XrML, it is expressed as an XML vocabulary. But a protocol is a different type of animal than a specification language, which is what XrML is. ICE not only determines how certain types of software should work (which is what a software specification does), but it also determines how these types of software should communicate with each other.

In ICE, two types of software communicate with each other: *syndicators* and *subscribers*. Syndicators make collections (*subscriptions)* of content available to subscribers over time by sending them packages periodically with instructions to add new content items to their collections or remove content items from them.

Figure 6-4 shows a basic example of this. The syndicator is Zingo, a restaurant reviewer, and the subscriber is TravelPace, a travel site. TravelPace has the Zingo subscription called "NYC Restaurant Reviews." TravelPace's collection of reviews, the result of various packages sent by Zingo previously, includes the restaurants Bistro Dordogne, Hoss's Steakhouse, Les Amateurs du Vin, Trattoria Il Duomo, and Adobe Café (presumably among many others).

In Figure 6-4, Zingo is sending TravelPace its May 2001 package. The package contains commands to add reviews for the new restaurants Thanos's Taverna, Bistro Dordogne, and Wursthalle Berlin. The review of Bistro Dordogne replaces the one that TravelPace already has because the restaurant got a new chef and the *pommes sarladais* are much improved. The package also contains a command to remove the review of Trattoria Il Duomo: The restaurant closed after the *New York Times* restaurant reviewer came down with salmonella after eating there. As a result of the operation, TravelPace has a new collection of restaurant reviews, which it can display on its Web site.

Using ICE, syndicators can do the following:

♦ Put up catalogs containing offers of content packages that they are making available for subscription, along with specifications about how often the packages will be updated.

♦ Accept messages from subscribers who want to subscribe to particular offers in the catalog and who want to negotiate terms of the subscription.

♦ *Push* content packages to subscribers according to predetermined schedules.

♦ Send unsolicited messages occasionally to subscribers — for example, to tell them about new content offerings or to inform them about scheduled service interruptions.

Meanwhile, subscribers can do the following:

♦ Browse syndicators' catalogs, choose offers to subscribe to, and negotiate subscription terms.

♦ *Pull* content packages from syndicators' Web sites.

ICE supports both push and pull methods of delivering content. It also defines two types of subscribers: weak and full. A *full* subscriber is assumed to have a server up and running at all times, ready to receive pushed content and unsolicited messages, as well as to pull content from the syndicator. A *weak* subscriber is one that only gets (pulls) content on demand, possibly on an ad hoc basis.

The basic unit of communication in ICE is a message called a *payload,* which is an XML document that conforms to the ICE DTD (Document Type Definition). Payloads contain messages that syndicators and subscribers pass back and forth. The messages use lots of unique ID numbers to keep track of things such as the identity of the syndicator, the identity of the subscriber, the type of message, the identity of a content package being requested or sent, and so on. The messages also contain either *requests,* which are commands being sent from the syndicator to the subscriber or vice versa, or *responses* to those requests.

Requests in ICE fall into two broad categories: those that have to do with syndicators' catalogs and subscriptions to the content and those that have to do with subscribers getting content to which they have subscribed.

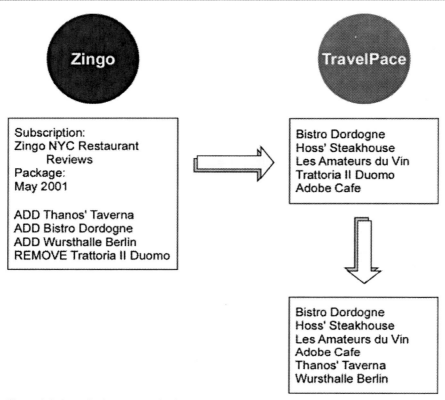

Figure 6-4: A syndication package in ICE.

Catalogs and subscriptions

The first thing that happens when a syndicator wants to make its content available is that the syndicator constructs a catalog of offers of content packages. A catalog consists of offers, which are descriptions of the content items available. Offers can be grouped into offer-groups, which can themselves contain offer-groups (allowing for hierarchical organization of offers).

Each offer contains several metadata fields, including an ID for the offer, a descriptive name of the product being offered, and fields that capture content rights information:

- ◆ Derivative work rights:
  - atomic-use: Tells whether the content must be used in its entirety or if subscribers can use parts. This is the converse of an *extract* right as defined in XrML and in Chapter 4.
  - editable: Tells whether the subscriber is allowed to edit the content before redistributing it. This is similar to an *edit* right as defined in XrML and in Chapter 4.
- ◆ ip-status: Specifies any licensing restrictions on the content. Possible ip-status values are
  - SEE-LICENSE: The content is covered under preexisting contractual terms; this is the default value if the field is omitted.
  - PUBLIC-DOMAIN: No licensing restrictions.
  - FREE-WITH-ACK: No licensing restrictions, except that the subscriber is required to display an acknowledgement string along with the content.

- SEVERE-RESTRICTIONS: This is meant to allow ICE processors to flag content items for special attention if their licensing terms fall outside of the preexisting license agreement.
- CONFIDENTIAL: The content is confidential and not meant for further distribution.
- rights-holder: Name of the entity that owns the syndication rights to the content.
- show-credit: If true, requires the subscriber to display the source of the content (as with the ACK above).
- usage-required: If true, requires the subscriber to return data on the usage of this content item.
- quantity: The number of times the subscriber is allowed to get an update of this content item; for example, if the content item is a stock quote on a given ticker symbol, the syndicator may limit the number of times a subscriber can access it.

An offer description also contains a *delivery rule,* which is a set of specifications about when the syndicator delivers packages to subscribers, and a list of *business terms,* which are pointers to explanations of different types of business relationships between the syndicator and subscriber.

Delivery rules contain several attributes that give syndicators a lot of flexibility as well as precision in defining delivery schedules for their content, including

- Whether the delivery is push (syndicator pushes content to subscribers) or pull (subscribers pull content from syndicator)
- The start and end time of the delivery
- The days of the week (Monday, Tuesday, Wednesday, and so on) or month (1st, 2nd, 3rd, and so on) that the delivery takes place
- The start time and duration of a specific time window on the above days when the delivery takes place
- The minimum and maximum time between updates of the content item
- The minimum and maximum number of updates of the content item

Business terms include the following:

- **Credit:** the required text crediting the source of the content that the subscriber must display
- **Licensing:** the terms of licensing
- **Payment:** the payment terms
- **Reporting:** the description of data on end-user content access that the subscriber is required to report
- **Usage:** the uses to which the subscriber may put the content

ICE doesn't contain any direct means of specifying the business terms. Instead, each of them can contain any of the following:

- A text string with the details of the business term, such as the credit string "Copyright 2000 XYZ Publishing, Inc."
- An ID number designating the business term, such as a reference to a payment schedule called MONTHLYSUB, as opposed to another one called ANNUALSUB or SINGLEITEMSUB.

 ◆ A URL that points to a file with the term's details; for example, the usage term can contain a URL pointing to an XrML description of the content's allowed usages.

This information framework for delivery schedules and business terms is intended to support automated negotiation between syndicators and subscribers. ICE contains an elaborate mechanism that allows the two parties to negotiate the details of these parameters.

For delivery schedules, a syndicator can specify which terms are negotiable and within what ranges. ICE includes a protocol by which subscribers can offer terms, syndicators can accept or reject them, and negotiation can proceed until either there is a set of mutually acceptable terms or there is no deal possible. ICE ensures this by requiring that only one parameter at a time is in play and that after a parameter value has been agreed to, it cannot be revisited later in the negotiation. A subscriber can offer a set of terms, and the syndicator can respond by saying, in effect, one of three things: "OK," "No, but feel free to try again," or "No deal is possible."

For business terms, the ICE specifications are merely a framework within which external software — or humans — can negotiate. There is no mechanism within ICE, for example, for negotiating the text of a credit line or the exact details of subscriber usage reporting.

ICE also allows the negotiation framework to be extended to include additional parameters, called *subscription extensions.* For example, a syndicator can specify a range of content formats from which subscribers can choose (such as Microsoft Word, PDF, or HTML for text or Real, Windows Media Player, or QuickTime for streaming video), or it can specify that an encryption-based DRM solution can be used to transmit the content.

When a subscriber wants to subscribe to content, it sends an `ice-get-catalog` message to the syndicator. The syndicator responds by sending the catalog in an `ice-catalog` message. Then both parties send a series of `ice-offer` messages until the negotiation is complete, at which time the subscriber has a subscription (assuming that the negotiation was successful).

After a subscriber has a subscription, it can cancel, ask for the susbscription status, or change the subscription. Changing the subscription starts a new negotiation process.

Content delivery

ICE provides a framework for delivering content that lets syndicators define ordered sequences of content packages and ensure that the packages are all delivered in the proper order. The framework is set up so that the syndicator has to keep track of the overall order of the sequence and where each subscriber is in the sequence; subscribers know only about the state they're in at any given moment. This gives syndicators a way of having more knowledge about their content than they may want to pass on to subscribers — which can be useful if, say, the content is a quiz sent as a series of questions, the number of which is to be kept secret.

Each package contains a lot of metadata, some of which overlaps with the information contained in subscriptions and overrides their values if they are set. Here are some of the metadata attributes unique to packages:

 ◆ `activation` and `expiration`: Start and end dates/times of the validity of the package.

 ◆ `fullupdate`: Specifies whether processing this package requires updating all the content that the subscription has delivered so far or (the default case) whether the package is incremental.

 ◆ `old-state` and `new-state`: Conveys state information by specifying the state of the package sequence immediately before (old-state) and after (new-state) this package is sent.

The subscriber is expected to know that it's in old-state before accepting the package; if it isn't, it can report an error.

Aside from the metadata, a package contains a set of ice-add and ice-remove instructions to add and remove content from the subscriber's collection. You can see the basics of how this works in Figure 6-4, earlier in this chapter.

The `ice-add` and `ice-remove` commands are associated with items. Items can be one of three things:

♦ Content (`ice-item`).

♦ A pointer to content (`ice-item-ref`).

♦ An item group (`ice-item-group`). Groups can contain groups, which makes it possible to organize items hierarchically.

`ice-items` contain the actual content within the ICE payload. They also include several metadata attributes that overlap with subscription metadata, such as rights information. Any attributes stored in `ice-items` override the corresponding attribute values of subscriptions. In addition, `ice-items` contain these attributes:

♦ `activation` and `expiration`: The start and end dates/times of the validity of the item.

♦ `content-filename`: This is a filename to be used as a destination name on the subscriber's site. It is often necessary to specify this attribute to ensure that file references in URLs across multiple content items are preserved properly on the subscriber's site.

♦ `content-type`: The MIME type of the content.

♦ `subscription-element`: An identifier for this content item that stays constant for the life of the subscription. This allows updates (adds where the content item already exists) and removes to work correctly.

♦ `update-attributes-only`: If true and this is an update (an add where the subscriber already has an item with the given `subscription-element`), don't update the content; just update the attributes.

`ice-item-refs` are more commonly used for content that doesn't comfortably fit into a delivered package, particularly streaming audio or video. They contain URLs that point to the content. An `ice-item-ref` can also contain a description of the time window during which the content is accessible, as well as access control parameters (such as user IDs, passwords, and cookie strings) that enable access to the content.

As mentioned previously, there are two ways of getting packages from syndicators to subscribers in ICE: push and pull. For push, syndicators send `ice-package` messages to subscribers, who are expected to be able to receive and possibly confirm the delivery of the packages. For pull, subscribers issue `ice-get-package` messages that contain the ID of the subscription.

ICE status

The ICE consortium has two levels of membership: regular member and authoring group. Each level has a handful of members, most of which are technology vendors. More importantly, several products on the market implement ICE. These are one flavor or another of syndication server — server products that enable content companies to syndicate their content and enable Web sites to subscribe to the syndicators' offerings. Some are designed as add-ons to existing

Web publishing systems or application servers, whereas others are standalone packages. Here are some current ICE-compliant products:

♦ Vignette Syndication Server: the original ICE server, designed to work with Vignette's StoryServer Web content management system

♦ HP Bluestone Total-e-Syndication: a Java-based application server component

♦ Kinecta Syndication Server: a standalone syndication server package

♦ Xenosys JICE: Java programming language components for ICE

♦ Intershop Enfinity: a Web content management system with ICE support

♦ Quark avenue.quark: a tool for exporting QuarkXPress page layouts to Vignette StoryServer in XML

♦ ArcadiaOne eSyndication: a standalone syndication server package

♦ Interwoven OpenSyndicate – a syndication server package designed to work with Interwoven's TeamSite Web content management system.

The products from Vignette, Kinecta, ArcadiaOne, and Interwoven are described in Chapter 12.

ICE's installed base of vendors and customers has been growing steadily. However, two forces act as barriers to ICE's further growth. The first is the expense and complexity of setting up ICE servers when compared to small-scale, ad hoc syndication. As mentioned previously, publishers who want to send their content to others have often been satisfied with simple FTP-based schemes. Some publishers who have been syndicating content for many years have a lot invested in legacy file formats for doing so: For example, McGraw-Hill has a standard tag format that they have used for many years to send content from titles such as *Business Week, Aviation Week,* and *Engineering News-Record* to online services such as Dialog and Lexis-Nexis.

Because publishers usually start out with one distribution partner and add others incrementally, it's unusual that one would think about building an architecture for scalable syndication from the start. More often, publishers build lots of ad hoc functionality and then, when it gets out of hand, decide to scrap it in favor of an extensible, robust architecture such as ICE. This kind of decision is neither lightly made nor easily executed.

The second barrier to ICE growth is the rise of third-party syndication networks such as Screaming Media and YellowBrix (see Chapter 12). These serve as hubs that sit between those who want to syndicate their content to others and those Web sites who want to use content from a variety of sources. The advantage of these services is that they make it very easy for publishers and subscribers — easier than adopting complex server software in-house. In particular, these services accept content in a variety of formats without requiring ICE-compliant payloads. (For example, Screaming Media accepts content in an XML tag set that is considerably simpler than ICE.) These syndication networks take the muss and fuss out of syndication. Of course, they do it for a price: They take large percentages of transaction revenue.

ICE remains the best solution for those publishers who want to build their own syndication architecture instead of trusting it to third parties. ICE enables them to build services that are more flexible and reliable than ad hoc FTP-type schemes, and it lets them keep the revenue in their own pockets. ICE is a vital part of the DRM standards landscape.

Secure Digital Music Initiative

The Secure Digital Music Initiative (SDMI) began in early 1999 as an initiative within the music industry that was analogous to the AAP's Enabling Technologies project, which resulted in DOI. The music industry wanted to forge a set of open standards for the online distribution of digital music with built-in rights management, and at the same time, create a viable marketplace for music encoded in accordance with the standards.

The record industry's trade association, the Recording Industry Association of America (RIAA), and representatives from the "Big 5" record labels that control the music industry (Sony, Warner, BMG, EMI, and Universal) called a conference of technology companies and consumer electronics makers in February 1999 to kick off SDMI. The initiative's motivation was clear: The MP3 file format, enabling good-quality digital music to be freely distributed over the Internet, was threatening the foundations of the music industry. The record companies had to do something, and fast.

As mentioned at the beginning of this chapter, when a trade association tries to create standards, there are significant legal constraints on the kinds of standards that they can impose: They must be procompetitive, not anticompetitive. Thus, it was not possible for the RIAA and the record labels to simply designate some vendor's technology as the endorsed standard for secure digital music distribution.

Instead, SDMI tried to set up a framework on which open, procompetitive standards could be built. This was the long-term goal. However, SDMI also needed a short-term goal to help stanch the flood of pirated music on the Internet. The SDMI participants decided not to concentrate on PC software, but instead to focus on portable music player devices, such as the cheap MP3 players that were beginning to flood the market at that time. Their short-term goal was to produce a specification for portable music players by June 1999 that consumer electronic makers could use, and they wanted the latter to get SDMI-compliant player devices out onto the market in time for that year's Christmas season.

This goal was incredibly ambitious. To help achieve it, they hired as SDMI executive director Dr. Leonardo Chiariglione (pronounced "kyar-ee-LYOHN-eh"), a brilliant engineer from Telecom Italia who had chaired MPEG. A growing number of organizations, currently exceeding 200, joined the effort.

The first version of the SDMI portable device specification met its June 1999 deadline . . . almost. However, the 35-page document was not a specification that multiple manufacturers could implement with interoperability; it was too high-level. Think of a group tasked with inventing a new written and spoken language, with the objective of getting poets to write poetry in the language. They put out a description that defines nouns, verbs, adjectives, and rules for putting them together into sentences but says nothing about what alphabet to use or how to pronounce the words. Then they distribute this language description to poets and tell them to write poetry that everyone can read.

Thus the first version of the SDMI specification served as a statement of design principles rather than a blueprint for manufacturers, although it was sufficient for Phase I implementations (see the following section, "SDMI Technology"). A good summary of the design principles, as well as SDMI's market objectives, is in the PowerPoint presentation "Secure Digital Music Initiative: Creating a Digital Music Marketplace," available on SDMI's Web site at `www.sdmi.org/download/create_dig_mktplace.ppt`. The specification itself, along with other supporting documentation, is at `www.sdmi.org/port_device_spec_overview.htm`.

Along with the release of the specification came announcements by many consumer electronics makers of the impending release of SDMI-compliant products, planned to be in time for Christmas shopping in 1999. Announcements came from the likes of Diamond (makers of the Rio MP3 players), Creative Labs, Matsushita (Panasonic), Toshiba, Mitsubishi, Lucent, Sanyo, Philips, Sony, Thomson (RCA), and Audiovox. SDMI created a logo and a licensing program for these vendors and any others who would sign on.

SDMI technology

The specification covers portable devices (PDs), which are the music players themselves; portable media (PM), which are the memory devices that store the music, and Licensed Compliant Modules (LCMs), which are hardware or software devices that process audio files and feed them to players and distribution channels.

LCMs are the main focus. Their job includes these functions:

♦ Convey audio from various types of media to PDs.

♦ Check for pirated content by testing for the presence of a watermark.

♦ Package content for secure distribution by using encryption and watermarking.

♦ Implement whatever business rules are defined — for example, for collecting payment or usage information from the consumer.

SDMI agreed that, initially at least, certified players would have to be allowed to play open formats such as MP3. This was necessary to avoid alienating consumers and device makers alike.

Figure 6-5, taken directly from the specification, shows how LCMs work. An LCM tests to see if the content is in an SDMI-compliant encrypted form. If it is, the LCM passes the content on to the business rules interpreter and eventually to an SDMI-compliant player or media device. If it is not encrypted, the LCM checks for the presence of a watermark, which in this case is an audio signal beyond the spectrum audible by humans. If the watermark is there, the content is legitimate; if not, it is rejected as pirated. Content produced by an SDMI-compliant device has a watermark that disappears if the content is copied by a non-SDMI-compliant device.

LCMs also have the capability of repackaging content for SDMI-compliant redistribution. To do so, they assign unique certificates, insert watermarks, and encrypt the content before making it available to the distribution channel, whether that's a media device, a file on someone's computer, or the Internet.

The SDMI architecture proceeded in two phases. In Phase I, players play music in any format; only in Phase II would players implement the protection mechanisms described earlier. Phase I players simply detect the SDMI watermark and, after Phase II devices become available, tell users to upgrade to a Phase II device. Eventually, Phase I devices would reject SDMI-watermarked content. Phase II devices would have all the watermarking and encryption technology necessary to implement the SDMI architecture.

In August 1999, SDMI selected watermarking technology from Aris Technologies for Phase I. (Aris has since merged with competitor Solana to form Verance Corp.) SDMI began Phase II by issuing a call for proposals from technology vendors in February 2000, from which it received over a dozen responses. SDMI chose five finalists, whose names have not been made public.

SDMI issued a public challenge (called "HackSDMI") to break the security of the proposed solutions. This showed that they took important lessons from the cryptography field to heart: A cryptography-related standard is much more likely to catch on and endure if its algorithm is subject to public examination and testing instead of being kept secret.

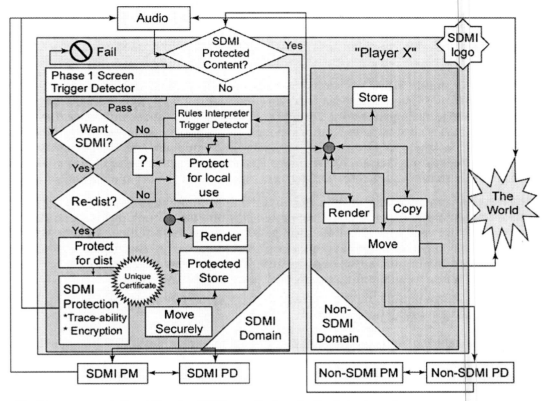

The ? box represents the ability of an SDMI-compliant application to implement a variety of licensed operations, including requiring an upgrade to Phase 2.

Figure 6-5: The SDMI licensed compliant module architecture.

However, when a team of people from Princeton University succeeded in cracking some of the proposed technologies in the fall of 2000, the RIAA lost its resolve. Prof. Edward Felten, the lead researcher on the Princeton team, had written a paper on how he cracked the SDMI solutions, which he intended to present at the Information Hiding Workshop conference in Pittsburgh, in April 2001. But instead of encouraging the publication of Felten's results as part of the natural process of strengthening SDMI's technology, the RIAA tried to muzzle him by invoking the Digital Millennium Copyright Act (see Chapter 3). He agreed not to deliver the paper at that particular conference, but the ensuing firestorm of media attention cast the RIAA in an unfavorable light. As a result, the RIAA backed down and let Felten deliver his paper at the USENIX Security Symposium in San Francisco in August 2001.

SDMI status

At this writing, SDMI has lost much of its momentum. Deadline after deadline has been missed. Despite all the announcements by consumer electronics makers, it appears that Sony is the only vendor that has actually marketed an SDMI-compliant device, the Sony VAIO Music Clip. The device is Phase I compatible, meaning that it functions as a generic digital music player.

The Phase II screening technology selection process concluded in early 2001 without a selection having been made. Around the same time, Leonardo Chiariglione resigned as executive director. SDMI continues on, but at this writing, has yet to appoint another leader. Functionally, SDMI is trying to move on by shifting its focus beyond portable music players to such devices as mobile phones, radios, and voice recorders — all devices that could play a part in the distribution of pirated music but have yet to do so.

What happened to impede SDMI's progress? Sources say that the main problem was fundamental conflicts of interest between the three constituencies: record companies, consumer device makers, and technology vendors. The latter, which included vendors of various flavors of DRM technology, wanted the specifications of their solutions to be endorsed as the standard so that they could sell their products immediately as "SDMI-compliant" and their competitors would have to retool their offerings. The resulting squabbles among technology vendors — however typical in technology standards initiatives — proved detrimental to progress.

Consumer electronics makers, meanwhile, did not want to be forced to produce devices that limited the types of music files that consumers could play; this would limit their appeal. The dichotomy of Phase I and Phase II enabled them to get a product to market quickly, but would have required them to put out two lines of products and, worse, would have required consumers to upgrade. Record companies had the opposite goal of the consumer electronics makers: They *did* want to limit music players' ability to play files under certain conditions.

The result was a virtual logjam. Each component of the industry had too much invested in the status quo to want to compromise.

Other recent events in the music industry put SDMI's future further in doubt. With important court decisions coming down in favor of the record labels, the shrinking market caps of many online music ventures, and the deals that the record labels have been doing with companies such as Napster, MP3.com, and myplay, the balance is shifting back to the record labels. They aren't particular about the need to use technology to protect their franchise; if they can get enough help through the legal system or the financial markets, they may no longer see the need for a technological solution.

Be that as it may, the record labels are taking matters into their own hands by launching subscription services that are based on existing DRM technology from Microsoft and RealNetworks: PressPlay, a joint venture of Sony and Universal, and MusicNet, which includes EMI, BMG, and Warners (the other three major labels). We discuss these in Chapters 2 and 7. It is possible that PressPlay and MusicNet will raise the hackles of antitrust regulators for reasons related to those stated in the section "The Role of Open Standards in DRM," earlier in this chapter. But otherwise, we believe that PressPlay and MusicNet represent the future – insofar as there is one – for online digital music.

Other Standards

We conclude this chapter with brief looks at a couple of other standards initiatives that are related to DRM, but which we believe will have less impact than the ones we have discussed in detail thus far.

eXtensible Media Commerce Language

The eXtensible Media Commerce Language (XMCL) was announced in June 2001 by RealNetworks, the vendor of streaming media technology, at the Streaming Media West trade show in Los Angeles. A Web site for the standard exists (www.xmcl.org), as does a draft specification (www.xmcl.org/specification.html).

XMCL, like XrML and ICE, is a technology for specifying content rights information based on the XML metalanguage. It is meant for describing "business rules" that govern access to content and the consideration for which that access is obtained – that is, rights models, as described in Chapter 4. XMCL is meant to be a standard language for communicating between DRM solutions and various systems, including e-commerce storefronts, payment systems, Web publishing, digital asset management, and customer relationship management systems. Although it was invented in the context of streaming media, XMCL was designed to apply to a wide range of content types and commerce models.

The most important top-level entity in an XMCL specification is the license. License specifications contain the following:

- Content metadata, including identification and keywords.

- A specification of the period during which the license is valid.

- Specifications of usage (render) rights, as well as copy and transfer (transport) rights, including rights extents.

The specification shows a compact design that is geared toward efficient implementation rather than comprehensiveness. It was presumably designed with RealNetworks' Media Commerce Suite in mind.

CROSS REFERENCE: See Chapter 7 for more on Media Commerce Suite.

From a purely technological standpoint, XMCL is a standard with its heart in the right place. It addresses the needs of technologists who have found XrML too heavyweight to implement and who are put off by the fact that an individual company, ContentGuard, holds patents to XrML. But more to the point, XMCL has been advanced by vendors who feel that XrML is really Microsoft's technology: As we point out in the section on XrML, earlier in this chapter, Microsoft is really the only vendor that has implemented XrML so far, although it's expressed its intention to advance it as an open standard.

RealNetworks has clearly been trying to rally companies around XMCL as an anti-Microsoft standard. A long list of companies became signatories to the press release that announced XMCL, including content providers (America Online, Bertelsmann, Clear Channel, EMI, MGM, Sony Pictures Digital Entertainment, and Starz Encore Group), technology vendors (Adobe, Artesia, Avid, eMotion, IBM, InterTrust, Rightsline, Sun Microsystems, and Virage), and various others. This makes XMCL yet another in the equally long list of "everyone against Microsoft" initiatives that have regularly appeared in the technology industry over the past years.

Unfortunately, very few such initiatives pan out. Of all the preceding press release signatories, we know of none that is actually working on its own implementations of XMCL, whether for in-house use or for its own product lines. A few that we talked to admitted that they contributed to the press release because they liked the *idea* of such a standard, not because they actually intended to devote any resources to implementing it.

Although the XMCL working group has stated its intentions to submit the specification to the World Wide Web Consortium (W3C) for ratification as an official Internet standard, we see XMCL losing what little momentum it had. At this writing, no updates have been posted to the original draft specification (dated June 19, 2001), no related product announcements have been made, and our attempts to get further information from the people responsible for XMCL at RealNetworks have not been productive. We suspect that XMCL will go the way of many well-intentioned initiatives in this ever-changing industry.

Open Digital Rights Language

The Open Digital Rights Language (ODRL) is the brainchild of Renato Iannella of IPR Systems, a vendor of digital asset management technology located in Sydney, Australia. Like XMCL, it is an XML-based language for expressing rights specifications that stays clear of implementation and rights enforcement issues.

ODRL contains an elegant rights-modeling language with components that map closely to the rights model elements discussed in Chapter 4:

- *Permissions*, including Usage, Reuse, and Transfer, which correspond roughly to render, derivative work, and transport rights as described in Chapter 4.

- *Constraints*, which correspond to the rights extents of Chapter 4.

- *Requirements*, which map to consideration in Chapter 4.

In addition, ODRL contains components that model rightsholders, their royalty obligations, and their agreements with other parties.

ODRL is more comprehensive in its rights modeling power than XMCL. In fact, it resembles a lighter-weight version of XrML, without some of XrML's features for security levels and other implementation-level concerns. It was clearly influenced by XrML's predecessor, DPRL, as well as by the massive metadata description language *<indecs>*.

> **CROSS REFERENCE:** See the section "Discovery metadata" earlier in this chapter for information on discovery metadata standards.

There is also an ODRL Web site (www.odrl.net) and a draft specification (www.odrl.net/0.9/ODRL-09.pdf) dated July 2001. However, ODRL appears to have gotten no traction outside of Australia and the Pacific Rim. Sponsors of the effort, in addition to IPR Systems, include two Australian intellectual property law firms, an E-book retail site that IPR built, and a Korean DRM startup vendor called ARPA (no relation to the Advanced Research Projects Agency of the U.S. Defense Department).

ODRL has been cited as influential by several organizations, including Hewlett-Packard Labs, the Open E-Book Forum, and Andersen Consulting (now Accenture), the latter in its study on eBooks for the Association of American Publishers. However, we do not expect ODRL to advance far beyond that in importance to the market.

World Wide Web Consortium

We conclude this section with a look at what the World Wide Web Consortium (W3C, www.w3.org) is doing about DRM. The W3C is, of course, the original governing body of the Web (insofar as any one organization could be said to govern it) and the ultimate arbiter of Web technology standards. DRM's ascent beyond the realm of publishers and other media companies into the mainstream of the Internet, which we believe is inevitable, is much more likely to happen through open standards if the W3C espouses them.

At this writing, several vendors and standards bodies have made presentations to the W3C or the unaffiliated Internet Engineering Task Force (IETF) to get them to endorse various DRM technologies as Internet standards. So far, nothing definitive has happened. The W3C held a workshop on DRM for the Web in Sophia Antipolis, the technology center in the south of France, in January 2001. People who delivered position papers at the workshop included representatives from DRM technology vendors, content providers, major technology firms, and standards bodies, as well as consultants and academics. Significantly, although most of the position papers espoused approaches that reflected their authors' own technologies, few of them took the position that DRM was antithetical to the original spirit of the Internet and, if espoused by the W3C, would induce a consumer backlash.

Since then, Renato Iannella of IPR Systems in Australia, author of the ODRL specification (see previous discussion), has been trying to gather support for a W3C DRM interest group. It remains to be seen how much momentum can be achieved. There is a fundamental conflict among people active in the W3C about whether DRM should even be considered a legitimate area of standardization at all. If that attitude prevails within the W3C, DRM standardization will fall to the narrower community of DRM technology vendors and content providers.

One thing is for sure: Standards are crucial. That is why we chose to go into so much detail about them in this book and why two of us have devoted significant chunks of our careers to working on them. We have more to say about the future and destiny of DRM standards in the final chapter of this book.

Chapter 7

Proprietary Core Technologies: The Heavyweights

This chapter discusses some of the most important proprietary core technologies in DRM from specific vendors. We present our generic DRM architecture in Chapter 5, which includes components such as repositories, packagers, DRM controllers, rendering applications, encryption algorithms, and watermarking schemes. In a perfect world, each of these components could be supplied by a number of different vendors, and the interfaces could be standardized, enabling complete DRM systems to be built that cobble together the best components for a given business situation.

Unfortunately, this standards-based Utopia hasn't been reached yet. It has been necessary to build end-to-end DRM solutions around component technologies, which make the components not very interoperable. For example, it's generally not possible to take Vendor A's encryption-based packaging technology and integrate it with Vendor B's rendering application.

As a result, there are three types of existing technologies that we would consider the "heavyweights" of DRM:

♦ DRM component technologies that have become de facto standards in certain market segments.

♦ DRM solutions from major vendors that are built around those vendors' file formats.

♦ DRM frameworks from major vendors that are designed to accommodate a variety of component technologies, now and into the future, and have gotten some traction in the marketplace.

We look at some of each of these in this chapter. Bear in mind that this chapter represents the status quo circa summer of 2001. Although it is unlikely that any of these vendors will be out of existence by the time you read this, remember that the industry is volatile, with developments taking place on a continual basis.

DRM Component Technologies

Although there is no such thing as a core DRM technology that is widely installed (compared, say, to rendering applications such as RealPlayer and Adobe Acrobat Reader), there are a few that have made some headway in niche markets or are well positioned to do so through distribution deals.

We discuss the following in this chapter, and these technologies aren't likely to disappear overnight:

- Image watermarking: Digimarc
- Audio watermarking: Verance
- Software packaging: Preview Systems

Image watermarking: Digimarc

Watermarking has succeeded in the market faster than encryption because it is far less intrusive to end users. The first type of digital content to see widespread use of watermarking was still images.

Digimarc Corp. (www.digimarc.com), of Tualatin, OR, makes technology that has become the de facto standard for still image watermarking. It has shipped its flagship PictureMarc technology since 1996. The story of how Digimarc developed PictureMarc reads like a textbook example of how a technology vendor should create a market around a core technology by integrating into users' tools and processes. Shortly after releasing PictureMarc, Digimarc shipped a Software Development Kit (SDK) that enables software tool developers to integrate watermark creation and detection into their applications. As we show in this chapter, many key tool vendors have done so, enabling Digimarc to achieve its present leadership position.

PictureMarc creates watermarks in still images that contain metadata about the images that are similar in nature to the types of metadata discussed in Chapter 5:

- **Identification metadata:** The image ID contains a unique identification number conceptually similar to the Digital Object Identifier (DOI) (see Chapter 6).
- **Discovery metadata:** Digimarc's watermarking scheme doesn't contain any discovery metadata, such as keywords or captions.

In addition, PictureMarc watermarks contain information about the image's rights, including IDs for the creator and distributor of the image, the year of copyright, and flags that specify whether the image has any restrictions on its use.

To use PictureMarc, you invoke a watermark insertion tool after you have scanned the image or created or modified it using a digital graphics program. Through Digimarc's SDK, vendors of several of the leading graphics programs have integrated watermark creation capabilities into their tools, including CorelDRAW, Adobe Photoshop, Micrografx Graphics Suite, and Equilibrium's DeBabelizer for processing images to be used on Web sites. In addition, these tools contain Digimarc's watermark detection tool, which lets them flag images with the flags that specify any usage restrictions. The resulting watermark is invisible to the naked eye.

Digimarc offers a Batch Embedder, which enables customers to embed watermarks into several images at once without having to go through a user interface. This has led to the adoption of ImageMarc watermarks by the two largest online stock image agencies, Getty Images and Corbis, as well as other online image sources such as Index Stock and Playboy.com. Digimarc also embedded its watermark technology into the FlashPix zoomable image format.

As mentioned in Chapter 5, the primary purpose of watermarks is to track usage of content through watermark detection. Presumably, if you own an image and you see a mysteriously similar image somewhere — say, in an ad in a magazine — you can scan it and have the Digimarc software test for a watermark that proves your ownership of the image. Digimarc's watermarks can survive some measure of conversion to analog (that is, print output) and back to digital again (that is, scanning).

However, that is quite a limited way of enforcing copyright. Digimarc tried to go one step better by automating the detection of watermarks in images on the Web. In 1997, it rolled out a system called MarcSpider that searches the entire Web for image files with Digimarc watermarks in them and reports on findings to content owners. MarcSpider uses a data feed from one of the major Web search engines, allowing it to crawl the Web looking for image files (in GIF, JPEG, and PNG format) and checking them for watermarks. MarcSpider continuously updates a database of watermarked image files and issues monthly reports from that database to the content owners identified in the watermarks.

MarcSpider finds unauthorized (or authorized) images, if they happen to be on the publicly accessible Web *and* if its Web-crawling technology can find them. MarcSpider won't find watermarked images under some circumstances, such as if the Web pages change too frequently or are password-protected. And it certainly won't find watermarked images if they are on hard drives or file servers that aren't attached to the Web. In other words, MarcSpider is better than nothing but doesn't approach encryption's capability to protect copyright; it merely serves as an "audit trail" to prove ownership.

Digimarc recognized this limitation and tried to address it by acquiring a company called NetRights in 1997. New Hampshire-based NetRights, one of the early encryption-based DRM solution vendors, originally attempted to create an online marketplace for creative artists' output. The acquisition didn't bear fruit, and NetRights's founder and chief scientist, Dr. John Erickson, now does DRM research for Hewlett-Packard Labs and is active on various DRM-related standards committees.

Having dominated watermarking in all aspects of the image creation and distribution value chain through successful partnerships with tool vendors and content distributors — and needing to grow its business substantially in the wake of a late-1999 initial public offering (NASDAQ: DMRC) — Digimarc began to look for additional business opportunities.

One such business opportunity was to tie print media to the Web using watermarks as the "string." Digimarc's MediaBridge, introduced in 2000, was a way of connecting printed images, such as ads in magazines, direct mail marketing, and even textbook covers and postage meter imprints, to Web pages. The way it works is that if a user sees an ad and wants to find more information, she holds it up to a Web camera. The camera detects the Digimarc watermark and sends a message to a Web browser — a URL that contains the metadata found in the watermark.. The Web site decodes the metadata, translating it into the address of a specific page on the site, and redirects the user to that page.

As a simple example, say that Voyage Bicycles has an ad for its latest 36-speed titanium mountain bike in the latest issue of the magazine *Cycle World.* The ad contains a picture of the bike with a watermark that has image ID 34987345. A cycling enthusiast, you pick up the latest *Cycle World* and see the ad. You want to find out more about the new bike, so you hold the ad up to your Web camera. The Web camera detects the watermark and passes a URL of the form `www.voyagebikes.com/.../ImageID=34987345` to your Web browser. Voyage Bicycles' Web site has a CGI script that interprets the image ID and directs your browser to the Web page for the new bike, where you can find out technical details, look at a 3D rendering of the bike, see what colors are available, find the nearest retailer, and so on.

The value of MediaBridge is supposedly that it makes it easy for users to get to specific pages on vendors' Web sites — for example, product purchase pages deep within e-commerce sites — without having to type in lengthy URLs. It's similar to the bar-code scanning technology that some newspapers use to associate Web content with printed articles. The success of the

MediaBridge technology depends on many factors: publishers agreeing to embed the watermarks in printed images, Web cameras containing watermark detection technology, and users actually using the cameras.

Toward this end, Digimarc managed to sign up several important magazine publishers as participants in MediaBridge and launched actual programs in the Hearst magazine titles *Popular Mechanics, SmartMoney,* and *Good Housekeeping,* as well as in *Wired.* Digimarc got its watermark detection technology embedded into Web cameras from Intel, IBM, and Creative Labs, composing almost half of the market for Web cameras, and it created watermark detection software that works with scanners that conform to the widespread TWAIN scanner and digital camera control standard. But the technology did not take off. According to an article in the April 1, 2001 issue of *The Seybold Report,* ". . . test runs all seem to be ending in wait-and-see decisions by publishers who have not found sufficient public interest or financial return to warrant wider rollouts."

Digimarc's other area of expansion is to other media formats, particularly audio and video watermarking. At the National Association of Broadcasters (NAB) 2001 conference, Digimarc announced a partnership with several of the leading makers of video playback equipment to build watermarking-based copy protection and broadcast monitoring solutions. It is too early to tell whether this partnership will lead to any products on the market.

Digimarc is bolstering its attempt to expand into the audio and video markets by extending its existing technology as well as its considerable patent portfolio. It is also waging a patent war against its principal competitor in the audio and video space, Verance Corp. (see the following subsection, "Audio watermarking: Verance"). The legal system must decide whether Digimarc's patents on image watermarking technology also apply to audio and video formats. Digimarc is pulling out all the stops to ensure that the decisions fall its way: After maxing out in the still image market, the company needs a major new revenue stream to keep its growth going.

Audio watermarking: Verance

Although still image watermarking has been around for several years, watermarking for audio formats is a more recent development. Most of the activity in audio watermarking has been prompted by the music industry, where the need to combat pirated content on the Internet is great and the Secure Digital Music Initiative (see Chapter 6) has given a boost to the technology.

Verance Corp., of San Diego, California, was formed in late 1999 as the merger of two principal competitors in the audio watermarking space: ARIS Technologies of Cambridge, Massachusetts, and Solana Technology Development Corp. of San Diego. Solana had, by that time, already made some headway into the digital music distribution market by licensing its Electronic DNA (E-DNA) technology to various software vendors, including Liquid Audio (see Chapter 11), which eventually replaced Solana's E-DNA with its own Liquid Watermark technology.

ARIS, meanwhile, received a major boost by having its MusiCode watermarking technology chosen by SDMI as the standard for SDMI Phase I, beating out Solana and several other competitors. In fact, it's fair to say that the SDMI decision forced the merger of the two competitors. The decision ostensibly united the five major recording labels (Universal, Sony, BMG, EMI, and Warner Bros.) behind the winning technology, leading the other vendors to believe that their opportunities would be sharply reduced. For SDMI purposes, ARIS — and later Verance — licensed its SDMI Phase I technology to all five labels, as well as to a company called PortalPlayer, which made secure music player hardware that it hoped to license to consumer electronics makers.

As mentioned in Chapter 6, SDMI Phase I was a transitional tactic on the part of the recording labels, as represented by the Recording Industry Association of America (RIAA). They wanted to fulfill their pledge to get SDMI-compliant products out on the market within their advertised deadlines, even though consumer electronics makers weren't ready to implement full-blown copyright-enforcing music players. Under Phase I, SDMI-compliant content has a watermark that simply says, "This is SDMI-compliant content." An SDMI Phase I player will just play the music, until such time as Phase II technology is available. At that point, the Phase I player will advise the user to upgrade to a Phase II player, and after a while, the Phase I player would presumably stop operating.

Verance also entered a proposal into the SDMI Phase II competition and became a finalist, but SDMI didn't choose a winner. Instead, SDMI is sticking with Phase I for now and has reaffirmed its selection of Verance's technology for that. Although it now looks like SDMI is on its way out, it has greatly enhanced Verance's visibility in the music community. Verance's watermarking technology is also the standard for DVD-audio, the portion of DVDs that holds audio material.

Like Digimarc, Verance's watermarking technology can embed identification numbers in content; these identification numbers can reference a database of rights metadata to enable rights transactions, as discussed in Chapter 4. Such identification numbers function like DOIs in the publishing world, as described in Chapter 6.

Verance's other significant product is ConfirMedia, which does for broadcasting roughly what Digimarc's MarcSpider does for images on the Web. ConfirMedia was launched in April 2001, at the same NAB conference in which Digimarc announced its own foray into audio and video watermarking. With ConfirMedia, content providers can monitor broadcast signals to confirm that certain audio clips aired. Verance has television and radio monitoring stations set up in the top 100 media markets in the United States. Content owners can embed Verance watermarks in their audio; ConfirMedia monitors detect the watermarks and measure the broadcasts.

The application of ConfirMedia with the biggest potential impact is in radio. As discussed in Chapter 1, ASCAP, BMI, and SESAC measure the airplay of songs in order to allocate music licensing fees from radio stations to performers and songwriters. In addition, magazines such as *Billboard* and *Friday Morning Quarterback (FMQB)* report radio airplay of hit songs in many genres. These organizations and others typically get reports from station program directors rather than actually measure airplay accurately, or they rely on tiny statistical samples: BMI, for example, requires stations to fill out logs of songs played on one day for each entire year. In other words, there is a lot of room for bad data and abuse in the way song airplay is currently reported.

A system such as ConfirMedia would let recording companies measure airplay accurately, thereby allowing artists to get the license fees and chart placements that they truly deserve. As far as ASCAP, BMI, and SESAC licensing fees are concerned, accurate measurement would be a boon to lesser-known artists, whose meager airplay tends not to appear in statistical samples and who, therefore, get no licensing fees at all instead of the modest ones to which they are entitled. This type of system would also eliminate the possibility of kickbacks from recording labels to radio stations for exaggerating about the airplay of certain specific songs.

In other words, ConfirMedia — or something like it — would do for radio broadcasting what SoundScan did for music retail in the 1980s, when it substituted actual record sales figures, based on bar codes scanned at cash registers, for the "Take my word for it" reports of record store owners. And just as SoundScan was vigorously opposed by some in the music distribution chain who had a vested interest in maintaining the status quo (such as the massive Tower Records retail chain), Verance is undoubtedly encountering resistance to ConfirMedia for airplay monitoring.

There are also logistical barriers to implementing ConfirMedia for the entire U.S. radio broadcasting industry. The main problem is that it would require that all music played by radio stations be watermarked with Verance's technology, a truly gargantuan undertaking. Despite that, SESAC became Verance's launch customer for ConfirMedia, agreeing to start using it in summer of 2001 and thereby confirming (pun intended) its potential for revolutionizing radio broadcasting.

ConfirMedia is of more near-term, pragmatic interest to radio and TV advertisers who want to ensure that their spots actually aired. Currently, broadcasters are required to issue affidavits, which are notarized documents that list dates and times when ads actually aired. If an ad that was scheduled didn't air, the broadcaster has to issue a "make-good" ad in compensation. But in many cases, the advertiser won't find out about a missed ad until it gets the affidavit, which is typically issued on a monthly basis. If the ad is of a time-critical nature — such as an ad for a holiday sale — the make-good ad will be far less valuable than the original ad.

ConfirMedia lets advertisers know immediately if an ad did or didn't air in several dozen cities simultaneously, allowing make-good ads to be issued during time-critical periods. It also enables advertisers to create special spots (or portions of spots, such as tag lines — for example, names of local retailers where a product is available) for certain markets, watermark them differently, and ensure that the right spots air in the right markets. In contrast to radio stations' libraries of music, it would be easy for advertisers to have their ads encoded with Verance watermarks before being sent to radio and TV stations.

All in all, Verance has found an exciting opportunity for watermarking in broadcast confirmation, rather than (or in addition to) Internet music distribution. For this and other reasons, Digimarc has been trying to muscle in on Verance's territory. As noted earlier, in "Image watermarking: Digimarc," Digimarc is also aggressively pursuing the broadcast monitoring market, although it is behind Verance in this area. Digimarc is trying to enhance its competitive position by suing Verance for patent infringement. At this writing, the U.S. Patent Office is deciding the case, with both sides claiming partial victory from the preliminary findings.

Software packaging: Preview Systems

Watermarking has become widespread in online distribution, especially of images, because of its lack of intrusiveness into the user's buying and viewing/playing experiences. Encryption-based DRM systems have been a much harder sell. As discussed in Chapter 5, they all require that users install special plug-in applications that act as DRM controllers and, in some cases, rendering applications. Distributing, installing, and using these plug-ins have all been problematic, both logistically and in terms of users' willingness to take extra steps to view or play content.

However, one market has been much quicker to adopt encryption-based DRM technology: the software market. Remember that software is just a collection of bits, just like any other type of content, and published software contains a lot of "regular" content as well, such as documentation and help files. Many software vendors put up e-commerce storefronts on the Internet to sell physically packaged software, and a few online retailers (such as buy.com, Egghead.com, and Amazon.com) set up shop to sell software from multiple vendors. Then, when broadband connections started to proliferate, it began to make sense to sell the software — which is typically in the tens or even hundreds of megabytes — in the form of digital downloads, eliminating the physical packaging entirely.

People who take the trouble to buy and install software are much less likely to be put off by such things as plug-ins and encryption. If you have to go through the rigmarole of installation — the InstallShield, the end-user license agreement, the "typical, minimal, and custom" options, the install directory, and most importantly, the user registration — you probably don't mind entering a decryption key or an account number as well. In fact, some vendors, such as Microsoft, make you enter a key (which it calls a product ID) when installing software from CD-ROMs as well. Furthermore, software vendors seem to have been more comfortable adopting encryption technology than have media companies.

So, while most of the early vendors of encryption-based DRM technology tried to concentrate on the publishing and image markets, a company called Portland Software (located in its namesake city in Oregon) focused on software. It released its encryption-based DRM technology, ZipLock, in 1996 and targeted it at the software industry (as well as at the music industry). Since then, ZipLock has become a de facto standard for secure software downloads, with marquis customers such as Symantec, Adobe, Corel, the distributor Ingram Micro, and the online retailer buy.com.

Meanwhile, another company, Preview Software of Sunnyvale, CA, had a technology around the same time called VBox that was complementary to ZipLock. VBox used encryption to package software files (executables, such as EXE files on Windows systems) for the purposes of easily creating trial versions — versions of the software that had certain features disabled or stopped working after a certain period of time or number of uses. Roughly speaking, VBox enabled "try before you buy," whereas ZipLock enabled the buy itself.

The two companies merged in 1998, forming Preview Systems.

The functionality that we call the DRM packager in the DRM reference architecture in Chapter 5 is embodied in the VBox Builder and the ZipLock Builder. These add try-before-you-buy and secure download capabilities, respectively. Preview's ZLM Builder creates a different type of package for music files. Both VBox and ZipLock packages use well-established encryption algorithms (RC4 and RC5 respectively; the latter is a faster alternative to DES, which is described in Chapter 5) licensed from RSA Security.

The ZipLock Server differs from other DRM repositories in that it allows for multitiered distribution. ZipLock was designed explicitly to enable software sales that involve manufacturers, distributors, and retailers. The ZipLock Server is useful for distributing volume-licensed software to corporate customers.

On the retailer side, the ZipLock Gateway is a set of functionality that integrates smoothly with popular e-commerce software packages such as Microsoft SiteServer, Broadvision, and Open Market Transact. Using the Gateway, it's possible for retailers to combine hard goods sales with digital downloads within a single user experience. Retailers can also set their own prices and insert their own graphics for branding purposes.

The VBox Download Manager creates the DRM-controlled executable on the customer side. The VBox Security Client acts like a DRM controller. The "rights model" for software is a bit different from the rights models for text, images, music, or video. To "render" the software is to execute it, the software acting as its own rendering application.

VBox takes this a step further, in effect controlling execute rights to specific features of the software that the vendor wants to make available as part of the trial package. With VBox Builder, software vendors can either go through a GUI-based packaging procedure that enables them to choose simple options (such as the length of the trial period), or they can use the VBox SDK to create an interface between the VBox and the application itself. This interface would enable precise control over features that are enabled, disabled, enabled for a period of time, enabled for a number of times, and so on.

As implied earlier, Preview Systems tried to extend its DRM technology from software to digital music distribution. In 1999, Preview jumped on the SDMI bandwagon and began to notch a few wins in the music space, starting with a joint announcement with EMI Records. Preview's music distribution technology was adopted by SuperTracks, which created an end-to-end paid-download service around it. This helped set the stage for Preview's successful December 1999 IPO (NASDAQ: PRVW).

In early 2000, SuperTracks licensed its Preview-powered music download service to the Musicland chain of record stores. A year later, Preview licensed its music technology to NTT, the Japanese telephone company, for use in an Internet music service.

However, Preview's music distribution technology didn't survive the loss of SDMI momentum and the increasing competition among DRM vendors in that space. In May 2001, Preview announced plans to shed its music technology and sell its original business, the software distribution technology, to Aladdin Knowledge Systems (NASDAQ: ALDN). Aladdin is the leading maker of several pre-Internet software security solutions, ranging from dongles to encryption schemes for offline media.

Single-Format DRM Solutions

The next important category of DRM solutions is those built (or acquired) by major vendors who control important content file formats. The two most important of these are Adobe's PDF and eBook format, and RealNetworks's RealMedia Secure for streaming audio and video. Microsoft also fits this category with its DRM systems for eBooks (Microsoft Reader .LIT format) and audio/video (Windows Media Player format), but because it is expanding its DRM technology so that it is applicable across all the media types that Microsoft supports, we treat Microsoft's technology as a DRM framework and examine it later in this chapter.

Documents and eBooks: Adobe

Together with its archrival Quark, Inc., Adobe Systems defines the market for graphics and desktop publishing, and it has done so for many years. In the mid-1990s, Adobe assumed a leadership role in the emerging market for electronically distributed documents by introducing the Portable Document Format (PDF) and its associated creator/reader application, Adobe Acrobat.

Acrobat got off to a slow start because of three factors: Adobe's reluctance to give away the Acrobat Reader in order to gain market share, the application's lack of tight integration with the Web browsers that were emerging at the time, and the format's lack of use in prepress processes. Adobe fixed the first two of these problems, and now PDF is the preferred format for many types of online documents, such as research reports and marketing brochures, that require better formatting than that which is available through HTML. More recently, PDF has been gaining in importance as a prepress format (supplanting PostScript), and even more recently, Adobe has been working hard to position PDF as the basis for eBooks.

When DRM solutions first came out on the market, their main focus was on text-and-image documents (as opposed to audio, video, or other formats). Of all the formats used for documents, PDF was a natural for DRM technology: PDF is a read-only format, thereby providing some implicit rights restrictions; the Acrobat Reader has a plug-in architecture that allows for DRM components to be added in; and PDFs are designed so that they can be generated from any document creation tool, thus enabling publishers to easily convert their existing material.

By 1998 or so, there must have been half a dozen DRM vendors with a PDF plug-in solution, every one of them trying to be licensed or acquired by Adobe. But in February 2000, Adobe introduced its own DRM solution for Acrobat, Adobe PDF Merchant. PDF Merchant was a fairly lightweight encryption-based solution that enabled publishers to charge for rights to PDF documents such as Print and View. Along with this, Adobe introduced a feature called Web Buy, which shipped with Acrobat Reader. Web Buy connected PDF files with e-commerce transaction servers, so a user who downloaded an encrypted PDF file could easily purchase a decryption key and read the file. Unfortunately, Web Buy failed to catch on in the market any faster than the third-party plug-in solutions.

Adobe entered the eBook market in 2000 through partnerships with Waltham, Massachusetts–based Glassbook, Inc., which made eBook reader software that read DRM-packaged PDFs and a server component called Glassbook Content Server, and another Boston-area vendor called Softlock, which changed its name to Digital Goods and then went under in May 2001.

Adobe got Simon & Schuster and Stephen King to agree to publish the best-selling author's novel *Riding the Bullet* in PDF format only. Adobe also became an eBook technology provider to Barnes & Noble's Web site (www.bn.com), whereas Microsoft put its focus on a partnership with its Seattle neighbor, Amazon.com, to sell eBooks in its .LIT format. (The two online book retailers now support both formats.) Adobe also struck a deal with Lightning Source, the print-on-demand subsidiary of book distributor Ingram Industries, to make eBook versions of many of Lightning Source's titles available in PDF.

But Adobe's biggest leap forward in the eBook market was its acquisition of Glassbook, which it timed to be announced at the Seybold publishing technology conference in August 2000. During the remainder of that year, Adobe retooled Glassbook's reader and server software, and in January 2001, Adobe released Adobe Acrobat eBook Reader and Adobe Content Server.

Adobe Content Server

Adobe Content Server is really a merger of Adobe's legacy PDF Merchant and the Glassbook Content Server technology. Its main components are a repository (content server database), packager (packaging module), a fulfillment server that distributes content upon user purchase, and a module called GBLink, which links e-commerce sites with fulfillment servers.

The repository can be any standard (ODBC-compliant) database, but it must be certified by Adobe before it can be used. Adobe generates digital certificates from a certificate authority (see Chapter 5) and installs them on the Content Server.

Figure 7-1 shows the packaging module. Notice that one of the pieces of metadata that it requires is a thumbnail of the book cover, which is one of several features of Content Server that facilitates use by eBook retail sites. The packaging module can create two types of packaged eBooks: PDF Merchant, using Adobe's proprietary DRM, and eBook Exchange (EBX), a putative standard that was proposed by the Open E-Book Forum but eventually abandoned.

The EBX standard lets publishers specify these rights:

♦ Read the book, with a time interval.

♦ Copy content from the eBook to the clipboard on the user's machine (a specific number of copies or time interval).

♦ Print pages from the eBook (a specific number of pages or time interval).

♦ Lend the eBook, plus rights to allow borrowers to lend it further.

EBX packaging lets you specify the length of the encryption key. There is little reason not to choose a long key length.

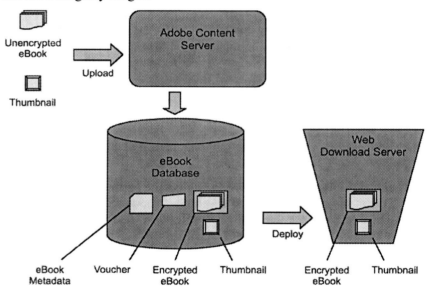

Illustration is courtesy of Adobe Systems Incorporated.

Figure 7-1: The Adobe Content Server packaging module.

PDF Merchant packaging requires that the publisher have an ID and a lock file (containing a digital signature), which can be obtained from Adobe. PDF Merchant rights are different from EBX rights; they include these:

♦ Print

♦ Copy

♦ Edit

♦ Annotate

♦ Export to another format

♦ Change any of these rights

For both PDF Merchant and EBX packaging, license generation is done at packaging time. The EBX term for a license is a *voucher.* Licenses are sent to users after purchases are complete, as explained shortly.

To sell eBooks, Adobe Content Server follows the process shown in Figure 7-2. The complexity of this process is necessary because it allows for the decoupling of e-commerce sites (bookstores) and fulfillment services so that they can be separate entities.

The GBLink module integrates e-commerce server software with the fulfillment server by providing query strings that identify packaged eBooks. The e-commerce server passes GBLink information about the eBook that was sold, along with a public key that identifies the selling bookstore as legitimate; GBLink returns an order entry URL that contains the location of the fulfillment server. The e-commerce server then sends the fulfillment server the order URL, along with the site's bookstore key; an ID for the eBook, which can be an ISBN, DOI, or other type; the time and date of the information; whether the eBook is PDF Merchant or EBX format; a digital signature (to provide tamper resistance); and other information.

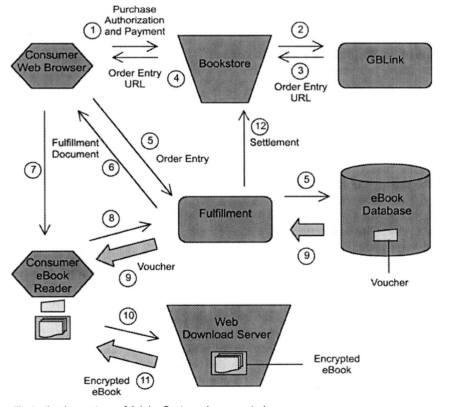

Illustration is courtesy of Adobe Systems Incorporated.

Figure 7-2: The Adobe Content Server fulfillment process.

After the fulfillment server has the request, it generates a fulfillment document for the user's eBook reader, which specifies the eBook requested along with a purchase authorization. The eBook reader sends the fulfillment document to the fulfillment server, which sends back a license that can be permanently associated with the actual eBook file. After this is done, the eBook reader can finally download the eBook content.

InterTrust partnership

Apart from Content Server, there are still several DRM vendors that have implemented Acrobat plug-ins. Of those, InterTrust is the most important. While building up its position in the eBook market, Adobe began to work with InterTrust to integrate its wide-ranging DRM solution with Acrobat Reader (which is a different application from Acrobat eBook Reader, the former Glassbook Reader). The two companies became technology providers to DigiHub, a now-defunct DRM service provider within PricewaterhouseCoopers, which the large consulting firm started to bolster its financial investment in InterTrust.

As noted in the section "DRM Frameworks," later in this chapter, InterTrust has a version of its Rights|Desktop technology called DocBox, which is implemented as an Acrobat plug-in and ships with every CD-ROM copy of Acrobat Reader 5.

In other words, Adobe is pursuing two different DRM strategies, one focused on eBooks, the other focused on plain PDF documents. The normal PDF format serves different markets, such as product brochures, research reports, corporate documents, technical white papers, forms, and legal documents. Regardless of this, Adobe will need to prevent consumer confusion by somehow consolidating its client software and its DRM technology into one strategy. Adobe has finally taken the step of endorsing a PDF plug-in vendor (InterTrust) by bundling it with Acrobat Reader. The company is aware of the need to consolidate its DRM technology strategy.

Streaming media: RealNetworks

RealNetworks was a pioneer in streaming audio whose CEO, Rob Glaser, was a former Microsoft executive. It started out in the mid-1990s as Progressive Networks and introduced its RealAudio format. Later on, it expanded to video with the RealVideo format and consolidated the two formats under the name *RealMedia.* Through sheer persistence, aggressiveness, and the quality of its technology, RealNetworks managed to vault past the several startup companies that had entered the streaming video market before it did, such as Vivo, Xing, VXtreme, and Graham Technology Solutions. The company went public in late 1997 (NASDAQ: RNWK). (It subsequently acquired two of its erstwhile competitors, Xing and Vivo.)

RealMedia and its client application RealPlayer constitute the most popular streaming media format today, despite Microsoft's efforts to unseat it with its Windows Media Player. RealNetworks has been looking for ways to expand its business beyond providing server software, client software, and network infrastructure services. In particular, it has made various attempts to become a content portal (the Web site Real.com and the RealJukebox application) that aggregates audio and video from various content providers, but without much success. In fact, RealNetworks got into some trouble in 1999 over privacy violations, when (as a class-action lawsuit alleged) it tried to snoop on users' music listening habits.

RealNetworks's latest strategy is to enter the DRM market as a partner of three of the five major recording companies, BMG, Warner Brothers, and EMI, in their MusicNet online initiative. RealNetworks has a financial stake in MusicNet, and the service will deliver audio exclusively in RealPlayer format. Although RealNetworks has had technology to enable pay-per-view of video and audio streams, which have mainly been used for high-profile live events (Webcasts), it has not had the technology to distribute streaming media securely nor any technology for controlling rights to downloaded content. As mentioned in Chapter 5, currently there is little need to protect streaming media from piracy, but there will be in the future as broadband Internet connections become more ubiquitous.

To fill this technological gap, and therefore to make RealNetworks more attractive to the major recording labels in the post-Napster era, RealNetworks acquired Rockville, MD–based Aegisoft Corp. in January 2001. Aegisoft was one of two companies focused on the encryption-based protection of streaming media; the other, PassEdge, was acquired by InterTrust in December 2000. RealNetworks integrated Aegisoft's MediaShield system with its own technology; the result is RealSystem Media Commerce Suite.

Media Commerce Suite works as an add-on to RealNetworks's existing server and client products, RealSystem IQ and RealPlayer, respectively. In place of RealMedia (.rm) files, the RealSystem packager creates RealMedia Secure (.rms) files. The files can sit on a streaming server or be distributed through downloads, on CD-ROM, DVD, and so on; however, playback is always done in a streaming fashion.

Media Commerce Suite includes another component called RealSystem License Server, which accepts purchase requests from the publisher's e-commerce server and creates licenses for it to send to the end user. When the end user has a license, she can then retrieve the content and, after the server validates the license (for example, making sure that the license hasn't expired), play it. The license contains the key necessary to decrypt the secure file.

RealMedia Secure files contain metadata, including a unique identifier (Globally Unique ID, or GUID) that is used to bind licenses to content, as well as user-defined metadata for discovery and other purposes. Although RealNetworks isn't specific about the encryption algorithms used, they are public (not proprietary) algorithms.

Users must download a piece of software called Media Commerce Upgrade for RealPlayer to play RealMedia Secure files. The Media Commerce Upgrade acts as a DRM controller in conjunction with the RealPlayer rendering application. Licenses bind a RealPlayer with Media Commerce Upgrade to a machine, not to a user. When a user tries to play a RealMedia Secure file and has RealPlayer but not the Media Commerce Upgrade, the Upgrade is seamlessly downloaded and installed.

RealNetworks Media Commerce Suite will surely become widespread in the months and years to come because of the dominance of RealNetworks in the streaming market; in the first half of 2001 alone, RealPlayer 8, with the DRM controller capability, was downloaded 15 million times.

DRM Frameworks

What constitutes a DRM framework? Refer to the generic DRM architecture (see Figure 5-1 in Chapter 5). A framework can be one of two things, which are roughly complementary: One is a suite of technology that implements DRM packaging and controlling functionality and that can integrate, via SDKs and other interfaces, with various different standard components in digital media and e-commerce, such as rendering applications, repositories, e-commerce packages, and so on. The other is a services offering that provides back-end functions for DRM deployments, such as repositories, e-commerce, and user authentication.

Early DRM systems generally didn't have SDKs: They were monolithic, end-to-end solutions that weren't designed to interoperate with other components. Nowadays, that's not a formula for success. The days of monolithic systems are long gone; in today's networked age, a new technology is never successful in the market unless it can integrate with technologies that customers are already using. This is especially true of DRM, which involves so many different types of systems.

Yet there are two downsides to creating SDKs instead of monolithic applications. First, designing good SDKs takes time, money, and expertise in system architecture in addition to expertise in the new technology. Second, SDKs must be designed to integrate with various types of third-party components; this means that the SDK builders must develop partnerships with those third parties to ensure that the integration is effective, as well as to jointly market and sell the new technology.

In other words, creating a good SDK requires significant investments of time, money, and staff. It's unlikely that a small startup will have as much of these as a large, existing vendor. Furthermore, if the technology is really going to define and dominate a new market, the vendor must be able to build successful relationships with integration partners — in the case of DRM, with vendors of Web server,
e-commerce, content creation, content rendering, and other types of software. Established vendors simply have a much better chance of building such relationships than startups do: Their names are attractive, and they may already have relationships in place that they can leverage.

This is not to say that startups have no chance against the Big Guys. But it does mean that, all else being equal, the major vendors have a better chance of becoming de facto standards in the DRM market or in other markets. Of course, a major vendor can adopt a startup's technology by licensing, marketing, and distributing it or acquiring the company outright. Developments such as this are happening in the DRM market on a monthly basis.

The second kind of DRM framework, the services offering, is a type of business whose success depends primarily on operational excellence, including a robust infrastructure and excellent customer support. It also depends on relationships with third-party technology firms, with whose products the service provider must integrate.

We start by examining one of the latter kinds of frameworks, from Reciprocal, followed by frameworks from InterTrust and Microsoft.

Reciprocal

Reciprocal, Inc., is the leading service provider in digital rights management. Its operational framework can integrate, but is independent of, specific DRM component technologies. This is a market position that should allow Reciprocal to survive the inevitable DRM format wars that will continue for the next couple of years.

Reciprocal's background

Reciprocal began life within the Japanese company Softbank Holdings, when Softbank wanted a means of distributing software securely to customers. Softbank built a system for doing this that included the InterTrust DigiBox DRM packaging technology and a back-end server farm.

Softbank spun the company out in 1996 under the name Rights Exchange, Inc. It changed its name to Reciprocal in March 1999 upon receiving a major investment from Microsoft and entering into a strategic partnership with the software giant. Shortly afterward, the Reciprocal acquired a group from within AT&T called a2b, which had been developing technology for secure music distribution. Reciprocal created two divisions: Reciprocal Publishing and

Reciprocal Music. Later, the divisions merged into one, although the company recognizes three distinct vertical markets: publishing, music and entertainment, and software.

Reciprocal Music began working with a number of music companies, including recording labels (the majors BMG and Sony, among others), retailers (the giant chain HMV), and marketing companies. Just as importantly, the company struck a deal with SoundScan, the definitive measurer of music sales, to count sales of digital downloads made through Reciprocal's service. It also announced a partnership with Loudeye Technologies, a service bureau that does digital encoding of audio and video, to provide audio-encoding services for Reciprocal Music customers.

Meanwhile, the company began to position itself away from the InterTrust DRM technology. Reciprocal had always maintained that it was capable of integrating any DRM system, but it took a while before Reciprocal actually implemented support for something other than InterTrust: Its integration with InterTrust proved to be too tight to be able to easily adapt it to other DRM systems. It may have become more necessary to lessen iReciprocal's dependence on InterTrust because of Microsoft's equity stake: InterTrust and Microsoft were becoming competitors in the music space.

In early 2000, Reciprocal formed a joint venture with Xerox called ePCS, for Electronic Publishers Clearinghouse Service. EPCS integrated Xerox's ContentGuard DRM technology (before Xerox spun it out into ContentGuard, Inc., which exited the DRM technology business in August 2001) with Reciprocal's back end. The service quickly landed pilot eBook distribution projects with major book publishers, including John Wiley & Sons and Houghton Mifflin.

Since then, Reciprocal has done projects with several more major book publishers, including Pearson Education, Random House, HarperCollins, Time Warner Books, and McGraw-Hill, on its own. Most of these projects involve distribution of eBooks. It has made a recent foray into the small-to-medium-size publishing market through a partnership with Texterity, Inc., a company that has tools to automate the creation of eBooks from legacy text formats.

Reciprocal has continually added support for more DRM technologies, including the following:

- Adobe PDF Merchant (now discontinued)
- Adobe Content Server (see "Documents and eBooks: Adobe," earlier in this chapter) for PDF eBooks
- Microsoft Windows Media for audio/video files (see "Microsoft," later in this chapter)
- Microsoft Digital Asset Server for Microsoft eBooks (see "Microsoft")
- Preview Systems technology for software distribution (see "DRM Component Technologies," earlier in this chapter)
- Franklin EbookMan format
- IBM Electronic Media Management System (EMMS; see Chapter 11)
- The DRM technology built into DataPlay, a consumer digital media storage device from DataPlay, Inc., that should be out by early 2002

In early 2001, Reciprocal landed the deal that most of the publishing-oriented DRM vendors had been coveting for some time: a partnership with Qpass (see Chapter 12). Qpass is a service that provides paid downloads of unencrypted content from the archives of some of the most important newspapers in the world, including the *New York Times,* the *Los Angeles Times, USA Today,* and the *Wall Street Journal.*

Back in 1999, Qpass had succeeded where DRM vendors failed: Newspaper readers were willing to pay for downloads of archived material, but neither they nor the newspaper companies themselves were willing to put up with the technological inconveniences of encryption-based DRM. But now that DRM is becoming more mainstream, e-commerce transaction costs are going down, and newspapers are looking to bolster online revenue in the face of unprofitable Web divisions, Qpass's customers began demanding support for DRM. In the Reciprocal-Qpass partnership, Qpass continues to provide paid download services and manage end-user accounts, while Reciprocal manages services that are specifically related to DRM.

Digital Clearing Service

Reciprocal's main offering is the Digital Clearing Service (DCS). DCS is a suite of online and support services built around the DRM technologies listed previously. In some respects, DCS is like a layer of abstraction built on top of those DRM technologies; the DCS documentation explains the service using terms that are common across the digital rights management field. Reciprocal has also built some technology that sits on top of and spans the various DRM systems, such as its offer management systems. In other respects, DCS is a service offering that depends on robust 24/7 operations and good customer support for its success.

Figure 7-3 shows the different modules that Reciprocal DCS comprises. Essentially, DCS acts as an intermediary between publishers and users, managing publishers' rights, transactions, and (sometimes) content in the same way in which an Internet service provider (ISP) manages its customers' Web sites or in which an e-mail outsourcer such as WebBox or 123Mail manages its customers' e-mail. The vogue term for this type of vendor, circa 1999-2000, was an *application service provider (ASP),* but that term went out of fashion when many of the highly capitalized ASP startups went under.

The best way to describe what Reciprocal DCS does is to discuss the sequence of events that take place when a publisher's customer wants to use content that is managed by DCS. A user must first create an account with Reciprocal. This can be done in one of two ways: The first way is for the user to go directly to a page on Reciprocal's Web site and fill out a registration form. Users need to do so only once: Typically, they do this the first time that they try to access an item of content that is distributed through Reciprocal. Users need to supply only a username, password, password reminder, e-mail address, and country of residence. Further demographic information can be collected later in the process.

The other way to create user accounts is through a recently added feature called *silent registration,* which enables publishers to send Reciprocal information about users, behind the scenes, that they may have already collected — thus sparing users the inconvenience of having to register again and giving publishers more control over information about their customers. It's also possible for all customers of a given publisher to use a single account with Reciprocal, although that makes it impossible for Reciprocal to track individual customers' use of content.

After a customer has registered with Reciprocal (whether explicitly or silently), she can place orders for content, either on the publisher's own Web site or on a site that Reciprocal runs for the publisher, called a Reciprocal storefront. If the publisher uses its own Web site to process orders, it communicates the details of the orders to Reciprocal using an XML protocol called Reciprocal Commerce Access Protocol. This enables a system integrator (such as Reciprocal's own Professional Services Organization) to integrate Reciprocal's order-processing system with the publisher's e-commerce software; however, Reciprocal doesn't provide any Plug-and-Play integration with any of the popular e-commerce packages. Publishers will also use the Commerce Access Protocol to do silent registration and to pass users' requests for order status information to Reciprocal.

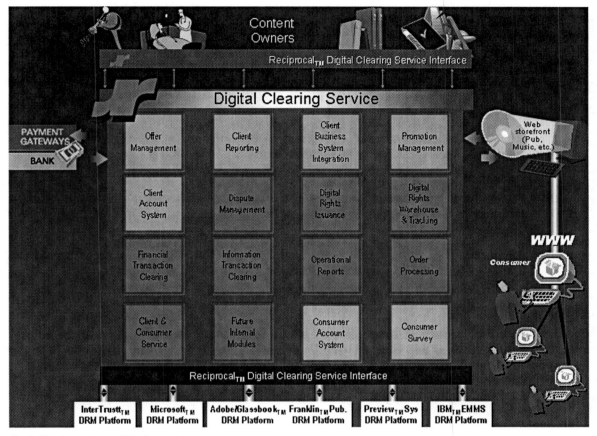

Illustration is courtesy of Reciprocal, Inc.

Figure 7-3: The architecture of Reciprocal's Digital Clearing Service.

If the publisher doesn't want to use its own Web site to process orders, Reciprocal can maintain a set of offers (HTML pages with product details) that the publisher wants to make available; the publisher creates and updates these through a Web-based user interface.

Reciprocal provides a few optional features that can be used during order processing: One of these is a survey that publishers can give to users before payment is processed, which enables publishers to collect more demographic information than the minimal set necessary to generate a Reciprocal user account. Reciprocal offers a standard survey form that asks a user for his full name, postal address, age, gender, and occupation. (The last three are optional.) Publishers can create customized surveys as well, especially if they want to use DCS to distribute content where the "payment" is the supplying of personal information rather than cash. If a publisher wants to create its own survey, it is responsible for creating the HTML form that the user fills out and for collecting the data.

The next step in processing orders is to process payment (if any). Publishers can do their own payment processing, or Reciprocal can do it for them. If Reciprocal does it, Reciprocal must ask for and store users' credit card numbers. It will calculate U.S. sales tax and, if desired, send a receipt e-mail to the user confirming the purchase.

Permits

When the order is complete, Reciprocal sends the user a license, or in its terminology, a *permit.* This is simply the license generated by whatever DRM technology is involved; hence, permits' properties and behaviors vary. For example, some tie the file to a machine, using an ID number for the machine that Reciprocal generates by "sniffing" the machine for various hardware attributes; others (such as licenses for Microsoft Reader format files) tie files to instances of the Microsoft Reader software instead. (See the subsection "Microsoft," later in this section, for details.)

Licenses have a few different ways of describing rights extents, or as Reciprocal calls them, *validity periods.* Reciprocal defines these rights extents:

- ♦ **Permanent:** The license never expires.
- ♦ **Fixed:** The license is valid for a fixed interval defined by a start date and an end date.
- ♦ **Counted use:** The license is valid for N uses of the content; not all DRM technologies support this.
- ♦ **Anchored:** The license is valid for a certain period of time after the license is created (regardless of when the user actually uses the content for the first time).

Reciprocal also supports a territory extent, which enables publishers to restrict distribution of content to a given geographic area, such as the United States.

Separating the license from the content file allows for a form of superdistribution (see Chapter 4). If User A sends an encrypted content file to User B, User B has to acquire her own license in order to use the file. If User B tries to open the file, the rendering application/DRM controller will take her to a Web page where she can purchase the license. Note that this works only for certain DRM technologies whose DRM controllers support this functionality; it doesn't work for Adobe and Microsoft eBook formats, nor for IBM EMMS. None of the formats supported by Reciprocal support the type of superdistribution that allows User A to resell content to User B and make a profit on it.

On the server side, Reciprocal defines *permit classes,* which are duplicate representations of the rights metadata in licenses. They are used to generate licenses (permits) at purchase time and to verify licenses when they are invoked. It is possible to use a single permit class for more than one content file — for example, for all tracks on an album or all modules in a curriculum. However, Reciprocal doesn't support permit classes that cover files of more than one type, such as Microsoft Windows Media Player for a music album and Adobe PDF for the album's cover art.

In most cases, the download of the content follows after the license has been issued; the exception is licenses for Microsoft format downloads, in which case the customer must go to another URL where she can download the file. Reciprocal doesn't supply DRM controllers to decrypt content files; that is the domain of the particular DRM technology chosen.

By default, the Web pages that Reciprocal provides to do order processing are branded with Reciprocal's logo, graphics, and so on. Reciprocal will let publishers substitute their own graphic identities, but only up to a point. Reciprocal can also translate the order-processing pages into a number of languages other than English.

Other services

Reciprocal provides various services that go beyond simply running DRM systems for publishers. It provides customer service for users as well as for publishers. It issues periodic reports to publishers on content sales, transactions, permits issued, and so on. Reciprocal also provides an infrastructure for distributing offline content on media such as CD-ROMs and DVDs. Toward that end, Reciprocal recently announced a partnership with Iomega that will allow downloaded content to be bound to Iomega portable storage devices, such as its Zip and Jaz drives.

InterTrust

InterTrust Technologies, Inc., of Santa Clara, CA, was in many ways the first digital rights management technology company. It began life as Electronic Publishing Resources (EPR) in 1990, at least four years before the Internet became known as a commercial distribution channel, and even longer before the idea of DRM was discussed among publishers. EPR's original aim was to develop a complete end-to-end solution for protected content delivery, which included a hardware component on the client side.

EPR operated in stealth mode for many years, spending tens of millions of dollars in developing a formidable war chest of intellectual property, which included many patents on the basic mechanisms of DRM. It also attracted some of the top consultants in the field, including Robert Weber and Douglas Armati, to executive positions. In 1997, EPR changed its name to InterTrust and began to publicize itself.

InterTrust went to market with a set of software technologies for Internet-based delivery of content onto Windows PCs. The client components were a DRM controller called InterRightsPoint and a packaging format called DigiBox. DigiBox, along with IBM's Cryptolope, was one of the original packaging formats of DRM. It could hold content in any format, and like other early DRM formats, it bundled rights metadata (license terms) along with the content. InterTrust's server-side components included InterTrust Commerce, an e-commerce server, and a disjoint set of packagers for publishers (Flying Media), music companies (PowerChord), and software vendors (SRM Packager).

Yet the InterRightsPoint and DigiBox technologies had significant obstacles to building an installed base. The main one was the size of the InterRightsPoint client — often a 5MB download in an era when almost all consumer Internet access was over dial-up lines. One reason for the large size was that InterRightsPoint was designed to be self-contained so that access could be controlled on the client side and didn't depend on communication with a server over the Internet. Another reason that it was difficult for InterTrust to establish an installed base was the overhead of the DigiBox file format. The publishing industry in particular was reluctant to adopt technology for which the file downloads were many times the size of the actual content involved.

As a result, in 1999 InterTrust turned up its marketing machine and turned to the music industry. Its IPO in October of that year (NASDAQ: ITRU) enabled InterTrust to spend a lot of money on two things that would help it get its message out: marketing and distribution. It marketed itself heavily to the music industry, which was reeling from the impact of pirated music in MP3 format on the Internet and just starting to get behind the SDMI standards initiative (see Chapter 6). Among other marketing tactics, the company took out full-page ads in *Billboard* magazine, the music industry's bible.

InterTrust also used its capital to finance distribution deals that would make its InterRightsPoint client easier to obtain than through Internet download. It sought out vendors of digital content-related software whose products were very widely distributed and attempted to get them to bundle InterRightsPoint with their offerings.

It is likely, though unconfirmed, that InterTrust paid dearly to get its distribution deals. Apart from financial considerations and the inherent worth of its technology, however, InterTrust's primary value to other software vendors was that it wasn't Microsoft. Even as early as 1999, it was clear to many vendors that Microsoft had an opportunity to own DRM as well as the rest of the technology for distributing and rendering digital media. Microsoft had started down the road to its own DRM solutions with Windows Media Player (see the subsection "Microsoft"). Other vendors of digital content technology needed to aggregate their offerings to mount a credible challenge to Microsoft.

One vendor that fit InterTrust's needs and saw the potential impact of Microsoft on the DRM market was America Online. Before its historic merger with Time Warner, AOL agreed to license InterTrust's technology on broad terms. The most important result of the agreement was AOL's bundling of InterRightsPoint with AOL 6 distributions on CD-ROM — although as an optional extra, not part of the default installation. This alone meant that millions of AOL users could install InterTrust's technology right off the CD-ROM, although they would have to take additional steps to do so.

The version of InterRightsPoint included with AOL is a plug-in to the Winamp music player that AOL uses. However, AOL seems to have made no effort to package any of its content, or that of its content partners, in the DigiBox format. Furthermore, Warner Brothers Records, now part of AOL Time Warner, joined with BMG and EMI in choosing RealNetworks's Media Commerce Suite over InterTrust's technology for their MusicNet digital service.

InterTrust's other key software distribution partner is Adobe, which has included a variant of its latest technology called DocBox in the Acrobat 5 distribution. We discuss DocBox in more detail in the following subsection, "Rights|System."

Rights|System

In July 2001, InterTrust introduced its new technology architecture and product suite, which it calls Rights|System. Rights|System is almost completely new technology; it is designed to position InterTrust with the broadest possible set of offerings in the DRM space.

Figure 7-4 shows the major components of Rights|System, which consists of packaged software products and APIs for building Rights|System components into other software. Rights|Packager is the DRM packaging component. It has two versions, one for downloadable files, the other for streaming media. Rights|Packager creates licenses, called Rights|Packs, which exist separately from the encrypted content.

For encryption, Rights|Packager uses several published algorithms, including AES (described in Chapter 5) to encrypt the content in a key length that is configurable up to 128 bits. Rights|Packager also uses 1024-bit asymmetric (public/private) key encryption to encrypt the AES keys, and it uses SHA-1 (Secure Hash Algorithm) to provide digital signatures for tamper resistance.

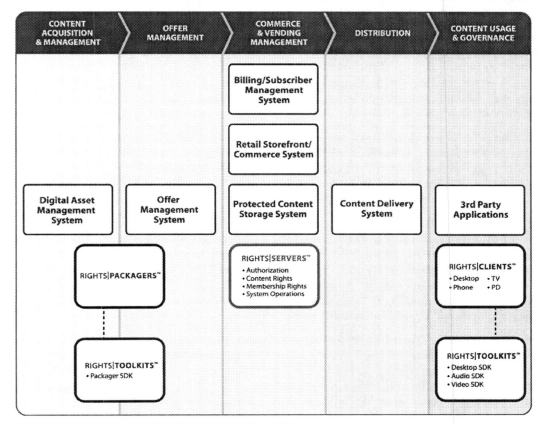

Illustration is courtesy of InterTrust Technologies Corporation.

Figure 7-4: InterTrust Rights|System components and the DRM value chain.

Rights|System has four different server components, which are called Rights|Servers. The most central of these is the System Operations Server, which manages user and client hardware identification, encryption keys, and software distribution, and it provides a user interface for administrative tasks.

The Authorization Generator and Content Rights Server work together to enable users to exercise rights to content. The Authorization Generator is called by a content provider's distribution system, such as a Web storefront or subscription system. It generates *authorizations*, which are like vouchers or receipts that contain identifying information about what the user has purchased or has rights to do. The user's client sends the voucher to an InterTrust Content Rights Server, which authenticates the authorization and issues a Rights|Pack, or license. The Rights|Pack resides on the client devices and lets the user access the content. Rights can be conferred on specific hardware devices, or they can be conferred on *certificates,* which bind user identities to more than one device (for example, a desktop computer and a portable music player). Content providers can specify how many devices a user can include under a single license.

The remaining server component is the Membership Rights Server, which content providers can use to maintain membership-based access to sets of content, supporting business models such as subscriptions and special promotions. It maintains a database of members along with their privileges, as well as content grouped into sets. InterTrust has realized that the most popular business models that are likely to emerge from the music industry's fracas with sites such as Napster and MP3.com are paid-subscription models rather then piecemeal paid downloads, so it is providing products to support such models rather than leave that to generic e-commerce or application server vendors. (Interestingly enough, Netscape used to have a product called Netscape Publishing Expert that provided some of this functionality, but the product has long been discontinued.)

On the client side, Rights|System has prepackaged DRM controllers for various types of platforms. Rights|Desktop runs on PC platforms. Unlike its predecessor, InterRightsPoint, which was designed to support offline access control, Rights|Desktop is designed to communicate with the aforementioned server components and, for that and other reasons, has a far smaller size — less than half a megabyte.

Rights|Desktop, like any DRM controller, needs to be integrated with rendering applications in order to work. InterTrust's first instantiation of Rights|Desktop is a product called DocBox, which ships with Adobe Acrobat Reader 5 (on CD-ROM) and supports the PDF format. InterTrust positions DocBox as a higher-end, more flexible DRM solution than Adobe's own Content Server (see the subsection "Documents and eBooks: Adobe"). InterTrust has also created Rights|Desktop interfaces to several music player applications, including Winamp (used by AOL), RioPort, and the MP3 player MusicMatch.

Rights|TV is InterTrust's DRM controller for television set-top box environments. It is designed to work with set-top boxes that support digital broadcasting using any of the MPEG standards (MPEG-1, MPEG-2, and MPEG-4). For portable music players and other handheld devices, there's Rights|PD, which works with devices powered by Cirrus Logic and Texas Instruments chips. Rights|Phone works on certain types of mobile phones, those that run the Symbian operating system. Symbian OS is a common operating platform used by most of the major wireless phone manufacturers, including Ericsson, Nokia, Motorola, Panasonic, and Psion.

All Rights|System's client components have modular subsystems that can be updated securely. For example, the encryption/decryption algorithms can be dynamically updated if one of them is cracked. In addition to their encryption schemes, the client components contain features for thwarting such attacks as license tampering, reverse engineering the code, and fooling the DRM controller by turning back the system clock (thereby making it think that an expiration time hasn't been reached yet).

InterTrust's Rights|System also includes SDKs for server and client functions, which it call Rights|Toolkits. The Packager SDK allows Rights|Packager functionality to be integrated with server components used by content providers, such as editorial systems, production tools, and Digital Asset Management (DAM) systems (see Chapter 10). InterTrust has demonstrated an integration of the Packager SDK with TEAMS, from Artesia Technologies, a leading DAM system that is used by publishers and broadcasters.

Rights|Toolkits for client development include the Rights|Audio, Rights|Video, and Rights|Desktop SDKs. The latter enables developers of rendering applications for PCs to integrate them with Rights|System. Rights|Audio enables developers to use Rights|System in conjunction with the X Audio format used by RioPort, Lycos's Sonique, and other music players; and it has built-in support for the MP3 and AAC audio formats. Rights|Video is designed to fit in with MPEG-4's IPMP (Intellectual Property Management and Protection) interface; (see Chapter 6).

Partnerships

InterTrust has been extremely aggressive in soliciting partnerships with a wide range of vendors. These include service providers who run InterTrust's technology for content providers who want to sell their content online, hardware device makers who embed the Rights|PD and Rights|Phone technologies into their products, and software distribution partners such as America Online and Adobe. InterTrust's service provider partners, at this writing, include the following firms.

Music and audio
- RioPort (www.rioport.com), a provider of online music download services
- Digital World Services (www.dwsco.com), a division of Bertelsmann's BMG recording company (see Chapter 11)
- AudioSoft (www.audiosoft.com), which compiles Internet music-usage tracking data
- MERCURiX (www.mercurix.com), a subsidiary of National Computer Systems of Singapore

Video
- Blockbuster (www.blockbuster.com), the major video rental chain, together with Enron (www.enron.com), the energy giant turned Internet bandwidth provider

Software
- Clickly (www.clickly.com), an online software retailer based in the Netherlands
- Waterfront Technologies (www.waterfronttechnologies.com), a provider of software license management services, also of the Netherlands

Images
- RightsWorks (www.rightsworks.com), a division of Mitsubishi Corp. of Japan

Corporate and enterprise
- Zero Gravity Technologies (www.zerogravitytech.com)

Multiple media
- Easy Systems Japan (www.easy.co.jp), a vendor of tools for creating CDs and DVDs
- Fasoo.com (www.fasoo.com), a division of Samsung located in Korea
- Magex (www.magex.com), a spin-off from National Westminster Bank's credit card division that bundles DRM-based content delivery with financial clearinghouse services
- Philips Digital Networks, a business unit of Philips Consumer Electronics (www.philips.com), which has demonstrated DRM-enabled delivery of multimedia content in MPEG-4 format
- Reciprocal, Inc. (www.reciprocal.com), discussed in the subsection "Reciprocal," earlier in this section
- Rumble Group (www.rumblegroup.com), a provider of brand asset management services, of Australia

Note that many of these firms' services aren't in production as of this writing. At least two InterTrust service providers — DigiHub, a service of the consulting giant Pricewaterhouse-Coopers, and the Hollywood startup Massive Media — have already ceased operations.

InterTrust's other primary type of partner is technology companies who build InterTrust's client functionality into hardware devices. These partnerships allow InterTrust to stake out territory in the post-PC Internet device world, including portable music players, PDAs, mobile phones, and set-top boxes.

The most significant hardware partner is Nokia, the wireless phone maker, which took a 5 percent stake in InterTrust as part of the partnership. Nokia has embedded Rights|Phone into a music player that is a companion device to some of its wireless phones. The player uses a protected version of the AAC audio format, into which users can "rip" music files from CDs on their PCs.

The semiconductor makers Texas Instruments, ARM, and Cirrus Logic have all implemented "DRM on a chip," mainly for embedding into Internet audio appliances and other post-PC devices. ARM's processors are embedded into many different wireless phones, portable computers, digital cameras, and PDAs (including future Palms). Cirrus Logic's Maverick processor is embedded in Diamond Multimedia's Rio portable audio player.

InterTrust has licensed Rights|PD to various other vendors of portable device technology, including big names such as Sony and Compaq, device makers such as Diamond and Creative Technologies, platform suppliers such as iObjects and Parthus, and Internet music appliance makers such as DigMedia and AudioRamp. Some of these vendors (such as AudioRamp) have products out on the market as of this writing, but not all those products actually have the Rights|PD technology embedded.

InterTrust clearly (and correctly) sees the emerging digital media distribution models as a networked marketplace, wherein solutions will come from combinations of interconnected vendors. It is trying to position itself as part of the landscape so that when the new content distribution models become widespread, InterTrust solutions will already be prevalent throughout all facets — as must be the case for DRM to succeed. InterTrust is particularly laying the groundwork for digital audio and video distribution through post-PC network appliances, which can be thought of as "end-to-end solutions" without the security holes that are so prevalent in the PC environment.

However, to paraphrase a cliché, a value chain is only as strong as its weakest link. Despite the number of vendors who have licensed InterTrust's technology for embedding into post-PC devices, not very many such devices are actually shipping with the technology in them. And despite the number of trials that InterTrust has done with major recording companies, such as BMG and Universal Music Group, and other content providers, precious little content in InterTrust's format has actually been downloaded by consumers.

Acquisitions

In addition to the staggering number of partnerships that InterTrust has developed over the years, the company also made a number of acquisitions. Two of these were attempts to address deficiencies in its position in the publishing market. PublishOne, acquired in January 2000, was a service provider that put PDF documents up for sale using Adobe's PDF Merchant solution (see the subsection "Documents and eBooks: Adobe," earlier in this chapter). InterTrust has positioned PublishOne as a one-stop solution for publishers who want to get their feet wet with DRM without acquiring and installing their own software. Infinite Ink, acquired shortly thereafter, had a proprietary DRM-based document viewing system that had its own document format and its own viewer application. Its primary advantage was a lightweight client, as opposed to InterRightsPoint's 5MG.

Another acquisition gave InterTrust key technology for use in the streaming media market: PassEdge, which was acquired in December 2000, had one of the two important DRM solutions for streaming media; the other, as discussed in "Streaming media: RealNetworks," earlier in this chapter, was Aegisoft, which was acquired at around the same time by RealNetworks. PassEdge focused exclusively on the video market. PassEdge's CEO, Mark Ashida, is now the COO of InterTrust.

InterTrust hasn't yet integrated any of these acquired technologies into its core offerings. Infinite Ink is being converted from its own proprietary format to Adobe PDFs, and PublishOne will migrate from PDF Merchant to become a service provider for InterTrust's Rights|System.

Apart from acquisitions and partnerships, InterTrust has various other components of its business that help bolster its competitive position. One is the MetaTrust Utility, which is an agency that certifies InterTrust-powered solutions — including service providers, devices, and rendering applications — to ensure that they implement security models properly. The MetaTrust Utility is supposed to act as a trusted third party, somewhat like a certificate authority (see Chapter 5), that has no hidden agenda in ensuring technology compliance. The other is STAR Lab (Strategic Technologies and Architectural Research Laboratory), a research lab in Princeton, NJ, that produces core intellectual property for the company.

Intellectual property is actually one of InterTrust's most important competitive weapons. It owns or has applied for dozens of patents, and it uses them aggressively to defend its turf. The company also has a legendarily tight nondisclosure policy when dealing with potential partners and customers. The most important current use of InterTrust's intellectual property is the lawsuit against Microsoft, filed in July 2001, in which InterTrust claims that certain internal features of Microsoft's then-new Windows XP operating system violate its patents. It isn't the first DRM company to attempt patent infringement actions against Microsoft (MediaDNA was another; see Chapter 12), but any victory greater than a token settlement that it achieves will be a first indeed. It's a long shot for InterTrust, but it's more than incidental to their business: it's a component of the company's survival strategy.

Microsoft

Microsoft is the heaviest of the heavyweights. Whatever it does in DRM will have enormous influence on the industry. Its first DRM offering was part of Windows Media Player, which became Microsoft's delivery platform for audio and video after a couple of earlier product strategies. The DRM component of Windows Media Player was a lightweight technology that came a couple of years after vendors such as IBM and InterTrust defined the market. Several security holes were found in Windows Media Player 7 in late 2000 through early 2001, although that was by no means the only DRM technology to be cracked. Also, the music and film industries didn't take Windows Media technology very seriously at first. RealNetworks was the acknowledged leader for music and video distribution. As far as DRM was concerned, the music industry was looking at a broader technological picture, one that focused more on portable music players than on PCs, as the focus for SDMI (see Chapter 6).

Digital Asset Server and Microsoft Reader

Microsoft's second and current DRM technology is part of its eBook offering, which consists of Microsoft Reader on the client side and Digital Asset Server (DAS) on the server side. Microsoft Reader is an eBook rendering technology that has implementations for Windows PCs and for Pocket PC handheld devices (although the two versions aren't entirely interoperable yet).

DAS has two components: DAS Server, which contains the repository and DRM packaging functionality, and DAS e-commerce components, which integrate into booksellers' e-commerce Web sites (storefronts). DAS can be deployed by service providers or by eBook retailers.

The DRM model in Microsoft's eBook technology is a very tight integration, not only of DAS and Microsoft Reader, but also of Microsoft's Passport user identity and registration system. In Chapter 5, we discuss how users are licensed to access content in a DRM system and the trade-offs in tying licenses to users versus tying them to machines. Some approaches to licensing use the machine as the point of identity by creating a unique ID for the machine and placing it, in encrypted form, in a cookie or other file. Others use the person as the point of identity via usernames and passwords. Microsoft uses the latter approach, but in a far more sophisticated way than many other DRM technologies.

Microsoft's Passport identity scheme should be familiar to anyone who uses Microsoft Network (MSN) or has a Hotmail account. It's a centralized database of users, containing e-mail addresses and other information. This enables your identity to work across all of Microsoft's network-enabled products and services, eliminating the need for you to re-register for each one.

Originally, Passport was a proprietary scheme: It appeared as though Microsoft was looking for ways to amass a gigantic database of information about users, which would give it ways of locking them into more Microsoft services by virtue of convenience — just as Qpass has done with online content archive sales (see Chapter 12). Privacy advocates sensed this and screamed "Big Brother." Yet in September 2001, Microsoft heeded privacy advocates' concerns, announcing that they would replace Passport's proprietary technology with Kerberos 5.0; Kerberos is an open standard Internet authentication technology that was invented at MIT. This would allow user identities to be understandable across multiple Internet service delivery systems, not just Microsoft's.

To read an eBook in Microsoft's format, you first download Microsoft Reader. Then you must activate it by registering it with your Passport ID, which is often your MSN or Hotmail e-mail address. From your Passport ID, Microsoft generates a unique user ID via a mathematical procedure known as a one-way hash function, which is similar to the function used to generate cryptographic digests that we discuss in Chapter 5. Microsoft calls this ID your *persona.*

If you don't activate Microsoft Reader, you will only be able to read unprotected eBooks. You can activate more than one instance of Microsoft Reader with a given persona; this enables you, for example, to treat your Microsoft Readers on your PC and your PDA as one and the same and to share files between them. Microsoft does keep track of each device that you activate using a given persona by generating another unique ID (again, via a one-way hash function) for each one. It imposes a limit of two devices for a given persona.

Note that it's also possible to have more than one instance of Microsoft Reader on a given machine. This allows the two readers to be activated using different personas, to store different sets of user preferences, and so on.

Microsoft's DRM technology uses a subset of XrML (see Chapter 6) to define rights. Currently, it provides for three levels of security:

♦ **Sealed:** The lowest level. The content is encrypted but can be read by any Microsoft Reader, regardless of whether it is activated. The primary purpose of the encryption at this level is to provide tamperproofing.

♦ **Inscribed:** These eBooks are sealed, as above, and then encrypted further. They are also customized so that the cover page contains the purchaser's name and personal information, such as a credit card number. Although eBooks with this level of security are still readable on unactivated Readers, the personal inscription provides some incentive for the purchaser to protect the content.

♦ **Owner-specific:** These eBooks are sealed, inscribed, and encrypted with public-key encryption using a public key derived from the persona of the user. A Reader activated with that persona is required to read eBooks secured at this level.

Microsoft's encryption technique revolves around something called a Black Box. The Black Box is a DRM controller that the DAS Server generates for a specific instance of Microsoft Reader when a user activates it. The Black Box, a separate file from the content, is designed to work with any rendering application, although it currently works with Microsoft Reader only. The Black Box also contains an encryption/decryption algorithm that is different each time a new one is created. It encrypts content using a symmetric-key algorithm, à la DES; then it encrypts the symmetric key multiple times using asymmetric keys (à la RSA). Key lengths and other details of the algorithms vary. Microsoft participated in an independent survey of eBook security done for the Association of American Publishers by Global Integrity (now part of Predictive Systems, Inc.) and fared very well with a score of 98 out of 100 in these categories:

♦ Publisher content delivery

♦ Copyright protection and content integrity

♦ Server security

♦ eBook security

♦ Consumer and bookstore authentication

♦ Consumer privacy

♦ Industry standard formats and protocols

♦ PC usage as intermediary

♦ Accountability and logging

♦ eBook device/software security

Unified DRM

The next phase in the evolution of Microsoft's DRM strategy is under currently under development, with the internal working name of Unified DRM, or uDRM. UDRM extends DRM in its eBook technology. It will have two major new features: First, it will complete the decoupling of the DRM controller functionality from the content package, enabling the controller to be used with any type of media, not just eBooks. Microsoft will undoubtedly create versions of its player applications, including Windows Media Player and perhaps versions of Microsoft Word Reader and PowerPoint Reader, that work with the Black Box. Users will able to use the same plug-in application and IDs (personas) for all media types.

Microsoft will publish APIs that will enable third-party rendering application vendors to use the Black Box as well. It will issue security guidelines for rendering applications and will do lightweight testing but not the type of rigorous certification that InterTrust does. By the time of this book's publication, the design of the API should be complete.

The second major feature of uDRM will be full support for the XrML rights specification language (see Chapter 6). Microsoft is the only vendor that currently supports XrML other than XrML's creator, ContentGuard, which dropped its own product line in August 2001 to concentrate on advancing XrML as a standard. Microsoft holds a significant minority stake in ContentGuard, and the two companies have been collaborating on research and development since ContentGuard's inception in early 2000.

Microsoft's support of the full XrML specification will do wonders for XrML's acceptance in the marketplace. For one thing, Microsoft's strategy includes a DAS service provider program. Microsoft is working with several companies who are running or will run DAS installations; it will be natural for them to upgrade to full XrML support and multiple media types. Current DAS service providers include the following:

- In the United States, Reciprocal (see the subsection "Reciprocal," earlier in this section), OverDrive (`www.overdrive.com`), and Lightning Source (`www.lightningsource.com`)
- In the United Kingdom and Ireland, Computer Bookshops Ltd. (`www.compbook.co.uk`).
- In the Scandinavian countries, eLib (`www.elib.se`)
- In France, Belgium, and Luxembourg, Info2clear (`www.info2clear.com`)
- In Spain and Latin America, Planeta (`www.planeta-actimedia.es`)
- In the United States, Spain, Portugal, and Latin America, Plaza Digital (`www.plazadigital.com`)

With the embrace of XrML as a standard rights modeling language, the promise of creating open APIs for uDRM so that rendering application developers can incorporate the technology, and its intent to use Kerberos for user authentication, Microsoft appears to be committing itself to an inclusive approach to the DRM marketplace. Indeed, provided that Microsoft lives up to these promises and delivers good technology for uDRM, it becomes hard to imagine a future in which other DRM vendors can compete on the PC platform, as well as on such other Microsoft-powered platforms as PocketPC, in arenas beyond specialized markets. This will be particularly true if Microsoft takes the next logical step in the evolution of its DRM technology: building it directly into its operating systems. We discuss what this means and implies in Chapter 13.

The Competitive Landscape

We end this chapter with some analysis of the competitive situation among the major players in media technology and their DRM strategies.

As noted earlier, Microsoft is in the proverbial catbird's seat in the industry. Although many media companies deliver products in some Microsoft format today, Microsoft cemented what could be its biggest deal in the entertainment industry in July 2001. At that time, Microsoft became the exclusive music format and DRM technology provider for pressplay, the online subscription service that is a joint venture between Universal Music and Sony Music. This deal draws the battle lines clearly: Of the five major recording labels, Universal and Sony have decided to throw in their lots with Microsoft and will be offering digital music exclusively in Windows Media format; the other three, BMG, EMI, and Warner Brothers, have an exclusive partnership with RealNetworks, as mentioned earlier.

The top level of the DRM industry is beginning to converge into major factions. Microsoft, by itself, is certainly one of them. At this writing, there appear to be two others: the axis of InterTrust, Adobe, and AOL Time Warner; and RealNetworks.

AOL Time Warner, InterTrust, and Adobe

Microsoft's biggest competitor is a de facto coalition led by AOL Time Warner that includes InterTrust, which in turn has a strong relationship with Adobe on the technology side.

InterTrust's primary competitive assets, apart from its technology per se, are its patent portfolio and cash position. The former enables it to keep Microsoft and other companies at bay through lawsuits for patent infringement; the latter enables it to generate more intellectual property through its research lab and to buy its way into distribution deals that make its DRM controller (client application) more ubiquitous. As mentioned earlier, InterTrust distributes its client applications in the latest releases of AOL and Adobe Acrobat, two of the most widely distributed non-Microsoft pieces of software. This overcomes InterTrust's biggest hurdle, the size of its client application, which has hindered its ability to achieve a large installed base. Its new technology, Rights|System, overcomes this hurdle technologically by decreasing the client size by an order of magnitude, although a client software install is still necessary, as it is with other DRM solutions.

Having lots of content available in InterTrust-packaged format is another matter. AOL agreed to distribute the DigiBox software but didn't make any commitments to distributing content in that format. Furthermore, AOL Time Warner's recording company, Warner Brothers, is part of MusicNet, which is using RealNetworks's DRM technology. InterTrust tried hard to get pressplay, MusicNet's rival, to include its technology, but it did not succeed.

InterTrust sees its future in the post-PC world of portable music players, wireless phones, and PDAs; it is aggressively pursuing partnerships with chip and hardware device makers. In this world, its only current, significant competition is IBM (see Chapter 11). However, even in this more wide-open market, content providers must still cooperate by making content available in the necessary formats, and ultimately, users must show willingness to consume content on DRM-enabled devices. The SDMI experience shows that device makers are highly reluctant to build devices that are restricted to playing DRM-protected content exclusively.

Adobe, meanwhile, has an unfocused DRM strategy, as we noted earlier in this chapter. It started with PDF Merchant and Web Buy, which have enjoyed only modest success in the market and whose futures seem uncertain. For eBooks, it uses DRM technology acquired from Glassbook and competes head-to-head with Microsoft. Its advantage over Microsoft is that it is a key player in the market for tools that publishers use to produce eBooks. This will presumably enable publishers to create eBooks with more enhanced features than those for Microsoft Reader, although this advantage may be offset by the move toward the XML-based Open eBook (OEB) standard for eBook layout. Another advantage is that Adobe's Acrobat and eBook readers run on Macintoshes, whereas Microsoft's don't.

The other part of Adobe's DRM strategy is its partnership with InterTrust, whose lightweight DocBox client is now distributed with Adobe Acrobat Reader (Version 5) on CD-ROM. This applies to documents, such as high-priced research reports, that aren't best distributed as eBooks. Adobe needs to migrate its DRM strategy to one solution to avoid user confusion.

Microsoft's advantage over Adobe is its commitment to a single DRM platform across all media types, not just documents and eBooks but audio, video, and other formats as well. However, InterTrust is also capable of providing a single DRM platform across all media types. A true technology integration of InterTrust's DRM technology— not only with Adobe, but with AOL's massive customer information database — would result in formidable competition to Microsoft throughout the media value chain.

RealNetworks

RealNetworks is still the number one format for the distribution of streaming audio and video — with an estimated 190 million players installed worldwide — despite Microsoft's aggressive attempts to displace it. As noted earlier, its DRM technology, acquired from Aegisoft, was chosen by BMG, EMI, and Warner Brothers for their MusicNet service. RealNetworks is also a 40 percent stakeholder in MusicNet.

Although RealNetworks has a number of allies on the content side, its only real technology ally is Sun Microsystems, whose industrial-strength server technology allows RealNetworks-based streaming server installations to be more robust and scalable than those based on Microsoft technology. Apart from that, RealNetworks is somewhat on its own.

To help bolster RealNetworks's position against Microsoft through partnerships with more of the major technology vendors, RealNetworks announced a standards initiative called Extensible Media Commerce Language (XMCL), which is mentioned in Chapter 6 and which has the nominal blessing of many technology companies, including Sun and IBM. XMCL is targeted squarely at XrML, which has Microsoft's support.

However, as mentioned in Chapter 6, there is a long road from announcing a standard to getting several vendors to implement anything based on it. We view XMCL as a well-intentioned piece of technology that is, however, merely the latest in a constant parade of "everyone but Microsoft" initiatives that tend to collapse under the weight of the many vendors involved.

Despite this, RealNetworks has the advantage — unlike InterTrust — of hundreds of thousands of hours of content already available in its own format. RealNetworks Media Commerce Suite takes advantage of RealNetworks's built-in infrastructure of installed players and servers: The new technology is an incremental add-on. Adoption of Media Commerce Suite should be easy for existing RealNetworks customers. It remains to be seen how easy Microsoft makes it for distributors of content in Windows Media format to upgrade to uDRM (or whatever Microsoft calls it after it is released) when it becomes available.

However, once again, it's important to mention that RealNetworks only applies to audio and video, whereas Microsoft's uDRM should provide a single DRM interface for all media types. Unless RealNetworks enters into an alliance that somehow ties its technology to other media formats or further strengthens its ties to content providers, RealNetworks is likely to find itself off the playing field as Microsoft and AOL Time Warner slug it out for world domination, especially if AOL realizes more of the potential of its partnership with InterTrust. A merger with Adobe, although it may seem far-fetched, could solidify RealNetworks's position as a technology provider by achieving more of a critical mass of media types under one technology.

We end this competitive analysis by noting that there are light rumors about a takeover of RealNetworks by AOL Time Warner. Although we won't speculate on the likelihood of such a deal, it would definitely upset the competitive balance of the DRM market. Most obviously, it would collapse the three factions into two — essentially AOL versus Microsoft, a competitive situation that already exists in many facets of technology today. With RealNetworks, AOL would have DRM technology for streaming audio and video, although not for other formats and not for the network devices that AOL is planning. In such an arrangement, there may not be room for InterTrust in the AOL family. If AOL does not find room, it's hard to see how InterTrust will survive over the long term.

Part III

DRM Solutions: Putting It All Together

Chapter 8

Get What You Need:
Determining Requirements

Every successful technology project starts the same way — with a clear, thoughtful, and complete statement of requirements. The only way a programmer or team of programmers can build something useful for you is when they understand what you need the "something" to do. This is true for even the simplest projects, and certainly for the most complex. You start by writing down what your requirements are in a way that a programmer can understand; then you begin to translate them into features and, ultimately, the code underneath those features.

This requirements-gathering may be somewhat difficult when it comes to digital rights management because DRM spans a broad array of technical and business requirements. It includes relatively specialized areas such as security and encryption, as well as areas that are near and dear to a publisher's heart — but perhaps new and foreign to software developers — such as pricing, terms, and conditions for use.

Created correctly, a statement of your requirements becomes the key step toward acquiring the right DRM system or services for your organization. Created incorrectly, this statement of requirements leaves you at square one, or worse — it leaves you choosing a system that does many things well, but few of them are things that you care about or need.

Fear not, though. This chapter arms you with the necessary information to analyze your own needs and to understand how consumers will likely want to work with your system. Each area of your potential requirements is discussed, and the concluding section outlines a checklist that you can prepare and review with potential vendors and suppliers of DRM systems and services.

Understanding Publishers' Needs

This section addresses the requirements publishers have for DRM software. Yet at the same time, this section deals with the consumer. One of the many ironies of DRM is that publishers need to do DRM well or not at all. Because in implementing DRM, publishers are placing themselves, for better or worse, directly between their product and the consumption of their product. So the publishers who are implementing DRM must understand their own requirements and those of the consumer and be prepared to balance those requirements in a way that meets the needs of both. This may be the crux of the DRM problem: What the consumer wants and the publisher needs may not always seem to be compatible. Publishers need to step forward and create the win-win situation that the consumer is demanding.

So although this section discusses DRM largely from the point of view of the publisher, it also discusses the consumer's point of view, highlighting key consumer concerns such as ease of use and privacy. This section goes on to suggest some ways that publishers can balance the need for a satisfying consumer experience and their own needs for revenue, reach, and the ability to do follow-on selling.

Where does requirements analysis fit into your project?

Determining your requirements is the first and most essential step in any software project. This is true whether the project involves developing the software yourself, integrating someone else's software, or adapting your business process to software being set up for you. This is also true no matter how easy you imagine the project to be — or, perhaps more importantly, how easy the person selling the software wants you to think the project is going to be.

The process of software project management is a book-length subject in and of itself and, in fact, is a somewhat contentious subject. Yet most practitioners of software development agree that the process follows these general phases:

1. **Requirements analysis:** The requirements of the potential users are analyzed, written down, and reviewed for completeness and accuracy. For example, you may capture a requirement and state it as, "The software should prevent unauthorized copying."

2. **Detailed specification:** The software developers translate the users' requirements into a detailed design. For example, a software developer translates the requirement of "preventing unauthorized copying" into a detailed specification for precisely how unauthorized copying will be prevented.

3. **Coding and integration:** The software components are developed (or customized) and integrated with other systems.

4. **Testing:** The software is tested to ensure that it meets all the original requirements.

It's clear that the earliest phase, requirements analysis, is arguably the most important, as all the other work flows from it. This phase is also the point at which the business requirements of the software are paramount. Beginning with the specification phase, software development enters into the mysterious and specialized world of the software developer, where mere mortals sometimes fear to tread. It is in the requirements phase that the customer wields the most influence and has the most input.

Software projects go wrong when the process loses track of the original, agreed-on requirements. "Feature creep" is exactly this kind of problem: The software developer begins to design or even code with one sense of what the requirements are, and then somehow new requirements are added. You should strive to leave the requirements analysis phase with a complete, accurate, and highly detailed document stating your requirements in your own language.

Why should you bother to protect your content at all?

Taken together, the materials protected under U.S. copyright have become the biggest sector of U.S. manufacturing. A recent report from the International Intellectual Property Alliance showed that the intellectual property sector outsells all major manufacturing sectors and continues to grow at an impressive pace. Between 1977 and 1997, U.S. employment in the intellectual property sector more than doubled to almost four million workers, and intellectual property became the single biggest U.S. export.

It's clear that, at minimum, DRM is tied to major business. As such, publishers' interest in DRM seems like a natural, although perhaps defensive, move to protect their commercial interest. Yet to view DRM as a purely defensive technology would be shortsighted for both the publisher and the consumer. Yes, copyrighted materials need to be protected from massive unauthorized copying and distribution. And, yes, an increasing percentage of copyrighted material is available in electronic form. But forward-thinking publishers view DRM as an essential component of online selling — for reasons well beyond its core capability of copy protection. More broadly, and perhaps more appropriately, DRM has the potential to establish the key component of trust between the buyer and seller, allowing for a growing market. Moving forward, DRM will be an essential tool in helping publishers better understand who uses their products and how they use them, creating an invaluable analytical and feedback tool for their ongoing product development.

As the music industry has learned all too well, the market for digitized content will only grow as a problem and opportunity. DRM increases in its potential importance along with ever-increasing bandwidth, the availability of more and more materials in digital form, and the increasing proliferation of computing power to include such things as mobile devices and home appliances.

File protection and access

As noted earlier, this book addresses the requirements of publishers in a broad sense. The first requirement for publishers to consider is, "What, specifically, are we trying to manage or protect with a DRM solution?" For a music publisher, it may be MP3 files containing its songs, and for an animator, it may be some combination of MPEG and other formats containing his creations. In short, the core requirement of DRM is to manage or protect content in digital form.

Although such a simple definition of DRM should be an obvious point at this point, it is worth reiterating as you begin to look at your own requirements for a DRM system. The key first steps to creating a digital product are intimately tied to the core requirements of DRM:

♦ **The product needs to be digitized and packaged for distribution.** Ideally, the packaged product is identified in a way that ensures its authenticity and uniqueness.

♦ **The product needs to be secured in a manner such that its usage can be controlled.** Although even the best encryption can eventually be broken, the existence of at least standard copy protection mechanisms can slow down the unlawful user and ward off the honest.

♦ **The product needs to be reliably associated with the rights information for how it can be used.** For example, an encrypted version of an eBook carries with it the "business rules" for the eBook. Say that it can be purchased for $17.95, read on a properly equipped machine, and then passed on to a second user (but no more). This is the product's rights specification, as discussed in Chapter 4.

Various industry groups, such as the Association of American Publishers (AAP) and the Secure Digital Music Initiative (SDMI), have looked at the issue of file protection and access (see Chapter 6 for more information). They have arrived at similar core requirements, including the need for security in the initial packaging, the need for some kind of digital signature to ensure authenticity, and the need to protect the material at all stages in the distribution channel.

As at least one publisher suggested, when publishers think about DRM, they're first thinking about file protection, but they're typically not very interested in how it works as long as it works. Although the DRM vendors are deeply interested in the details of their solutions, publishers take a broader view. Many of the publishers that we interviewed had a similar view — make mass copying and distribution difficult.

One more aspect of protection that is worth discussing is the notion of persistence. Security has traditionally dealt with the security of data interchange and access within a given system. Even with Web access, security typically worries only about firewall-style access and not about what happens to the data that you have downloaded or copies of that data. Publishers need to consider seriously their requirements for persistent, or offline, protection. That is, when your content gets beyond your walls (and firewalls), do you still need to protect it?

Note, though, that *the flip side of protection is access.* After all, publishers create products to be consumed, not to be put in a safe and forgotten forever. DRM software and systems then must create the correct balance between security and access. Indeed, it is in this critical area of managing access that DRM earns its keep. The business of selling and managing content is increasingly about access and not about copying per se: It's not so much about copying something and how many copies can be made but about the many things that can be done with content after it is accessed. Publishers have increasing opportunities (and problems) managing content that can be incorporated wholesale into other products and content that can be divided up and reused.

Publishers by and large have let the existence of a satisfactory business lull them into not pushing the technology envelope. In other words, if the current technology is supporting the business, there is less of a determination to innovate, especially if the current technology meets the publishers' needs for protection. In book publishing, for example, publishers have relied on the inconvenience pirates faced in copying and distributing the whole book (which has, of course, been done). But this is still a kind of rough justice, capable of protecting the existing business model and revenue stream, but not perhaps truly indicative of the real use of the product.

Take college textbooks as one example of how a kind of rough justice has traditionally prevailed. College textbook publishers know that their books are resold and passed along for free. The sale of 10,000 books likely begets 40,000 readers. To better protect their investment, they publish an expensive, targeted product with a built-in obsolescence. If a book does well, the publisher updates it, creating a second edition that replaces the old one and, temporarily at least, eliminates the used book problem for that title.

College textbook publishers especially are driven to try new methods of marketing their materials online and are experimenting with DRM technologies to support their marketing. Take the Biology Place (www.biology.com), for example, a leading site for teaching college-level biology. This Pearson Education site has a subscription model for membership. Some students subscribe on their own, some subscribe at the urging (or requirement) of their instructors, and some subscribe when their schools buy a subscription for them. In all cases, the subscriptions are time-limited and typically run for the academic year or the semester. Interestingly, Pearson has experimented with tying the purchase of print books to the Web site subscriptions. For example, one bound book is shrink-wrapped with a coupon good for a semester-long subscription. Such a model gives Pearson options for cross-selling to related sites (such as the Chemistry Place and the Psychology Place) and enables them to experiment with different selling models.

All these examples go to the point of access being as important as protection and the realization that your DRM system needs to recognize and balance these two needs. Your requirements for protection are largely defensive, yet your requirements for access are directly related to your business models and, as significant, a more sophisticated notion of the needs and concerns of users. For example, a college textbook publisher wants to easily give evaluation copies of materials to professors but wants the student to always buy everything. A trade publisher wants to prevent wholesale copying and distribution but is happy to allow what is normally considered "fair use" of its material.

Indeed, in some instances, you may want to exploit copying rather than suppress it. The software industry has learned well from the practice of encouraging copying, especially when it can control later usage or do follow-on selling. The deployment and copying of the initial object can be used to gain further insight into the true usage of the product and affect future product development.

At a minimum, your DRM solution should tie your organization to the primary channels for selling and distribution. Publishers clearly have distribution in mind, and DRM vendors and service providers have developed marketing agreements with major selling channels. In teaming with DRM services and providers, publishers see themselves as gaining the technical expertise to deal with arcane issues such as security together with access to the desired channel. Book publishers, for example, also are looking to tie eBook distribution to mechanisms for print-on-demand. Although print-on-demand is not in and of itself a digital product, it typically can be derived from a digital product (Portable Document Format — PDF) and is also part of the same competitive picture that has publishers trying to make content available to consumers when they want it, where they want it, and in the form that they want it.

Types of content

The first core requirement of DRM is content types or, more specifically, file types or file formats. The key with this requirement is to err on the side of caution. Begin by listing all the possible formats that your content could be rendered in, on all the possible platforms, with as many variables as you can reasonably anticipate. You can later decide if some formats are unimportant, or less important, than others.

Why all the attention to such a seemingly mundane topic as file formats? Unfortunately, there is no such thing as a "universal viewer," so it is critical to find out which formats are supported by a given DRM solution. This is especially true for the publisher who deals in many media, such as an entertainment company that produces music and video. But even within a relatively narrow domain such as eBooks, for example, multiple formats and standards proliferate. For now, at least, DRM systems must deal with a multitude of formats. In the case of this requirement, your job is to determine what formats you need to do business and then to determine which of the many DRM solutions successfully meet your requirements.

You may eventually winnow out other solutions because of other requirements, but understanding whether a given DRM system handles your required formats is an excellent first step. You will find that this enables you to focus your competitive analysis later on. If you are a music publisher and a given DRM system doesn't support the major formats for distributing music, you can rule them out early on.

The final section of this chapter lists many of the possible requirements in a checklist. There are at least three primary areas to consider; you can later augment the checklist for your own needs:

♦ **File formats:** To begin with, outline all the known binary and (if appropriate) ASCII formats that the content may be stored in for distribution. For eBooks, for example, this may include PDF, the Open eBook (OEB) standard, and Microsoft's `.lit` format, to name a few, but it can also include some other, lesser-known formats.

♦ **Platforms:** In addition to file formats, list the platforms and operating systems that the content may be stored on. List all major operating systems, including various flavors of Windows, Macintosh, and Linux, that are important to your market (where appropriate) as well as specialized devices such as Palms, media players, and other handheld devices.

♦ **File size and complexity:** Spell out whether you require support for extremely large files or complex file types that include in and of themselves multiple media (for example, a document file that contains embedded images or sounds).

What are your business models?

Chapter 2 discusses the various business models that DRM technology enables you to employ and support. These models form an important part of your requirements analysis, as you need to spell out the ways in which you want the DRM solution to support your business. Business models, though, are closely tied to rights models, so your thinking about business models needs to be grounded in the reality of the rights models that DRM solutions can support.

> **CROSS REFERENCE:** See Chapter 4 for more information on rights models.

Publishers are increasingly moving away from the "all or nothing" mode of selling. This has resulted from a variety of market pressures that have built up over time:

♦ Publishers face shorter development time and shelf life. Products need to be developed more quickly, updated more quickly, and retired more quickly.

♦ Customers demand an expanding choice of delivery media. (For example, print publishers may well be supporting print, Web, PDF, and CD/DVD output even before they begin to look at the long list of potential eBook formats.)

♦ Publishers must deal with the downward pressure on price, causing them to look at reducing cost over time.

♦ Yet at the same time, publishers face the normal pressures of business, notably the requirement to increase existing revenue streams and develop new ones.

Examples of this sort of change in the publishing business abound. Consider the publishers who sell high-value reference material, such as Lexis-Nexis, Standard & Poor's, or Elsevier Science. Until the early 1990s, they published only in print. In the mid-1990s, publishers added a CD-ROM. By the late 1990s, publishers were facing continued pressure to publish their content over the Web. Questions of protection and access were relatively easy to solve in the worlds of print and CD-ROM, but the Web has created whole new problems — and whole new opportunities.

Why? These pressures have combined to create a pent-up need for publishers to be "lean manufacturers," capable of creating flexible, just-in-time inventory to balance the shifting demands of their customers against their own needs to lower production, warehousing, and distribution costs and lessen or eliminate the costs associated with returns.

As a result, publishers need to develop and quickly assess new business models. Publishers are increasingly open to new approaches ranging from time-limited subscriptions to "viral marketing" programs, in which portions of a product — or even the entire product — are distributed for free as part of gaining market intelligence or farming prospects. The possible models are limited only by the imagination of the publishers. The two components of rights models presented in Chapter 4 bear repeating here:

♦ **Types of rights:** Render rights, transport rights, and derivative work rights

♦ **Rights attributes:** Attributes of the primary types of rights, including consideration (what is offered for granting the rights), extent (how long, how many times, or in what places the right applies), and the types of users (for example, students or senior citizens)

The challenge is to articulate these business models as requirements and to fit these requirements into your larger matrix of requirements. For example, if you list PDF and Open eBook as required formats, encryption and persistence as protection requirements, and a mix of selling approaches as business model requirements, you have gone a long way to matching your requirements to potential solutions — and eliminating many others. Stephen King's *Riding the Bullet*, for example, is sold on Amazon.com in both Microsoft Reader and Adobe Reader formats. *Harvard Business Review* provides reprints of articles, also via Amazon.com, in Adobe Reader format as well. These publishers have clearly identified these formats and these channels as important to them.

As you consider your requirements, keep in mind the kinds of business models that you can employ, which may include the following:

♦ Subscription

♦ Pay-per-view

♦ Time-based access

♦ Slice and dice/mix and match

♦ Metering (demographics-per-view)

> **CROSS REFERENCE:** Chapter 2 discusses business models in detail.

The nitty-gritty: Payment, clearinghouse functions, and business intelligence

At the end of the day, money usually has to change hands. Someone has to pay, someone has to be paid, and, usually, someone has to secure and clear payments. From publishers' perspectives, the requirements are straightforward: Payment should be accurate, timely, and accompanied by reports that mesh well with their existing back-office systems.

Beyond these requirements of payment processing, there is a potential use of DRM that is of great interest to publishers. The "killer app" inside DRM may be the use of DRM as a tool for marketing or, more specifically, as a tool for developing market intelligence. Many DRM applications include robust features for tracking how protected content is being used and who is using it. As such, DRM systems can give publishers a highly accurate view of how their products are actually being used. This differs markedly from nondigital content, where products are sold and distributed but publishers typically then end up with more ad hoc understanding of actual usage patterns. This is precisely the approach of lean manufacturing applied to publishing — analyzing and responding to what is really in demand (or not), what is viewed as having the highest value (or not), and, potentially, what you should be building more of and charging more for. So your job in looking at payment and clearinghouse requirements is to view them with a larger goal in mind — developing an increasingly accurate picture of your customers and your products.

Another DRM vendor echoed this point: "DRM solutions allow you to develop knowledge of the users and how they are using the products. Think of it as usage profiling, with a specific segmentation or orientation — how is this particular material being used?" In particular, you can look for the system to monitor and report on who is making the initial purchase, who is getting the content later, and how is it being used.

Depending on the published products and the markets, such profiling can be a simple or complex undertaking. The use of a simple, mass-market product such as an eBook or music title is, in some ways, easier to profile than the use of a modular, reusable product such as a reference database for accountants. A more extreme example, and one that may indeed not even be worth handling in a general purpose DRM tool, is the use of a software library or component in other software products (such as a spell-checking library used in a number of larger, more complex programs). Currently, such complex usage arrangements are largely monitored "by hand," and a lot of mutual trust between the parties truly governs the relationships.

Why do all this profiling? Done well, this profiling can lead to improved input to the product development cycle. If you understand the true use of your products — what works and what doesn't, what is popular and what is not — you can eventually build a more useful, more marketable, and ultimately more profitable product. Precise monitoring and reporting can give publishers a very accurate picture of how their products are selling and, as such, can help them better understand the true profitability of their products.

Many new selling models are possible, but little hard data is available yet on how successful each new model may be. So it becomes difficult for publishers to know where and how to place their bets. Would a new eBook sold only on Amazon.com be profitable, or should it be offered on more sites and in more formats? Could a record company profit from distributing some tracks free with the hope that the customers buy more? In truth, publishers are just starting to learn. The results are just emerging. How would DRM solutions help with this problem? By allowing this publisher to economically deploy and test different models and to then assess the results of those models with meaningful feedback, analytic tools, and reporting.

Some other considerations

Much of the focus in this chapter has been on so-called business-to-consumer (B-to-C) applications of DRM in selling content. But some publishers (those that cater to the legal and medical professions and technical training come to mind) are very focused on business-to-business (B-to-B) selling, and most publishers do at least some selling through B-to-B channels.

Professional audiences are significant, and they may well be accessing and purchasing through their organization or company. An individual consumer may be accessing content from an organization as an individual subscriber or as one of many subscribers eligible to view the content. That same individual accessing the content may be an ad hoc user or may be the key person in the subscription process (for example, the executive who approves the sale or the librarian who evaluates the content).

The various education markets have aspects of B-to-B commerce: Consider a school adoption in which a math program from a single publisher is selected for a whole school system, or the college professor who, after reviewing a free teacher's edition of an English text, orders copies for his 75 incoming freshmen.

You should consider the mix of B-to-C and B-to-B channels in your total requirements and document your reporting and business intelligence requirements accordingly.

Being Realistic about Your Audience and Competition

In the preceding few chapters of this book, we spend time with the more theoretical and technological aspects of DRM. As fascinating as those topics may be, it shouldn't hurt to remind you that you have a business to support. Two vital aspects of your business are your customers (the audience for your content) and your competitors.

How much will your audience tolerate?: "Frictionless" commerce and DRM

First and foremost, make it easy for your consumer to locate what he wants and to conclude the transaction. The ascension of Napster taught the recording industry many things, but the most important lesson is that, in simple terms, water flows downhill. In software terms, this can be translated to mean that the ease of use rules. In other words, if you put something in front of motivated consumers and make it easy to use, they will use it.

The buzzword, and it is perhaps a useful one, is to create "frictionless" commerce, where *friction* is defined as anything that slows down the process for the buyer. Friction can include slow performance, the need to download cumbersome client applications, and forms or cookies that suggest an invasion of privacy.

Yet DRM, at least in some of its early forms, is viewed as adding precisely to this friction. The more rigorous the security, the more difficult an experience the consumer may have, when in fact the goal for many publishers is to have the digital product be at least as good as its analog counterpart. Looking at eBooks, a publisher would want to make the eBook experience in all aspects to meet all the subtle pleasures of a real book. Features such as pass-along and library-style lending would make sense to most readers and may be expected. The DRM solution should balance the publishers' needs to adequately collect for their intellectual property against the consumers' desire to easily purchase the material and dispense with it as they normally would, such as pass along the read copy to a friend (but not a thousand friends).

Publishers' and consumers' early experiences have been mixed. One publisher reported confusion among its buyers. After they purchased and downloaded materials in one eBook format to a computer, it was not clear that the purchase was tied to that precise computer. After the consumer tried to then copy the purchase from the office computer to a laptop, the consumer couldn't access the purchased material on the laptop. The publisher ended up granting the consumer rights to use the content on both machines, but it took extra work on the part of the consumer and the publisher to enable this.

Ease of use

In an ideal world, consumers should be able to easily purchase and download any object — from any source — and use it immediately on any device. Clearly we are a long way from that ideal world, but DRM needs to be viewed as an enabler of commerce and not as part of the friction.

Publishers who have been early adopters of certain DRM systems have met resistance beginning with this question of ease of use. The InterTrust DigiBox client application initially required an initial download of more than five megabytes on the part of the consumer, over and above whatever content product was being purchased. This burdensome download has proven to be a barrier to acceptance for InterTrust and has led it to work hard to mitigate the problem. InterTrust has been able to make the overall download smaller, and, perhaps as significantly, has developed marketing partnerships so that its client will be installed as part of more popular and more standard software installations, such as AOL 6 and Acrobat 5.

Some other considerations for the publisher in viewing how to make the purchasing experience more palatable to the consumer include the following (and notice that some of these may end up being more the purview of the retailer and not necessarily the publisher, as the retailer may be the direct interface to the consumer):

- **The size of the overall download should be as reasonable as possible.** Some content is destined to be large and cumbersome to download, but publishers should employ the best possible compression and avoid any DRM techniques that add needlessly to the overall size of the download.

- **The content should be easy to find, establish the cost of, download, and use**. Aspects of "finding" content can include things such as a notification that the consumer has already purchased this content or has already bought a related product that entitles her to a discount.

- **It should be easy to determine what rights apply.** For example, the system should make it obvious whether an object is available for download and distribution, whether it can be copied, and if it can be copied, how many copies can be made or passed along.

- **What the consumer has bought and what rules apply to its use should be obvious.** Did the consumer buy this product for download to a single PC or for others? Can it be also copied to a portable device? Can the consumer copy it only to her own device or others? And if it turns out that the consumer wants to acquire additional rights, it should be obvious and easy to her how she can do it.

- **The consumer should be able to easily determine what he or she has bought in the past and when.** Ideally, the consumer should be able to view and understand the "bank" of content from a variety of devices (his or her PC at home versus the one at work or school, as well as a portable device such as an eBook reader or music player).

Value

Beyond ease of use, consumers should be able to easily recognize the value of the products available to them. This begins with such obvious characteristics as the selection, breadth, and quality of the materials themselves. This may seem obvious, but it is surprisingly lacking in today's e-commerce environment for high-value content.

For example, some of the most popular and profitable financial organizations, such as brokerage houses and investment banks, are very difficult to buy from online. Not only can a consumer not easily purchase content that he may be interested in, but he may not even be able to find relevant content or confirm the existence of content that he has heard about. Why? Because the financial organization has acted protectively first and has erected impenetrable firewalls to protect the content itself and even the content metadata, which includes such information as the report title, abstract, and price.

Other considerations of value include the following. (This list is both practical and notional. Some of these features and capabilities exist already. Some are under consideration or being developed by vendors. And some are more of a wish list.)

- **Helping consumers avoid device and data obsolescence:** Content purchased for a valid device today should be compatible with the DRM system on an upgraded device available tomorrow. Whenever possible, publishers should also avoid upgrading the DRM systems and formats themselves so that a valid DRM device today can at least enforce its current rules on future data, even when that data contains DRM information beyond the scope of the older device.

- **Giving consumers mechanisms to easily store and retrieve their purchased content:** The assumption of the DRM system should be that, over time, users will acquire an expanding personal library of content that they will want to catalog, retrieve, annotate, and continue to use. The DRM system should encourage this kind of personal knowledge store, all within the appropriate, licensed rights to the content.

- **Giving consumers the analogous experience of the nondigital world:** For example, users may find value in lending-library features that enable them to share (but not copy) favorite digital products. Indeed, some people may even want to profit from such arrangements — for example, the consultant who recommends an industry study to a client, who then proceeds to buy it, or the lawyer or accountant who provides authoritative material to a client to help him better understand a pending matter or recommendation.

- **Giving consumers the ability to buy an enhanced product or related product, leveraging their prior purchase or license:** For example, users may initially download and install an abridged version of a book for a low price but then be able to buy the full version at a discount.

In a 2000 report entitled "Digital Rights Management for eBooks: Publisher Requirements," the Association of American Publishers squarely backed this notion that consumers' perception of value clearly begins with the current experience with, in this case, the eBooks' analog counterpart (in other words, a printed book). "Consumers know that using paper-based books is a fairly straightforward process," the report reads. "Buy a book at the bookstore. Read it. Store it on the shelf or maybe give it to a friend. No interoperability issues here." The AAP report goes to quite vividly compare the satisfaction of the analog world with the difficulties in the nascent eBook business. "To read an eBook," the report continues, "the consumer must be sure that her reading device will work with the eBook's DRM format. Some combinations work, others don't. Moreover, some books are available in one DRM format but not in another. . . . And when the consumer finishes her eBook and gives it to her friend, another layer in interoperability enters the picture."

This is not a pretty picture, but it's a challenge that needs to be addressed quickly if consumers' expectations are to be met. Indeed, consumers may be reasonable to expect a satisfying experience with their new electronic content. They also often realize the benefits that digital distribution can perhaps bring to the publisher, in the form of, dare we suggest, lower costs and eventually lower prices to the consumers. Even the AAP's own research suggests that cost savings will potentially be passed on to the consumer.

Trust

The Internet is slowly but surely benefiting from maturation in the understanding of what *trust* means in electronic commerce. For the buyer, *trust* means knowing what he is buying, from whom he is buying it, that he will receive the product as presented, and that the transaction is auditable and secure. For the seller, *trust* means knowing that the buyer can complete the transaction, has taken delivery of the shipped product, and will make sure that the seller receives payment promptly.

Moreover, for buyers concerned about privacy, there is a growing movement to allow the buyer to control personal information, including how it is obtained and how it is shared or used (if at all).

DRM systems have the advantage of coming to market when at least the majority of these trust components are in place. All of them are essential to the consumer experience of DRM. Indeed, the content marketplace has added some additional requirements to how trust is established and maintained in an electronic transaction:

- ♦ In the case of specialized or high-value information, the consumer and publisher can benefit from authentication technology that guarantees the source of the information.

- ♦ In the case of sensitive information, consumers should be able to purchase content without uniquely identifying themselves. Consider the person recently diagnosed with a serious illness who wants to ensure his privacy when he downloads certain information. Consider also the person involved in a legal dispute who seeks to research the topic without fear of reprisal.

- ♦ Personalization becomes a sensitive issue when connected to privacy and DRM. Consider the once-pregnant woman who visits a book-shopping site, only to be reminded again and again of available books for naming babies.

In all, DRM-based e-commerce has all the requirements that generic e-commerce has — and many of its own. Your requirements analysis should include these generic e-commerce requirements, the ones specific to DRM-based e-commerce, and the specific needs your market or organizations may have.

Your competition: The same worries, legacy, concerns

If you're worried about your competition being way ahead of you, stop right now. DRM is still very much a nascent market. Unless you are in a specialized area with many early adopters of DRM (for example, you're a popular music site that features MP3 files), you have time to thoughtfully consider your requirements, engage with a vendor or supplier of DRM services, and deploy your initial DRM-based application.

In fact, even if you have competition in the DRM space, the competition may not be faring that well yet. Early adopters of new technology tend to struggle mightily for success, and early adopters of DRM are perhaps no exception.

It is worth looking at some representative sites and how they have attempted to solve the problem of protecting their content, either with commercial DRM solutions, "homegrown" solutions, or partial solutions based on traditional "perimeter" security.

Homegrown and partial solutions abound

In general, content sites that have developed their own protection schemes solutions outnumber sites that have employed commercial DRM solutions. Like many other markets for Web software (the content management of a few years ago comes to mind), homegrown solutions abound, and the pace of adoption for commercial DRM solutions has only recently begun an upsurge.

The ones who have been successful have, thus far, typically focused on a few features and had a very specific goal in mind. This section looks at two examples in particular.

Case Study 1: A publisher of high-value research

DRM vendors have often looked at high-value research — including financial, technical, and market research — as prototypical applications for the deployment of DRM. Indeed, a few such organizations have deployed DRM solutions. One successful implementation of DRM was at a research company that focuses on high-value market research related to technology trends, and its DRM solution went as follows:

♦ The company began with an established audience for its content that had thus far been accustomed to ordering print and waiting for it. Recent trends and some of its own customer feedback showed the company that customers were eager to move to a new model.

♦ The company began by digitizing its content in PDF, a form that is sufficiently universal and easy to use, which honored its requirements for quality and similarity to its print products and was relatively easy to produce and deploy for distribution.

♦ With the DRM solution in place, the publisher's consumers began receiving material faster; at the same time, the publisher realized cost savings in production and distribution. It didn't have to charge substantially less for the electronic product, giving it the option of increasing margin on its core products.

♦ As more commerce moved to it DRM-enabled Web site, the publisher began to get more specific and potentially more useful information about its consumers and about the actual use of the material. No longer was it simply printing and throwing material over the wall. The enhanced profiling of its customers and use of its products has enabled it to begin targeting future content development and marketing efforts.

♦ The publisher is beginning to experiment with different special offers, such as discounted and bundled content, time-limited use, and pass-along. As it experiments and analyzes the results of these experiments, it can add to its growing intelligence about its audience and how they use its products.

Case Study 2: Music

Buying music often represents a prototypical community of interest. Whether music buyers are attracted to a genre, a particular artist, or a particular instrument, they are indeed a small, focused community of interest. A DRM-backed music site can become a powerful and yet easy means by which an artist or a publisher can market to fans, and the fans can find all they want to listen to and know about a particular topic. Along with many of the practical benefits listed in the publishing case study, the music site can also take advantage of the following features and trends:

♦ As with the publishing site, the music site can experiment with different offerings and trends, but it can also establish relatively easy mechanisms with which the consumers can develop their own collections. This kind of "burn-to-own" offering is already taking hold and can be encouraged even more.

♦ Because music is often tied to events, there are many opportunities for cross-selling. The buyer of a music product can be offered a discount to an upcoming, related event. Attendees of a recent concert can "opt in" to receive special offers for downloadable music and other products.

♦ Moderately priced and scalable solutions could work well for the individual artist or the niche music publisher.

Adoption has been slow

Despite the pockets of success, adoption of commercial DRM solutions has been slow and success relatively discrete. There are many possible explanations for this, beginning with practical issues that seem to be slowing all e-commerce (such as the lack of uniform systems for micropayments and electronic cash) as well as some issues unique to DRM-backed e-commerce, such as concerns about cost and complexity. In addition, some publishers worry about the potential for the sale of digital products to cannibalize existing analog markets. Moreover, as formats such as digitized music and eBooks take hold in the popular imagination, the question of who holds the rights seems to have been opened anew. Authors and artists are working harder to maintain electronic rights in situations where they don't feel the publisher has a clear and compelling plan for marketing the electronic product. Finally, the courts may decide some of the fundamental questions, and traditional publishers may be losing their grip on some of these rights.

Yet the nascent DRM market seems to be showing signs of life. Despite the recent softness in the economy and spotty results among some of the DRM-focused vendors, the larger trends are encouraging. Vendors seem to be recognizing and dealing with some of their barriers to growth. They recognize the need to move forward with a consistent, standards-based approach.

From the publishers' perspective, they are in agreement that there are large potential markets for digital products. Yet they are stymied by the lack of specifics. They are looking for low cost, low risk approaches that can help them better identify and approach this market, while at the same time not losing focus on their core business and core opportunities.

Matching Needs to DRM Capabilities: A Checklist

The goal of this section is to kick-start a process where you develop a requirements checklist for your DRM needs. This is by no means exhaustive; we hope the chapter has made the point that your requirements will be unique to your market and your organization. Indeed, the requirements listed here represent a "brain dump" of possible requirements and in some cases may be overlapping or conflicting. But we do hope that this section outlines some of the main areas of your requirements analysis and provides a useful starting point for you.

Protection features: Encryption, watermarking, authentication

The first section of the checklist should include requirements for how your content must be protected. Weigh your organization's needs for security against the expectations of customers.

We suggest that you organize your checklist into a table with three columns, with the first column describing the feature, the second column giving a particular vendor a rating of "full compliance," "partial compliance," or "noncompliance," and the third column offering comments (see Table 8-1). As you rate additional vendors, you can include additional ratings columns for each vendor.

Table 8-1: Protection Requirements

Feature	Vendor A Rating	Comments
Encryption	Full compliance (for example)	
Public/private keys		
Watermarking		
Authentication		
Secure server storage		
Secure transmission		
Persistence		
Protection levels for different users		
Subcomponent protection (granularization)		
Unique identification of an object		
Alert if compromised		
Secure transactions		
Trust infrastructure for transaction		

Content types: eBooks, streaming media, and multimedia

The second portion of your checklist, shown in Table 8-2, addresses the types of content that the DRM solution can work with. Again, this list is by no means exhaustive, and you should take care to include all your required content types.

Table 8-2: Content Type Requirements

Feature	Vendor A Rating	Comments
Open eBook	Full compliance (for example)	
PDF		
GEMStar		
Glassbook		
Microsoft Reader		
Palm		
XML		
HTML		
WAP and other wireless formats		
Other text formats		
GIF		
JPEG		
Other image formats		
MP3		
Other audio formats		
JPEG		
Streaming audio		
Streaming video		
Other formats unique to your organization or market		

Business model enabling features: Distribution, pass-along, pay-per-view, and superdistribution

The third section of your checklist should detail any requirements that you have for the types of business models you would like to employ with your DRM solution. Be creative in your thinking here, as you want to include many possible business models and not inadvertently exclude any key ones. This part of the checklist, as shown in Table 8-3, begins with a set of requirements based on Chapter 4, which introduces the multidimensional view of rights, and then moves on to include elements of the business models discussed in Chapter 2.

The key to this section of your checklist is to determine the flexibility of the potential DRM solution, as well as its general appropriateness to your organization and your market. Your DRM solution shouldn't favor a single business model to the exclusion of others; it should support the business models that you see as key to your success, while also having the flexibility to allow you to experiment with new ones.

Table 8-3: Business Model Requirements

Feature	Vendor A Rating	Comments
Enable/restrict viewing	Full compliance (for example)	
Enable/restrict printing		
Enable/restrict playing		
Enable/restrict copying		
Enable/restrict moving		
Enable/restrict loaning		
Enable/restrict extracting		
Including abstracting		
Including fair use		
Including slice and dice or mix and match		
Enable/restrict editing		
Enable/restrict embedding		
Enable/restrict backing up		
Enable/restrict caching		
Enforce payment or another consideration		
Including one-time payments (pay-per-view)		
Including subscription processing		
Enable time limits (time-based access)		
Enable limits by geographical region		
Enable limits by IP address		
Enable limits by other business rules		
Support varying rights by user type		

Table 8-3: (continued)

Feature	Vendor A Rating	Comments
Support varying rights by individual user		
Enable/restrict pay-per-view		
Enable/restrict pass-along		
Enable/restrict superdistribution		
Enable/restrict lending		
Support metering		

The nitty gritty: Payment, clearinghouse, and business intelligence

The fourth section of your checklist, as shown in Table 8-4, deals with the core issues of payment and reporting and outlines some requirements for business intelligence, including profiling, reporting, and feedback mechanisms.

Table 8-4: Business Enabling Requirements

Feature	Vendor A Rating	Comments
Automated payment	Full compliance (for example)	
Other clearinghouse functions		
Payment auditing		
Payment reporting		
Automated transmission of reports		
Other required interoperability		
Allow other clearinghouses to be swapped in		
Business intelligence		
Profiling by user		
Profiling by product		
Granularity of product usage (for example, by section or page)		
Other feedback mechanisms		

Other requirements

The fifth section of your checklist, shown in Table 8-5, details other, mainly general, requirements that you should include in your analysis. It includes some general information technology (IT) concerns that others in your organization may want to weigh in on, as well as some general business requirements such as cost.

Table 8-5: Other Requirements

Feature	Vendor A Rating	Comments
Fits into budget	Full compliance (for example)	
Available for lease instead of purchase		
Available through Application Service Provider (ASP)		
General IT requirements		
Runs on standard operating systems		
Uses existing network infrastructure		
Relies on open standards for programming (application program interfaces — APIs)		
Is scalable		
Has a track record for integration		
Can integrate with existing back office systems		
Adheres to major standards		
ICE		
DOI		
XrML		
Has existing relationships with key channels		
Supports syndication		
Provides (or integrates with) automated tools for promotion		
Viral distribution		
E-mail campaigns		
Enhances indexing with major search engines		

As noted earlier, these tables are neither exhaustive nor necessarily consistent with your organizational needs. They are a good starting point, however, for discussions with potential vendors or service providers. They can also be used by a consultant who is helping you with your analysis.

Chapter 9

Implementation Options: Build, Buy, Integrate, and Outsource

Chapter 8 deals with understanding your requirements for DRM technology. This chapter brings you even closer to a technology decision by discussing options for implementing DRM. As with other technologies, you have several options for putting DRM into place. At minimum, you have the following options:

- ◆ You can develop and deploy your own technology solution from scratch.
- ◆ You can customize a solution based on core technology provided by a vendor.
- ◆ You can buy a total solution from a vendor and integrate it with your other systems.
- ◆ You can outsource the whole DRM problem, either by itself or in combination with other technology and services, such as syndication and fulfillment.

In fact, there are many variations and combinations of these approaches. Outsourcing itself can actually be a spectrum of approaches; an outsourcing arrangement can be limited in scope or all encompassing. Indeed, one of the challenges of the DRM landscape is not only deciding which technology or technologies are right for you, but also deciding whether you want to build it, buy it, lease it, or have a trusted partner solve the problem for you.

Building, Buying, or Integrating

The DRM space is crowded with technology and with options for acquiring the technology. Deciding whether to develop your own software or buy commercial software is a useful first step in helping to clarify the landscape for you. In truth, the "build or buy" question should perhaps more accurately be "build or otherwise acquire" because there are so many options for leasing and outsourcing. But you should make this "build or acquire" decision first; after you decide that, you can look at all the ramifications of your decision.

Why build?

Some organizations have staff for ongoing software development and maintenance and raise the "build or buy" question for both small and large projects. Organizations that develop their own software solutions do so for a variety of reasons, ranging from the economic to the technical:

- ◆ **They believe that they can get precisely what they want by building it themselves.** This is perhaps the most common reason organizations cite for building their own software. Some organizations have thoroughly evaluated commercial offerings and found there is too much of a gap between their requirements and the functionality of the commercial solutions. As a result, they decide to build precisely what they need.

- **They believe that they can save money by building new applications on top of an existing software infrastructure.** Some organizations are well aware that very little software is shrink-wrapped these days and that the real cost of software is often in the customization and integration. As a result, they have developed methodologies in which they build business applications on top of, for example, core libraries or a general platform such as an application server or a portal platform. They then evaluate a new application, such as DRM, to see if it can be built for a reasonable cost on top of their core software foundation.

- **They have the technical competency to develop, deploy, and support the applications.** Some organizations are appropriately staffed and organized to do software development and deployment themselves, though the trend is moving away from this.

- **They see the developed application as a key piece of their added value.** Organizations may see a certain application as intrinsic to their business and value proposition. For example, a distance learning company may decide to develop its own course registration software, even though commercial software is available. It may want to develop unique features that the commercial tools don't have, ensuring their unique value in that part of its business.

- **They believe that they can do the software development and deployment more inexpensively than the vendors.** Even lacking a general infrastructure to build on and leverage, some organizations may decide that a given application or tool can be developed for less in-house than by purchasing it from a vendor.

Keep in mind that it is a major undertaking to develop custom software for any kind of application, and such a decision should not be entered into lightly. If your organization doesn't have experience developing its own software applications, chances are this is not the time to start, and DRM is not the first application to try to build yourself.

Why not build?

Although there may be compelling reasons to build your own DRM software, such an approach works for few organizations because there are many reasons to not develop your own software:

- **Chances are, no matter how much DRM knowledge you have, there are people out there who have more.** In other words, why reinvent the wheel — and not as well as the first guy? Indeed, some building blocks of DRM, notably encryption, are mature specialties in computer science that knowledgeable people have been thinking about and working on for a long time. Some commercial solutions for DRM represent scores of engineering years of effort in and of themselves. On top of this, building blocks such as encryption are often standards-based, and the development of the standard also represents significant accrued intellectual effort.

- **Software development is a risk-intensive undertaking that can dramatically affect your schedule and budget.** You may be dealing yourself a wildcard that your business model simply cannot withstand. If you are planning on a third-quarter launch of a product that needs DRM protection, why not focus on getting the product out and have someone else worry about the DRM solution?

- **Your core business is something besides software development.** Why dilute your focus?

As discussed later, in the section "Outsourcing," there is some overlap between the "why not build" and the "why outsource" question. Both raise strategic questions of focus and staffing.

Why integrate?

As Chapter 5 illustrates, many component technologies compose DRM. These include security technologies, such as encryption and authentication, and tools for packaging, distribution, and rendering. Short of building your own components, doesn't it make sense that you can select various component technologies and integrate them into your own solution?

The short answer is yes, of course, and some organizations have done this already. The DRM vendors themselves recognize this potential, and many offer their tools as Software Development Kits, or SDKs. These SDKs provide programmers with libraries of core code and sample integration code for implementing the core libraries in larger applications. Thus, a programmer who needs an encryption scheme doesn't need to write it himself. He can license an encryption software company's SDK and integrate the core libraries into the application that he is writing. Indeed, there are public domain (including open source) libraries for various programming tasks, and programmers often try various libraries to solve a problem before choosing either a commercial or public domain one. This is a common practice among programmers and is the foundation for much application development today.

The potential to customize can be a nice middle ground between building your own software and buying something shrink-wrapped. As you know, some shrink-wrapped applications may do almost everything, but not quite everything. And, more significantly, they may not do many things precisely the way that you need them done. Hence the need to be able to at least customize the applications.

The key is the software buyer's need for a competitive advantage. To gain an advantage, technology buyers may want to look at SDKs that support rapid prototyping and deployment and allow them to develop finished applications that meet key business objectives.

Outsourcing

It's likely that you won't decide to build your own DRM software and will instead look to the marketplace of commercial products. As the subsection "Why Integrate?" intimated, you are also faced with questions of how much to customize what you acquire and how many different component technologies may be part of the mix. This section addresses the many questions that arise if you decide not to build your own solution, such as how you decide how much of the commercial solution to undertake yourself and how much you depend on outside partners. Your decision could include outsourcing the entire problem to a qualified third party, several of which already exist to do just that for publishers and entertainment companies.

In a series of interviews with senior management at publishing companies, we determined that there was a great deal of interest in outsourcing for technology in general but that DRM technology itself may not always be viewed as a prime candidate for outsourcing. At a strategic level, management views the outsourcing question as a relatively "clean" one, especially if it is already outsourcing other technologies. Upper management is increasingly open-minded about whether its organization needs to run a given technology itself. On the other hand, DRM is sometimes viewed as being part of the organization's security infrastructure, and IT organizations have traditionally been reluctant to outsource security technology and other core services such as e-mail.

Why outsource?

Outsourcing is a growing trend for organizations. One specific trend is to outsource one or more technology needs to an application service provider, or ASP. In this model, the ASP provides the hardware, applications, and networking to the organization and its customers — in effect, all the components to successfully run a given application or applications. Although the market for ASPs is facing some consolidation, it is still a rapidly growing trend. With more and larger companies turning to ASPs, Forrester Research projects that the market for application hosting will reach $11.3 billion in 2003, with a compound annual growth rate of 86 percent.

Many organizations have a first inclination to do the implementation work in-house and run the finished application in-house. Yet you are well advised to consider all the issues and risks that come with such a project and weigh them against the possibility of handing the problem over to a qualified partner. Beginning with the technology selection itself, bringing technology in-house is fraught with risk.

Avoiding the difficulty of choosing the right DRM solution

Right now, the DRM market is in its earliest stages, with perhaps a few better bets among the competing vendors — but no clear winner. At this writing, one DRM vendor ceased operations, and another announced that it was looking for a buyer. It is a difficult market in which to make a confident decision.

What complicates matters is that DRM companies often offer point solutions. A given DRM tool may work only with a certain medium. Thus, you may be fortunate enough to pick the eventual market winner for the technology that protects your PDF files, but the company that makes your audio DRM technology may go belly up. And it's the rare publisher that deals with precisely one medium. For example, an educational book publisher, moving to an increasingly electronic marketplace, may well find himself or herself needing to distribute and protect text files, audio, video, and animation, just for starters. Determining the right technology for each of these formats is a daunting task; in baseball terms, it would be very hard to bat 1000 and get all your choices right.

Companies to which you can outsource, such as Reciprocal, have implemented not just one but several DRM technologies. They have gone through the process of testing and selecting various DRM technologies and may well know which DRM solutions are best for your needs. If they have a comprehensive offering of several DRM technologies to choose from, this may mitigate the risk of your betting on selecting and acquiring the technology yourself.

Remember too that, besides being risky, analyzing and selecting DRM tools can in and of itself be a complex and costly undertaking. Some organizations are staffed with analysts who are expert in making such decisions, but other organizations aren't. Even if you do have such a staff, they may be busy with other projects or have higher priorities. If DRM is central to your future, you may well want to invest in such analysis. But if you are unsure about DRM's importance to your organization and are looking to simply work with it for a particular business opportunity, an outsourcing partner may even make more sense, as it will have done this analysis already.

Finally, working with an outsource partner mitigates the particular risk of technology selection by helping you avoid *technology lock-in*. Organizations that choose a technology, implement it, and go on to use it for a period of time have all kinds of good reasons to simply continue using it, even when better and less expensive solutions emerge. They simply have too much cost sunk in, and too many existing processes, to make the switch over to a new system worth their while.

An outsourcing partner may be able to help you economically begin with one solution and then switch over to a better one when it emerges. This enables you to continue to focus on your organization's business needs, while your outsource partner focuses on the best fit industry standard technologies to meet those needs.

Decreasing time to market

Unless you have been living on a desert island for the last 20 years, you know that software development and integration are time-consuming. If you are facing a firm deadline to launch a product that needs DRM protection, you have to be realistic about the schedule impact of implementing and testing the DRM software. Because nothing is shrink-wrapped anymore, even the simplest software projects are most comfortably measured in days and not hours — and often in weeks. If there is significant customization involved, the length of the schedule increases dramatically.

And that is the best case. Only that same desert island could protect you from having suffered with the impact of some delay in a software project. Add to this that the DRM products are relatively new and still somewhat unstable, with many product revisions, and you face a higher risk of schedule delays. Such delays can be relatively discrete and have little impact, or they can prevent you from establishing an e-commerce presence in time for you busiest selling season.

A qualified outsourcing partner can help you mitigate schedule risks and reduce time to market if it has solutions in place that meet your needs. Look for an experienced organization with a proven track record with companies much like your own and solid reference accounts that can speak to the question of how quickly they were up and running. Look to strike an agreement with incentives for on-time or early deployment and penalties for delays in implementation.

Getting ready solutions to complex technical problems

No matter what the DRM vendors tell you, implementing, rolling out, and supporting commercial software is an expensive, complicated proposition. Each phase of implementation, from determining requirements to rollout and support, raises technical challenges that your organization may or may not be ready to deal with.

Keep in mind also that a DRM solution may be unlike other systems a publisher has implemented in that it has a major component that deals directly with the customer. Most of the DRM solutions require the end user to download a client application. Such a solution brings with it issues of supporting geographically dispersed customers with heterogeneous systems and varying abilities to troubleshoot and deal with technical problems. End users of such systems have high expectations of reliability and, because a financial transaction is often involved, expect customer support 24 hours a day, 7 days a week.

Moreover, because a DRM solution is customer-facing, it must be engineered with a customer in mind; this is fundamentally different from in-house tools and systems that an organization may have put in place for its own use. With in-house solutions, you can depend on internal training, a growing pool of experienced users, and some commitment from employees to make the system work, despite its glitches and shortcomings. This is not the case with a software solution that will be used by customers. The user's experience with the DRM solution needs to be straightforward, easy to use, and self-revealing. Otherwise, the deployment of the system will lead to, at best, a customer-support nightmare and, at worse, lost business and disgruntled customers. Ironically, developing such easy-to-use software is very hard work. Hemingway said about writing, "Easy writing makes hard reading" — the message being, of course, that if you work hard as a writer, you make your reader's job easier. The same can be said for software development: Work very hard at implementing a solution, and your user's experience will be that much better.

Part of this complexity risk can be mitigated, of course, by well-chosen and well-implemented solutions. The DRM provider Authentica, for example, tries to avoid part of the customer-support problem by providing a "silent install" for its client tool. The users of its client tool can enable a process in which updates to the client tool are "pushed" to them on a regular basis without their having to do anything.

Even with such useful tools to make the deployment problem easier, outsourcing may still make sense for many organizations. Even assuming that you can engineer and deploy an easy-to-use customer solution, you still have your other main constituency to consider — your publishing organization. Another piece of the complexity puzzle is the software used on the publisher side. Whereas the customer's side is complex precisely because it needs to be easy to use, the publisher's side of the DRM system is complex because of the need to integrate with so many other key systems, most notably an electronic storefront and various back-office systems. Any of these integrations can be a complex piece of programming. A qualified outsource organization may well have solved many of these problems already.

Finally, supporting any software solution has the risk of putting you on the proverbial technology treadmill. You will always need to work hard to keep the solution up-to-date and running smoothly. Again, because DRM is a relatively early software market, you can expect more changes to the software, more updates, and more need to pay close attention to the software's care and feeding.

Avoiding a major capital investment

An obvious and compelling advantage of outsourcing is that your organization can avoid the sometimes-staggering up-front capital investment and integration cost of a new software system. Outsourcing arrangements can often mean a much more modest up-front cost, together with a monthly or quarterly fee.

In addition to potentially lower up-front costs, an outsourcing arrangement also helps you accurately predict costs over time. Indeed, you may be able to lock in costs over a period of time. Software projects have many risks beyond the schedule and complexity risks, as discussed earlier, and cost is perhaps the paramount risk. The cost of implementing complex software merely begins with the acquisition cost of the software itself. Research from companies such as Gartner Group and Forrester Research suggests that the cost of integrating major software platforms typically ranges from three to six times the cost of the software itself. The bulk of this cost can be fees for professional services firms and contract programmers as organizations race to deploy systems on time after not realizing how complex the implementation would be.

Because DRM is not yet viewed as central to many organizations' IT needs, organizations may take an even closer look at the up-front and ongoing costs for DRM. Some technologies, such as e-mail and networking, are central to an organization and are viewed as part of the cost of doing business. DRM is not viewed that way yet. Because of this, organizations may feel even more compelled to minimize investment and arrive at an accurate estimate of costs over time.

Publishers who are unsure of DRM's role in their enterprise, or who are experimenting with a DRM-backed e-commerce system, may view outsourcing even more favorably if they are convinced that the costs of an outsourcing arrangement can be very accurately predicted.

Traditionally, publishers operate in a model in which they can accurately estimate costs going into a venture, even if the potential revenue is a projection. Deploying a new technology such as DRM can be expensive in and of itself. In addition, unplanned and hidden costs can arise. The end result can lead to overspending in a venture that ultimately yields too little revenue.

Hidden costs arise from a variety of factors:

♦ The difficulty in predicting the costs to create and manage custom applications or integrate packaged applications

♦ Poorly scoped projects, which lead to overlooked necessary functionality or expensive deployed functionality that isn't really necessary

♦ A customer demand that exposes problems in the the deployed DRM-based e-commerce system and leads to increased customer-support costs

Despite competitive pressure to deploy e-business solutions, publishers need to return to a product development model in which they can accurately predict costs of development, distribution, and marketing, even when they have to guess at projected revenues. Ideally, they should also be able to accurately predict the initial costs of such a venture but also have the ability to predict lifecycle costs as well as incremental costs for adding major new features or for extending the DRM support to other brands.

Given these vagaries of deploying DRM with either commercial or home-grown applications, publishers may be able to mitigate the economic risk by teaming with an outsourcing partner.

Avoiding adding staff

After schedule, technical complexity, and cost, the other often-cited reason for outsourcing is staffing. Some publishers don't have extensive technical staff for deploying a solution such as DRM, and some do have the technical staff but would rather deploy them elsewhere. In either case, organizations may look at the staff required for deploying and supporting a DRM solution and decide that an outsourcing arrangement makes more sense.

You would need the following kind of internal staffing to deploy and support a DRM system:

1. During integration and deployment, you need someone focused on the project management of the deployment — someone who decides who is responsible for the different elements of the integration and deployment and when the internal and vendor resources (if applicable) are available to perform the tasks and who makes sure that the schedule is being met.

2. You may need technical specialists, including programmers, to undertake aspects of the customization.

3. You need production specialists to prepare the content for packaging and distribution.

4. You need personnel connected with back-office operations to ensure that the correct business information is collected from the DRM-based e-commerce system.

5. You need customer-support personnel to deal with technical problems encountered by customers.

If your organization partners with an outsourcing company for DRM, it is reasonable to assume that you need none of the personnel listed in item 2, none of the personnel listed in item 5, and probably none of the personnel listed in item 3. You can decide whether to project manage the process yourself (item 1) or depend on the outsource partner. Of course, your business people will still perform the due diligence (item 4) to ensure that the proper information is collected from the outsource partner's e-commerce system.

Keep in mind that, even if you outsource the DRM solution, you're still likely to need project management on your side. In addition, the publisher also needs someone to act as product manager — to meet requirements, control budgets, articulate the marketing message, and to plan campaigns. It is absolutely critical that the technical efforts of implementing DRM happen in conjunction with well-thought-out product marketing.

This is a significant saving in technical resources, which may be precisely what some organizations are after. In certain job markets, in which technical personnel are available only at a premium, this ability to outsource can be very attractive. And again, even in a case in which an organization does have technical staff, it may well not want to deploy them on a DRM project when the organization has other projects that it deems more important. Among all of these personnel areas, customer support may be the biggest surprise for publishers. Keep in mind that most DRM solutions require a piece of client software and that the end users can end up requiring technical support when they upgrade or change computers or when they purchase new material and have difficulty with existing licenses or keys. Some early adopters of DRM systems have had problems with qualified customers getting access to content that they have already purchased. Customers will want that sort of problem resolved quickly and painlessly.

Keeping new business separate from existing business

Keeping a new venture separate from your existing business is a piece of business wisdom that may make particular sense for DRM-backed e-commerce. In many cases, the business models for electronic content are still unfounded. In the case of eBooks, for example, many publishers are certain that there will be some level of business, but exactly how much is pure speculation. It also remains to be seen what publishers should charge, precisely how they should market eBooks, and what they should do with issues such as pass-along and library lending.

As a result, it makes good sense to have a clean separation of your existing business from the new DRM-backed business. The publishers that we interviewed liked the idea of outsourcing the DRM efforts as part of having the new business work within its own profit and loss statement, where costs and revenues can be scrutinized on their own.

One publisher that we interviewed discussed the unique challenges of marketing electronic content. The publisher has been in the business of marketing print materials for close to a hundred years and has very well-established marketing and pricing guidelines. Its management staff knows in detail the costs of print content development, production, manufacturing, and distribution, making it a straightforward task to accurately determine the profitability of a product or a line of business. In the past year, this company has begun marketing online, first using a DRM solution that it selected and later teaming with an outsourcing partner. Its initial efforts to implement the DRM technology itself was eye-opening, as the company had numerous customer-support issues and found itself troubleshooting and debugging the customer's PCs and networks as part of supporting the new electronic product. The lesson for this publisher was to use the outsource partner to cleanly separate the costs and revenues for the new product line from its existing business.

Such separation may be especially useful to the publisher who is brand new to developing and marketing electronic content. If you aren't already developing and marketing an electronic product, you may not want to take on the new product line and the DRM implementation all at once. This may simply be too much for your organization to absorb, making outsourcing an even more sensible option.

Focusing on core competencies while the experts handle the specialized system

Focusing on your core competencies is a corollary to keeping new business separate from existing business. The thinking here is that the DRM technology and specialized operations are outside your current expertise, which is developing and marketing the content. By outsourcing the DRM technology and operations, you can continue to focus on the business itself. The advantages can be impressive. The company to whom the publisher outsources the DRM solution does the following:

♦ Makes the capital and human investment in the technical solutions that compose a DRM system.

♦ Provides all the integration work for the DRM system and e-commerce components so that they work together as one complete, preintegrated solution.

♦ Provides round-the-clock staffing and technical expertise in all aspects of DRM deployment, integration, and operation.

♦ Provides fixed, predictable costs for all features and functions associated with the system.

♦ Continues to invest in underlying technical solutions, providing the publisher with ongoing and systematic upgrades to its environment.

In such an environment, the publisher can focus on the core business process of developing the editorial product and accompanying business model, leaving the technical details to a qualified partner whose sole business is to provide the infrastructure without trying to usurp the publisher's business.

Maintaining flexible capacity

One television commercial related to the Internet is a favorite, perhaps because the anxiety it portrays is so well understood. In this commercial, a team of young dot-com types gathers around a computer screen, watching their site launch, and the first few orders start to trickle in. Small smiles turn to broad ones and just as quickly to looks of horror as the orders then start pouring in. The commercial doesn't even really have to state the problem (although it does). Is the site ready for this kind of traffic? Will it collapse under its own weight?

Many things affect whether a Web site will hold up under pressure, but often it is the most mundane problems that kill you. Frequently, the core problem is poor performance caused by an inadequate capacity to handle the traffic. And a slow site will soon be a dead site. According to Jupiter Research, poor performance can lead directly to a lost audience — more than half of the people surveyed by Jupiter had at least temporarily stopped using a site because of performance problems, and some of those people never come back.

Yet solving performance is not an easy problem. You can try to spend your way out of it, with more and better hardware and increased bandwidth, but you may still have challenges. The heavy traffic you predict today will likely not be enough as the Internet grows. One publisher built a fine Web presence, with excellent hardware and bandwidth, only to be swamped the very day their content was linked to a promotion on America Online. For the publisher, it presented a Catch 22; the publisher needs to grow its business by promoting its site, but promoting it means spending enough on infrastructure to be able to accommodate traffic that it may get only sporadically.

Of course, you hope that you have such a problem of increasing demand. But what if you don't? You may have spent your way to an expensive solution that is never used. Outsourcing is an almost certain way to get the flexible capacity that you are likely to need. If you are planning a promotion that you are hopeful will bring increased traffic over a defined period, some planning with your outsource partner will get you the capacity you need.

Tying to other outsourced services

Publishers who are considering an outsource arrangement for DRM services likely already outsource other technology and professional services. This raises the question of combining the DRM outsourcing with other outsourced services. One example is tying the production of the electronic content itself to the DRM services. One outsourcing company, Reciprocal, seems to have established the market leadership, at least in the publishing space. At the time of writing, Reciprocal and the eBook conversion and production company Texterity announced a new service for small- and medium-size publishers. Using this joint service, publishers can use Texterity's Text Café eBook services and then house their eBooks and make use of Reciprocal's DRM services, which include solutions from Adobe, Microsoft, and InterTrust. The goal of the joint offering is to provide small- and medium-size publishers with economical access to an end-to-end digital distribution solution.

It follows that other technologies and services may well be outsourced with the core DRM solution. These include the following:

- Conversion and packaging
- Subscription management
- Other list management
- Payment clearing and reporting
- Asset management
- Inventory management
- Data warehousing
- Print on demand
- CD-ROM production and shipping
- Site design and hosting
- Reporting
- Campaign planning
- Content syndication

Syndication is important to mention here as an allied service because there is often an important overlap between DRM and syndication. Several DRM-focused companies, including DigitalOwl and MediaDNA, in fact offer services and technology that bridge DRM and syndication. Among other things, these companies focus on helping publishers define and apply subject taxonomies. These improved taxonomies are then used to make the publishers' content more visible to search engines and to better organize the content for placement on partner sites. Reciprocal makes a similar point about the Digital Asset Management services, which it feels are able improve how publishers can create and manage catalogs of their content for their own sites and for partner sites.

When you think through what other services may be sensibly outsourced with DRM, we advise you to not lose track of the fact that DRM is ultimately about business models and marketing in its broadest sense. To this end, you should consider organizations that are attuned to helping you market your products best, while experimenting with different business models and fully understanding the success and challenges of each model.

If anything, publishers have too many options for partnering and not too few. Some professional publishers, for example, have long-established arrangements with document fulfillment houses that essentially act as resellers, printing materials on demand as orders come in. One large professional publisher takes all orders through its central Web site and 800 number, but then the printing and fulfillment is done elsewhere by a network of partners. What happens to such an arrangement if DRM can be added to the mix and the partners can also distribute electronic content? This particular publisher foresees a time when DRM systems can even help its largest customers deal with internal tracking and accounting.

Things to watch out for when outsourcing

If you decide to pursue outsourcing as an option, there are some issues to consider. Some of these issues, such as cost and reliability, are generic to any outsourcing arrangement. You will want to make sure that you get the best possible level of service at the most reasonable price. Some of the issues, though, are unique to DRM because of its importance to your business models and marketing efforts.

Relationships with key channels

You know where your content needs to be. If customers are already coming to your site and most of your sales will continue to emanate from there, your outsource partner will only have to make your DRM system work on your site. Chances are, though, that you have some key channels you need to work with, so you need to ensure that the outsource partners already work with or are prepared to work with your key channels. As an example, in the eBook world, this would mean Amazon.com and Barnes & Noble.com, at a minimum. Whatever you view as key sales channels, make sure that your potential outsourcing partner is able to connect you with these channels.

In addition, your outsource partner may have additional sales channels for you. DigitalOwl, for example, has a retail network of niche Web sites and vertical marketplaces, mainly focused on business topics and job hunting. Other potential outsourcing partners have created electronic storefronts that can be quickly integrated into your partner sites. For example, if you are a publisher of specialized gardening books, you may be able to quickly establish storefronts on major gardening portals, as well as specialized portals for niche gardening interests. The key is expanded reach, and your outsourcing partner may be able to quickly help you market through your primary channels and add additional, potentially fruitful ones.

Flexibility in implementation

When examining outsource partners, look for some flexibility in how they implement the various pieces of the DRM puzzle. Keep in mind that a comprehensive DRM solution starts with content conversion and packaging and often includes content hosting, payment clearing, and distribution. Because of your own needs, or your selling partner's needs, you may need some flexibility in precisely how your outsource partner implements each of these pieces. What if you have the opportunity to work with a major new channel, but it wants you to use its e-commerce system and payment clearing process? Would your outsource partner be able to accommodate this?

It's likely that both your existing channels and potential new ones may present some implementation challenges to your outsourcing partner. One scientific publisher that we interviewed already has in place an arrangement in which other Web sites can sell its materials, but the publisher itself currently handles all the fulfillment. This includes the sales of both electronic content and printed materials. Ideally, the publisher would like to allow the partner sites to handle fulfillment as well and to extend the DRM solution to these partner sites.

Service-level agreements

ASP-type outsourcing arrangements often include some type of service-level agreements. These service-level agreements commonly address issues such as a guaranteed level of network availability and the rate of data transmission. Avoid service-level agreements that are too general and try to ensure that the agreements include up time for the specific DRM and e-commerce features.

Branding cohesiveness

One last consideration is the issue of branding. Outsource arrangements sometimes lack the level of customization that a customer wants. Remember that your outsource partner may be presenting your products in a variety of channels, including major retail sites, general-purpose portals, and specialized catalogs. You want to ensure that you can control all the details of branding that you are concerned about, including logos, colors, and other features. Your customers should be presented with your product precisely the way that you want them to see it.

ROI: Can the DRM System Pay for Itself?

Return on investment (ROI) is a lively topic these days. Management has a keen new interest in ROI for technology projects, after a period of time when ROI was viewed by some as an outdated, 20th century concern that new economy companies didn't need to worry about. In the wake of the high-tech slowdown of 2000-2001, we have arrived at a more mature notion of ROI, which includes a number of factors:

♦ ROI still begins with the traditional notion of savings through capital investment. Some organizations are still able to measure what they've spent on the new technology against, for example, the burdened labor cost of continuing to perform the work the old way. In some cases, they can also add derived revenue. So, in the simplest analysis, a $1 million capital investment that saves $400 thousand per year in burdened labor pays for itself in 2.5 years — or faster if the investment also leads to increased revenue.

♦ The key in traditional ROI analysis has been to arrive at the appropriate metric for measurement. In a print publishing environment, for example, publishers may have arrived at a very accurate metric. For example, they may know that it costs $12 to typeset each page with their current system. If they are preparing to invest in a new system that promises to reduce costs to $8 per page, they can begin to make some meaningful calculations. How much would they be willing to spend to arrive at the $8 per page figure? If they can get to $8 per page, how many more books would they be able to produce at their current level of spending? How much more income could be derived from the additional books? And so forth.

Admittedly, the post-Information Age has added some new factors to ROI analysis and has perhaps even spawned new measures:

♦ Some technological innovations — e-mail and a basic Web presence come to mind — are an integral part of today's business process. So a traditional ROI analysis doesn't necessarily apply.

♦ The need to keep up with competitors or move ahead may also be a factor that doesn't fit nicely into a simplistic equation and has more recently been considered an almost distinct calculation — "return on opportunity (ROO)," or, more negatively, "opportunity cost." But some investments may not have as much bottom line ROI as they do top line ROO, such as retaining customers, attracting new ones, and building new value for the company.

♦ Other, less tangible and measurable factors apply, such as customer satisfaction, employee satisfaction, and success through innovation.

Fortunately, we are beyond the stage where ROI was viewed as meaningless. Instead, analysts, consultants, and IT management are beginning to view ROI as a key element in a broader analysis of how to make and justify technology spending decisions.

A traditional cost analysis

So if you are a publisher and are looking to implement DRM, how do you view ROI? To begin with, you need to look at your current situation and where you are with DRM as a component of your business:

♦ If you are an established user of DRM using "home-grown" or first-generation DRM solutions, your ROI analysis will largely be a traditional one of determining cost savings with the new investment and how quickly the new technology can pay for itself.

♦ If you are convinced that DRM-supported e-commerce is a viable business for you but you are not firmly in the business yet, focus your ROI analysis on a low-cost, highly reliable solution that will pay for itself quickly and allow you to easily scale and increase your DRM-supported system with predictable, incremental technology investments.

♦ If you are exploring DRM-supported e-commerce but aren't yet sure that it will be a significant business for you, base your ROI analysis on making a small and predictable investment. With this small, fixed cost in hand, you can then focus your analysis on how much revenue you will be able to derive by looking closely at the business models that make the most sense for you.

Whether you are planning to build, buy, or outsource your DRM-enabled commerce system, you will be well served when you have an accurate metric to measure current productivity and security against the potential productivity and security of the new system. In a DRM-supported commerce system, the metric could be something like cost per transaction; in addition, publishers could begin to estimate whether the improved security is resulting in some captured sales that had previously been lost. Publishers can then look at major cost categories such as labor costs, with an eye toward better understanding the true cost of the many manual steps that they are now performing:

♦ Costs associated with packaging content, including human and IT resources

♦ Costs associated with managing the delivery of content — the matrix of managing who gets what content, and when

♦ Costs of errors, including the need for redelivery

Larger publishers, at least ones with multiple product lines and locations, will also be able to calculate potential ROI from eliminating overlapping and/or redundant functions, as well as the benefits of combining production operations into a single process.

Less tangible ROI factors

In addition to the preceding cost factors, DRM has a number of less tangible factors that you need to consider in your ROI analysis. Many of these fall into the area of "return on opportunity," and some are unique to DRM itself.

Publishers that successfully implement a DRM-supported commerce system should be able to realize the following advantages over their current operations. They should be able to do the following:

- ♦ Protect their content after the point of purchase.

- ♦ More accurately monitor information use. This enables them to determine unsuccessful content and discontinue it, increase market exposure for successful content, and develop new offers based on use. This type of improved analysis is both an investment and return factor that affects content development.

- ♦ Improve brand recognition and brand loyalty through more easily accessed and accurate information. Brands can be efficiently and accurately maintained and propagated.

- ♦ Add or improve customer self-service in which agreements can be established and then customers can select and purchase content automatically.

In our interviews, several publishing executives spoke about ROI for DRM being much more about increased revenue. Several of them voiced cautious optimism about the DRM-based systems being able to yield revenue that they are otherwise not getting because of unauthorized copying. One executive of a firm that already sells a significant amount of content in electronic form talked about at least being able to prevent the "network" copy, where one legitimately purchased copy of a document somehow ends up on several desktops or on a networked server. For these executives, the ROI from a DRM-based e-commerce system will be proven mainly by increased revenue.

Chapter 10

Plug and Play: Integrating DRM

Chapter 9 deals with understanding your options for working with DRM technology, ranging from developing your own tools to outsourcing the entire technology solution to a qualified partner. Chances are — no matter what your approach — you still need to consider integration issues. At a minimum, you will need to consider the following:

- ♦ Whether your production processes lend themselves to producing finished goods that are ready for DRM systems
- ♦ Whether your DRM solution is easily integrated with your core production systems
- ♦ Whether you have other systems that need to be integrated, such as e-commerce systems and technology for features such as usage metering
- ♦ Whether your end users face challenges integrating your client tools with their desktops

The core issues are indeed related to production processes. As indicated in other chapters, one key to successfully implementing DRM is doing it with reasonable and predictable costs. Your organization needs to be able to economically create electronic products, "DRM them," and make them available to your chosen markets. Having such an economical process has as much to do with rationalizing your production process as it does with choosing the right DRM technology or outsourcing partner.

Yet production, although the primary challenge, is only part of the integration puzzle. A myriad of other systems may well need to integrate with your DRM system, including back-office and reporting software. Also, significantly, DRM integration raises fundamental questions about your organization's methods and goals for data protection, and, as such, DRM may bump up against other security issues. Finally, the manner in which you deploy your DRM system to your end users raises a number of practical and oftentimes frustrating issues.

This chapter discusses these issues, focusing especially on production processes, security, and end-user deployment.

Integrating DRM into Production Processes

Whether you are a book publisher, recording company, or video producer, production processes for electronic products ultimately require you to arrive at two things — finished goods in the formats that the market expects and metadata or supporting data for catalogs, commerce systems, Web sites that sell and promote your product, and such. A book publisher, for example, likely needs to produce the publication metadata that goes along with a format such as Open eBook (OEB), and a recording company often needs to produce track-by-track metadata for Web sites that list or sell the track. To complicate matters, a given publisher may be producing the same product in several formats, and each format may require different metadata and several delivery methods to different distribution outlets. If production processes aren't refined and automated, they will remain burdensome and inefficient, making it difficult or impossible for a company to profitably explore DRM-based e-commerce.

Finished goods production

When figuring out the impact of DRM integration on production, begin by looking at how you produce finished goods for electronic products. How is the content managed from creation to production? What systems are used in your production workflow, and how may these systems hook up with the DRM process?

Take print publishers as an example. Their current production workflow is likely centered around a desktop publishing application such as Quark Express. When they are done with editorial and production processes, their final format may well be the Quark Express file itself, which, although well suited to be sent out to the printer, stops short of the finished good that they may need for creating their electronic product, which may be in an XML-based eBook format such as OEB or in a format such as Portable Document Format (PDF). Indeed, some publishers may be going one step further in-house by producing a PostScript or PDF file ready for reproduction, but many publishers aren't at that stage yet. At the completion of their process for producing a printed book, for example, they may be left with a combination of the Quark Express binary file, TIFF or EPS files for finished artwork, and an assortment of other raw materials.

This kind of workflow is indeed less than ideal for seamless integration with a DRM solution. Much handwork would remain to be done, first to produce the finished goods formats and then to connect with a DRM solution. Yet it is likely that you have a similar production workflow in that it is somewhat disjointed. Music and video producers may have a similar problem, with finished goods left still needing to be digitized.

This is not to say that you should immediately change what you are doing and create a seamless, all-digital workflow for each and every product you produce. To begin with, lots of organizations exist to do this digital capture for you, and you should look at the cost of changing your internal processes versus the very real possibility that you could use outside services. For example, companies such as Texterity (www.texterity.com) and OverDrive (www.overdrive.com) in the eBook space, and the Sonopress division of Bertelsmann (www.sonopress.de) in the music space, focus on blending their digitization services with the practical realities of how publishers and music companies produce finished goods.

Yet you should at the very least perform the following three tasks:

♦ Look at the economics and throughput of your current production processes and determine how they will fare with producing both your current finished goods and electronic product. Include some analysis of unit cost and the potential return on investment for doing things in-house versus outside.

♦ Decide whether some fine-tuning is in order. A book publisher, for example, may want to modify its production process to include the production of PDF as the final form instead of something like the Quark Express binary that they are currently producing. A music producer may want to begin doing some digitization upstream.

♦ Begin to get your house in order by looking at your assets and beginning a process of inventorying and evaluating them, with an eye toward creating an overarching plan for Digital Asset Management (DAM) that will take into consideration what assets you have, what value they have, and what digital forms they should be available in.

This third point is the most important one. Over the long term, electronic products can be most effectively created and marketed when the products themselves, and the raw materials from which they are created, are efficiently managed. You could argue that publishers have a DAM problem first and a DRM problem second.

The typical publisher has lots of materials, in both digital form and not, originating from several sources. These materials include diverse formats such as compound documents, audio and video files, image files of many formats, databases, raw text files, and so on. The materials themselves may reflect uncomplicated rights, such as material that the publisher itself has created or has had created as work for hire, or may be bound to complex rights — author manuscripts, commissioned photos, licensed music and videos, and so on. A single Quark file or video could include material from more than one source, with multiple rights needing to be managed.

We discuss the DAM question in more detail later in this chapter in the section "Moving from Today's Processes to Tomorrow's." But as you begin to look at your production processes for finished goods, you should look at your intellectual property assets and how they are being managed, stored, and produced.

The first questions in looking at finished goods are quite concrete: What do you produce, what formats do you produce it in, and where are the final products stored and managed? You should answer these questions as specifically as they need to be. List the software and operating systems that you use, the precise formats used for storage, and the locations of everything on file systems and servers if in-house or with partner organizations or offsite storage facilities. (Note that this will instantly raise questions about long-term storage and archiving if they haven't already been answered.)

Then map out your current workflow or workflows for producing finished goods. This should be oriented by task (for example, write, edit, copy edit, layout, and so on). Indicate in the workflow if and where content is digitized (or initially created in digital form) and where any electronic transformation occurs (for example, the production person converts the finished manuscript files from Microsoft Word to Quark Express). The workflow should also indicate what software is used, including desktop applications and more enterprise applications, such as manuscripts that are controlled by a document management system.

This kind of bird's-eye view of your production process can help you begin to explore questions about integrating DRM into production. For example, where would the DRM process be introduced into the editorial and production workflow? Does the current workflow result in finished goods ready for the DRM system? Where would the DRM conversion and packaging processes be introduced into the current workflow, and who would apply them? Would this happen in the production process? Or as a back-end process after finished goods are complete? Could some of the conversion and packaging be somehow done automatically? If a document management system is used, could it be somehow integrated with the DRM system?

Such a workflow exercise may not only help answer these DRM questions but may also help rationalize your workflow to better accommodate digital production in general — not just for DRM. It may identify potential efficiencies and steps in the workflow that can be automated, outsourced, or eliminated. At the very least, such a workflow analysis will identify how efficiently finished goods can be made available for DRM processes and whether the finished goods need to be further processes or converted.

Packaging

After you have created finished goods, most DRM systems involve a process in which the finished goods are packaged into a form suitable for distribution under the control of the DRM system, as shown in the generic DRM architecture in Chapter 5. The packaged product typically includes the finished goods, often in some kind of encrypted form; the DRM server software also produces a license that identifies the product and the rights information assigned to it.

Packaging and encrypting the finished goods may involve some conversion beforehand, and the process itself may be automatic or may require some human intervention. As you look at DRM solutions and your own workflow, consider how your production systems and processes will integrate with your potential DRM solution at this point of packaging:

- How would your content be packaged for the DRM system and distribution?

- Is this process manual? Semi-automatic? Can it be scripted or done with some kind of batch file?

- Can the publisher's workflow processes and systems be fine-tuned to better automate conversion and packaging?

Depending on your market and industry, packaging may also include making available certain supporting information and materials. For book publishing, it may include preparing catalog information and a sample chapter, along with the finished book. For a music publisher, the supporting materials may include the finished tracks, catalog information, and samples from the tracks. These additional details of the packaging process have proven to be frustratingly difficult to master and often result in time-consuming, inefficient processes for the publisher.

One music publisher, for example, reports a number of problems keeping various partners' catalogs up-to-date. Partners look for the music publisher to provide the track, a clip, and certain selling information and then to keep all this information up-to-date. The initial packaging and loading of data on each partner site has, in some instances, proven to be difficult and time-consuming. What is also difficult is updating or revising the data. There are no standards yet for such information, so sites have typically designed their own data types and data formats, which usually vary widely from site to site. Although we do expect some standard to emerge for such data, some adoption of the standards is some time away. In the meantime, publishers need to have open, flexible processes for generating the necessary data to economically package and distribute their products.

Once again here, outside companies offer services to help with this end of the problem. It may be enough for you to produce the finished goods and then have a third party take care of the packaging. As you will see, though, whether you do the packaging yourself or have a third party do it for you, the key will be to have a production process that lends itself to flexible, high-volume output.

Here are some other questions to consider as you look at your production workflow and how it lends itself to packaging:

- What materials need to be included in the packaging process? Given your current production systems and processes, are these materials all available electronically? Will you have to design new processes or tools to create these materials?

- Do your potential partners require widely different materials and formats?

- Would you be required to update information after you have packaged it? How would you provide updates?

- Are processes for conversion and packaging easy to modify for different selling channels?

- Do you have any specialized requirements for packaging, such as the need to combine multiple files into one or to chunk the content into smaller files?

- Do you or your partners also have requirements for specialized processes such as compression or watermarking?

Metadata production

It's impossible to look at DRM integration without looking at issues of metadata creation and maintenance, as well as how metadata will be communicated to the DRM system or DRM provider. After all, DRM is largely about metadata — about the business rules and usage rules associated with intellectual property.

The preceding subsection, "Packaging," necessarily discussed some of the issues of metadata. The packaging process especially is tied intimately to DRM metadata because it involves packaging the finished goods and generating the necessary license that the DRM system requires. So just as you looked at your workflow for finished goods production with an eye toward how it could be optimized for DRM integration, you will want to undertake a similar process with an eye toward how metadata production can be optimized for DRM integration.

In particular, ask yourself the following questions related to DRM metadata and your current workflow:

- Where would the DRM rules be applied, and who would apply them?

- Would the application of DRM rules happen in the editorial process? As a back-end process after finished goods are complete?

- Could some of the rules be somehow applied automatically?

- Do you have systems or databases in-house that could be used in creating and maintaining DRM metadata? Could these be integrated with potential DRM solutions?

- Do you currently use DAM systems or Media Asset Management (MAM) systems that already maintain metadata about finished goods and/or raw materials?

- Do you currently use royalty tracking systems or other databases that contain information about the use of intellectual property?

Ultimately, the metadata needs to flow to the DRM system and/or provider to be available to the DRM system at the time of packaging. You need to know the requirements of the DRM system as to the required format of the metadata at the time of packaging and whether the DRM packaging system can be tightly integrated with your business and production systems. These can be fairly complex issues that get right to the heart of the DRM matter for some publishers.

One publishing client that we worked with had a comprehensive database of information about every book that it had published, organized by the ISBN number of the book, that included such data as subject matter, date of creation, author information, and rights-related information such as royalty attribution. The publisher was able to automatically extract this information in a format suitable for conversion to the publication metadata required for the OEB format. Interestingly, not all the required publication metadata was stored in the publisher's product database, so the automatic processes needed to be supplemented by some editorial review and data entry. Still, that particular publisher was able to get a leg up on the creation of a complex set of metadata, which accelerated its launch of the electronic products.

With such possible automation in mind, include in your workflow analysis some ideas of what metadata is available at different points in the workflow and how it can be accessed if it is in some kind of electronic form. DRM vendors and outsource partners can assist with this kind of analysis, but you are well advised to do some of this thinking before you look at particular DRM solutions or partners. Such an analysis of your available metadata should be part and parcel of the overarching plan for DAM mentioned earlier. When making this plan, take into consideration what assets you have and what digital forms they are and should be available in. Along with these assets, you will need the metadata that describes these assets.

Complex metadata for complex products

Having such a careful and well-thought-out process for metadata is easier said than done, of course. It is the rare organization that has assembled all its assets in digital form, clearly indexed and categorized, ready for packaging and distribution. Chances are, your organization has a more complex picture — some assets in digital form and some not, some metadata captured in an organized form and some not. Perhaps more significantly, you likely have some clearly understood rules and plans for using certain assets and only a vague idea of what you may want or may be able to do with other assets.

Metadata is complicated by the fact that many assets are compound. A book, for example, may contain multiple images, each of which may have different rights associated with it. A book publisher may have obtained rights to use one picture in only the printed form, another picture in print and eBook form, and a third image in all forms. Video producers face the same challenge; a given video may include footage, sounds, and images, each of which could carry its own rights.

Indeed, the multimedia CD-ROM industry was one of the first industries to run into these challenges. You could make the argument that one of the limiting factors of that industry was its inability to solve the implementation and integration problems in a straightforward, economical, and scalable manner. For some CD-ROM developers, each product involved facing a morass of rights issues, with complex and costly efforts to secure rights for the materials used in the product. In an Internet-based version of content distribution, such rights issues need to be addressed up front, allowing publishers to readily market product with technology that secures the rights the publisher already has.

The need for clearly understood and articulated rights extends beyond Internet distribution per se. The same file used for eBook distribution could also be used as a source file for print-on-demand. The same music file could be used for downloading or for burning onto a CD to be shipped overnight. Ideally, a customer would be able to locate content that she is interested in,

determine the forms in which it is available for purchasing, and then purchase it in one of those forms. Then there is superdistribution, as discussed in Chapter 4: There could be applications in which that very same customer becomes a reseller of the content. For example, a college professor who has selected and organized materials for a class can then become the distributor of that same material to the students enrolled in the class. In these instances and others, the key ingredient is clear rights information that can be understood and acted on by the DRM solutions.

In fact, one of the complicating factors of DRM is that the potential application of DRM technology is endless, and each application could quite reasonably develop many business models. This complicates the process of creating and maintaining metadata and eventually of tying the metadata to the controlling DRM technology.

Take college textbook publishing again as just one example. College professors are accustomed today to receiving, gratis, review copies of textbooks that they may end up using in the classroom. Although the publishers hope that the professors adopt their textbooks, there is no requirement that they do, so professors are given unfettered access to reviewing the books themselves. Later, if a professor begins using one such reviewed textbook in his class, he may well be granted rights to use ancillary materials in the classroom, such as worksheets and tests.

When these materials move increasingly to electronic distribution, a controlling DRM system can face complex and subtle rules of usage; for example, what is the professor free to use as a reviewer, and how to do those rights change when he adopts the book for classroom use? And what if the professor were to stop using the book? Should rights previously granted then be revoked? And what of the students in the class? College publishers already are experimenting with systems that give students access to Web-based materials after they have purchased a book or while they are attending a given class.

This is but one example, but it suggests the complex business rules that a publisher may face when launching an electronic product that it intends to enable for DRM. This example suggests that the process of integrating metadata into the production and packaging workflow may well be a complex and subtle matter, but one that is worth exploring if publishers want to be well positioned to explore new forms of electronic commerce.

Among the publishers that we interviewed, there was some consensus that niche markets will drive this sort of "business-rule-heavy" application of DRM. As one music company executive put it, "Music doesn't have time to be methodical." But high-value, specialized material, such as for the professions and for educational publishing, will benefit from publishers being able to create and enforce complex rules of usage and sharing.

Not that music doesn't have metadata issues of its own. Music shopping and downloading Web sites live and die by the quality of their metadata — track-specific metadata that identifies artist, title, and more. This is also true of sites that specialize in selling and indexing video products. The search engines behind sites such as the video and DVD section of Amazon.com are in fact killer metadata search engines, fueled by authoritative databases created and maintained by companies such as Muze. As more commerce goes to the Web and more electronic products become digitized and downloadable, more publishers need to have well-maintained databases and efficient processes for delivering data to their marketing partners. The more well integrated such metadata is, the better.

Moving metadata capture upstream

According to at least one music publisher that we interviewed, metadata for music products can be reasonably and efficiently added at the point of digitization and packaging; indeed, there may not be enough of a workflow prior to the digitization process that would allow for metadata to be created further upstream. Publishers of print materials, however, may have more of a *requirement* to move the creation and capture of metadata upstream. A book, for example, presents a more complex picture for metadata than a single audio track. The files are deeper, potentially involving compound documents and multiple points of entry. There may well be a richness of content that would require lengthier and more complex metadata.

Print publishers may also have more of an opportunity to capture metadata upstream. A print publisher that uses a document management or workflow tool may well be maintaining a great deal of document-specific metadata, including permissions information. One DRM vendor that we interviewed has a client that has integrated its document management system with its DRM solution. Policy information about each document is maintained in the document management system. When the document is exported to the DRM system, the policy information is exported with it. The customer has written a tool to automatically map the policy information inside its document management system with the policy information that the DRM system needs. The document is then sent to the DRM system, a license is automatically created, and the newly published document is automatically packaged with the appropriate license.

Keep in mind that metadata is as much about marketing products as it is about controlling access to them. Think of the Muze example again. The quality of the metadata available through the likes of Muze is a boon to marketing products both online and through in-store information kiosks. Indeed, several DRM vendors have a broader solution that ties the DRM technology to search engines and other means of providing broader reach to the DRM-enabled content. The vendor DigitalOwl, for example (see Chapter 12), integrates its solution with syndication technology in such a way that the taxonomy used in the DigitalOwl system can be mapped to the syndication system, enabling automatic syndication of the content after it is in the DigitalOwl DRM system. MediaDNA's eLuminator technology (also discussed in Chapter 12) exposes text index terms to search engines while still allowing the content to be protected with MediaDNA's own DRM technology.

Music publishers have many options for this kind of marketing, with many selling and partner sites already established. With the growing convergence of media and devices such as set-top boxes, such opportunities will only increase. Standards for metadata will need to be developed and codified so that materials from different media (video, audio, eBook, and so on) can share a common set of metadata, especially for those user-centric fields that can be used for searching, such as subject matter, keyword, artist or author name, and the like.

CROSS REFERENCE: Chapter 6 lists some of the established and emerging standards for metadata.

The preceding are just a few examples of how a DRM system, and specifically the metadata in a DRM system, can tie directly to vehicles for marketing and promoting content. This is important to keep in mind when looking at your workflow and where in the workflow you have opportunities to add or enhance DRM.

One specialty publisher that we interviewed distributes its material in both print and electronic form. During the editorial workflow, the material is indexed for both forms. When the materials are complete, a PDF of the product is sent to the Web site, along with a set of keywords and other metadata that feeds a search engine. Customers are then able to search for products using a fairly complex set of keywords suitable to the specialized material. As this publisher explores DRM solutions, it is considering how well the potential DRM solutions can take advantage of the keyword system that it has established.

Again, there are many ways to approach how to add appropriate metadata. You don't necessarily have to bring this process in-house, change your existing workflow, or develop specialized databases. The entire problem can be outsourced, and companies such as Texterity on the publishing side and Sonopress on the music side stand ready to help you effectively add metadata to your digital products or to add it for you. Yet your analysis should at least look at steps such as adding metadata and determine what can be done effectively in-house and what you may consider doing with an outside partner.

As a final note, you should be realistic about what amount of metadata is ultimately useful and necessary. Would customers want to search by artist hair color? If they do, and it will increase your sales, go for it. But your efforts of collecting and maintaining metadata will be an expense against your potential revenue, so you should have solid reasons for incurring the costs. The best efforts that we have seen of enhancing content with metadata for applications such as search and syndication have been very specific:

◆ A publisher of engineering standards enhances its Web site with a keyword-driven search. Each standard is indexed by a professional indexer after all other editorial work has been completed.

◆ A publisher of market research indexes its articles by company name and product name, taking care to index all products mentioned and whether they were mentioned favorably or unfavorably. A customized program initially indexes the articles; it scans each text file for company and product names. An editor then reviews the results, refines the indexing, and adds new company and product names as she encounters them.

◆ A reseller of business books and reports creates brief, informative abstracts that are then indexed by keyword and major subject area. Some abstracts are created manually, and many are purchased from an outside source. The abstracts are then indexed automatically with a customized version of a commercial search engine.

These examples have several things in common. Each publisher took care to identify some specific metadata that it knew would be valuable in the selling process and then focused on creating and maintaining that metadata economically and at the appropriate point in the editorial and production workflow. Also, as each of these publishers looked at DRM solutions, they looked at how the DRM solutions would integrate with their current metadata processes and technology.

Moving from Today's Processes to Tomorrow's

As the previous section, "Integrating DRM into Production Processes," showed, there are many ways to approach the production of finished goods and metadata. There are at least two questions to consider:

◆ How much work do you want to do in-house versus out of house?

◆ How much do you want to integrate digital production and metadata creation into your current workflow?

The New Workflow

At the very least, digital production changes three steps in your "analog" workflow — capturing, managing, and distributing — and DRM itself adds a fourth process — packaging. Figure 10-1 shows this workflow generically.

If you think of these added processes in the context of your current workflow, you can consider where in your workflow they can logically, efficiently, and economically fit in. Clearly, the distribution process is a back-end one, as is much of what happens in packaging. But the capturing and managing processes are candidates to be integrated into your current workflow.

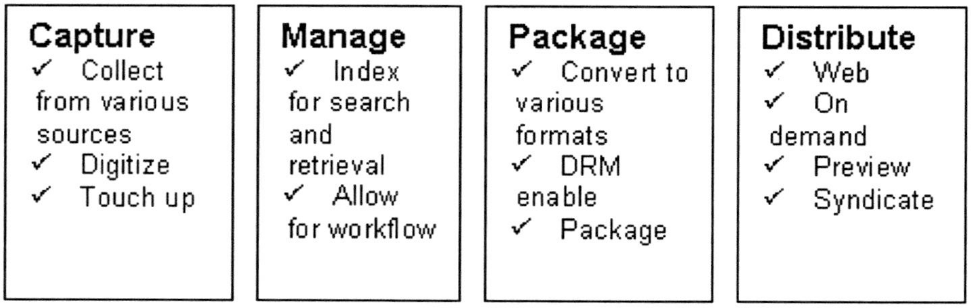

Capture	**Manage**	**Package**	**Distribute**
✓ Collect from various sources ✓ Digitize ✓ Touch up	✓ Index for search and retrieval ✓ Allow for workflow	✓ Convert to various formats ✓ DRM enable ✓ Package	✓ Web ✓ On demand ✓ Preview ✓ Syndicate

Figure 10-1: Adding DRM packaging to the production workflow.

Moreover, as the previous section showed, you can create and maintain the metadata needed for packaging during the earlier processes and then map it to the DRM packaging software automatically or semiautomatically. In a world where 90 percent of your product sales are "analog" and 10 percent are digital, you are wise to keep the processes separate and not disrupt your current workflow. But if your business is shifting to an increasingly digital one, you would be wise to modify your workflow so that it adds more of the digital production into your dominant workflow.

Digital Asset Management

A key consideration as you look at your workflow is to determine where you may have opportunities to integrate the content production with the metadata production. Many organizations are looking at or are already using systems for document management, content management, and Digital Asset Management. Each of these technologies, despite many differences, has certain key features in common: They all feature some kind of repository for storing and managing content, and they all bind the stored content to some amount of metadata.

A document management system, for example, allows for the storage of documents, often in many revisions, with workflow and metadata for document tracking and management. Content management systems vary widely in functionality and purpose, but many of them allow for the storage and management of documents and individual components such as image files, links, and other media. A publisher with a wide variety of content types, including text, images, multimedia, and streaming media, may consider Digital Asset Management technology in the mix.

Unfortunately, when it comes to the subject of managing digital assets, the industry can't seem to get comfortable with less than three or four acronyms, starting with DAM (for Digital Asset Management), MAM (for Media Asset Management), and DMM (for Digital Media Management). *DAM* seems to be gaining the most ground, though, so we'll stick with that term, despite its rather unfortunate pronunciation.

The proliferation of acronyms is revealing. There are many approaches to the problem of Digital Asset Management and many interested parties, from giant storage-focused vendors such as IBM and EMC to a long list of "end-to-end" and niche DAM vendors specializing in areas such as video, audio, and graphics management. Many blue-chip customers, including cable and broadcast networks such as CNN, have partnered with more than one vendor to solve their DAM needs, beginning with the need for high-speed storage and networking and moving to the front lines where content is digitized and indexed for storage and retrieval.

Indeed, if you have recently begun looking at the issue of managing digital assets, you will encounter a blizzard of terminology and acronyms for data storage, networking, analog-to-digital capture and encoding, metadata, indexing, and distribution. The March 2001 Bear Stearns research report "Maximizing the Value of Content: A Primer on the Digital Asset Management Industry" includes a 12-page glossary of terms and a table of over 100 technologies that fit somewhere in the DAM mix. And that is only on the technology side. The other important considerations here are the business case for using such technology and adoption of processes and workflows that will maximize such an investment.

The intention of this book, of course, is to introduce you to DRM and not to DAM. Yet the two issues are intrinsically linked, whether you end up attempting these things yourself, relying on an outsource partner, or delaying the decision until later. This section, then, serves as an introduction to DAM technology, focusing on the overall problem of Digital Asset Management, the major vendors in the market, and some first steps that you can take as you consider whether you need to introduce more technology to the work involved in managing your digital assets.

Going from analog to digital

The world is going digital. The production and management of new text, audio, and video material are increasingly digital, and new mediums such as the Web are constantly raising the question of whether existing assets should be digitized. This is true for companies whose first business is communication, such as entertainment companies, networks, and publishers, as well as any business with a growing need to communicate with customers, employees, and other partners.

Moreover, you likely have already felt some pain from not having your assets in digital form, or, even if they are in digital form, not being managed appropriately. Consider the last time that you had to provide a digitized version of one of your products after it had previously existed only in analog form. Chances are, there was some scrambling to make it happen — some additional manual work, and a few phone calls, and, voilà, a few hours or a day or two later, the work was done. Wouldn't it make sense to predict such needs, plan for them, make the materials available in the correct formats, and put them, for example, on a server where the right people can find and access them?

That, in a nutshell, is the DAM problem and solution. For the average company, it affects such areas as sales, marketing, public relations, and investor relations. It can cut right to issues such as the length of the sales cycle and the capability of the company to promote shareholder value. For the company that owns significant creative assets, such as a broadcast company, television network, or publisher, DAM goes right to such top-line questions as what assets are available for selling and such bottom-line questions as the cost of product development.

Because DAM is right in the middle of such important issues for organization, it is no surprise that so many vendors are looking to claim this space. The research and consulting company GISTICS focuses on the DAM market and is projecting sales in this market to grow to over $4 billion by 2004.

Understanding your DAM needs

Understanding your requirements for DAM technology begins with developing a clear, documented sense of what your organization needs from its digital assets. The first step for companies is to develop a plan for why and how they will use DAM and how DRM fits into this larger plan. Companies need an overarching strategy for these technologies, focusing on what products they want to be marketing and what their key channels will be.

Understanding how DAM may integrate with DRM and fit into your technology planning begins with a process of inventorying and evaluating what assets are on hand. Many companies are tempted to plunge right into the digitization process without much consideration of precisely *what* should be digitized. For an entertainment company or publisher, such an inventory should consider the normal parameters of supply and demand, what value an asset may have in digital form, what opportunities there are to market it, and so on.

After a plan for your digital assets is in place, you need to begin the technical steps of digitizing and managing your assets. You may well face the need to digitize and manage an array of materials, including text, graphics, multimedia, and streaming media — with the goal of being able to easily access, repurpose, and distribute these assets at any time. End-to-end solution vendors such as Artesia Technologies (www.artesia.com), with its TEAMS product, talk about the need to have a DAM product that can "ingest, index, categorize, secure, search, transform, assemble, and export" content in as many forms as you require.

Artesia's list is a good one. After content is digitized, it needs to be made widely available to many people and processes along a variety of workflows, from the simple to the long and complex. An organization may have individual components, such as photos and sound files, as well as compound documents in word processing and desktop publishing formats and finished goods in formats such as PDF. The DAM system should be ready to ingest, store, and index these assets in such a way that they can be later found, modified, reassembled, and eventually exported. Once exported, the assets need to be distributed; vendors such as Artmachine focus on the distribution side of the DAM problem.

Why would you consider moving to a DAM solution? Both Bear Stearns and GISTICS point to lower costs, faster product development cycles, reduced labor costs, and opportunities for increased revenues through additional licensing opportunities. Indeed, after an asset is digitized and properly managed, it is available for repurposing and reselling in ways not before possible.

The enterprising company can develop whole new markets for products that had been effectively dormant or at least underused. When such assets are then tied to a DRM solution, the opportunities are close at hand and ready to be exploited.

Examining the range of approaches

As mentioned earlier, many vendors have product, service, and mixed product-service offerings for Digital Asset Management. Larger, storage-focused companies, such as IBM, Sony, and EMC, offer customizable solutions and services that center on their hardware and networking solutions. Among them, these larger companies have significant installations with blue-chip customers such as CNN, Entertainment Tonight, and Starz Encore Group. Sony and IBM, for example, installed an asset management system at CNN, allowing CNN to begin the process of digitizing over 120,000 hours of its video archive.

After the large, storage-focused companies, there are a number of DAM-only companies that offer either "end-to-end" or more niche solutions. Among the end-to-end offerings, Artesia's TEAMS stands out as the most full-featured product, with support for both rich media and a wide range of text formats, databases, Quark files, and finished good formats such as PDF. TEAMS is also a highly extensible product that is suitable for enterprise deployment and has flexible support for many things that IT organizations are looking for, such as Java, XML, and contemporary programming interfaces based on approaches such as CORBA.

Another company with a broad offering is eMotion (www.emotion.com), with its MediaPartner product. MediaPartner boasts enhanced features for "ingesting" and archiving assets, with a natural language search engine and project management tools to support a flexible, open workflow. North Plains Systems (www.northplains.com), with its TeleScope product, tracks, manages, and retrieves a wide variety of files. Like most other DAM products, TeleScope is integrated with several commercial databases, including Oracle and Microsoft SQL server. TeleScope also offers I-Piece plug-ins for specialized requirements such as digital rights management and watermarking.

More typically, though, products focus on a particular medium and do it exceedingly well. Convera's Screening Room, for example, manages video content and continues to add more and more features to an already impressive list. (Convera [www.convera.com] is the company resulting from the merger of Excalibur and the Interactive Media Services group at Intel.) Like many DAM vendors, Convera offers both a product and a hosted service. Toronto-based Bulldog (www.bulldog.com) is another attractive offering for managing video content, and it integrates well with VideoLogger from Virage (www.virage.com), which is a best-in-breed tool for cataloging video content.

Keep in mind that many of these technology companies offer hosted services, and some companies, such as Artmachine (www.artmachine.com), focus almost exclusively on the hosting end of the business. Also, many vendors work together to provide a "total solution"; for example, Artesia teams with specialized companies such as Virage and Web-content management vendors such as Vignette and Interwoven, and Bulldog integrates with both Virage's VideoLogger and Convera's RetrievalWare search engine.

Understanding what DAM products do

When all is said and done, the products discussed in the previous subsection, "Examining the range of approaches," offer some or all of the following features, for one or more of the media types that you require:

- **They help you capture and digitize assets.** This can include tasks such as converting assets, encoding them, and logging them in the system. This can also include the tools involved in the original creation and editing of the assets.

- **They help you manage the assets once captured.** This includes core features such as storage, indexing, and retrieval, but can also include more sophisticated tools for DRM. Storage should be flexible, allowing for the repurposing of assets over time.

- **They help you distribute the assets to all interested parties.** This includes people inside and outside the firewall as appropriate, across the Internet, and people using all manner of client devices (PCs, wireless devices, and so on), as well as content distribution networks such as those from Akamai.

When you begin to look at specific vendor offerings, do so with these core features in mind. If you have articulated both your business goals and your blueprint for DAM and DRM technology, you should be able to understand which offerings will be helpful to you and which will not be. And no matter what you do on the technology side, the first logical step is to inventory your assets and understand what assets you have and what business use you may have for them.

Do you need to tackle DAM and DRM?

Do you *have to* look at DAM technology in the process of looking at your DRM integration needs? Of course not. You don't *have to* do anything. You may have some systems in place, such as a document management system, that do some of this asset management for you already. But there are some compelling reasons to consider a move to a DAM solution, over and above the ideas already listed:

♦ Your DRM needs will likely include the management of raw materials (individual files) as well as compound documents and finished goods formats such as PDF. A DAM solution could be an excellent repository for such a mix of materials and save you a great deal of work and rework down the road.

♦ A DAM system doesn't have to entail huge expense or effort. As with DRM solutions, you can outsource the entire problem. DRM-focused service providers such as Reciprocal (see Chapter 7), for example, are adding DAM capabilities to their core services. Even in-house, you can look to lower-cost and "lower-tech" solutions, such as using an existing repository such as Lotus Notes and improving on it with some best practices for storage and archiving. One electronic publisher that we interviewed maintained digital assets on a server, with an easy-to-use database form available for querying about which titles were available and in what formats.

DAM and DRM, taken together, are a logical solution to the compelling challenge of the new economy for content. What do you have to sell? What form is it in? Where does it reside? How can you make it widely and instantaneously available yet still protect it? The unique combination of DAM and DRM technologies answers all these questions.

Examining Other Related Technologies

So far, this chapter has focused on the technology surrounding DRM prior to the creation of the DRM-enabled product — mainly the production tools and processes used, with some attention paid to how these processes and tools can evolve with the use of both DRM and DAM technology. The remainder of this chapter focuses on the technology and integration issues that arise after the product is DRM enabled and ready for distribution.

Keep in mind that DRM is still an emerging technology, without an abundance of documented case studies and deployed systems in the field. Still, there are two areas where some clear integration issues are emerging — in security integration and end-user deployment. We interviewed both vendors and early adopters of DRM technology to see what some of their integration challenges were. Some lessons learned from early adopters are offered here, along with some guidance for your potential projects.

Security integration

The paradox of better security is, seemingly, a more difficult customer experience. Internet message boards and discussion groups on eBooks and music downloading run white-hot with messages condemning the DRM efforts of publishers, and the conventional wisdom, as of this writing, is that Napster is doomed to fail as it institutes a secure model for transactions. Put DRM in the way, people say, and gone are the simple pleasures of a "real" book — reading it again years later, passing it along, selling it when you are done with it, and such.

Publishers need to think through the issues of "how much" security is enough and how it will be enforced and supported. Security is a central issue in DRM. It goes to the heart of why publishers look to acquire DRM technology — for protection of their digital assets — but it is also a cruel master. Provide too little security, and users can walk away with the store; provide too much, and you will create much ill will with current and prospective customers.

As you look at how your DRM system will integrate with your other security systems, keep the following points in mind:

- **Authentication:** How is authentication supported on your current Web site and other places where the DRM solution will be deployed? What level of integration is sought here? Will it be enough to have logins based on domain authentication? Or will more precise identification be needed? What is too burdensome?

- **Digital certificates:** Do you have other systems in place that require or use digital certificates?

- **LDAP and other schemes:** Is your authentication process or any of your other systems reliant on LDAP? Will the DRM solution need to integrate with any such systems?

- **Other policy schemes:** Do you have any other systems, including proprietary ones, that maintain security or policy data? One DRM vendor we interviewed works with a customer that maintains data about access to documents in a separate policy server. This other server has information on all users, what their rights are to each document, and so on. The contents of this separate policy server are then piped to the DRM policy server via an API that enables mapping of the users' policy data to the form that the DRM policy server needs. The DRM policy server then generates the keys for the documents to be shared under the control of the DRM software.

As with your workflow analysis suggested earlier, in which you look at what metadata may be available along your normal production workflow, you should look at what metadata may be available related to users, privilege information, and document access. User/privilege information maintained in a document management system can be communicated to a DRM policy server in much the same way as the example cited in the preceding list, using APIs available on both the document management server and DRM server.

In the end, the question of security integration, as with DRM security itself, is one of balance. You could integrate your DRM solution in very complex ways with other internal systems, just as you could require your users to use more rigorous login methods. But how far do you reasonably need to go, and how much infrastructure and overhead do you really need?

In researching this chapter, we heard a range of requirements from users of DRM solutions. Some publishers didn't want to burden end users with complex processes, for fear of creating ill will. This was a consistent message from publishers, echoing some of the frustrations that end users have voiced. Yet in another instance — a manufacturing company needing to protect access to sensitive specifications — the manufacturer was instituting very specific and strict controls and was tightly integrating their DRM solution with other internal databases. Likewise, your specific integration should reflect the goals that you have for the system.

In looking at DRM solutions and how they may integrate with your security infrastructure, look closely at how the DRM solution handles two key requirements: authentication and identification. These are two key infrastructure issues that need to be part of the DRM solution today or a key part of the vendor's product development roadmap. From a buyer's perspective, make sure that the DRM vendor's approach to authentication and identification hook up with your own requirements.

End-user deployment

As discussed in Chapter 8, DRM technology has two key groups of users: the publishers who need their content protected and the eventual consumers of the content. This second group of users represents an integration challenge for the publisher. Among other factors, consider the following:

♦ The end users likely have little or no motivation to work at making the DRM solution work and may indeed be hostile to it. Their primary interest is obtaining access to content that they are interested in, and they may view the DRM solution as an impediment to that end.

♦ The end users are on the distant end of what is likely a long and thin connection to the publisher. They may be accessing the publisher's content over a low bandwidth connection, via third-party sites, with little or no immediate connection to the publisher.

♦ The end users are on a wide variety of heterogeneous systems — using different hardware, operating systems, browsers, and media players. They may be completely unaware of required hardware and software, as well as required revisions, service packs, and patches.

♦ The end users will likely be impatient with lengthy downloads, complex installation instructions, and installations that require rebooting and reconfiguring their systems. They are likely to give up rather than debug download or installation problems. If they are able to successfully install a given solution, they will be unlikely to upgrade it without significant motivation.

♦ The end users may well be using other readers, other DRM solutions, and other supporting applications, in addition to or instead of your chosen solution.

It should be no surprise then that end-user implementation issues stand out as some of the major complaints among early adopters of DRM solutions. Our own interviews bore this out, as did a comprehensive study from IDC, "The DRM Landscape: Technologies, Vendors, and Markets," published in June 2001. In the IDC study, analyst Joshua Duhl cited end-user issues such as the following as significant complaints:

♦ Too many screens to navigate in order to purchase content

♦ Large client downloads and difficult setups

♦ Unreliable connections and partial downloads

♦ Lack of adequate support for restoring keys

This last problem was cited in a number of interviews that we conducted. In the case of one publisher, its DRM solution bound the key to the particular machine that had been used when the purchased content was downloaded. Later, the same user would attempt to access the purchased content on a different machine, not realizing that the terms of sale had bound the copy to that particular machine. This can be viewed as less of a technical support issue and more of a problem with the selling process, but as far as the end user is concerned, all she knows is that she can't easily view the content that she legitimately purchased. As discussed in Chapter 5, DRM vendors take different approaches to user authentication; some authenticate the user via a username and password or other means, others authenticate to the hardware, and yet others (such as Microsoft) authenticate to a combination of the two. Most end users aren't comfortable or don't want to be bothered with the subtleties of these authentication schemes.

The other problems are just as significant and need to be carefully considered when looking to deploy a DRM solution. Take the size of the client download. Despite the growing number of users accessing the Internet via broadband solutions, many users still access the Internet over modems with speeds of 56kbps and slower, with actual download rates being significantly slower, at times, than the baud rate. A 7MB to 10MB client download can be a tough sell when the purchased content is significantly smaller or when the content is being downloaded for trial or previewing.

Complex installations are also an issue. An eBook consumer, for example, may need to have multiple readers and multiple DRM solutions on the same machine. If a publisher's DRM solution then requires another download, with an upgrade of a certain reader and of the DRM software itself, the installation process can begin to look very complex. Installation processes are improving all the time, but some installations still require the end user to reboot the machine. Take some care to ensure that your solution has an installation procedure that is as seamless and failure-proof as possible.

Here are some other issues to consider in terms of end-user deployment and integration:

♦ Client availability on the Macintosh continues to be a limiting factor. This may change with the rollout of the new Macintosh operating system and increasing Java compatibility with Macs, but it is still an issue.

♦ The various media players and readers become an important element in the installation and deployment to end users. What versions of popular readers such as Adobe Acrobat are required in order to be compatible with your DRM solution? Are your end users already using a version of a media player or reader, and will you be requiring them to upgrade that?

♦ What requirements will you have for end users to upgrade the DRM solution itself? Will you somehow make it automatic or easy for them to receive updates without their having to do anything explicit?

♦ Will customers be downloading and installing both applications and content from the Internet always? Will some components and content be installed from other media, such as CD-ROM? Some music publishers have been distributing CDs with sample tracks and the DRM client software, which is then installed when the end users use the CD. Future tracks, and upgrades to the DRM software, are then downloadable.

Plan to resolve these issues before you expect to do any kind of wide-scale deployment. Be prepared as well to get phone calls and e-mails looking for help installing software. Are you prepared as an organization to act as technical support, or will someone be doing that for you?

In interviews with other organizations that have deployed DRM solutions to their end users, we collected some other guidelines and observations about end-user deployment. You should use these as guidelines when selecting a DRM solution in general:

♦ The download of the client DRM application needs to be as lightweight as possible, allowing for a rapid download.

♦ As one recording company executive said, "The user does not want to know about DRM." The installation should be as simple and unobtrusive as possible.

♦ One product manager for a DRM company told us that he considers the end user's tolerance level for the installation process to be "about 30 seconds to a minute." The installation should take no more than "three or four clicks" and should be "simple, obvious, and with big buttons."

♦ The same product manager emphasized that consumers "shouldn't have to learn or do new things" during the installation process. He recommended that the client installation process be handled by a commercial tool such as InstallShield, which is now widely used and very familiar to end users.

♦ Several people that we interviewed highlighted avoiding anything that would "challenge the patience" of end users, such as installations screens that require them to scroll horizontally or vertically, "read anything," or make it difficult for them to scroll forward or back.

♦ Installation and access requirements should be flexible and familiar to the consumer. For example, it may make sense to allow the consumer to install the content on two machines, presuming that she would typically have a home machine and an office machine or an office machine and a laptop.

♦ Think carefully about how updates to the client application are deployed. More and more contemporary applications have an auto-update feature that can be made completely invisible and nonintrusive to the end user.

♦ Look at successful examples of easy-to-use consumer applications and learn from them, such as Napster and AOL.

♦ Rigorously test your end-user deployment on a variety of operating systems and with different readers and media players installed. The ideal client application will have no conflicts with operating system features or other applications. This suggests that client applications need to be tested extensively in a variety of potential customer installation environments.

♦ Be ready to provide customer support and expect to help consumers with varying technical backgrounds and varying abilities and inclination to debug technical problems.

♦ Provide obvious and attractive feedback about download progress and installation progress.

Financial and CRM Systems

Content providers should have systems for processing financial transactions and keeping track of customers' use of their content. Remember that one of the most important benefits of DRM is that it enables you to find out more about how your customers use your content. A customer relationship management (CRM) system can compile that information and perform useful tasks with it, such as produce reports, target special offers to certain customers, and help determine what future product offerings are likely to have the most appeal. CRM systems are essentially supersets of legacy sales and marketing systems. (Many books on the market discuss CRM in more detail than we can possibly hope to do here.)

Some DRM offerings have their own e-commerce financial systems built in, whereas others are designed to be integrated with standard e-commerce storefront packages from vendors such as Microsoft, Open Market, ATG, and so on. DRM service providers often outsource the financial component. The usual way of integrating e-commerce packages with DRM is as follows: Content products for sale are passed to the e-commerce system for inclusion into its product catalog. Entries in the product catalog include IDs that uniquely identify the content – the same ones that we introduce in Chapter 5. Users browse the Web site and put items into their shopping carts.

At checkout time, the e-commerce system sends the IDs of the content purchased, together with information about the user (such as an e-mail address), to the DRM system. The DRM system then takes over and fulfills the transaction. This can happen through an immediate file download (via HTTP) or by sending the user an e-mail with a URL to click or with the actual file (content package) attached. The rest of the process takes place as described in Chapter 5. This type of integration with e-commerce packages is quite common.

CRM integration is another matter. Whereas financial systems have been around almost as long as computers have, and e-commerce systems have been around almost as long as the Web, CRM systems are a more recent development — and they are multifarious and quite complex. Although all publishers have sales and marketing systems, which can be based on old technology, not many have adopted the newer breed of high-end e-CRM packages, such as those from Siebel, Oracle, and ePiphany. Accordingly, it's rare to see a DRM solution designed to integrate with one of those packages. Any such integration is more likely to be performed by custom development; otherwise, some DRM packages may have their own modest CRM functionality.

Other integration issues

Over time, DRM systems will be more tightly integrated with back-office systems, e-commerce systems, and other business software, including royalty tracking. To date, though, our research shows us that such integration has been largely customized, or implementers have settled for loose coupling of systems. For example, several publishers that we interviewed, who relied on outsource partners for DRM, received printed selling reports or spreadsheets via e-mail or floppy disk.

Indeed, the real payoff when integrating DRM solutions and business systems is some time off, although publishers and DRM vendors both can foresee significant applications of DRM to business planning, marketing, and business intelligence. Among the ideas that we heard are the following:

- ♦ Publishers would like to see tight integration between DRM systems and software for royalty tracking, contract administration, and sales administration.
- ♦ Publishers would like to see more ready means for DRM systems to manage or tie into subscription lists.
- ♦ Publishers would like to see the DRM systems produce more comprehensive feedback on what content is being used and how it is being used. One publisher would like to see integration with customer relationship management (CRM) software, profiling tools, and analytical tools.

At least one vendor, Savantech (see Chapter 12), is developing a framework for publishing companies that ties back-office software components — and others, such as DAM systems — together into a cohesive architecture.

Summing Up

As this chapter shows, the key issues surrounding the integration of DRM technology are tied to the processes and technology that you now use to create finished goods and the metadata surrounding the finished goods. We can't stress enough that the key to success in implementing DRM is doing it with reasonable and predictable costs. Your organization needs to be able to economically create digital products, apply DRM technology to them, and market them. Developing an efficient system for content development has as much to do with rationalizing your production process as it does with choosing the right DRM technology or outsourcing partner.

But production is only part of the challenge. DRM integration raises fundamental questions about your organization's methods for security and data protection, and the manner in which you integrate DRM with other security technology needs to be examined closely. Finally, deploying a DRM solution to end users may well be a whole new challenge for publishers, and this chapter offers some items for consideration.

Chapter 11

Additional DRM Solutions

In Chapter 7, we discuss the major DRM vendors (Microsoft, Adobe, InterTrust, RealNetworks, Reciprocal, and Preview Systems), as well as the watermarking vendors Digimarc and Verance. In this chapter, we look at the digital rights management solutions that, to a greater or lesser degree, conform to the generic DRM architecture presented in Chapter 5. Several other vendors' technologies and solutions are related to DRM but lie outside of the generic architecture; Chapter 12 covers those. Note that (with a few choice exceptions), we have chosen not to include descriptions of DRM businesses that act as service providers for one of the technologies described here or in Chapter 7.

Allow us a brief disclaimer: This is a snapshot of the market as of Summer 2001. DRM is a young, volatile industry, and as we have been researching and writing this book, there have been business failures, reorganizations, acquisitions, new companies, and new product offerings. In addition, companies are positioning and repositioning their products and adding features and supported data formats. We have made every effort to make this material current as of this writing, but are certain that there will be some changes in the marketplace over the next several months.

Text and PDF Solutions

We start out our survey of DRM vendors by looking at those that handle the formats that DRM solutions have focused on from the very beginning: text documents, along with still images and PDF files.

DocuRights (Aries Systems)

DocuRights (www.docurights.com) is the Web-based DRM service from privately held Aries Systems Corporation, a North Andover, Massachusetts–based technology company with a long history of developing search and publishing tools for the STM (scientific, technical, and medical) marketplace. Aries's flagship product, Knowledge Finder, is a natural language query engine tuned to the vocabulary of medical literature and has been used by STM publishers such as Lippincott Williams & Wilkins since its introduction in 1986.

DocuRights is a full-featured DRM offering for STM publishers. It offers persistent protection of PDF files and supports business models such as pay-per-view, subscriptions, and prepaid delivery. DocuRights uses 56-bit RC5 encryption for the content itself and standard 128-bit Secure Socket Layer (SSL) encryption for the transfer of certificates. The DRM client, which includes an Adobe Acrobat plug-in, runs on all major releases of Windows and Macintosh OS, and DocuRights is adding support for a Linux client. The DocuRights server runs on Windows 2000 Server and Microsoft SQL Server and uses Microsoft IIS for a Web server.

E-commerce is provided as a DocuRights service, but rights grants may also be triggered by external e-commerce systems. Publishers can integrate DocuRights with their own document delivery processes and content management systems. Aries also offers Editorial Manager, a manuscript submission and tracking system. Review copies of PDFs generated by Editorial Manager may be protected and secured with DocuRights to ensure content protection and confidentiality. DocuRights can also be integrated with the Aries's Knowledge Finder medical literature search service for enhanced searching and distribution.

Credit Aries Systems with recognizing early on the revolutionary effect the Internet would have on scholarly publishing. Its range of tools is well suited for the creation, review, and intelligent, secured distribution of high-value, scholarly materials. Its move into the DRM space, with DocuRights, is another smart step for Aries Systems.

DocuRights is well positioned for the current STM market, where publishers have a realistic approach to how much effort they — and their consumers — are willing to go through in order to participate in DRM-driven commerce. This begins with the fact that DocuRights is a hosted service, which appeals to many publishers. Aries's focus on PDF is also pragmatic because PDF is the format of choice in this market, with its complex publishing requirements, such as equations and its need for page fidelity.

DocuRights default usage rules are well tuned to the needs of STM publishers. Purchasers are allowed to pass along content, for example, but the secondary recipient won't have immediate access to the article contents. Instead, the DocuRights system solicits repurchase information from the secondary recipient.

The DocuRights system is currently in use by 20 publishers, including the *New England Journal of Medicine,* Lippincott Williams & Wilkins, the *Journal of Bone and Joint Surgery,* and the *Journal of Bone and Mineral Research.*

FileOpen

FileOpen Systems, Inc. (www.fileopen.com), is a privately held New York City company in operation since 1997 that has been solely focused on the DRM space.

FileOpen Publisher is a DRM solution offering persistent protection for PDF files. FileOpen Publisher supports a number of business models and has features such as absolute or relative document expiration, locking to specific media such as CD-ROM, and restrictions on printing to a specific period of time or number of printouts. Customizable watermarks can be used to extend copyright protection to printed documents.

The DRM client application is a plug-in to Adobe Acrobat Reader and protects the secured content in both online and offline environments. FileOpen Publisher offers a combination of RSA RC4 and a proprietary cipher for encryption; and the Web-enabled tool, FileOpen WebPublisher, uses RC4 encryption and the HTTPS protocol.

The DRM client runs on both Windows and the Macintosh, with a Linux client in development. The DRM server runs on Windows NT, Sun Solaris, Linux, Compaq Tru64 Unix, any ODBC-compliant database, and any major Web server.

FileOpen's primary market is the traditional publishing space, but it is also used in applications such as corporate information, libraries, and government agencies. It currently includes among its installed customers publishers such as Hungry Minds, Inc., and corporations such as Arthur Anderson and BEA Systems.

FileOpen is a mature offering in a relatively new market, with established products that are into their second and third revisions. It has achieved particular success in the CD-ROM market, although it also has offerings for Web-content distribution. FileOpen comes in at a modest price point, with a flat price scheme that is notable for its simplicity. Unlike DocuRights, which is focused solely on the STM publishing market, FileOpen has some features that appeal to a broader market, such as corporate information.

RightsMarket

RightsMarket, Inc. (www.rightsmarket.com), is an Alberta, Calgary, Canada–based company that has been in operation since the early 1990s, making it one of the earliest DRM players. Formerly TragoeS, Inc., the company has been focused on the DRM space since launching RightsMarket.com in 1997, and it is traded on the Canadian Dealing Network under the symbol RTSM.

RightsMarket offers persistent protection of PDF and MP3 files and offers built-in support for standards such as Digital Object Identifier (DOI), Secure Digital Music Initiative (SDMI), and Open eBook (OEB). RightsMarket's primary product offering, RightsPublish, supports business models such as subscription, membership, per-seat licensing, and time-limited viewing. RightsPublish is billed as an end-to-end solution that includes packaging, encryption, and distribution, but also adds an online catalog, shopping cart, payment, and reporting mechanisms. RightsPublish is available as a service and as a product that publishers can license and integrate into their own Web sites.

The DRM client runs on Windows, Windows CE, and Palm, and the DRM server runs on Windows NT and Microsoft SQL Server. Encryption is proprietary. E-commerce features, the Web server, and content management capabilities are included as part of the product.

RightsMarket currently has 60 customers, concentrated in STM publishers, trade associations, and copyright collectives. It is also looking to offer a print-on-demand service in the near future. But its long-term plans may lie elsewhere; RightsMarket is looking into the large corporate market and applications such as the secure handling of medical records. Its newer product offering, RightsVault, is aimed squarely at the corporate market, and it emphasizes auditing, access, and authorization, over the more commercial positioning of RightsPublish.

Corporate and E-mail Solutions

The corporate enterprise market is the next major territory for DRM vendors to conquer, after they gain success in the traditional content-provider markets. Many corporations, particularly those with high numbers of knowledge workers, such as banks and consulting firms, have very sensitive information that must be protected. Corporations are also highly reliant on e-mail as a primary means of communicating this sensitive information. Furthermore, one of the most attractive aspects of the corporate market for DRM vendors is that, unlike the media markets, in which vendors must give away client software to consumers for free, these vendors can charge per-seat licensing fees for their software.

Alchemedia

Alchemedia (www.alchemedia.com) is an Israeli company, founded in 1998, with U.S. operations based in San Francisco. A private company with venture backing, Alchemedia has been shipping its Clever Content products since November 1999.

Clever Content is a full-featured DRM product for image files (GIF and JPEG), PDF files, and through extensions, text files. Clever Content is a suite of three products:

♦ **Clever Content Server:** Image protection software for Windows NT and Solaris, installed on the site's host server

♦ **Clever Content Manager:** A Java-based, remote management tool used to select which images are to be protected

♦ **Clever Content Viewer:** A browser plug-in supporting both Windows and Macintosh browsers, implemented as an ActiveX control for Microsoft Internet Explorer and a SmartUpdate for Netscape Navigator

The DRM client runs on Windows and the Macintosh. The DRM server runs on Windows NT, Windows 2000, and Sun Solaris. Supported Web servers are IIS, Netscape Enterprise Server, and Apache.

With its focus on image files, Alchemedia's earliest customers included Terra*Server* (www.terraserver.com), the company that sells Russian spy satellite images, and Cahners's show business magazine *Variety* (www.variety.com). In August 2000, Alchemedia began offering a retail version of its product through a Web site, www.clevercontent.com. The retail site enables small businesses and individuals to enable up to 50 image files for DRM using the full features of the Clever Content platform.

More recently, though, Alchemedia has had an increasing focus on the corporate enterprise and has aligned itself with portal-focused vendors such as CoVia, Sybase, and Oracle. Alchemedia's positioning, too, has changed, with more of an emphasis on information security (using a tagline of "Secure Display") and less on its earlier positioning of using DRM as a means of connecting commerce and content. Alchemedia has won some business from large companies such as Ford Motor; for example, Ford can solicit comments on proposed designs for cars without worrying about the proposed designs ending up in the wrong hands. Alchemedia's technology is finding a similar use at America Online's Digital Marketing Services (DMS) division, which does online research for major clients.

ATABOK

ATABOK (www.atabok.com), a privately held company based in Newton, Massachusetts, began as the e-parcel division of Mitsubishi in 1996. In 1998 it was spun off from Mitsubishi and took with it a suite of core technologies for DRM and secure data delivery.

ATABOK's products for DRM include the ATABOK File Protection System (FPS) and the ATABOK Digital Wrapper. The FPS system provides a "closed loop" system for controlling assets within an organization, and the Digital Wrapper technology enables an organization to extend DRM protection beyond its walls. ATABOK's tools work closely with major e-mail platforms such as Microsoft Outlook and Lotus Notes and provide DRM services for the e-mail itself and for attachments, including options that control printing, forwarding, and copying. ATABOK supports a wide range of file types, including JPEG, HTML, and Microsoft Word DOC files, along with a number of multimedia formats.

ATABOK's client applications are Microsoft based, running on all flavors of Windows, with support for e-mail platforms such as Microsoft Outlook 2000 and Lotus Notes. Encryption is 256-bit symmetric key, using a proprietary algorithm. ATABOK focuses on outsourced solutions for secure e-mail and DRM.

ATABOK strikes us as superior technology. It has capabilities beyond those of secure e-mail, extending to DRM through its flexible application of business rules and excellent reporting capabilities. It doesn't seem to have much of a track record yet in pure DRM applications, especially in commerce-focused situations. However, with the growing awareness of DRM needs within organizations, ATABOK should find more situations in which its DRM solutions will have a role.

Authentica

Waltham, Massachusetts–based Authentica, Inc. (www.authentica.com), was founded in 1998 and has been solely focused on the DRM space. A privately held company, Authentica was founded by the same individuals who founded Raptor, the makers of the first software firewall. (Aside from a small ownership interest, Raptor has no relationship with Authentica.)

Authentica offers full-featured DRM solutions for electronic documents, Web sites, and e-mail. Authentica's products can be used on their own as a DRM solution, or they can be integrated with document management systems, workflow software, or e-mail systems. Authentica's PageRecall, MailRecall, and NetRecall products support PDF, HTML, and any Simple Mail Transfer Protocol (SMTP) e-mail message for Windows platforms, Microsoft Outlook, Lotus Notes, Eudora Pro, Internet Explorer, and Netscape Navigator. Authentica provides 128-bit RSA RC4 encryption.

The PageRecall client runs on Windows, Macintosh, and Sun Solaris, whereas the MailRecall and NetRecall clients run on Windows only. The DRM server software runs on Windows NT and Sun Solaris, with database access from Oracle and Microsoft SQL Server. Authentica's products come with both COM and C APIs for integrating with other systems such as e-commerce, document management, and other databases.

Authentica has developed an active rights-management architecture that enables organizations to set policy permissions, change the permissions any time, and audit all activities associated with the information from a centralized server. Authentica's emphasis on recall is in line with its focus on critical corporate information and sensitive applications such as government intelligence, financial services, pharmaceuticals, and health care. Authentica has 35 active customers for its DRM solutions, including a major semiconductor manufacturer and the U.S. House and Senate Subcommittees on Intelligence.

Like ATABOK, Authentica has excellent technology, with capabilities from e-mail to Web sites and electronic documents. Unlike ATABOK, Authentica seems to have more of a track record in DRM-specific applications. It also has made its DRM server a product, and it doesn't rely so heavily on a model that requires it to be the hosting organization.

Infraworks

Infraworks Corporation (www.infraworks.com) is an Austin, Texas–based company that was founded in 1997. Originally named STRATFOR Systems, Inc., Infraworks is privately held.

Infraworks's products are centered on its InTether technology. The technology enables the owners of digital property to establish permissions on any files, which are enforced by the client-side InTether Receiver. Infraworks considers InTether technology unique in the DRM space, in that no proprietary reader is required for accessing the protected property. InTether allows the protected property to open in its native application. Infraworks's foundation products are InTether Point-to-Point, a desktop application that enables owners of digital property to control usage and redistribution of their property, and AutoTether, a server-based application that performs the same task. After permissions have been established and the files packaged, the protected files can be downloaded from intranets and the Internet.

Infraworks's technology works with all major document file types, most common multimedia file types, Microsoft Office applications, HTML, and other supporting files such as included image files. Infraworks uses standard blowfish encryption.

The client application runs on most flavors of Windows, and the server application runs on Windows NT and Windows 2000 and requires a Java server (Allaire's JRUN, Sun Microsystems's Java Web Server 2, or Tomcat) and a Web Server (Microsoft IIS or Netscape's I-Planet/Enterprise Server).

Infraworks is still a very new offering and was at the outset aiming for the publishing and entertainment market. But its recent positioning is clearly aimed at a broad market, and most of its trade show focus in late 2001 has been in the corporate security arena.

Phocis

Phocis Ltd. (www.phocis.com) is a private, U.K.–based company established in 1996 with a focus on the DRM market.

Phocis combines DRM encryption and licensing technology, and it has recently developed the Secure Digital Exchange (SDX) and Secure Publishing Exchange (SPX). Originally the product was known as "authorit-e." SDX was launched in March 2001, and Phocis will launch SPX in the third quarter of 2001. SDX and SPX support any digital media type, and they use Macrovision's proprietary algorithms to secure content.

The Phocis SDX client runs on all 32-bit versions of Microsoft Windows, and the server runs on Windows NT, Sun Solaris, and Linux, with support from Oracle and Microsoft SQL Server databases through an ODBC interface. The server product runs with the Apache Web server and the BEA Weblogic application server. The Phocis SDX and SPX systems are XML-based, so integration with other technologies (such as e-commerce) is done through XML adapters. Phocis also provides a Simple Object Access Protocol (SOAP) interface that makes its packaging and licensing facilities available to a wide range of third-party systems for content management and workflow.

Phocis has concentrated on professional markets such as law, financial services, and consulting (with SDX), as well as publishing and e-learning (with SPX). Phocis currently has ten customers using its production systems. Phocis SDX is available as a hosted service and as a product that organizations can integrate with their own systems.

Phocis, like Infraworks, is a relatively new company that offers a DRM capability without the need to use certain rendering applications such as Acrobat or a browser. This may prove to be an important feature in enterprise deployment.

Music Solutions

The music market has been an obvious candidate for DRM, especially since free distribution of MP3 files became all the rage through Napster and others. Although Microsoft and RealNetworks will probably claim a large chunk of this market through their partnerships with the major recording labels' subscription services, MusicNet and pressplay, other vendors have been plying their DRM technologies for the music market successfully as well.

Liquid Audio

Liquid Audio, Inc (www.liquidaudio.com), is a Redwood City, California–based company founded in 1996 with some blue-chip venture backing, including money from Intel and Paul Allen's Vulcan Ventures. Liquid Audio went public in July 1999 (NASDAQ: LQID). It has been a key player in the SDMI initiative (see Chapter 6).

As mentioned in Chapter 2, Liquid Audio is currently the leading end-to-end DRM offering for the music industry, with global distribution and arrangements with major recording labels such as Warner, EMI, and Zomba and more than 1,500 independent labels. More than 150,000 music tracks are protected by Liquid Audio technology, and Liquid Audio provides distribution to consumers through major sites such as Amazon.com and Yahoo!. In addition to working on Windows and Macintosh systems, Liquid Audio also announced new technology to enable chipset vendors and portable device manufacturers to add digital music to their devices, including new devices from Sanyo, Sony, Palm, Toshiba, and Aiwa.

Liquid Player software supports MP3, AAC, ATRAC3, AC3, and Windows Media, and it includes support for multiple formats including Liquid, Sony's OpenMG, and SD. Liquid Player includes SDMI support and uses a variety of encryption schemes (DES, RC5, Blowfish, Twofish, and SHA) ranging from 56 bit to 512 bit, depending on the application and export restrictions. The DRM client runs on Windows 98 and higher and Macintosh 7.6.1 and higher, and the server software runs on Windows NT, Solaris, and Linux, with database support from Oracle 8*i* and MySQL. On the client side, Liquid Player operates with RealPlayer, RealJukebox, Winamp, and Windows Media Player.

Liquid Media is a mature, comprehensive offering of both technology and services necessary to meet the digital distribution requirements of major and independent content companies. These include encoding, hosting, clearinghouse, distribution, and promotion. The technology has been in use since 1997, with hundreds of thousands of downloads of the client technology.

Like many Web-focused companies, Liquid Audio has had to trim its sails over the recent months, as the explosive growth hoped for at the time of its IPO has leveled off. However, this is a proven technology and service, and the service has been designed to allow for more than one DRM technology. It will be interesting to see how Liquid Audio broadens its technology offerings beyond its own solutions. It will be necessary for it to do so, given that the major recording labels have aligned themselves with Microsoft and RealNetworks DRM solutions for their subscription services, pressplay and MusicNet. Liquid Audio will have to continue diversifying its offerings to stay afloat amid that heavy competition.

Musicrypt.com

Musicrypt, Inc. (www.musicrypt.com), is an Ontario, Canada–based company and is privately held; it has been in business since 1999 with a sole focus on DRM solutions for the music industry.

Musicrypt bills its offerings as a "DRM framework" and, in fact, is composed of a suite of component technologies that together are called Musicrypt's BRM (for Biometric Rights Management) Solution. Its chief innovation with respect to most other DRM technologies is its use of biometrics for user identification, as opposed to username and password combinations or a universal ID scheme such as Microsoft's Passport. Musicrypt's BioPassword software creates a custom signature for each user based on the user's highly individual typing rhythms. This permits users to port their music from machine to machine, without the restrictions inherent in single-device, lock-down systems. No biometric password is required on the user's default machine if the user selects this option.

The BRM Solution includes the following:

- **The DRUM server:** Assigns rights to users with respect to their digital media purchases made online and enables online or offline auditing of those materials. The DRUM server routes signals to each user's local client module whenever an appropriate Internet connection is established. The server runs on Microsoft Windows 2000 Advanced Server, with database support for Microsoft SQL Server 2000.

- **The DRUM client:** Contacts the server if required rights aren't available in the stored, encrypted local profile and updates that profile accordingly. The client runs on various flavors of Windows, with ports to Macintosh and various portable devices in the works. The client software primarily supports MP3 as a format (but is billed as format independent) and integrates with Windows Media Player and RealPlayer.

- **The DRUM db:** Also includes both a client and server component. The server portion of the db is located on an Internet server network system, and the local db (client rights portfolio) is located on the user's computer.

- **The Virtual Matrix Encryption (VME) encryption module:** A proprietary encryption technology offering up to million-bit encryption.

- **The BioPassword software:** Incorporated into Musicrypt's DRM solution, this ensures that only validated users are accessing the available media files.

The BRM Solution is currently integrated with an e-commerce system developed by Logistix Technologies, but it can be securely coupled to any type of electronic transaction system by means of XML communication or to any ODBC-compatible database. Web services are currently available via Microsoft IIS, but any ASP-compatible server can be used. Future support is planned for interfacing with content management and production systems.

Although Musicrypt is unproven (it is scheduled to go live close to the time that this book is published), it is an intriguing new offering, both for its open architecture and its approach known as *biometric authentication.* If successful, this approach could solve one of the thornier problems of DRM — namely, how to authenticate a user on different machines without placing artificial limitations on how many devices the user can claim as his own.

Multiple Media Solutions

Several DRM solutions are appearing that don't focus on one particular format or type of content. These solutions can be deployed by content providers that offer a mix of content in many different formats, as more and more are doing nowadays.

Digital Media on Demand

Digital Media on Demand (DMOD; www.dmod.com) is a Boston, Massachusetts–based company that was founded in 1996. DMOD has been exclusively focused on the DRM space since its inception.

DMOD provides secure distribution and DRM solutions for all types of digital assets, including music, video, and text. The system employs on-the-fly encryption and watermarking of assets, using multiple encryption keys, and it supports a number of business models, including pay-per-download, pay-per-view, subscriptions, and advertising-supported. DMOD's solution enables consumers to preview a song before purchase, using a lower-quality sample before the production-quality song is encrypted and downloaded.

DMOD's technology is integrated with the UltraPlayer audio software and the Sonique Media Player. DMOD also offers technology companies a software development kit (SDK) to allow the DMOD system to be embedded in Internet applications and other multimedia clients.

LockStream

LockStream Corporation (www.lockstream.com) is an application service provider (ASP) for the DRM market, founded in 1999, with offices in New York, Los Angeles, and Redmond, Washington. LockStream's backers include AOL Time Warner.

LockStream bills itself as an end-to-end solution combining DRM and asset distribution with a full range of services for publishers. It supports a full range of media — audio, video, and eBooks — and distribution over the Internet and wireless. LockStream has developed a proprietary solution that includes the Morphing Player, a private-label media player that can be highly customized in look and feel, as well as proprietary DRM technology.

The Morphing Player can be customized in both look and feel and functionality. LockStream has developed a number of customized versions, such as a comic book viewer; an audio player that also links to multimedia, photos, and lyrics; and a script player that combines the movie script with linked footage. The DRM protection is based on encrypting the content and encapsulating it in an XML wrapper, allowing access when the user enters her own key (her credit card number, typically). On the back end, LockStream provides the DRM technology, clearinghouse functions, and reporting.

LockStream has had a successful start, with key customer wins in a variety of businesses. It has also been able to broaden its offering as it goes, announcing added features and security for audio and video. LockStream's Morphing Player applications are clever and show its commitment to the "customer experience," as LockStream calls it. LockStream would be smart to begin offering a Morphing Player toolkit, allowing other organizations to develop customized players.

SealedMedia

SealedMedia (www.sealedmedia.com) is a well-established U.K. company that has been in business and focused on the DRM space since 1996. SealedMedia had U.S. operations based in San Francisco until Summer 2001, when it cut back its U.S. operation and retrenched to its U.K. headquarters under its original CTO and founder, Dr. Martin Lambert.

SealedMedia provides persistent protection for many types of digital content, including PDF, HTML, GIF, JPEG, MP3, and QuickTime. SealedMedia's DRM client is a browser plug-in for the Macintosh and Windows, supporting both Netscape Navigator and Microsoft Internet Explorer. The license server supports a variety of business models, including preview and purchase, pay-per-view, subscription, and "event tickets." SealedMedia also offers content management tools that enable publishers to integrate combinations of files, in various formats, into content sets for customized and individualized offerings.

SealedMedia's technology is mature, open, and well designed for integration. SealedMedia also offers a toolkit, enabling the customer to more tightly integrate the server components with his own system. Publishers can integrate the content management tools with their own workflow, allowing for batch creation and packaging of content sets. After the content is deployed, publishers can communicate with the license server through a Web interface, an e-mail gateway, or programmatically through an API.

SealedMedia has a solid customer base, representing publishers of all types, and has recently developed more business in the corporate space, with applications such as online documentation. It has also been broadening its technology partnerships, adding vendors focused on areas such as content management, audio and video distribution, and electronic billing.

Macrovision

Macrovision Corporation (www.macrovision.com) is a publicly held company (NASDAQ: MVSN) headquartered in Sunnyvale, California with sales and development offices near London and in Tokyo. Macrovision has a number of offerings in the DRM space, recent developments and acquisitions that complement the company's original strength: copy protection technologies for video, software, and audio content on physical media such as prerecorded videocassettes, CDs, and CD-ROMs, as well as computer software and content delivered over the Internet.

Macrovision's core technologies are copy protection, electronic licensing and rights management, and encryption. Macrovision is the most important vendor of copy protection solutions for physical media; it holds many pieces of intellectual property in those areas, including 98 issued or pending U.S. patents and 648 issued or pending international patents. The company is constantly increasing its patent portfolio.

Macrovision is the result of several acquisitions, which are represented as the following divisions:

- **The Video Technology Division:** Develops and licenses technologies to prevent the unauthorized duplication, reception, or use of copyrighted video materials on videocassette, DVD, and digital pay-per-view

- **The GLOBEtrotter Software Division:** Provides electronic license management (ELM) and electronic license distribution (ELD) solutions

- **The Consumer Software Division:** Develops and licenses copy protection and rights management technologies for consumer entertainment and application software publishers

Macrovision's SafeCast product is a comprehensive DRM and security solution for a variety of application, content, and entertainment products. It includes a wide range of tools that help publishers encourage trials and generate incremental sales using either CD-ROM or electronic software distribution (ESD) and electronic license distribution technology. Macrovision's SafeDisc CD-ROM copy protection solution has been licensed to over 100 mastering and replication facilities worldwide and is used by many major interactive software publishers. Its SafeWrap product provides tamperproofing for digital properties. Its SafeAudio copy protection solution prevents exact copying of audio CDs.

In 2001, Macrovision has been in the news for its role in helping the major recording labels manufacture and distribute "copy-proof" CDs that still enable consumers to copy their CDs to audiocassettes but not to other digital media. Macrovision's approach, which includes third-party technology, adds distortion when consumers make additional digital copies.

ViaTech

ViaTech Technologies, Inc. (www.elicense.com), is a Natick, Massachusetts–based business that was formed in 1996 with a sole focus on the DRM space.

ViaTech is a DRM service provider, offering technology and services to sell, secure, and protect software, music, video, publishing, and any other proprietary content electronically distributed over the Internet. ViaTech's eLicense System provides security to ensure authorized use and flexibility to accommodate a wide range of distribution, e-commerce, and data-gathering models, including subscription licensing, mobile licensing, multiple licenses, and volume purchases. Post-installation security uses ViaTech's Adaptive Fingerprint Technology to ensure license control specific to the computer where a product is licensed.

The eLicense System provides the following:

- Usage control for software and digital content on the user's desktop. The execution of applications, functionality within applications, and access to digital content are allowed according to the conditions fixed in an installed license.

- Tools for publishers to include eLicense controls with their distributed software and content products, including self-generated, secure trial-use licensing.

- Automated acquisition and installation of licenses via the Web (with optional phone and e-mail acquisition as well).

- Web-accessible database accounts for publishers and resellers to configure product and license settings from which licenses are delivered.

- Flexibility in implementation to support e-commerce models for desktop purchase, Web store purchase, and prepaid (purchase order) license acquisition.

- Data gathering, management, and mining tools associated with trial registration, superdistribution, sales, and licensing activities.

The eLicense client runs on both Windows and the Macintosh and is integrated with RealPlayer and Acrobat Reader. The client application doesn't have to be in contact with the license server after the content has been deployed. Encryption is a combination of DES, RSA, and RC5.

eLicense is a mature product offering, with established business from Electronic Arts, General Electric, and edel Entertainment. Future plans include increased support for video protection and distribution.

OS-Level Tools and Frameworks

Our final group of vendors are those that offer DRM frameworks and solutions that attack the problem at the level of the operating system or that provide DRM services across a wide range of devices, both present and future. These are perhaps the most ambitious ones of all. Instead of going after a niche market such as music downloads or STM publishing (although they may start out by targeting markets like these), the following vendors are positioning themselves for the day when DRM truly goes mainstream.

Digital World Services

Digital World Services (DWS; www.dwsco.com) is a company that provides DRM services to the entertainment and publishing industries. To that extent, it can be viewed as a service provider, but it is also in a unique situation because it is right in the middle of the changeover of

Napster from a free to a commercial service, as explained in Chapter 2. Operating with offices in New York and Hamburg, Germany, Digital World Services is a subsidiary of Bertelsmann AG, one of the world's largest media companies.

As a service provider, DWS uses both the InterTrust and Adobe technology for DRM protection, supporting secure delivery of music, publishing, video, games, and software. DWS also provides tailored services, including end-to-end project management, system integration, and ongoing consulting. DWS actually provides two related offerings: "DWS Rights Clearing" and professional services. DWS Rights Clearing is the technology suite that includes digitization, packaging, distribution, rights clearing, payment, and reporting. DWS has engineered a technical hub for DWS Rights Clearing that uses the third-party DRM technology at its core, but is bolstered by DWS's own engineering.

As DWS has built out its own technology suite and integrated more third-party tools, it has built up an impressive level of experience with DRM integration, both on the server side and the client side. On the client side, it developed a tool, DWS Content Manager, to help the experience of the consumer acquiring digital products. A single tool to negotiate the download and use of digital products, DWS Content Manager brings together all media types and associated players with the capability to interact with DRM-secured content. It provides consumers with a unified visual display of download information as well as specific product information, and it gives them a single library view of their acquired content, which can be activated directly from the interface. Although the tool is brand new, this strikes us as precisely the kind of work that should be done for consumers. As our research and the work of others shows, many of the problems with DRM happen precisely at the point of end-user installation.

DWS was launched in January 2000 and has been busy first building out a DRM environment for BMG Music, and more recently, with the Napster project. But it has won business outside of Bertelsmann proper, mainly with music companies and mainly in Europe. However, it is increasing its U.S. presence and broadening its marketing message to other entertainment companies and publishing companies.

Elisar

Elisar Software Corporation (www.elisar.com) is an Albuquerque, New Mexico–based company that was founded in 1999 with a sole focus on the DRM space. Elisar is a private company, and it launched its MediaRights product at Seybold Boston in April 2001.

The MediaRights client doesn't reside at the application level, but instead exists in the operating system as an OS extension. As an OS extension, the MediaRights client leverages the OS to limit access to protected content. This also gives MediaRights the flexibility to work across applications. Because it is not tied to a particular application (unlike plug-ins), MediaRights can work with any file format. To add support for a new application, Elisar must "register" the application to prevent spoofing. The registration is completed in days, and every version of MediaRights contains an auto-update feature that will update itself to support the new application at regular intervals or whenever protected content is received or downloaded.

The MediaRights client enables end users to access and view protected content by downloading a lightweight device driver. The client, which resides in the end user's computer operating system, provides the secure container through which users gain access to content. The server technology is offered as both an Internet-based server and enterprise server.

In addition, MediaRights consists of these components:

♦ **Internet Content Server (ICS):** Encrypts, hosts, packs, and serves files from Elisar's content servers. Content is uploaded through Elisar's online Web application and is then encrypted and hosted on the ICS. The interface to the protected content (such as a public Web site) is hosted on the user's own Web server or ISP.

♦ **Enterprise Content Server:** Encrypts, hosts, packs, and serves files from within your own organization or enterprise's servers. Content is uploaded and managed through the software interface packaged with the server.

MediaRights supports a broad array of file formats, including image, video, and document formats. MediaRights uses symmetric encryption and supports the National Institute for Standards and Technology's (NIST) Advanced Encryption Standard (AES) encryption and both private and public key encryption, depending on the distribution method selected. In the United States, MediaRights supports 128-bit encryption. The MediaRights client software operates on Windows 95 and higher and on MacOS 8/9. Ports to PalmOS and PocketPC are planned. MediaRights Enterprise Content Server operates on Windows 2000 Server and will support Apache Linux by 2002. The database is Microsoft SQL server, but it can use any ODBC-compliant database.

MediaRights has been focused on certain market segments, notably images, publishing, and streaming media. To date, its primary focus has been on the image industry, in which content volumes are high, copyright awareness is high, and digital distribution is more mature. Moving forward, Elisar will focus on business-to-business (B-to-B) for medium-to-large business concerned with Internet security for the distribution of confidential and valuable information ranging from stock images to market reports to executive video conferences.

Elisar's technology is unique in that it handles DRM protection at the operating-system level, which is fundamentally a more effective approach to security than other technologies that handle it at the application level.

IBM EMMS

IBM has been involved in DRM for a long time. Its first DRM program, which appeared on the market in 1996, was infoMarket. InfoMarket was highly advanced technology, containing some features that future DRM solutions would abandon for the sake of simplicity. It was an end-to-end solution for text, images, and HTML that contained a clearinghouse, a search engine that could search multiple text repositories simultaneously, and support for superdistribution.

At the heart of infoMarket was a DRM-packaging technology called *Cryptolope*. Like the contemporary InterTrust DigiBox, Cryptolope contained both packaged content and DRM controller functionality. It was designed in an era when network connectivity wasn't ubiquitous, so it allowed for controlled access to content on computers that were disconnected from the network. As a result, the packages were quite large: Cryptolopes took up 4MB, plus another 1MB for a utility application that users used to view their rights and other metadata.

IBM signed up a few pilot customers for infoMarket, including Reuters New Media, the research firm Jupiter Communications (now Jupiter Media Metrix), and the computer magazine chain CMP Publications (now part of United News & Media). However, infoMarket didn't catch on. Despite an attempt to revive it under the name Cryptolope Live! a couple of years later, as part of IBM's Digital Library (digital asset management) offering, the technology died.

EMMS (Electronic Media Management System; www.ibm.com/software/emms) is IBM's second-generation DRM offering. Originally called the Madison Project, it is the result of research and development at IBM's Advanced Technology Center in Ft. Lauderdale, FL; Almaden Research Center in California; and Hawthorn Labs in the New York City suburbs, between 1991 and 1999.

The EMMS technology is billed as an end-to-end solution for the preparation, delivery, and consumption of high-value encrypted and watermarked content via open networks. The solution includes five software components that were designed to work together, but are also separately licensed:

- ♦ **EMMS Content Mastering:** Provides tools for format conversion, compression, and packaging
- ♦ **EMMS Web Commerce Enabler:** Provides the framework for e-commerce
- ♦ **EMMS Clearinghouse:** Provides secure clearinghouse features and comprehensive reporting
- ♦ **EMMS Content Hosting:** Provides secure hosting and distribution of protected content
- ♦ **EMMS Player SDK:** Provides publishers with a toolkit for developing custom client applications

The EMMS product line was announced in February 1999, in conjunction with the AlbumDirect consumer music distribution trial, which was cosponsored by IBM and the major recording labels such asEMI Music, Sony Music Entertainment, Universal Music Group, and Warner Music Group. Conducted for six months from June to December 1999, the AlbumDirect trial examined consumer experience in purchasing and receiving music online and tested the security features and viability of EMMS in downloading music from the Internet. AlbumDirect was the most broad-based of the many DRM trials in which the major labels have engaged — for one thing, it involved all five, not just one or two — but like most of the other trials, it didn't result in permanent service offerings. Around the same time, IBM became one of the vendors most heavily involved in the Secure Digital Music Initiative.

EMMS supports most media file formats and RealPlayer, Acrobat Reader, Labelgate Player, Toshiba-iVC Du ub Player, Sony Open Magic Gate Jukebox, Music Match, VDE (Vedalabs Media Engine), Sony Memory Stick Technology devices (for example, Walkman, CyberShot digital camera, and PHS wireless phone), and Toshiba Memory Card Technology devices.

The EMMS technology uses both public and private key encryption, including RSA, RC4, and an IBM proprietary algorithm. The client software is based on a Windows SDK that allows partners to develop unique players. The server software runs on Windows 2000 and Windows NT. The Web Commerce Enabler APIs are supported on a number of operating systems, including Windows, IBM AIX, Sun Solaris, HP-UX, and DEC-UNIX. Database support is currently with IBM's own DB2 database.

IBM has a broad market focus for EMMS, but has had some initial success with music downloading applications for portable devices, notably in the Japanese market. It has also been targeting the DRM service providers, with some success. Moving forward, IBM, like many of the other vendors, is targeting the corporate market, but more broadly, it is moving to an industry-independent platform that supports music, video, games, documents, and imaging. This cross-device approach puts IBM squarely in competition with Microsoft and InterTrust as the focus of DRM shifts from the PC to portable media players, Internet appliances, and other post-PC devices.

Chapter 12

DRM-Related Solutions

In Chapter 11, we discuss a wide range of digital rights management solutions that, to a greater or lesser degree, conform to the DRM reference architecture presented in Chapter 5. Several other vendors' technologies and solutions are related to DRM but lie outside of the generic architecture. We examine many of these vendors in this chapter.

Note that this is a snapshot of the market as of summer 2001. As we stated in Chapter 11, DRM is a young, volatile industry. We have made every effort to make this material current as of this writing, but we're certain that there will be some changes in the marketplace over the next several months.

Internal Rights Management

We mention in Chapter 1 that publishers and other content providers must expend a great deal of effort in tracking the intellectual property rights that flow through their organizations. These property rights include content created for them under contract by authors, musicians, filmmakers, illustrators, and so on, as well as content licensed from other publishers, agencies, and such. Often, content providers also license their material to other publishers and distributors.

Content providers can license various types of rights. Foremost is the primary right, such as the right to publish a book in print. So-called *subsidiary rights* (or *subrights* for short) include all the rights to content that a publisher can confer apart from the primary right, such as translation, film rights, audio book rights, and so on. In the film industry, the analogs of subrights are things such as cable TV and videocassette distribution. There are also *permissions,* which are for cases such as using a small piece of one content item (for example, a graphic or table) in another item or making reprints of a magazine article or photo.

Just about all the DRM solutions discussed in Chapters 7 and 11 are focused on consumer content distribution. Yet the area of rights tracking and business-to-business (B-to-B) distribution is a huge area unto itself. For large media organizations, internal rights tracking can be a bureaucratic nightmare. Large departments of administrators exist to keep track of contracts, rights acquired from other publishers, and rights requested of them by others.

As discussed in Chapter 1, tracking rights and permissions internally is difficult to automate because each publisher does it differently — and, of course, the nuances of these processes vary even more across different segments of the media industry, such as film and book publishing. The video (film and television) industry has led the curve among the larger types of content providers in deploying internal rights management solutions. This is not surprising, given that many major-studio motion pictures make more and more of their money not from box office sales but from rights transactions for television distribution, videocassettes, books, theme park rides, clothing, and other sorts of product tie-ins. Off-the-shelf (that is, non–custom-built) solutions for internal rights management in the film and television industry have been around for well over a decade; some of the vendors have more recently been retooling their systems for publishing and other types of media.

In publishing, years of attempts to create automated rights and permissions systems have borne little fruit until quite recently. The demand among publishing companies for such functionality has increased dramatically because rights and permissions processes have become significant bottlenecks to the deployment of new digital media-based business models.

Essentially, it ought to be possible for an automated system to determine whether a certain piece of content can be used in a dynamically assembled online product and, if so, what rights clearance procedure has to take place to do so. Production of such a product can't stop while a rights and permissions administrator wades through spreadsheets and hard-copy files to determine whether the appropriate rights are in place to use a particular piece of content or prepares letters to send through postal mail to obtain clearance for it.

Some internal rights management systems include a closely related function: that of royalty payments. Royalties are elements of contract terms between content packagers, such as publishers, and content creators, such as authors or photographers. A stream of royalty payments is little more than a special case of a content rights transaction — it's sort of the flip side of product sales — but it's one that has been in existence in publishing (and other segments of the media industry) for a long time and is fairly standard across the industry. Furthermore, royalty schemes can be quite complex in the ways that they are calculated according to various conditions, such as distribution medium (for example, hardback, paperback, and eBook), geography, retail price, and so on. For these reasons, most publishers already have royalty systems in place and are often reluctant to replace them; therefore, some internal rights management systems are designed to "fit around" royalty systems rather than subsume them.

Here, then, are some of the vendors with solutions to the bugbear of internal rights management.

Savantech

Savantech, of Redondo Beach, California (www.savantech.com), was founded in 2000 by Dr. Prasad Ram, who had managed the group at Xerox that commercialized Mark Stefik's Digital Property Rights Language (DPRL), which is now known as XrML and is owned by the spin-off company ContentGuard. The other principal of Savantech is Carol Risher, the former vice president of copyright and new technology at the Association of American Publishers, who was instrumental in developing such book and journal industry standards as DOI (Digital Object Identifier) and ONIX (Online Information Exchange).

> **CROSS REFERENCE:** See Chapter 6 to find out more about DOI and ONIX.

Savantech started out as a system integrator specializing in DRM and related technologies and providing services to DRM vendors. Among others, it integrated ContentGuard's DRM technology (now abandoned) with Reciprocal's service infrastructure to create ePCS (Electronic Publishers Clearinghouse Service). ePCS has been deployed at publishers such as John Wiley & Sons and Houghton Mifflin.

Savantech has been developing an overall digital content commerce, or "d-commerce," framework for publishers, which it calls dCI (d-commerce integration). It has defined an architecture for dCI and is building a suite of products called Photon that fits into the architecture. The first of these products, Photon Rights, is an internal rights management application designed especially for book and journal publishing, created with the help of Risher's deep experience in those areas.

Photon Rights handles both sides of a publisher's internal rights management function: rights granting (responding to external requests for rights on content that the publisher owns) and rights acquisition (acquiring rights to content from authors, agencies, or other publishers). It consists of four applications:

♦ **Rights and permissions:** Automates rights-granting functions and provides Web-based forms for third parties to use to request rights, automatic responses to requests, status tracking, storage of terms and conditions, and invoice generation.

♦ **Rights acquisition:** Supplies standard forms for acquiring rights from other publishers and other sources, tracks the status of requests, associates rights metadata with the actual content, and generates payment reminders.

♦ **Subsidiary rights:** Automates subsidiary rights-granting functions.

♦ **Contract management:** Manages contracts with authors and other content sources, stores terms and conditions, analyzes rights metadata, and manages scanned images of legacy contracts.

Photon Rights can be integrated with a publisher's content management systems, payment processors, content distribution systems, and other functions. Specifically, it interfaces with various e-commerce servers from Microsoft and IBM, third-party payment processors, and DRM systems from Microsoft, Adobe, and MediaDNA. It handles product metadata based on the ONIX standard.

In addition to Photon Rights, Savantech is developing Photon Commerce, which is a solution for content distribution management. With Photon Commerce, a publisher can manage various types of distribution paradigms, including on-demand distribution, scheduled distribution, and several different types of DRM packaging. Photon Commerce should be available by the end of 2001.

REAL Software Systems

REAL Software Systems, of Woodland Hills, California (www.elcamino.com/rss/), is a subsidiary of El Camino Resources, Inc., a company whose primary business is large computer system leasing. It is unrelated to RealNetworks, and its name is pronounced the Spanish way, "ray-AHL."

The company originally (in the mid-1980s) produced a solution for the film and television industries that covered internal rights management. That solution ran on IBM mainframes; more recently, it has been ported to Windows NT. REAL's current applications for film and television include Alliant Royalties, Alliant Participations, and Rights Licensing.

Rights Licensing is REAL's original application for licensing video properties to theaters, TV stations, pay-per-view, satellite TV, cable TV, videocassettes, and so on. It allows rights holders to track terms that are unique to each type of content distribution, such as market shares of broadcast TV stations and sizes of markets, which are factors in determining license fees. Rights Licensing is meant to integrate with accounting systems.

Rights Licensing also has a feature for setting up a worldwide marketing schedule for a given property so that users can set up release dates for various media along with asking prices. For example, a movie studio can set up a schedule for a theatrical release on a given day, a release to videocassette and pay-per-view TV six months later, and a release to broadcast TV six months after that.

Alliant Royalties and Alliant Participations are two separate products built on a common base of functionality. Alliant Royalties tracks royalty payments to authors, agents, and other parties. It applies to film, publishing, game, software, and other industries. Alliant Royalties provides flexible ways of representing royalty terms from contracts, even when the contract terms are convoluted and have many different sets of conditions.

Alliant Royalties also includes a specially designed calculation language called DealScript, in which royalty terms can be calculated based on changing factors. The DealScript language is like a spreadsheet calculation engine with functions that are specialized for the entertainment industry. It lets users define calculations that determine deal terms — for example, Adjusted Gross, Cash Break Even, or Net. It also lets users set up templates in which results of DealScript calculations can be used. If you change a DealScript variable, the template dynamically revises itself, resulting in new deal terms.

Alliant Royalties can take dynamic data feeds from a wide variety of external systems, such as accounting and enterprise resource planning (ERP). It also feeds royalty payment requests to accounting systems after routing them for approval.

Alliant Participations is unique to the film industry, in which "participations" are the slices of box-office revenue that studios and other parties receive under contract. Participations are treated as a different flavor of royalties, and the system has most of the same components as Alliant Royalties.

REAL's customers include large movie studios (such as MGM, Disney, and Universal Studios), broadcasters (such as Cox and the BBC), publishers (such as International Thomson, Houghton Mifflin, *Reader's Digest,* and Hungry Minds, the publisher of this book), and various other organizations.

RightsLine

RightsLine, Inc., of Beverly Hills, California (www.rightsline.com), is another internal rights management software vendor focusing on the film industry. The company was formed in 1999 by Russell Reeder, a former application sales executive at Oracle Corp. Reeder recruited a management team that included other Oracle alums.

RightsLine's suite of software products goes beyond the kind of internal rights tracking that REAL's Rights Licensing system does: It is designed to interface with e-commerce storefronts to enable online sales of rights that are tracked internally. RightsLine's Rights Intelligence System (RIS) is the internal application for defining and tracking rights. A content provider uses it to maintain a database of rights information, which RightsLine calls a *rights repository.*

RIS includes workflow management capabilities for automating rights-granting processes, sophisticated reporting and access control mechanisms, and a calculation engine for computing deal prices. RIS is meant to interface with internal business systems (such as accounting); this requires assistance from RightsLine's professional services group.

The other major component of RightsLine's software is Rights Licensing Server (RLS). RLS sits between the rights repository and an e-commerce site, on which customers can purchase rights. RLS lets users search and browse a content provider's selection of rights for sale, and it interfaces with an e-commerce package's shopping cart (or other purchasing function) to enable purchases.

RightsLine's first customer was Universal Studios, which signed on in February 2001.

VISTA International

VISTA International, of Northwood, Middlesex, U.K. (www.vistacomp.com), is perhaps the original software systems provider to the book and journal publishing industry, dating back to 1977. VISTA had minicomputer-based software for book and journal publishers' back-office functions, such as financials, customer service, and fulfillment. Nowadays, its customer list includes just about every major publisher in the United Kingdom, several small-to-medium-sized publishers in the United States (as well as a couple of big ones), and several more in Canada, Australia, New Zealand, and continental Europe.

More recently, VISTA has been developing a product suite called author2reader. VISTA's intent is to have functionality for every aspect of publishing, from dealing with authors through to production workflow, warehousing, and finance. VISTA has slowly been building a portfolio of integrated products that fits the author2reader framework.

One of these products is Rights & Royalties, which deals with the rights-granting part of the internal rights management equation: It enables publishers to enter rights information about content that they own so that they can manage incremental revenue opportunities from the content, including subsidiary rights, electronic rights, and permission requests from third parties, as well as royalties due authors from rights sales.

The system enables publishers to take rights sales into account more easily when doing revenue forecasts — just as a movie studio can take sales of videocassettes and TV rights into account. Together with other components of VISTA's author2reader suite, Rights & Royalties can consolidate reporting of revenues from rights sales as well as normal book or journal sales. It can also feed rights metadata to extranet systems for buying and selling rights — rights exchanges, as discussed in the following section. VISTA has a partnership with one of these, Rightscenter.com, the first customer for which is Orion Publishing in the UK.

Internal rights management systems are vitally important, as mentioned throughout this book. They are fairly well entrenched in the entertainment industry, but the area remains a problem for many publishers. Some refuse to admit that they have an internal rights management problem, but an increasing number are beginning to understand the increasing implications of the bottlenecks that they have in this area. The problem is very complex, but not so complex that it can't be solved. Potential vendors are not bringing solutions to market because they believe that they can't make a profit from internal rights management. They realize that one solution is not applicable to all publishers and sales and implementation cyles are quite long.

Good internal rights management solutions for publishing companies will ultimately be original applications and not those that are repurposed from the entertainment industry. For that reason, it is good to see companies such as VISTA and Savantech working to bring solutions to market.

Rights Exchanges

Internal rights management systems enable content providers to organize rights information for their own use in making internal processes more efficient. If the systems are equipped with a Web browser interface (as Savantech's and VISTA's are), outsiders can also view the information, as long as the content provider has set up an extranet through a virtual private network or some other means.

The next logical step beyond that is a single Web site that lists many content providers' available rights and enables people to purchase them. Such services exist today; they are called *rights exchanges* (not to be confused with Rights Exchange, Inc., the original name of the company that is now Reciprocal, Inc.).

In the 1999-2000 timeframe, online B-to-B exchanges of industrial goods such as chemicals, steel, and aircraft parts became all the rage, especially among venture capitalists and Internet entrepreneurs. Like any business fad during the Internet bubble, many of these exchanges didn't succeed. One of the primary reasons for the failures was the overcomplexity of rules about pricing and negotiations, making buying processes too difficult to replicate online.

Commerce in content rights has this problem, to be sure — meaning that no matter how successful rights exchanges get, there will always be room for personal negotiations, whether over the phone or at large conferences such as the Frankfurt Book Fair or Western Cable. Another difficult problem with automating rights commerce, as mentioned earlier, is that every content provider does it differently. Among other things, this means that each content provider has its own way of describing its content and the rights that it has to sell — that is, each publisher uses different metadata. Although some standards efforts are under way for the kind of DRM solutions that distribute content to consumers (see Chapter 6), there are none for B-to-B rights commerce.

This lack of standardization is both a hurdle and an opportunity for online rights exchanges. It's a hurdle because it makes it that much more difficult for a rights exchange to sign up publishers; the publishers have to take whatever rights metadata they have and make it fit the rights exchange's metadata scheme. But this lack of standardization is also an opportunity because if a rights exchange achieves critical mass in the marketplace, its own metadata scheme becomes a de facto standard, which enhances its ability to charge for its services, sign up even more customers, and increase its leverage in partnership deals.

The size of the opportunity hasn't been lost on the handful of companies who have launched rights exchanges, but more importantly, neither has the need among content providers for such services. Studies have suggested that it costs over $1,000 for a buyer and seller of rights to find each other and complete a deal using offline methods.

Rightscenter.com

Rightscenter.com, of Palo Alto, CA (`www.rightscenter.com.com`), is an online rights exchange for publishing, which has recently expanded to the film industry. The company was founded in 1999 by a pair of Silicon Valley veterans — unlikely backgrounds for entry into the publishing arena, where people expect to deal with members of their own tribe. Jim McHugh is a veteran of Apple and Encanto Networks with a marketing background, and Kip Parent's credentials include working at SGI (Silicon Graphics Inc.), where he was the company's Internet evangelist, and the large Web development firm iXL (now Scient).

Rightscenter.com has two primary components: the Global Literary Marketplace and the Global Rights Directory. The Global Literary Marketplace is a listing of who's who in the publishing world, including publisher personnel, agents, and other publishing professionals. The Global Rights Directory is an online catalog of rights that publishers and agents have put up for sale.

Rightscenter.com's business model is to charge publishers $250 per year to list a title in the Global Rights Directory. There is no charge for looking in the directory, nor is there one for being listed in the Global Literary Marketplace; in fact, Rightscenter.com has access to lists of publishing people for inclusion in the directory from companies that produce the important trade shows in the book industry, such as BookExpo America and the London Book Fair, where rights buying and selling traditionally take place. For the $250, publishers also get tools for such tasks as title management and sales tracking (essentially a lightweight version of internal rights management, as described earlier). Publishers who put up title listings can choose to limit access to them: They can group them into catalogs, make them available only to named parties, or make them available to all.

In addition to listing rights offers, publishers can also use Rightscenter.com to manage the buying and selling processes. Like other online exchanges, Rightscenter.com has a facility for automating the negotiation process, including sending offers and counteroffers back and forth. Publishers can find out who has been looking at their titles and manage multiple simultaneous offers through negotiation (important for, say, selling the movie rights to the brand-new Stephen King novel).

Rightscenter.com signed up HarperCollins, Bloomberg Press, and — once again — Hungry Minds, the publisher of this book, as marquee publishing clients. More recently, it has expanded into the film industry by putting up the Film Rights Directory, a catalog of books' rights that are available for film or television adaptation. Its movie industry customers include Samuel Goldwyn Films and Lightstorm Entertainment (of *Titanic* fame). In all, the company boasts over 300 paid rights sellers listing titles in the directories.

The company's most recent direction is to move into the territory of internal rights management systems by offering permissions management and other internal rights management functions.

Rightsworld.com

Rightsworld.com, based in New York City, is another rights exchange that focuses on the publishing industry. It was founded by Eric Miller and Nick Bogaty, two alumni of Web publishing tools vendor SOHOnet (now Runtime Technologies) and the Web-based on-demand publisher iUniverse, and launched at the London Book Fair in March 2000.

Whereas Rightscenter.com uses a B-to-B exchange model, rightsworld.com uses an auction model à la eBay. (Another similar service, SubRights.com, was launched around the same time but did not survive.) Buyers and sellers both open accounts on rightsworld.com by supplying information, which is verified by rightsworld.com staff. Sellers can list titles on the system for $20 to $100 per title, no matter how many different rights to that title they want to sell. The price for listing a title depends on the prominence of the listing on Rightsworld.com; this is similar to many B-to-B directories, which charge vendors more for prominent placement in search results.

Sellers put up rights for auction; buyers bid on them during a predetermined time period, just as on eBay. When the auction is over, the buyers and sellers are introduced to each other and have ten days to close the deal. Rightsworld.com takes 5 percent of the selling price as a commission.

Rightsworld.com started out amid some controversy that helped it get publicity in the trade press. It offered on its site the rights to *Fortunate Son,* a biography of then-candidate George W. Bush that was dropped by its original publisher, St. Martin's Press, because of allegations concerning its author, J.H. Hatfield. After St. Martin's dropped the title, the small publisher Soft

Skull Press picked it up and put it up on Rightsworld.com, in addition to a print run of 45,000 copies.

Currently, rightsworld.com has agreements with iUniverse, Routledge, and several other publishers, mostly of eBook material. It is unclear how much actual bid volume the site handles.

iCopyright

Somewhat related to the idea of the rights exchange is the business of Renton, WA-based iCopyright (www.icopyright.com). iCopyright's business is sort of the converse of copy protection: Instead of protecting copyrighted material from piracy, it makes it easy to comply with copyright. iCopyright addresses itself to the fact that in certain publishing markets, it's a hassle to obtain rights to use content, and therefore many people elect to cheat because it's the easiest way. (As mentioned in Chapter 2, often it's not the price; it's the process.)

iCopyright makes it easy to license content on the Web for reuse. The canonical example is ordering reprints of a magazine article. Let's say that you do public-relations work for a company, and a noted business magazine writes a favorable article about the company. You want a thousand glossy color reprints of the article, in order to include it in your press kit. You have two choices:

♦ Print the Web page from your browser, go over to a copying machine or your local copy shop, and run off 1,000 copies — despite the fact that there is a copyright notice at the bottom of the Web page, along with banner ads and a lot of other extraneous features.

♦ Call the magazine's publisher, get the runaround trying to find the reprints department, fill out a form that they fax to you, fax it back, and wait six weeks until glossy color reprints come in a box via UPS.

With iCopyright's Instant Clearance Service, there is a third way:

♦ Click on the iCopyright icon at the bottom of the Web page, fill out an HTML form, and download a PDF that you can print in color.

The Instant Clearance Center enables publishers to set up Web forms through iCopyright that allow users to purchase as many copies as they want, in PDF, HTML (without banner ads or other extraneous content), or bulk e-mail formats, for free or fee. The reprints all contain an identifier (analogous to a DOI; see Chapter 6) that users can reference to obtain further licensing on the content through iCopyright.

iCopyright hosts the content and processes the transactions, taking a 50 percent fee from the revenue. iCopyright also charges monthly subscription fees for the Instant Clearance Center and the Publisher Central tool for managing content licensing offers.

In July 2001, iCopyright announced a partnership with Reprint Management Services (RMS, www.reprintbuyer.com), a leading source of magazine article reprints. RMS has relationships with over 250 publications, for which it manages the entire reprint process; and it has the capability to navigate traditional reprint processes on behalf of users to obtain permissions on any article from any magazine. By the end of 2001, RMS's Custom Reprint Service will be available to iCopyright users. The two services are quite complementary.

iCopyright has a rather tortuous history. It was founded in 1998 by Mike O'Donnell, the founder of the early ISP SpryNet and chairman of the e-business division of the Software and Information Industry Association, and Andrew Cameron, a former Xerox PARC employee and executive at Silicon Graphics. O'Donnell was ousted in 2000, when the board of directors decided that they wanted someone running the company who could bring them a quick IPO. O'Donnell formed Data Depth Corp., which attempted to do for commercial databases (such as credit reports) what iCopyright was doing for online articles.

In early 2001, with the market for Internet IPOs turning sour, the company trimmed staff, fired management, and was bought by Data Depth Corp. O'Donnell resumed his role as CEO as the company refocused on its original business and ramped up for the long haul.

Over 200 publishers license their online content through iCopyright. Its partnership with RMS will give it continued competitive advantage against its nearest competitor, the Copyright Clearance Center (see Chapter 1 and the following subsection), which has been unable to launch a similarly compelling Web service for permissions granting.

Copyright Clearance Center

iCopyright's only real competitor is the Copyright Clearance Center (CCC, www.copyright.com), which is discussed in Chapter 1. In early 2000, CCC launched RightsLink, which enables publishers to make permissions transactions online. Despite Yesteryear's (a fictitious name that we use in Chapter 2 for a real-life failed business) failed attempt to do something similar for book content, CCC is building a niche for the service in the news business. Its launch customer was Dow Jones, which is using the service for the *Wall Street Journal's* and *Barron's* content. CCC supports transactions for permissions as well as reprints in PDF. Since launching RightsLink, CCC has also signed the *New York Times*.

More recently, CCC acquired the assets of the small, failed DRM vendor Vyou, whose technology it intends to integrate with RightsLink to support commerce in pay-per-view rights to the content.

Rights exchanges are inevitable in all media businesses, but like their counterparts in other industries, they will be slow to take off. We saw early evidence of this with yesterlicense, discussed in Chapter 2. Phone and face-to-face negotiations for big-ticket items, whether for a shipment of vanadium steel or the novelization rights to *Star Trek: The Next Generation* episodes, have been around for decades and will take some time to dislodge from today's business practices. Look for rights exchanges to find niches in smaller transactions. The big fish will require humans to land for some time to come.

Searchable DRM-Enabled Content

The interface between digital rights management and search is problematic. You can put encrypted files up on your Web site, allow restricted viewing, and make them available for purchase, but how do you get users to find the content in the first place without exposing it?

At least two companies — MediaDNA and ebrary — have figured out a simple yet effective way around this conundrum. You can create a full-text index of a document, which is really just a list of all the words in the document (minus the trivial ones, such as *a* and *the*), along with their frequency of occurrence. Text indexes are at the heart of every search engine. After you have a full-text index, you can expose the *index terms* to search engines without exposing the actual *document* until the user has provided proper consideration (purchased it, subscribed to the service, and so on).

MediaDNA's eLuminator

MediaDNA, Inc., of La Jolla, CA (www.eluminator.com), was one of the original DRM vendors. It grew out of the Sweden-based Optitech, a multimedia production company that produced CD-ROMs for professional publishers such as Thomson Corp. Optitech invented a way of copy-protecting multimedia content, which it called MediaDNA. Optitech applied for patents on its technology and spun it out as a separate business, originally called Global Media and then renamed MediaDNA, Inc. The company was founded in 1997 by Greg Benson, founder of Optitech. Benson is now MediaDNA's nonexecutive chairman; the CEO is Ralph Koehrer, a former executive of various document management concerns.

MediaDNA's original product was a DRM technology called eMediator. The product didn't have many takers and was up for sale as of September 2001. eLuminator is a service offering that was originally developed (in 1999) as a way of creating demand for the company's core DRM offering, but it rapidly took on a life of its own and surpassed eMediator in revenue and installed base.

eLuminator was originally a solution to the search/DRM conundrum discussed earlier. The technology examined files protected in MediaDNA's eMediator DRM format and constructed full-text indexes of them. It then exposed the index terms (keywords) to the major search engines by creating metatags (invisible HTML tags containing the keywords) on the Web pages in which the DRM-packaged files were embedded; the major search engines then picked up and indexed the Web pages. This scheme solved the conundrum, allowing documents to be protected from copyright infringement but also able to be found through search engines.

eLuminator subsequently evolved to create Web pages with index terms from many different types of content — not just files in eMediator format, but also PDF files and Web pages generated by dynamic Web publishing systems such as Vignette StoryServer. eLuminator essentially became an enhanced and automated solution to a problem known in the Web-development community as search engine optimization, or SEO. SEO denotes a bunch of techniques to get Web pages to turn up prominently in results lists of search engines such as Yahoo!, MSN, Google, Excite, and Lycos. Because the vast majority of Web surfing starts with searches from these search engines, Web sites often do whatever they can to be listed prominently in their results lists.

Many online marketing consultancies have developed expertise in SEO. The most common techniques of SEO are metatagging, as described earlier, and creating "landing" or "doorway" pages, which are Web pages meant to serve as entry points to a site's interior pages, in addition to the normal entry point, which is the home page. Landing pages are peppered with metatags intended to attract the big search engines.

eLuminator automatically creates a landing page, with metatags, for each piece of premium content on your site. It contains a description of the content item, a list of related content items (that is, those on your site that have similar index terms), and a button that the user can click to access the content item.

What happens when the user clicks the button varies according to the type of content. If the content is in a DRM format, a window may pop up asking the user if she wants to purchase the item, subscribe to the journal, or whatever. If the content is stored in a dynamic Web publishing system, the button will cause the publishing system to generate the proper page on demand.

MediaDNA runs eLuminator as a hosted service offering. If a publisher sends MediaDNA its files, tagged with MediaDNA's XML tag set, MediaDNA will construct the necessary indexes to make the system work. MediaDNA charges for eLuminator based on the amount of traffic that the service causes to be drawn to the customer's Web site. It produces regular reports on usage statistics.

One big advantage of MediaDNA running the service itself — as opposed to licensing the software for publishers to use themselves — is that MediaDNA can continually tweak the technology to keep up with improvements in the search engines' Web crawling and indexing schemes. MediaDNA has an alliance with Inktomi, a vendor of search engine technology to portals such as MSN, AOL, HotBot, and iWon, to ensure that eLuminator has access to developments in Inktomi's search technology.

eLuminator's installed base includes professional publishers such as McGraw-Hill's AviationNow, EducationWorld, Penton Media, G2 Computer Intelligence, Computer Publishing Group, MightyWords, and Hoover's.

Ebrary

Ebrary is a service provider for selling content on the Web in a way that protects copyright while allowing users to search and browse content. The company was founded in February 1999 by Christopher Warnock, son of the legendary John Warnock, chairman of Adobe Systems (who serves on the company's board of directors), and Kevin Sayar, a lawyer from the powerhouse Silicon Valley firm Wilson Sonsini Goodrich & Rosati.

Ebrary doesn't really compete with other DRM solutions; its most direct competitors are subscription-based research services such as Questia and Infonautics' Electric Library. However, ebrary's technology has the same basic principle as MediaDNA's original eLuminator: protect publishers' content using encryption, while exposing index terms to allow users to search and browse it. However, whereas eLuminator applies to content on its customers' Web sites in a number of different formats, ebrary stores content on a single server in PDF format (not surprising, given Warnock's Adobe heritage).

Publishers submit PDF documents to ebrary and provide instructions on how users should be allowed to purchase them— whether by the paragraph, section, or entire document. Ebrary indexes the text in the documents and collects metadata about them (for example, publisher and ISBN). Users can search the ebrary site and see search results, but then they must purchase the complete text for copying or printing. Publishers share in the revenue from purchases.

Ebrary provides tools for users, called InfoTools, which enhance their reading of the documents, once purchased. These tools perform actions such as linking individual words in documents to searches of reference material (for example, dictionaries or encyclopedias, which provide definitions) or to additional commerce opportunities for the publisher.

Financial backers of ebrary include some of the biggest names in professional and educational publishing: Random House, McGraw-Hill, and Pearson. The service has been slow to launch. Its first beta customer, announced in July 2001, was Pearson's Learning Network. It has also announced that it will support McGraw-Hill's Primis Online eBook courseware delivery service. Ebrary should begin commercial deployments in late 2001 and early 2002. The list of publishers that have submitted material to ebrary exceeds 50, including many university presses. Ebrary started out as a single-hosted content repository; but more recently, it has been exploring ways to license its server software in three different offerings: one for general Internet portals, one for online learning environments, and the other for professional reference sites.

Paid download services

Paid content download services involve search, but very few of them actually involve DRM. Nevertheless, we discuss them here because DRM has great potential when integrated with them.

The original paid download services are far, far older than the Internet. In ancient times, people would enter the closed environments of online services such as Dialog and Lexis-Nexis, perform searches, and purchase articles. The Internet was extremely disruptive to such services (although they continue to exist), in two ways: First, the Internet provided a platform for delivering information — HTML-encoded Web pages and the HTTP protocol — that obviated and improved upon much of the infrastructure that those online services had to develop and maintain. Second, some of the information for which those services charged became available for free from various sources.

No one will suggest that the old user interfaces and technical infrastructures of Dialog, Lexis-Nexis, and their ilk are going to stage a comeback. Yet their economic models seem to be doing just that. Providers of certain types of content are finding that it's no longer possible to sustain a business based on either advertising revenue or on charging for fancy search features. Around 1999, a funny thing happened: A critical mass of major name-brand news publishers decided that enough was enough. They kept their free Web sites, which gave users access to their latest editions, but started to charge for access to archived content. However, they had not prepared themselves by building the internal content management and e-commerce capabilities that were necessary to build these paid services, so they turned to outsourcers to manage everything for them.

The two most important of these outsourcers are Qpass and ProQuest, a new and old company, respectively. The two are separate businesses; their functions overlap, yet they are strategic partners.

Qpass

Qpass (www.qpass.com) is a recent startup, having begun in 1997 and launching its service in March 1999. The company, based in Seattle, was founded by former Microsoft executive Chase Franklin, who remains chairman and CEO, and two others who have since retreated to advisory board positions. Qpass is privately held, its corporate backers including Accenture (formerly Andersen Consulting) and American Express.

The company built infrastructure for outsourcing fee-based transaction processing, such as for content downloads — which became their core business. Users who want to download content from any publisher that uses Qpass first need to open an account with Qpass, which includes a credit card number. Then whenever they purchase articles (or subscriptions, or anything else), they log in to Qpass, which processes the payment and delivers the goods.

This scheme is a win-win one for users and Qpass: It requires users to register only once for access to content from all publishers that use the service, instead of having to register separately for each publisher; and Qpass gets to build a huge database of all the users that have accounts and their activity history. For publishers, the advantage is that the single registration makes it easier for users to buy content on many different sites. The disadvantage is that Qpass, not the publisher, has ultimate control over customer info, although it supplies reports on customer activity to publishers.

Qpass has built up a who's-who list of news publishers that use its service, including the *New York Times,* the *Los Angeles Times,* the *Wall Street Journal, USA Today,* Factiva (the Dow Jones-Reuters joint venture that competes with Lexis-Nexis), *Consumer Reports,* the *New York Post,* the *Houston Chronicle,* and about 100 others. Qpass has also made a foray into the music industry through a partnership with ArtistDirect, which runs Web sites for pop stars such as Metallica and the Beastie Boys. Over half a million users have Qpass accounts.

Qpass was in the right place at the right time with the right infrastructure. It has astounded many in the publishing industry with its ability to sign up a list of news publishers so influential that the cumulative effect is to legitimize paid downloads as a business model throughout the industry.

ProQuest

ProQuest (www.proquest.com), on the other hand, has assets dating back decades, which it is leveraging well for the Internet age. ProQuest is a new name, but it has a heritage dating back to 1938. The Ann Arbor, Michigan–based company was formerly known as Bell & Howell Information and Learning, which in turn was the result of Bell & Howell's acquisition of University Microfilm, Inc. (UMI) in 1985. The acquisition united the premier maker of microform creation and viewing equipment with a huge source of academic material in microform. The move to the Web was the vision of Joseph Reynolds, ProQuest's CEO, who is the former COO of International Thomson Publishing's educational publishing group.

ProQuest owns the rights to several important periodicals and text databases, which it hosts on various digital archive services, including the following:

- ♦ **Digital Vault Initiative:** An ongoing initiative to create an archive of some 5.5 billion pages of historical and literary works
- ♦ **ProQuest Newsstand:** Full-text access to the archives of 150 newspapers from around the world
- ♦ **ProQuest News & Magazines:** General-reference periodicals and a selection of regional newspapers tailored to the installation (usually public libraries)
- ♦ **H.W. Wilson:** Databases of social science information
- ♦ **American Film Institute:** Information about movies
- ♦ **Periodical Contents Index:** Periodicals in the social sciences and humanities
- ♦ **Computing and Telecommunications:** Periodicals and databases in those fields
- ♦ **ProQuest Career and Technical Education:** Periodicals about vocational and technical skills
- ♦ **LION (Literature Online):** More than 290,000 English-language literary works
- ♦ **INSPEC:** Engineering content

In addition, ProQuest is amassing various software tools that enable their customers — typically public and academic libraries — to customize their subscriptions to ProQuest databases by selecting specific sources of content. All the content in ProQuest's databases is precleared for copyright.

ProQuest also has ProQuest Archiver, which is a hosted solution for turning a publisher's existing content archive into a paid download service on the Internet. ProQuest's partner in Archiver is Qpass, which provides payment-processing services.

Although ProQuest's core customer base is libraries, ProQuest is clearly branching out into ways of offering content to the masses — although it does this through partners, not by itself. More and more publishers are giving their content archives over to ProQuest to host through Archiver. For example, *Business Week* magazine hosts its own paid downloads for recent articles, but customers who want articles from before 1994 must get them through ProQuest, via a link from *Business Week*'s Web site.

Paid download services and DRM

The fact that (for the most part and for the time being) neither Qpass nor ProQuest involve digital rights management is worth discussing and why these companies are included here. When you buy an article using one of these services, you get it in unencrypted form, in HTML, PDF, plain text, or some other format. Although the content invariably has copyright notices on it, making it clear that it's illegal to make unauthorized copies of the material, there's nothing technologically preventing you from doing so.

Clearly, companies such as Qpass and ProQuest could add DRM technology to their service offerings. Every DRM vendor on earth has beaten a path to their doors, trying to get technology partnership deals — and failing. Why? Mainly, because the publishers feel that they aren't ready for it.

Remember that most of the content offered through Qpass is low-value content, such as newspaper articles, with price tags in the low single dollars. It is not the type of high-value content, such as boutique journals and market research, which is typically considered early-adopter material for DRM. Publishers are willing to accept some modicum of bleed to offset the downside of forcing users to install and use DRM controllers on their machines. They may even build a "bleed factor" into their pricing for archived articles. It is most likely that these publishers anticipate a time in the near future when they will add DRM to these services, but not until their audience is comfortable with paying for archived articles and not until the technology becomes easier to use.

Qpass sees this future and is preparing for it. However, instead of integrating with a specific DRM technology vendor, Qpass announced a partnership with DRM service provider Reciprocal in January 2001. This enables Qpass to avoid choosing any one particular DRM technology (recall from Chapter 7 that Reciprocal supports many different ones) and to avoid actually supporting it (Reciprocal does that). Qpass also has a partnership with MediaDNA that makes the company's eLuminator service available to Qpass-affiliated publishers who want to expose articles in their archives to Internet search engines.

With these arrangements, publishers will have the option of DRM-protecting content that is to be downloaded through Qpass. The rate at which those publishers exercise that option will be an important barometer of the penetration of DRM into mainstream publishing.

Syndication Software

Many media companies that have defined an overall architecture for their products and services refer to distribution as a key component of the architecture. DRM is an enabler for a specific type of distribution — between content providers and consumers under controlled, metered circumstances. Yet there are many other models of online content distribution that are just as relevant. Business-to-consumer (B-to-C) models get the most press, but one of the aims of this book is to give more equal weight to business-to-business distribution models.

Earlier in this chapter, we discuss B-to-B rights management and rights exchanges (in the sections "Internal Rights Management" and "Rights Exchanges") — mechanisms for content providers to internally track the rights that they own and to buy and sell those rights online. In this section, we discuss technology that supports online content distribution between businesses.

As mentioned in Chapter 6, *syndication* is a generic term that covers many cases of B-to-B content distribution, generally involving publishers and subscribers. News-gathering organizations such as the *New York Times* and the *Los Angeles Times* syndicate stories to their membership; companies such as King Features and United Media syndicate comic strips and opinion columns to newspapers.

The Internet opens up many opportunities for Web sites to syndicate content to each other. Underlying each syndication deal are two things: a set of logistics that governs the distribution and receipt of content and a contractual arrangement that dictates what the publisher allows the subscriber to do with the content and what the subscriber must pay for it.

Syndication technology allows both of these concerns to be automated, thereby letting both publishers and subscribers participate in growing numbers of syndication schemes without expending undue manual effort. Just as there are DRM software packages, which you can run within your own organization, and DRM service providers, which run them for you, there are two approaches to the technology of syndication: software packages and services. Each one has its place, depending on who you are and what you are trying to achieve.

Syndication software packages have grown around the Information and Content Exchange (ICE) standard, which is discussed in detail in Chapter 6. ICE provides a specific protocol for automating both the logistics and business aspects of content distribution, but it's not the only way to perform syndication. Many publishers have been effectively doing syndication by means of the Internet's standard File Transfer Protocol (FTP), which is a simple way of moving or copying files from one place to another. If you're a publisher whose content is in demand by large organizations with plenty of technical resources at their disposal, you can simply put up your content on an FTP server and have your subscribers "harvest" it on a periodic basis. That's the logistical part. The business arrangement would normally be managed by written contract and all the paperwork that goes along with it. Each such syndication arrangement is relatively tedious and time-consuming to set up, but if you really only plan to have a handful of them, that may be okay.

Yet you never know what other businesses may want your content. One of us advises a small publisher that produces legal journalism in text and audio formats. The publisher had never thought of distributing its content in any way other than direct subscriptions to lawyers. Then one day, an insurance company came calling, saying that it wanted some of the publisher's material on liability issues in text format to put up on its Web site on a regular basis. The insurance company wanted to put up the content for free, as a way of attracting those who are interested in liability insurance to its site and to show expertise on the subject.

The logistics of the content distribution were simple: The publisher just needed to send the insurance company a text file every month, and the insurance company's Webmaster would insert the text into an HTML page. But the publisher's CEO had no idea how to price such a deal or what terms and conditions to attach to it. Eventually he figured it out, but the resulting deal had no applicability to the next one, which involved a vendor of online CLE (continuing legal education) courses.

The point is that if you produce content, you need to be able to get it to wherever an audience for it might be. Given the proliferation and fluid state of the Internet itself, the number of sites that are potential showplaces for your content must surely be increasing; and you need to think about ways of feeding content to those sites that are scalable — meaning that they don't involve much extra effort for each distribution partner.

Syndication software packages fill this need. These began within the context of Web content management solutions. As discussed in Chapter 6, it has become evident that although ICE is a great idea, implementing it requires a major commitment to process and technology that organizations must make for themselves and must convince their customers to make as well (albeit to a lesser extent); therefore, many potential adopters of syndication software consider ICE to be overkill. As a result, syndication software vendors have made it possible for their customers to syndicate software via other methods, such as FTP and e-mail.

Vignette

It's hard to say when the first software package that performed syndication in some shape or form was created. But as mentioned in Chapter 6, the first ICE-compliant software package came from one of the originators of ICE itself: Vignette Corp. (www.vignette.com; NASDAQ: VIGN), makers of StoryServer, the popular high-end Web content management system. Vignette's initial syndication software product was Vignette Syndication Server (VSS), which it sold as an add-on to StoryServer.

More recently, Vignette's product line has proliferated beyond content management to a range of products for B-to-B and B-to-C e-commerce. Content management and related products became only one part of Vignette's portfolio. As part of its V/5 suite of products, Vignette offered V/5 Syndication Server, which was discontinued in early 2001. Its latest product, its third-generation syndication software system, is Vignette Content Syndication Server (CSS).

Vignette suffered some criticism in the market because its products included its own, proprietary application server technology instead of working with the leading third-party application server products. (*Application servers* are software components that interface between Web server and databases.) Vignette responded, and as a result, its latest technology, including CSS, is a complete Java reimplementation that is based on standards such as J2EE (Java 2 Enterprise Edition) and EJB (Enterprise Java Beans) and runs with leading application servers such as BEA WebLogic. Unlike Vignette's earlier syndication software products, CSS is designed to run standalone and doesn't require Vignette's content management software.

Content Syndication Server normally uses ICE as the protocol for providing content to subscribers. As explained in Chapter 6, ICE has two delivery models: request-reply and subscribe. Subscribers need to install a small software client, called VS Agent, on their servers in order to receive content. ICE packages can contain content in XML or plain text, or they can refer to content elsewhere in another format (for example, PDF or database records).

To use CSS, a publisher uses a server-side console application to choose content to syndicate and to set up subscribers. Subscribers are set up according to the content that they will receive, the communication protocols that they use, the method of delivery (scheduled push, on-demand push, or subscriber pull), the frequency of delivery, pricing, and other options.

In addition to using ICE, CSS can syndicate content in FTP, e-mail, HTTP, and various formats common in the product catalog industry, such as Commerce Extensible Markup Language (cXML) and CIF (Catalog Interchange Format). On the content provider's back end, CSS can take content directly from Vignette's Content Management Server and, through an interface component called Vignette Business Integration Server, can take data directly from financial systems such as Oracle, SAP, PeopleSoft, and JD Edwards.

Although Vignette originally intended both its syndication software products and the ICE protocol to apply to publishers — one of its first customers was Preview Travel, which syndicated travel destination information to other Web sites — it has found a bigger business in syndicating product-catalog entries, for example, from manufacturers to resellers. For example, one of its customers in this vein is ICG Commerce, a company that provides online procurement services to large businesses. ICG Commerce needs to get its customers information about products that they can purchase through ICG, and it uses Vignette CSS to ensure that they always have the latest product information from their suppliers.

Interwoven

Recently, it has become clear that Internet content syndication makes the most sense in the way that Vignette originally intended it: as an adjunct to Web content management systems. Interwoven, Inc. (www.interwoven.com, NASDAQ:IWOV), of Sunnyvale, CA, is another leading vendor of content management solutions for Web sites, a key rival to Vignette. Probably due to competitive pressure, Interwoven threw its hat into the syndication software ring in June 2001 with its OpenSyndicate product.

OpenSyndicate is meant to be used with other Interwoven products, including TeamSite, Interwoven's flagship content management tool; TeamXML, an XML content management system (also announced in June 2001); and OpenChannel, a tool for repurposing XML content to multiple distribution channels, including WAP phones. Like Vignette CSS, Interwoven's OpenSyndicate can publish content using the ICE protocol, or via FTP, standard Web HTTP, or e-mail.

Kinecta

Kinecta (www.kinecta.com), of San Francisco, is another provider of standalone ICE-compliant syndication software. The company was formed as ShiftKey in 1998 by Adam Souzis, a Web publishing tools developer, and Arthur Do, a technical consultant who had developed the core technology that became Kinecta's flagship product. Souzis was a key contributor to the ICE standard.

ShiftKey's original product, SiClone, had Reuters and TheStreet.com as its first customers. David Mathison, Reuters's global head of syndication, jumped the fence in March 1999 to become ShiftKey's CEO. (He is now chairman.) ShiftKey introduced its ICE-compliant product, SiClone 2, at the same time. In February 2000, the company renamed itself Kinecta and changed its flagship product's name to Interact.

Kinecta Interact is now called Kinecta Syndication Server. Its feature set is similar to that of Vignette CSS. Its companion product, Kinecta Subscription Agent, is the piece of software that subscribers use to receive content. Both are browser-based Java applications and can run on Windows or Sun Solaris platforms.

Kinecta Syndication Server can handle a wide range of content formats, including Real and Microsoft streaming audio and video. It can monitor sources of content, including file directories, FTP servers, and Web servers for syndication to subscribers, and it has a set of APIs that developers, such as Kinecta's own services organization, can use to interface the Syndication Server to other data sources, such as databases, content management systems, and ERP systems. Kinecta has KTL (Kinecta Transformation Language), which is a utility for translating content into an appropriate format for syndication — for example, removing graphics from articles and keeping only the text. (Content providers can also use the standard XSL style-sheet language for doing content transformations.) Its content delivery methods include FTP and e-mail in addition to the ICE protocol.

In addition to Syndication Server and Subscription Agent, Kinecta has an application called Kinecta Content Directory, which Kinecta hosts itself. Content Directory is a catalog of all content that a content provider wants to make available to subscribers via ICE offers (see Chapter 6), along with descriptions of the content that can include graphics. Companies that want to subscribe to content can simply go to the Content Directory and sign up for whatever they want by clicking on a license agreement. Kinecta can give a publisher's area on the Content Directory a branded look and feel. It can also deliver content from the Content Directory using a DRM packaging application; Kinecta's DRM partner of choice is SealedMedia (see Chapter 11).

Finally, Kinecta also hosts a content access measuring tool called Kinecta Content Metrics. Content Metrics is similar to the type of outsourced Web site traffic measurement service that many ISPs run, such as HitBox or Urchin, but instead of measuring access to individual HTML pages or the site in general, Content Metrics measures end-user access to specific items (offers) that appear on subscribers' Web sites.

Unlike Vignette and Interwoven, Kinecta doesn't make its own content management tool (which is admittedly a rather lopsided statement, rather like saying that unlike Microsoft and Sun, Lotus does not make its own operating system). Instead, Kinecta integrates with content management through partnerships with most of the important vendors of Web content management solutions in the world *other than* Vignette and Interwoven. Kinecta has partnerships with the content management vendors EasyPress, Eprise, MediaSurface, Open Market, Percussion Software, Tridion, and WorldWeb.net.

Kinecta has an impressive array of content providers as customers; in addition to Reuters, its launch customer, it has as customers the *Economist,* the *Financial Times* (the latter two being divisions of the publishing conglomerate Pearson), computer and entertainment magazine publisher Future Publishing, and the financial research giant Fidelity Investments. In addition, Web portals including Yahoo!, Excite, and Lycos use Kinecta's products to aggregate content from multiple sources onto their sites.

ArcadiaOne

ArcadiaOne (www.arcadiaone.com), of Sunnyvale, California, is another provider of ICE-compliant syndication software. It was founded in 1998 by Ahmed Farooq, a Stanford PhD who had been at Calico Commerce, an early e-commerce vendor.

ArcadiaOne's calls its technology eSyndication. Its flagship product is arcadiaOne Enterprise, whose feature set is similar to all the products discussed in this section. However, the company is staking out a niche for eSyndication that is somewhat different from the target markets of most of the other syndication packages. Instead of focusing on content providers, as we would understand them in the context of this book, arcadiaOne targets the B-to-B e-commerce and supply chain management market. It has integration partnerships with leading B-to-B e-commerce and supply chain management systems, such as I2, Vitria, and CommerceOne. Its customers include Forbes and Cahners, two publishers of B-to-B directories, and e-procurement vendors such as Industria (process manufacturing) and American Wholesale (building materials).

In addition to its eSyndication product, arcadiaOne offers a low-end package, arcadiaOne Lite, which allows one-to-one syndication over dial-up lines, and a hosted solution called arcadiaOne Online.

The survival of these syndication software engines depends on two external factors: the survival of their associated content management systems and the adoption rate of the ICE protocol in general. Just as publishers need to manage rights internally before they are really ready to participate in B-to-B exchanges for content rights, publishers need to manage content before they are really ready to syndicate via ICE or some other method. ICE syndication is a good idea, but it's a hard sell; and it's unclear whether a standalone business can be built on it.

Syndication Hubs and Distribution Services

In addition to the hosted services of syndication software providers (such as Kinecta Content Directory and arcadiaOne Online), there are a few service providers who serve as syndication hubs — bringing together content providers and those who would want their content.

The original syndication hubs, Screaming Media and iSyndicate, had two types of customers: "little guys," such as individual authors, who wanted to distribute their content but didn't have the wherewithal to build the necessary relationships or technology, and established content providers who were looking for new outlets for their content. By the late 1990s, it had become clear to most media companies — as mentioned earlier — that success on the Internet wasn't limited to driving traffic to your own Web site, but also included finding your audience and getting your brand and content to them, wherever on the Web they may be.

Syndication hubs helped both individual content providers and large publishers do this. There were (and are) two basic models of syndication that the hubs support:

- **Syndicate for traffic:** Sends headlines to syndicatees, with the headlines hyperlinked to the syndicator's site. Syndicatees get compensated for driving traffic to syndicators' sites.
- **Syndicate for revenue:** Sends content items (articles, graphics, video clips, and so on) to other Web sites in exchange for money. This is what the legal publisher did with the insurance company mentioned in the preceding section, "Syndication Software."

In the latter case, the syndication hubs typically take 50 percent of the money paid in the transaction.

Screaming Media

New York–based Screaming Media (www.screamingmedia.com) was the brainchild of Alan Ellman, formerly of ABC television. He originated the business back in 1993 as Interactive Connection, a Web advertising firm. In 1998, he was joined by Jay Chiat, a legendary figure in the advertising business (his firm created the "1984" Super Bowl ad campaign for Apple Computer), who invested in the company and became CEO for a while, until yielding the reigns to Kevin Clark, another former advertising executive. The company went public in March 2000 (NASDAQ: SCRM).

Screaming Media's original business was to strike distribution deals with the Associated Press and other major sources of news content and syndicate the content to Web sites of corporations who wanted to post relevant news stories but didn't want to license entire wire services, let alone do their own news-gathering. An important early customer was Sun Microsystems, which used the technology to obtain news stories about Java technology for its Java Web site.

Now Screaming Media has a huge variety of content providers contributing content to its hosted syndication hub. It has a wide variety of content feed offerings that are packaged by type of content, such as news, business information, weather, and vertical-industry content. At the center of it all is its technology operations center, called the Content Engine.

The Content Engine harvests thousands of content items per day from FTP servers or other means, such as Web pages and satellites. For each one of these, The Content Engine strips all markup codes. Then it adds metadata elements according to a standard XML tag set that it maintains. It creates category keywords by using the Autonomy automated categorization tool, which uses statistical analysis of the text and artificial intelligence techniques to do its work. After that, the Content Engine inserts the content item into its database.

Clients who want to receive content from Screaming Media use an application called SiteWare. SiteWare contains a tool called Editor's Desk, which enables syndicatees to choose content from the package(s) that they purchased from Screaming Media, create headlines, add graphics, and route them to their own Web sites. SiteWare is a Java application that can run on any flavor of Windows, Sun Solaris, and many freeware versions of Unix. It can feed content directly into many content management and Web publishing systems.

SiteWare comes in three versions. The basic version is designed for small Web sites. SiteWare Pro adds a component called Writer's Desk, which allows syndicatees to integrate their own content with content from Screaming Media. The top-of-the-line version, SiteWare XE, is designed for large enterprises. It adds editorial workflow capabilities to Writer's Desk; it also contains an XML-based tool called Digital Press, which provides multipurposing capabilities so that articles chosen from the Screaming Media network (and original content items) can be distributed through Web sites, wireless devices, and feeds in various standard formats such as NITF and NewsML.

Screaming Media has expanded from its original niche business to be a general Internet-based content distributor, a virtual one-stop shopping experience for content of all types. It goes well beyond news-only aggregators such as NewsEdge and Individual. At this writing, Screaming Media has content from over 2,900 sources in 12 different languages. Its customers include a wide range of content portals, Fortune 500 companies, and so on.

YellowBrix and iSyndicate

YellowBrix (`www.yellowbrix.com`), based in Alexandria, Virginia, was spun-off in 1997 from the Web portal Infoseek's Corporate Information division. Founded by Jeffrey Massa, the former CTO of that Infoseek division (which was subsequently acquired by Disney), Massa is currently president and COO; CFO Randy Lampert took the helm as CEO in 2001.

YellowBrix's primary asset is its proprietary technology, which is an artificial intelligence–based engine that takes content feeds and categorizes them, removes duplicates, introduces hyperlinks, and does other processing that adds value to the body of content as a whole. This type of information retrieval technology, often the product of someone's Ph.D. thesis on information retrieval, is potentially interesting to information professionals, but it generally has little value to the general Internet user population.

Yet YellowBrix found an interesting application for this technology: feeding the value-added content to corporate Web sites. In other words, YellowBrix is similar to Screaming Media, but with fancier technology for processing content items compensating for a previous lack (relative to Screaming Media) of content sources. YellowBrix's service is of interest to Web sites whose readers do more than just browse content. In June 2001, YellowBrix fixed its lack of sources by acquiring iSyndicate, along with its over 1,200 content sources. Now YellowBrix has about as many content sources as Screaming Media does.

iSyndicate, based in New York City, was the other original syndication hub. Its model, as suggested earlier, included distributing individual content creators' material in addition to that from known content brands. The company began in 1997 as NetEvents and changed its name to iSyndicate in 1998. Its original two services, RapidContent Express and RapidContent Network, corresponded to the two syndication models listed earlier: syndicate headlines for traffic and syndicate content for revenue.

During 1999 and 2000, iSyndicate ran a hard race against Screaming Media, signing up both content providers and syndicatees as rapidly as possible, packaging content into various offerings for different types of Web sites, offering an XML feed so that the content could be more easily repurposed, and producing a content service for wireless devices. During the time when Screaming Media went public, iSyndicate closed a mezzanine funding round with strategic investors such as Microsoft, NBC, and News Corp. In late 2000, iSyndicate started licensing its content network technology to companies who wanted to set up their own private syndication networks; for example, Major League Baseball used it to syndicate sports news and scores to individual baseball teams' Web sites.

iSyndicate's Content Manager tool is similar to Screaming Media's SiteWare. Its infrastructure, unlike that of Screaming Media, supports content submissions via the ICE protocol — not surprising given that Vignette Corp. was an early investor in the company.

We view the merger of iSyndicate and YellowBrix as merely a consolidation in the syndication hub market. Although YellowBrix has pledged to integrate iSyndicate's technology into its own offerings, the consolidation of customer bases is more the point. The ultimate aim is to stop the Screaming Media juggernaut, which is a daunting task indeed.

DigitalOwl

Whereas syndication software packages and syndication hubs provide functionality that is designed to appeal to a broad range of content providers and users, Winter Park, Florida–based DigitalOwl (www.digitalowl.com) offers a more vertically oriented suite of services targeted at certain high-value niches in the publishing market. The company was founded in August 1999 by Kirstie Chadwick and Robin Phelps, former cofounders of the consulting firm Vantage360 and sales executives in the telecom and computer industries.

DigitalOwl has two products, KineticEdge and TitleFusion. KineticEdge combines DRM packaging with multichannel distribution. Its DRM packaging tool can be used from a desktop user interface or through a batch tool that allows multiple pieces of content in XML, HTML, or PDF repositories to be packaged at once. The packaging process assigns discovery and rights metadata (see Chapter 5) to content, and it allows content items to be split up into components (for example, book chapters). KineticEdge also enables publishers to set up IDs for users that can receive licenses to the content after it is distributed.

The rights model in DigitalOwl's proprietary DRM technology supports several different business models, including the following:

♦ Paid downloads

♦ Paid subscriptions with secure downloads of individual content items

♦ Pay-per-view

♦ Check-in/check-out (for distribution of content to libraries)

♦ Institutional (multiuser) site licensing

KineticEdge passes content directly to retail users and to publishers' corporate intranets, as well as to a number of different types of distributors, including the following:

♦ **Syndicators:** DigitalOwl has a partnership with iSyndicate (now YellowBrix) to distribute content through its network.

♦ **Print-on-demand services:** DigitalOwl has a partnership with Kinkos.com to enable printing of content on demand from users' desktops.

♦ **Libraries:** DigitalOwl has teamed up with Informata.com, a service of the major book distributor Baker & Taylor, to distribute eBook content to academic and public libraries.

DigitalOwl's other product is TitleVision, a desktop client. TitleVision lets users click and drag to reformat content in a variety of formats, including the TealPoint and Aportis eBook readers for Palm handheld devices, Adobe Acrobat, and Web pages. TitleVision uses encryption technology from Certicom as part of its DRM solution for handheld devices. A unique aspect of TitleVision is that unlike other format conversion packages, it manages and maintains rights through the conversion processes, using DigitalOwl's proprietary DRM technology, in a way that is opaque to users. In addition, TitleVision helps users organize and search through information that is distributed to them through KineticEdge.

DigitalOwl's customers are the typical early adopters of DRM technology, such as market researchers and publishers of boutique newsletters, eBooks, and professional books. They include McGraw-Hill Professional books; iPublish, the eBook division of Time Warner Books; Keesing's, publishers of the Record of World Events archive of international news reports, "Dilbert" cartoonist Scott Adams (publishing an eBook himself, without a publisher), and various market research and professional publishing concerns.

DigitalOwl's business is predicated on being able to charge significant money for high-value services targeted to specific, well-chosen market niches. DigitalOwl offers itself as an alternative to publishers building (or cobbling together) their own solutions for DRM packaging and distribution in multiple formats and to multiple channels. Like the syndication hubs, DigitalOwl appeals mostly to publishers who don't want to package and distribute content themselves — and that includes most of the publishers in DigitalOwl's chosen markets.

Therefore, DigitalOwl should have a solid niche business. It will run into growth limitations if and when certain aspects of its value add become commodities or free, so it will no longer be able to charge enough for them. It is also hard to see how DigitalOwl will be able to serve markets beyond the ones that it has chosen. Its most likely growth path is through merger with or acquisition by a company that serves complementary markets or provides broader services.

Chapter 13

Epilogue: The Future of DRM

The market for digital rights management solutions is indeed a tumultuous one. During the period in which we wrote this book (spring and summer of 2001), several DRM vendors cut back or went out of business entirely, such as the following:

- Liquid Audio cut its staff by 40 percent.
- Reciprocal sustained two rounds of layoffs, resulting in total staff reductions of about 75 percent.
- Digital Goods, formerly Softlock, ceased operations.
- Vyou declared bankruptcy, and its assets were bought by the Copyright Clearance Center.
- ContentGuard, the Xerox spin-off, discontinued its software product and service offerings, reduced staff by two-thirds, and narrowed focus to licensing its XrML rights modeling language.
- MediaDNA put its core DRM technology business up for sale.
- Preview Systems sold its Ziplock DRM system for software to Aladdin Knowledge Systems and discontinued its other lines of business.
- SealedMedia dismissed most of its U.S.-based management team and retrenched to its original headquarters in the United Kingdom.
- The content syndication hub market consolidated with YellowBrix's acquisition of iSyndicate.

As another indication of the direction that the market is taking, we counted the number of DRM vendors that exhibited at Seybold Seminars, the largest trade show for publishing technology, held twice a year in Boston and San Francisco:

Seybold Show	DRM Vendors
Spring of 1999	2
Fall of 1999	5
Spring of 2000	8
Fall of 2000	13
Spring of 2001	16
Fall of 2001	7

These statistics certainly tell a tale; however, two things must also be said: First, the drop-off of DRM vendors in 2001 is as much due to the overall downturn in the economy as to consolidation in the DRM market, and lack of trade show attendance is also due to cutbacks in corporate travel budgets. Second, several vendors are being born as well as dying: We knew of a handful at the point of this writing, but they were at such an early stage in their development that they chose to keep their technology confidential.

In September 2001, Seybold Research published the results of a survey, *Digital Rights Management: Usage, Attitudes, and Profiles of Users* (see the Bibliography). It showed that publishers are increasingly interested in pursuing DRM but have reservations about the market as it is today. In particular, 27 percent of respondents said that they planned to build the infrastructure necessary to sell content via DRM technology. Among current providers of paid digital content, although only 18 percent are implementing a DRM solution now, two-thirds expect to do so in the future.

However, the survey also shows that half of the respondents feel that the market is confusing, that vendors are not succeeding at explaining the value of their solutions; and nearly three-quarters feel that choosing a DRM solution is difficult. More troubling is that half of the respondents feel that DRM is not worthwhile because it's impossible to protect content completely. Apart from that, the most commonly cited obstacles to adoption are cost of the solution, inconvenience for users, and lack of widely supported standards. The messages for DRM vendors from these statistics could not be clearer.

What is likely to happen to the DRM market in 2002 and beyond? The following sections look at it from three perspectives: the business models, the technology, and the marketplace.

The Business Models

The first trend that we can predict with confidence is that DRM-enabled business models — some of those discussed in Chapter 2 — will grow dramatically. The biggest industry development that ensured that DRM-enabled business models will grow was, ironically, the bursting of the Internet bubble in 2000. Web businesses that were based on content grew on the premise of developing audiences and then, maybe later, figuring out how to make money from them. Advertising, the facile answer to this question, turned out to be far less lucrative a source of revenue than required. Selling the content directly didn't work either, for the reasons stated in other chapters: The technology was too clunky, and, in many cases, there were free alternatives to paid content that were good enough or even better.

Yet the spectacular crashes of so many content-based Web businesses has emboldened the survivors to start charging for content because their stark choice is that or certain death. On 20 February 2001, an event occurred that is an inflection point for Internet content models. On that day, New York Times Co., parent of its namesake newspaper as well as the *Boston Globe,* the *International Herald Tribune* (jointly with the *Washington Post*), and many smaller papers in the southeast United States and California, announced an equity investment in the Austin, TX–based company NewsStand.

NewsStand is building a system for delivering digital copies of newspapers in a modified version of PDF with proprietary DRM technology built in. These digital newspapers are electronic facsimiles of the print versions. By the time this book is in print, customers should be able to go to www.newsstand.com or to the sites of its customers, like some of the Times' papers, *the Daily Deal,* and *the Harvard Business Review,* and purchase single issues of or subscriptions to the papers.

In the magazine business, the New York–based company Qiosk.com (`www.qmags.com`) is doing something similar with its qMags service, although with standard PDF and the Adobe PDF Merchant DRM technology. At this writing, qMags has *Popular Mechanics* and a few other titles in production. qMags doesn't have financial backing from a company such as Time Inc., Primedia, or Conde Nast, but its advisory board is an all-star lineup of some of the most respected executives in the business. Another company with an electronic facsimile system for magazines is Brisbane, CA-based Zinio, which has its own format and reader technology. Zinio also has some magazine-industry luminaries on its advisory board and is backed by Silicon Valley venture capital. At this writing, Zinio has yet to put its service into production.

There are various problems with the technology of electronic facsimile editions that will take some time to fix. For one thing, many would argue that a facsimile version of the print edition isn't necessarily the best format for reading on a PC. One reason why these newspapers and magazines chose to do it that way has to do with the Audit Bureau of Circulations (ABC), the organization that issues official measurements of newspaper and magazine circulation, which periodicals use in their formulas for advertising rates. ABC is beginning to count "electronic circulation" as a category separate from print subscription and single-copy sales, and it is currently only willing to consider electronic products that substantially resemble their print counterparts.

Other drawbacks with electronic facsimile editions are long download times for the content and the difficulty that these vendors (especially NewsStand and Zinio, with their nonstandard formats) will have making their content readable on the inevitable handheld devices. But one thing is clear: The backing of these vendors by companies such as New York Times Co. sends a signal to the industry. The Times is willing to experiment with this new type of electronic product. It can't sustain its current digital content delivery organization, Times Company Digital, at its current rates of financial loss. There must be a new direction. Many other publishers will follow the Times' lead and go in this direction.

A similar watershed event is taking place around the time of writing in the music industry: the launch of the five major recording labels' subscription services, pressplay and MusicNet, which are discussed in various chapters in this book. These services are expected to launch in fall of 2001, but we predict that technical, regulatory, and licensing issues may hold them up for a while. Nevertheless, these are important developments.

The music industry has tried many different DRM-based business models and has never gotten beyond very limited rollouts. Why? Simply because it has been easier to get equivalent products either through traditional media (CDs, cassettes, and LPs) or for free on Napster-type Internet services. There have been a few artists who released songs on the Internet only, or on the Internet first, and a couple of attempts have been made to create recording labels that distribute only online (such as N2K Encoded Music, now part of CDNow). But the sum total of content generated in those ways is but a drop in the ocean. Moving music to the Internet in that way is laudable, but not scalable.

The only way that the music industry can use the Internet to add real, appreciable value to its content is by offering up entire catalogs in online digital form, for licensing direct to consumers through subscription services or to other businesses for repackaging. Recording labels have been holding back on doing this because they won't make money in direct proportion to the popularity of individual titles, because the licensing issues (as mentioned in Chapter 2) are problematic, and because the idea of subscribing to a music service is alien to most end users.

They also may be afraid that the total revenue from such services will be less than the revenue from single-title sales.

Yet the licensing of entire catalogs digitally enables totally new classes of music services that will be refined and that consumers will surely embrace over time. Before the Internet, you basically had two choices for listening to recorded music: buying albums or listening to the radio. A wide range of possibilities exists between those extremes. Internet radio services such as Shoutcast, Radio SonicNet, and Live365.com point the way but only scratch the surface because of their low budgets and music licensing restrictions.

Subscription services such as MusicNet and pressplay will finally add enough value to content to justify restricting its usage through DRM technology. That, in a nutshell, was the problem with the Secure Digital Music Initiative (SDMI): It was based on restricting access to content on the promise of future content that is available only in SDMI-compliant format. The added value wasn't high enough, so consumers weren't willing to put up with the restrictions — or at least that's the way consumer electronics makers viewed it, which is one of the reasons why SDMI has failed to catch on.

CROSS REFERENCE: For a more detailed discussion of SDMI, see Chapter 6.

Different business models will succeed in different segments of the industry. As discussed in Chapter 2, there is a movement from single-copy sales to subscriptions, just as there has been in other industries like telecommunications. The publishing industry has come to realize that single-copy sales (paid downloads) of small items, such as newspaper and magazine articles, will probably never be viable. The only place where such a model works is in business-to-business (B-to-B) arrangements, such as syndication, where the mechanics can be automated.

Importing business models from the physical-media world is important from the standpoint of customer expectations. The successful DRM-enabled business models will represent a gradual synthesis of legacy business models with the new possibilities of the Internet. It won't be a discontinuous leap, as early Internet pioneers have suggested.

The Technology

DRM technology will certainly improve over time, as it takes on new features, supports business models that are endorsed by content providers, and provides a more secure and seamless user experience. Yet DRM technology has had mostly difficult relationships with the technologies underlying the devices on which it must run. The root of the problem is that DRM technology should be a low-level service built into the devices, instead of being an add-on application, but most of the time it isn't. The ramifications of this include security holes and poor usability.

This isn't a new type of problem. If you look at the history of the development of PC software, you can see a number of examples of technology that was first made available through third-party add-ons and then later absorbed into the underlying system. The best examples of this are graphical user interfaces (GUIs) and networking. The first graphical user interfaces were add-ons to command-line operating systems such as MS-DOS and UNIX. The Macintosh showed the benefits of building support for GUIs directly into the operating system. Microsoft finally released operating systems with fully integrated GUI capabilities several years later; the UNIX/Linux community has yet to produce something similar.

Networking used to be available through clunky add-ons that didn't integrate with PC file systems very well; now (particularly in UNIX environments), the user perceives no difference between files on a network and files on her local hard drive. Other lower-level capabilities such as virtual memory management and disk compression have also migrated from third-party add-ons to operating system built-ins or even hardware features.

The same thing must happen with DRM in order for it to really succeed in the PC world: DRM must be built into PCs. There are essentially three ways that this could happen:

♦ **Build DRM into the PC's hardware.** This is the most effective way to do it with respect to security. We mention one attempt in the book's preface: Wave Systems, of Lee, MA, put DRM functions on a chip and attempted to sell it to PC makers. This wasn't successful, mainly because the PC hardware industry isn't a monopoly like PC operating-system software. If you're a PC maker such as Compaq, Dell, or Hewlett-Packard, in effect, you would be *paying more* to build a machine (or charging more for it) that restricts what it can do compared to other similar machines. This makes sense only if you have some other incentive to produce such machines.

The only major company that seems to have such an incentive is Sony because it produces content (it owns a major movie studio and a major recording label) as well as PCs: Imagine a Sony PC that is the only way to play certain Sony content. However, Sony hasn't pursued this, primarily because there are legal constraints against doing so, but also because it is unlikely to think of PCs as a major platform for playing music and movies; Sony has hundreds of consumer electronics products better suited to doing that. It is significant that Sony is virtually the only device maker to actually produce an SDMI-compliant music player and bring it to market. It is certainly possible that Sony may have produced an SDMI-compliant PC (or, more likely, PC add-on) if SDMI had taken off.

♦ **Bundle the software into operating system distributions.** With this method, every PC that comes with some new version of Windows includes a DRM controller that applies to all content types. Microsoft could certainly do this with its next-generation DRM technology, as described in Chapter 7, and it probably will. Microsoft now includes a version of DRM in Windows Media Player, which ships with current versions of Windows, anyway. This solves the problem of getting the DRM controller software onto the machine — as opposed to making users download it from a Web site or install it from a CD-ROM. But it doesn't necessarily solve the security problem, and it doesn't do much about ease of use.

♦ **Build DRM controller functions directly into the operating system.** Let's examine what this implies. When you use any file on your PC, you initiate a *system call,* an instruction to the underlying operating system (for example, Windows 2000 or Windows XP) to grab the file and open it up for reading or modification. This happens regardless of whether you open the file in a word processor, spreadsheet program, or other application; attach the file to an e-mail; send it to your Web site for publication; or whatever. The system call to open files, not a separate DRM controller application, should determine whether you have rights to the file and then make the file available, possibly decrypting it in the process.

There are other system calls that correspond to rights exercise operations, such as the calls to write information into files, to copy files, and to delete them. These system calls could also be extended to become full-fledged DRM controller functions. Additionally, DRM functionality would need to be applied to operations such as taking backups and making temporary copies of files in cache directories — the so-called utility rights mentioned in Chapter 4.

By building DRM controller functionality in at the system call level, Microsoft could reduce the potential number of security holes and provide a more seamless user experience.

This third way seems like the most effective way to bundle DRM into PCs. Microsoft is the overwhelmingly dominant provider of PC operating systems, so if it starts shipping a version of Windows that includes DRM functionality — let's call it "Windows DRM" — then content providers can start taking advantage of it by producing content that requires the functionality without worrying too much about limiting their audience.

On the face of it, it seems as if Microsoft could just release Windows DRM, and a wide swath of the DRM software industry would be put out of business at a stroke. (Chapter 11 of this book would then be very aptly numbered.) Of course, it's not quite that simple; several things could get in the way of this happening:

♦ Unified DRM (as it has been called internally at Microsoft) could suffer mounting delays in its release. Already, Microsoft has had trouble keeping its DRM releases current among PC and Pocket PC platforms.

♦ Crackers could blow holes in Unified DRM's security. As mentioned in Chapter 5, the more popular a platform is, the more attention it will get from crackers.

♦ Microsoft would have to migrate its Unified DRM technology from an application to the operating system. That may be a difficult engineering task, although if that doesn't work, Microsoft could always integrate a third-party technology, such as Elisar (see Chapter 11), that does essentially the same thing.

♦ Microsoft's operating systems group would have to judge the feature worthy of inclusion in its core product; it probably gets hundreds of suggestions per year of new features to include in Windows.

♦ There will always be room for third-party vendors that provide advanced or specialized features for niche markets.

Finally, let's not forget that Microsoft's product model creates plenty of opportunities for service providers to add value, and it's based on the putative standard XrML (see Chapter 6), so it provides potential for some level of interoperability with other DRM technologies.

Yet there is another factor that is in Microsoft's favor: its Passport user identification system. Chapter 5 discusses that there are two fundamental ways to authenticate users when they want to exercise rights on content: by machine and by user. Microsoft is the only DRM vendor with a system that allows the flexibility of authenticating both ways and is already widely installed. More importantly, Passport gives Microsoft the unique ability to tie DRM authentication to the same scheme that enables users to do their online shopping through MSN, read their e-mail through Hotmail, get plane tickets through Expedia, and use many other services that Microsoft intends to introduce in the coming months through its .NET strategy. Thus Microsoft has the unique ability to remove one of the usability hurdles that plague DRM.

Passport will have to survive a growing number of challenges by privacy and antitrust advocates, but we predict that it will, particularly as Microsoft has announced its intention to migrate the proprietary technology it built for Passport to the open-standard Kerberos authentication scheme, which can then interoperate with other Kerberos-based services.

Furthermore, Microsoft isn't the only vendor that can deliver a universal or quasi-universal network services ID scheme. AOL is in an excellent position to do so, as is Yahoo! to a lesser extent. A few DRM vendors, including InterTrust, have the capability of authenticating to both machines and personal IDs.

Most DRM technology development has focused on the PC because of its ubiquity as a network access device. But as Mark Stefik of Xerox PARC pointed out in his seminal "Letting Loose the Light" white paper, the PC was never designed for DRM. In general, DRM will succeed on devices where it's built in from the ground up. We need only compare eBook readers with portable music players to understand this.

Most eBook readers have DRM built in; portable MP3 players don't. The eBook is a new type of product. eBook reader makers had to get buy-in from the major book publishers to get them to produce titles in eBook formats, and the publishers wouldn't accept a solution that didn't involve at least simple copy protection.

In contrast, portable MP3 players evolved outside of the realm of the major recording labels. Antitrust law closed off most of the options the recording companies could have pursued to stop the already-moving train: Any activity described by the phrase "the major recording labels get together and . . ." is subject to heavy regulatory scrutiny. Given that the makers of the first generation of portable MP3 players, such as Diamond Multimedia, openly produced products that were hostile to the interests of the music industry, the recording labels weren't likely to get much voluntary cooperation from them. SDMI was the best that regulatory constraints would let them do, and it wasn't enough.

In contrast, the way the eBook industry has evolved, eBook reader vendors are dependent on the major book publishers for their very existence. The vendors aren't likely to ignore the book publishers' dictates, which come through the auspices of the Association of American Publishers and other trade associations.

Both content providers and DRM technology vendors will undoubtedly pin their hopes on new kinds of media-consuming devices. If they are designed in cooperation with content providers, as eBook readers were, then it's virtually guaranteed that they will be built from the start with DRM functionality. In the good old days of vertically integrated media companies, this wasn't a problem; for example, the audiocassette was developed by Philips, and the CD was invented jointly by Philips and Sony. Both produced recording/playback equipment and had their own recording labels (Philips sold its label to what is now Universal Music Group). Other device makers licensed technology from those companies to produce their own CD players and cassette machines.

More recently, Sony has tried a few times to produce its own formats and playback devices as outlets for its own content. From the Betamax videocassette format to the current Memory Stick, none have been very successful. There is a possibility that Sony could build music- or video-playing features with DRM for its PlayStation gaming platform; certainly the PlayStation has enough computing power to support that functionality. But overall, no one media company can succeed at verticalization anymore. They must entrust playback, and more often than not, distribution, to third parties. DRM technology vendors such as InterTrust and IBM are ready to embrace new devices; they should hope that such devices are made to play DRM-friendly formats.

We close off our look at the future of DRM technology by talking about open standards of the type that are discussed in Chapter 6. We can't overstate the importance of open standards in fostering the growth of the industry in a way that doesn't unfairly benefit certain parties at the expense of others. Yet there are issues with each of the current open-standards initiatives that need to be addressed.

The Digital Object Identifier (DOI) is vitally important (although in the interest of disclosure, we repeat here that one of us participated in its creation). It is almost a no-brainer choice as a standard content identifier that also allows online reference. Certain segments of the publishing industry already treat it as a given, even if they may not have implemented many services with it yet. Yet DOI risks being pigeonholed as a standard that applies only to book and journal publishing. Efforts are underway to get other content industries — including magazines, financial researchers, motion pictures, and television — to adopt it. Some of these other industries will greet DOI with skepticism, as do some people in the broader Internet standards community. If the International DOI Foundation steps up its efforts to bring these other segments into the fold, DOI will take its rightful place as a general Internet standard, not just a niche technology for the book and journal community.

XrML, which is owned by ContentGuard, is on a better path than before to becoming a true open standard. The industry has looked somewhat askance at it because it is under patent protection and is being adopted by Microsoft. However, ContentGuard's retrenchment in August 2001 from a DRM technology vendor to focus solely on XrML is a good thing for the technology. More recent announcements that ContentGuard will hand XrML over to a standards body are also encouraging, even if they are not yet very specific. These developments will decrease the number of axes that ContentGuard has to grind about XrML vis-à-vis its former sources of revenue, its now-defunct DRM products and services. Unfortunately, much of the industry still views XrML as a Microsoft-centric initiative. ContentGuard must work actively to show its independence from Microsoft and sign up other vendors who aren't Microsoft service providers. This may be difficult because XrML is not an easy technology to adopt.

RealNetworks's competition to XrML, eXtensible Media Commerce Language (XMCL), is a pragmatic technology that is destined to fail as a standard, as discussed in Chapter 6. It will do so because of the sheer number of vendors involved with it, some of whom merely signed a press release and otherwise made no contribution. We don't expect to hear much about XMCL from vendors other than RealNetworks, although we would enjoy being proven wrong.

Information and Content Exchange (ICE) is a great piece of technology for B-to-B content exchange, especially in the context of ICE-compliant products such as those from Vignette, Interwoven, Kinecta, and arcadiaOne that complement their ICE support with other ways of syndicating content. But it's unclear whether there is enough money to be made from selling ICE servers to sustain these vendors and products. We expect ICE servers to end up where they began: as components of larger Web publishing and content distribution solutions.

Finally, the music industry's SDMI is all but dead. In all, standards bodies have a lot of work to do to ensure that the DRM market takes off in an egalitarian way before it's too late, but they deserve whatever support people in the industry can give them.

The Market

We designed this book so as to minimize the portion of it that is spent on analysis of individual vendors' solutions. One reason for this is that the market is, as noted earlier, changing rapidly and consolidating. It is likely that several of the vendors described in this book will be gone, be acquired, or change radically by the time that you read this. Yet research, like IDC's June 2001 report on the DRM market, indicates that DRM will grow to a multibillion-dollar market within five years. Which is correct?

Both are, of course. The ubiquity of DRM will definitely grow, but the number of vendors who supply the technology will continue to consolidate. Let's see how this can happen.

For any technology-driven market, the best way to look at its current status and predict its course of future development is through the lens of a marketing concept called the *technology adoption lifecycle*. This is a model that predicts how society adopts any sort of technology over time — what types of people adopt it when and what kinds of products and services based on the technology will succeed during certain phases of the lifecycle.

The technology adoption lifecycle has been a standard part of business-school marketing curricula for decades (where the canonical application of it is invariably the automobile), but a few consultants and academics have adapted it specifically for information technology. The best known of these is Geoffrey Moore, through his books *Crossing the Chasm* and *Inside the Tornado*.

The lifecycle starts with a phase in which vendors offer nothing but raw technology, and the only customers are those with the vision and technical resources to take it in its raw form and try to make it work themselves. In the second phase, vendors work closely with their customers to develop customized end-to-end solutions to business problems. Although many of these solutions turn out to be one-offs, vendors hope that they are replicable for other customers.

The third phase is one in which the technology gets built into end-to-end solutions that vendors can offer to multiple customers. The first group of such solutions applies in vertical niche markets, or what Moore calls "bowling alleys." After that, the luckiest and/or most skillful vendors break out of niche markets into the mainstream and become what Moore calls "gorillas" — rich and powerful industry heavyweights.

The transition from the second phase to the third phase is what Moore calls the "chasm." As the name suggests, it is where many vendors fall down. They cannot embed their technology in end-to-end solutions that are stable, provide benefits to customers, are profitable to the vendor, and are better (or better marketed) than the competition.

So which phase is the DRM market in? It varies, but for the most part, our determination is that much of the DRM market is in the chasm now. Despite the overall downturn in the technology sector in 2001, the events cited at the beginning of this chapter are the classic symptoms of a chasm.

Yet certain subsegments of the market are in bowling alleys. For example, Liquid Audio's (see Chapter 11) end-to-end solution for music is a bowling-alley solution, as is Preview Systems' solution for software (see Chapter 7). Both of these vendors have reached the outer limits of their growth; neither of them stands much chance of breaking out of its bowling alley and going mainstream. Preview Systems tried to expand into another bowling alley (the music market) and failed; Liquid Audio's solution is overshadowed by the fact that the major labels have thrown their massive weight behind RealNetworks and Microsoft. Internal rights management (see Chapter 12) is in the bowling alley for movie studios, although in the prechasm phase for publishing companies. NewsStand, qMags, and Zinio (see the section "The Business Models," earlier in this chapter) are also classic bowling-alley solutions.

Many of the first-generation raw technologies have died off. A few others are being acquired by companies that can place them into end-to-end solutions. For example, Aegisoft, with its solution for streaming media DRM, was bought by RealNetworks for use in MusicNet. We expect the latter trend to continue.

A few lucky vendors will make it all the way through the bowling-alley phase of the market to the mainstream — which we estimate will hit in the 2003 timeframe.

Which ones will make it? Clearly, the most likely are the ones who can leverage existing marketing channels and installed bases. Owners of rendering applications, such as Adobe, Microsoft, and RealNetworks, are in good positions by this criterion. They have content creation tools as well as rendering applications that are very widely installed. Yet even these major powers aren't without risk. Adobe has to focus its scattered DRM strategy; Microsoft has a convincing plan with Unified DRM but must get a lot of buy-in throughout a large organization to execute it; RealNetworks has the hot breath of Microsoft at the back of its neck 24 hours a day.

Third-party DRM vendors have had an uphill battle in achieving strategic partnerships with makers of existing links in the content value chain, including content creation and distribution tools as well as rendering applications. But the battle is winnable. Digimarc is perhaps the best example of a DRM-related technology vendor that has fit in so smoothly with image creation applications that it has become part of the landscape in that segment of the market.

No matter whether the winners turn out to be the major software vendors or DRM-specializing third parties (who will probably win by having one of the majors acquire them), one thing is for sure: The winners won't be vendors of *DRM technology*; they will be vendors of *digital media solutions* that contain DRM technology. It is hard to see how DRM technology by itself can generate more than modest profits. To achieve escape velocity and reach the mainstream, the technology is better situated in a larger organization that can subsidize it as part of a more lucrative solution, just as Sun Microsystems subsidizes the development of Java technology through sales of its server hardware.

An important component of DRM's move into the mainstream is its success in the corporate enterprise market. Vendors such as Authentica, ATABOK, InfraWorks, and Phocis (see Chapter 11) are trying to sell their solutions to large corporations that have sensitive information to protect, rather than (or in addition to) customers in the media and publishing industries. The stakes here are high: Unlike media companies, who must give DRM controllers away to their customers, corporate buyers may be willing to pay per-seat licensing charges for DRM technology that controls corporate documents and e-mail.

The platform for the corporate enterprise market is likely to remain the PC for some time — unlike the market for consumer media, which is moving more and more to portable devices. This means that there is even more of a need for DRM vendors to improve their solutions for the PC. The early adopters for corporate DRM solutions are likely to be the same as those for technologies like groupware, document management, and knowledge management: consultancies, banks, and other groups of knowledge workers, who have content as core assets, just like media companies.

Solutions of the types mentioned (such as Lotus Notes or the Documentum document management system) have sophisticated security models that control access to information to a good extent. These are often extensions of file-permission schemes in operating systems. These vendors will incorporate more and more DRM-like features — such as content encryption — into their solutions. However, that paradigm reaches its limits as information gets cut loose from those systems and exposed to outsiders, such as customers and business partners, through e-mail or by being published on corporate extranets. True network-based DRM technology will be necessary to restrict access to sensitive corporate information.

Accordingly, the latest crop of DRM vendors who are serving the corporate market are solving these problems and integrating with widely-installed e-mail, groupware, and document management platforms. Look for this trend to continue; in fact, we would not be surprised to see major strategic partnerships between corporate-oriented DRM vendors and established vendors of e-mail, groupware, and document management systems — if not outright acquisitions by the latter.

Yet adoption of corporate DRM solutions isn't any more guaranteed than it is in the media industries. One of the reasons why systems such as Lotus Notes and Documentum haven't become more ubiquitous within corporations is that their security models are complex and not very comprehensible to users. The same obstacles of transparency and user-friendliness stand in the way of DRM vendors in the corporate market.

Conclusion

If we sound pessimistic about the future of DRM, it is because we have lived with it personally for several years during its awkward startup phases; most of what we have seen is the failure of vendors' solutions to be adopted and the traditional media industries' slowness at adapting their businesses to embrace online digital distribution. Nothing about this is abnormal or cause for alarm. The "information wants to be free" theory of the Internet hasn't been proven, but it hasn't been disproved either. The Internet has lowered the intrinsic value of certain types of information, but information is still valuable; it is the basis for our economies and our societies. Content providers need to find new ways of adding value to their core products.

We also reject the idea that the Internet is a "discontinuity." It is a force of huge change, but it only repeats patterns that we have seen in the content industries for decades. Technological developments have always caused media companies to lose control over certain links in the content value chain; those companies adapt and survive. The dramatic drop in cost of recording a music album caused independent labels to flourish in the 1980s, but that didn't kill the major record companies. Neither did the advent of xerography kill the publishing industry. The Internet is causing content providers to run to catch up with the easy spread of their proprietary information, but run they will. Digital rights management is the vehicle.

References

"AAP, Andersen release E-book recommendations." *The Bulletin: Seybold News & Views on Electronic Publishing,* Volume 6, Number 9; 29 Nov. 2000 <www.seyboldreports.com/Bulletin/subs/vol6/issv6n09.html>.

Alattar, Adnan M. "'Smart Images' Using Digimarc's Watermarking Technology." Proceedings of the IS&T/SPIE's 12th International Symposium on Electronic Imaging, San Jose, CA 25 Jan. 2000, Volume 3971, Number 25 <www.digimarc.com/news/SPIE2000-8.PDF>.

Association of American Publishers. *Digital Rights Management for Ebooks: Publisher Requirements, Version 1.0.* Nov. 2000 <www.publishers.org/home/drm.pdf>.

Association of American Publishers Copyright Committee. *Contractual Licensing, Technological Measures and Copyright Law.* Washington, DC: Association of American Publishers, 2000 <www.publishers.org/home/abouta/copy/licensing.htm>.

Association of American Publishers Rights and Permissions Advisory Committee. *The New & Updated Copyright Primer: A Survival Guide to Copyright and the Permissions Process.* <www.publishers.org/home/abouta/copy/primer.htm>.

Brodsky, Jay, et al. *ICE Network — ICE Standard Version 1.1 (Final Review Draft).* <www.icestandard.com/spec/SPEC-ICE1.01-20000511.html>.

Burns, Christopher. *Copyright Management and the NII: Report to the Enabling Technologies Committee of the Association of American Publishers.* Washington, DC: Association of American Publishers, 1995.

Cox, Brad J. "Superdistribution." *Wired* 2.09, Sept. 1994 <www.wired.com/wired/archive/2.09/superdis.html>.

Cox, Brad J. *Superdistribution; Objects as Property on the Electronic Frontier.* New York: Addison Wesley, 1996.

Duhl, Joshua. *The DRM Landscape: Technologies, Vendors, and Markets.* IDC Report #24891, Jun. 2001 <www.itresearch.com/alfatst4.nsf/unitabsx/W24891?openDocument>.

Gervais, Daniel J. "Electronic Rights Management and Digital Identifier Systems." *Journal of Electronic Publishing,* Volume 4 Number 3, Mar. 1997 <www.press.umich.edu/jep/04-03/gervais.html>. Ann Arbor, MI: University of Michigan Press.

Hughes, C.J. "Pay-to-Play: RealNetworks and its label partners hope to make the Net safe for music." *Silicon Alley Reporter,* Issue 47, September 2001:42-46.

Industry Survey: Digital Rights Management: Usage, Attitude and Profile of Users. Foster City, CA: Seybold Seminars & Publications, Sep. 2001 <www.seyboldreports.com/Specials/DRMsurvey/summary.html>.

Kahin, Brian and Kate Arms, eds. *Forum on Technology-Based Intellectual Property Management: Electronic Commerce for Content.* Special issue of *Interactive Multimedia News,* Volume 2, Aug. 1996.

Katzenbeisser, Stefan, ed. *Information Hiding Techniques for Steganography and Digital Watermarking.* Norwood, MA: Artech House, 2000.

Levy, Steven. *Crypto: How the Code Rebels Beat the Government — Saving Privacy in the Digital Age.* New York: Viking, 2001.

Lyman, Rick. "Hollywood Moves to Rent Movies Online." *The New York Times,* August 17, 2001:A1+.

Moore Geoffrey A. *Crossing the Chasm: Marketing and Selling High-Tech Products to Mainstream Customers,* Revised Edition. New York: Harperbusiness, 1999.

Moore, Geoffrey A. *Inside the Tornado: Marketing Strategies from Silicon Valley's Cutting Edge.* New York: Harperbusiness, 1995.

Northrup, Kerry J. "Technology Ahead of Its Time." *The Seybold Report*, Volume 1 Number 1, April 2001:5-7 <www.seyboldreports.com/TSR/free/0101/techwatch.pdf>.

Risher, Carol A. and William R. Rosenblatt. "The Digital Object Identifier — An Electronic Publishing Tool for the Entire Information Community." *Serials Review,* Volume 24 Number.3/4, Dec. 1998:13-21. Stamford, CT: JAI Press, Inc.

Rosenblatt, William R. "The Digital Object Identifier: Solving the Dilemma of Copyright Protection Online." *Journal of Electronic Publishing,* Volume 3 Number 2, Dec. 1997 <www.press.umich.edu/jep/03-02/doi.html>. Ann Arbor, MI: University of Michigan Press.

Rosenblatt, William R. "Two Sides of the Coin: Publishers' Requirements for Digital Intellectual Property Management." Inter-Industry Forum on Technology-Based Intellectual Property Management, Washington, DC, Mar. 1996. Slides available from the author.

Samtani, Rajan. "Following the Money: Managing Intellectual Property in the Digital Age." <www.elcamino.com/rss/news/news_money.html>.

Schneier, Bruce. *Applied Cryptography: Protocols, Algorithms, and Source Code in C,* 2nd Edition. New York: John Wiley & Sons, 1996.

Secure Digital Music Initiative: Creating a Digital Marketplace. Sept. 1999 <www.sdmi.org/download/create_dig_mktplace.ppt>.

Secure Digital Music Initiative: SDMI Portable Device Specification, Part 1, Version 1.0. Jul. 1999 <www.sdmi.org/download/port_device_spec_part1.pdf>.

"Shiver me timbers; Software-piracy rates." *The Economist,* Jun. 2, 2001:106.

Souzis, Adam, et al. *ICE Implementation Cookbook: Getting Started with Web Syndication.* Nov. 2000 <www.icestandard.com/spec/icecookbook2.pdf>.

Stefik, Mark. *The Internet Edge: Social, Technical, and Legal Challenges for a Networked World.* Cambridge, MA: MIT Press, 1999.

Stefik, Mark. "Letting Loose the Light: Igniting Commerce in Electronic Publication." *Internet Dreams: Archetypes, Myths, and Metaphors.* Cambridge, MA: MIT Press, 1996.

Van Tassel, Joan. *Digital Content Management: Creating and Distributing Media Assets by Broadcasters.* Washington, DC: NAB Research and Planning Department, 2001. Available from National Association of Broadcasters at (202)429-5373 or <www.nab.org/nabstore/>.

Vilensky, Jeffrey A., Raymond Lee Katz, and John T. Williams. *Maximizing the Value of Content: A Primer on the Digital Asset Management Industry.* Bear Stearns Equity Research report, Mar. 2001. Abridged version: <wpinter2.bearstearns.com/eweek/200103141.htm>.

XrML: eXtensible Rights Markup Language, Specifications v. 1.03, Aug. 2000 <www.xrml.org/get_XrML.asp>.

Index

Printed in the United States
98454LV00004B/196/A

9 780764 548895